Ius Gentium: Comparative Perspectives on Law and Justice

Volume 127

Ius Gentium is a book series which discusses the central questions of law and justice from a comparative perspective. The books in this series collect the contrasting and overlapping perspectives of lawyers, judges, philosophers and scholars of law from the world's many different jurisdictions for the purposes of comparison, harmonisation, and the progressive development of law and legal institutions. Each volume makes a new comparative study of an important area of law. This book series continues the work of the well-known journal of the same name and provides the basis for a better understanding of all areas of legal science.

The *Ius Gentium* series provides a valuable resource for lawyers, judges, legislators, scholars, and both graduate students and researchers in globalisation, comparative law, legal theory and legal practice. The series has a special focus on the development of international legal standards and transnational legal cooperation.

Nauman Reayat • Hakeem O. Yusuf
Editors

Constitutionalism in Africa and Beyond

Challenges and Opportunities

Springer

Editors
Nauman Reayat
Leicester Law School
University of Leicester
Leicester, UK

Hakeem O. Yusuf
Centre for Justice, Law, and Society
University of Derby
Derby, UK

ISSN 1534-6781 ISSN 2214-9902 (electronic)
Ius Gentium: Comparative Perspectives on Law and Justice
ISBN 978-3-032-01179-4 ISBN 978-3-032-01180-0 (eBook)
https://doi.org/10.1007/978-3-032-01180-0

This Springer imprint is published by the registered company Springer Nature Switzerland AG
The registered company address is: Gewerbestrasse 11, 6330 Cham, Switzerland

Foreword

"A judiciary of undisputed integrity is the bedrock of democracy and the rule of law . . . even when all other protections fail, the judiciary provides a bulwark to the public against any encroachments on rights and freedoms under the law"—thus declares the United Nations Bangalore Principles of Judicial Conduct.

The truism that the rule of law and judicial independence are inextricably linked, and at the epicentre of democracy, faces critical challenges on the African continent. Diverse challenges confront judicial officers across the continent, but in essence the central challenge is the same—undue interference with or influencing of judges to subvert judicial independence and integrity. The attempts at interference and influencing may these days be less brazen than in the past, but it is no less insidious. Generally speaking, but in Africa in particular, the judiciary is often seen as the last bulwark against tyranny and oppression. The increasing democratisation of political systems in Africa, with progressive constitutions, often containing strong bills of rights, and courts bestowed with powers of judicial review is refreshing, but has concomitantly given rise to renewed and increased threats against judicial independence. Checks and balances in any political system axiomatically create fertile breeding ground for the contestation of power, and as Africa continues to democratise, that contestation will also increase exponentially.

The critical role played by courts on the continent is compellingly illustrated in the landmark decisions following election outcome challenges. Examples that come to mind are Uganda in 2006, Ghana and Kenya in 2013, Malawi in 2014, Burundi in 2015 and Zambia in 2016. Some see this as the "politicisation" of courts. Judicial interference, judicial independence and judicial politicisation are features of political contestation as democratisation expands.

This book comprehensively and incisively explores these challenges across the length and breadth of the continent. It ranges from South Africa's "judicialisation of politics" as some call it, denoting the increasing tendency of a migration of politics into the courts with an exponential increase in the number of highly political matters that are being adjudicated in courtrooms, instead of being resolved politically (others call it "lawfare"). As the authors demonstrate, while this may justifiably be cited as a triumph for accountability and the vindication of the Constitution and the rule of law, this is not without any cost to the South African constitutional project.

It extends to the Ethiopian challenges of what is described as a federation without constitutionalism. The author demonstrates the urgent need for an impartial constitutional court that ensures the supremacy of the constitution, resolves disputes impartially, enforces human rights and sets limits on executive power. The book includes a critique of the institutional design of Cameroon's judicial appointment body, the Higher Judicial Council, and its capacity to enhance or protect judicial independence in Cameroon. It has a thoughtful and critical analysis of Madagascar's challenges and how a state-centred approach to rule of law may well be ill-suited for attaining justice or effective governance within developing countries with weak state institutions and strong non-state normative systems like Madagascar.

There is a perspicacious analysis of the Nigerian judiciary's contribution as a strategic role player across diverse and critical aspects of governance in that country and the continuing blight on it due to an unaccounted institutional legacy. The book also provides an insightful, intriguing comparison between Egypt and Pakistan regarding judicial populism and judicial independence in developing democracies.

This continental overview of the beleaguered judicial independence and rule of law in Africa is meticulously researched, well-articulated and closely analysed. It is a panoptic examination of the challenges Africa faces to ensure the continuance or restoration of those central fundamental precepts in functioning democracies. This book is a very welcome new resource and it will be invaluable to constitutional scholars, comparative constitutional lawyers, judges as well as political scientists.

Africa has a sad, chequered history as far as democracy and constitutionalism generally are concerned, but particularly in respect of the rule of law and judicial independence. Readers of this book will be acutely cognisant of the continuing challenges that face the continent. From north to south, east to west, the narrative is grim, but not irremediable. In many of the contributions, the authors make useful suggestions to ensure the continuance or restoration of judicial independence and the rule of law in Africa. In the case of Ethiopia, the author concludes that it demonstrates the shortcomings when there are efforts to federalise power without putting in place the necessary judicial institutions for checking political power. It is pointed out that federalism without active constitutionalism is open either to authoritarian centralisation or subversion, depending on the political dynamics of the particular context. In respect of Cameroon, there are some reflections on the potentials for institutional transformations in political systems where institutional interdependence is deeply entrenched and underpinned by an established political culture.

An insightful observation of the Egyptian and Pakistani positions is that the contestation between people and elites and the presence of a strategic judicial leader willing and able to exploit the contestation are essential for judicial populism and its contribution to the increase in judicial independence in developing democracies. When any of the above features of judicial populism is absent, judicial independence in countries like Pakistan and Egypt begins to face limitations.

This book is a very welcome addition to the important transnational and trans-continental debate about Africa as the so-called "basket case" of the planet. A continent ravaged by colonialist and imperialist pillaging finds itself well into the twenty-first century faced with rampant tyranny, oligarchism and authoritarianism. The debate around the re-establishment or prolongation of the rule of law and judicial independence amidst this atrociously challenging environment must continue. This book admirably succeeds in doing exactly that.

The Constitutional Court of South Africa
Johannesburg, South Africa
November 2023

Steven Arnold Majiedt

Contents

About the Contributors

Abdul-Wahab Egbewole is a legal practitioner and academic. He was called to the Nigerian Bar as a Solicitor and Advocate on 20 August 1985 and is currently a Professor in the Department of Jurisprudence and International Law at the University of Ilorin. He served in various capacities in the faculty, including the office of Dean between 2010 and 2012. He is a member of the Governing Council of the University of Ilorin representing the Senate. Between 2015 and 2018, he served as the Director of General Studies Division of the University of Ilorin and is currently the Research Manager for the Faculty of Law. He is a member of several learned societies including The Chartered Institute of Arbitrators (UK) which he joined in 2016. He has served as the Newsletter Editor and Vice Chair of the IBA Committee on Negligence and Damages and elected as the Chair of the Committee in 2020. He has published widely in the areas of Jurisprudence and Legal Theory, Juvenile Justice, Arbitration, Child Rights, Public International Law, Judicial Process, Law, and Development and has many books in his name. He has also secured numerous research grants in Law and Society and has served as the Principal Researcher on the Law and Disability Rights grant awarded by the Open Society Initiative for West Africa. On 24 September 2018, he was sworn in by the Chief Justice of Nigeria as a Senior Advocate of Nigeria (SAN), the highest professional ranking for lawyers in Nigeria. His wealth of experience in the Law sector has been of immense benefit to Welfare Microfinance Bank Ltd where he served the bank as a member of the Board of Director and as a Chairman of Board Credit/Risk Management Committee till August 2022. In September 2022, he was appointed the 11th Vice-Chancellor of the University of Ilorin.

Dr Laura-Stella Enonchong is a Senior Lecturer in Law at SOAS University of London. Her research interests are in comparative constitutional studies and human rights. She has published widely in those areas and her research has featured in reputable academic platforms and distinguished media outlets. Laura is a co-director of Post-graduate Research in the School of Law at SOAS. She is also a Distinguished Research Fellow in the Constitutional Studies Program at the University of Texas at Austin and a Secretary General of the African Network of Constitutional Lawyers.

Assefa Fiseha (PhD, Professor) is a leading expert in comparative federalism and devolution in Africa and has been engaged in teaching and research in higher education since 1996. He has published numerous articles, book chapters, and a book related to these fields both in Ethiopia and reputable international journals. He has been engaged in constitution making processes and dialogues in several countries (Sudan, South Sudan, Ethiopia, Yemen, and Malawi). He has worked in joint research and training projects run by the Max Planck Institute (Heidelberg, Germany), the European Institute of Peace, the Forum of Federations (an international network of experts in Federalism based in Canada), Berghof Foundation (Germany), InterAfrica Group (Ethiopia), and the Netherlands Institute for Multiparty Democracy (NIMD) among others. Previously, he has served as the Dean of the Faculty of Law and designed MA/LL.M and PhD programmes run by Addis Ababa University. He has served as a lead research team in different research projects both at Addis Ababa University and other partner research institutions based in South Africa, Canada, and Switzerland. He was a Principal Investigator in a three-year project (2020–2023) titled "Addressing the Crisis of Governance in the Horn of Africa". This collaborative research initiative, conducted with the University of Aberdeen (UK) and partner institutions in South Africa, combined research and capacity-building activities. An edited volume featuring ten chapters arising from the project was published in September 2022. https://www.routledge.com/Contemporary-Governance-Challenges-in-the-Horn-of-Africa/Fombad-Fiseha-Steytler/p/book/9781032207926

Dr Olivia Lwabukuna is a Senior Lecturer in International Human Rights and Development at the Institute of Commonwealth Studies, School of Advanced Study, University of London, UK. She is also a Research Associate in the Africa, Law and Development cluster at the School of Law, SOAS University of London; a Research Fellow at the Free State Centre for Human Rights, University of the Free State, South Africa; and serves as an Editor of the *Journal of African Law*. Dr Lwabukuna, who is an Advocate of the High Court of Tanzania, obtained her LL.B from the University of Swaziland, LL.M from the University of Cape Town, and an LL.D from the University of Pretoria. Before SOAS, she was a policy research specialist in the Africa Programme of the South African Human Sciences Research Council. She has lectured law at Tumaini University (Tanzania) and the University of Pretoria (South Africa) and practiced in Swaziland and Tanzania. Dr Lwabukuna has also been a Fellow in the Center for West African Studies, College of Arts and Law - University of Birmingham and an associate in the Nyerere Center for Peace Research - East African Community, and the National Competitiveness Council of Nigeria. She has consulted for Konrad Adenauer Stiftung's Rule of Law Programme for sub-Saharan Africa, Advocates for International Development's ROLE UK (Rule of Law Expertise), and the UK Open University.

Dan Mafora is a lecturer in public law at the University of Cape Town, South Africa. He is also the author of *Capture in the Court: In Defence of Judges and the Constitution* (Tafelberg, 2023). He is a former law clerk of the Constitutional Court of South Africa and holds a Bachelor of Laws from the University of Pretoria and an LLM in constitutional theory from the University of Cape Town.

Justice Steven Arnold Majiedt is a Justice of the Constitutional Court, Johannesburg, South Africa (October 2019 to present), a Chancellor of Sol Plaatje University, Kimberley (2015 to present), and an Honorary Professor of Law, University of the Western Cape, Cape Town (2021 to present). Previously, he was the Chief State Law Adviser, Northern Cape Province in the Office of the Premier, Kimberley (1997–1999), a judge of the High Court, Northern Cape Division, Kimberley (May 2000–November 2010), and a judge of Appeal, Supreme Court of Appeal, Bloemfontein (1 December 2010–September 2019). He is the former Chairperson of the South African Rules Board for Courts of Law, the former Council Member, South African Judicial Education Institute (SAJEI), and the former Council Member, Hugo de Groot Society, University of Pretoria.

Sfiso Benard Nxumalo is an advocate of the High Court of South Africa and is currently reading for a Doctor of Philosophy (DPhil) in Law at the Faculty of Law, University of Oxford. He holds a Bachelor of Civil Laws (BCL) from the University of Oxford and a Bachelor of Laws from the University of the Witwatersrand. His research for the DPhil concerns the philosophical purviews of the African Charter on Human and People's Rights and African Legal Theory. He taught constitutional law and administrative law at Brasenose College as a stipendiary lecturer and contract law at Balliol College as a tutor.

Dr Nauman Reayat is a Lecturer in Law at the Leicester Law School, University of Leicester. Prior to joining Leicester, he obtained the Certificate of Qualification from the National Committee on Accreditation of the Federation of Law Societies of Canada in 2022. From 2021 to 2022, he held an Economic and Social Research Council Postdoctoral Fellowship at the School of Law and Politics, Cardiff University, where he led the project titled "Judicial Independence in Authoritarian and Hybrid Regimes" (ES/W007223/1). This edited book, along with Nauman's contribution to it, is based on the conferences and workshops conducted during that project. Before undertaking the fellowship, he completed his PhD at the University of York in 2022 on the topic "Judicial Independence in Authoritarian and Hybrid Regimes: Lessons from Pakistan" (2005–2013). Nauman is also the Founder and the Chief Convener of the Global South Network (GSN) (www.globalsouthnetwork.com) which is an interdisciplinary forum for research students, scholars, practitioners, and civil society organisations from different regions of the Global South including but not limited to Africa, Latin America, Asia, East Europe, and the Middle East.

Dr Rhona Smith is a Professor of International Human Rights at Newcastle University in the UK. She has a background in academia, and extensive experience in human rights capacity development and technical assistance particularly in academic and justice sectors. Her academic work has focussed on the UN systems as well as rights of disadvantaged and marginalised people and groups. She has also supported human rights education more generally through introductory texts on human rights, human rights education, and human rights research methods. Her practical work has been centred in China and Southeast Asia. Rhona also served as the UN Special Rapporteur about Human Rights in Cambodia from 2015 to 2021.

Professor Hakeem O. Yusuf is a Professor of Global Law at the University of Derby. Hakeem's research interests are in comparative constitutionalism, colonial (rule of) law, transitional justice, and business and human rights. His works in transitional justice, colonial (rule of) law, and comparative constitutional law have won international recognition. In 2011, he served on a Truth and Reconciliation Commission in Osun State, Nigeria. His article in the *International Journal of Transitional Justice* provided a pioneering account of the truth-telling process in Nigeria (the Oputa Panel). His second book, *Colonial and Post-Colonial Constitutionalism in the Commonwealth: Peace, Order and Good Government* (Routledge Abingdon 2014), was awarded the prestigious John T. Saywell Prize for Canadian Constitutional Legal History for 2015 and shortlisted for the Kevin Boyle Prize 2015 by the Irish Association of Law Teachers (IALT). His first book *Transitional Justice, Judicial Accountability, and the Rule of Law* (2010) was shortlisted for the 2010 Kevin Boyle Prize by IALT. His article "The Judiciary and Constitutionalism in Transitions: A Critique" won the Silver Medal in the Global Jurist 2007 Awards. In 2009, he won the Highly Commended Award, Emerald Literati Network Awards for his article "Democratic Transition, Judicial Accountability and Judicialisation of Politics in Africa: The Nigerian Experience" published in (2008) 50 (5) *International Journal of Law and Management* pp. 236–261. Hakeem is also the Co-Convener of the Global South Network (GSN) (www.globalsouthnetwork.com).

Introduction

Nauman Reayat

Abstract Limits on governmental power are essential for safeguarding fundamental rights, upholding the rule of law, and preserving judicial independence. While this issue is a global concern, it is particularly acute in jurisdictions marked by gross human rights violations, non-transparent and unfair elections, the concentration of power in individual leaders or small groups, and frequent constitutional overhauls. In such contexts, the absence of effective checks on power creates systemic risks: investors become wary of investing capital, marginalized groups face exclusion from political and economic participation due to unequal opportunities, and individuals are driven to migrate in search of better opportunities, placing unsustainable pressures on destination economies. The introductory chapter establishes the volume's central focus on constitutionalism in Africa and beyond, situating its analysis within gaps in existing scholarship while presenting the book's overarching framework. The growth or decline of constitutionalism stems from a combination of factors. These include, but are not limited to historical legacies, the strength of judicial leadership, the presence of socio-legal movements, the adequacy of constitutional design, the degree of political cohesion, and the alignment between formal constitutions and informal practices.

This edited book is based on activities and collaboration done during Economic Social Research Council Postdoctoral Fellowship (ES/W007223/1 Judicial independence in authoritarian and hybrid regimes) of the author at the School of Law and Politics, Cardiff University. The author began work on this edited collection during the fellowship and completed it after joining the University of Leicester, Leicester Law School, in 2022.

N. Reayat (✉)
Leicester Law School, University of Leicester, Leicester, UK
e-mail: nr210@leicester.ac.uk

N. Reayat, H. O. Yusuf (eds.), *Constitutionalism in Africa and Beyond*, Ius Gentium: Comparative Perspectives on Law and Justice 127,
https://doi.org/10.1007/978-3-032-01180-0_1

In August 2025, the United States (U.S.) President Donald Trump suggested that a Russia–Ukraine peace deal would require territorial exchange.[1] However, such recognition would necessitate constitutional amendment in Ukraine, approved by referendum and parliament, posing a major hurdle for President Zelensky and threatening his government's stability.[2] In March 2025, Judge James Boasberg, Chief Judge of the U.S. District Court for the District of Columbia, issued a temporary restraining order halting the deportation of alleged Venezuelan gang members, prompting the U.S. President to call for his impeachment.[3] Chief Justice John Roberts of the U.S. Supreme Court subsequently responded to these remarks, asserting that "impeachment is not an appropriate response to disagreement with a judicial decision."[4]

In January 2025, security was withdrawn from the Chief Justice of Kenya, leaving the head of the judiciary unprotected against potential retaliation from individuals dissatisfied with rulings issued by the Supreme Court of Kenya. This move not only endangered the Chief Justice's life but also created an environment of fear among other judges, threatening judicial independence.

In March 2024, judges of Islamabad High Court, Pakistan, suggested in a letter to the Chief Justice of Pakistan that they are being intimidated by spy agencies. In November 2023, the UK Supreme Court supported the Court of Appeal's decision and overturned the government's decision to deport asylum seekers to Rwanda.[5] In October 2023, the Supreme Court of Nigeria dismissed the opposition's challenge to President Bola Tinubu's election win.[6] In Chile, two constitution-making processes failed between 2021 and 2023, even though more than a million people actively participated in their formulation.[7] In 2020, a national vote approved amendments to the Russian Constitution further empowering President Vladimir Putin.[8] In light of these global instances, there is no better time than now to discuss constitutionalism, what are limits to state power, and who and how to hold the government to account.

What is Constitutionalism? There is no universally accepted definition of constitutionalism. Different studies define constitutionalism and classify it in different ways. Constitutionalism encompasses a range of aspects, including majority rule, the ability of politicians to organize into political parties to gain public support, broad consensus on certain policies that cannot be altered by a simple majority, and judicial independence.[9] Of these, judicial independence is one of the core elements.

[1] Gozzi (2025).

[2] Ibid.

[3] Lowell and Gedeon (2025).

[4] Epstein (2025).

[5] R(on the application of AAA (Syria) and others) (Respondents/Cross Appellants) v Secretary of State for the Home Department (Appellant/Cross Respondent) [2023] UKSC 42 https://supremecourt.uk/uploads/uksc_2023_0093_etc_judgment_636270e30e.pdf

[6] Ewokor and Chibelushi (2023).

[7] Soto Barrientos et al (2025)

[8] Hutcheson and McAllister (2021).

[9] Tushnet and Bugarič (2022).

It has two kinds: *de jure* and *de facto* judicial independence.[10] *De jure* judicial independence refers to constitutional guarantees given to the judiciary.[11] *De facto* judicial independence is highly contested but mainly involves judicial power. Some scholars view *de facto* judicial independence as the judiciary's increased ability to protect itself against the regime's court-packing and court-curbing activities, while others characterize it through observable judicial outcomes—specifically, rulings against other state branches and their subsequent enforcement.[12] However, at its core, constitutionalism revolves around holding the government accountable and imposing limits on its powers.

Depending on who holds the government accountable, to what extent, and through what means, there are various forms of constitutionalism, including but not limited to liberal constitutionalism, transformative constitutionalism, and abusive constitutionalism. Transformative constitutionalism requires commitment of both judges and politicians[13] to substantive equality and improving socio-economic conditions whereas abusive constitutionalism involves the misuse of liberal constitutionalism to achieve illiberal goals.[14] Liberal Constitutionalism advocates for a constitutional order that upholds and reflects key political ideals, including democracy, free-market capitalism, individual equality and liberty, and the protection of private property. Central to this framework are periodic elections, the separation of powers, and the prioritization of civil and political rights.

There is no single definition of what constitutes liberal constitutionalism or a definitive answer as to who holds the government accountable within this framework. Some studies argue that liberal constitutionalism comprises two complementary components: legal (or judicial) constitutionalism and political constitutionalism.[15] As evident, some features, such as democracy and elections, involve politicians, while others, like the protection of rights, rely on judges through judicial review. Politicians contribute to the separation of powers, free and fair elections, and other democratic processes via constitutional amendments, constitution making, or ordinary legislation in legislature. This list of constitutionalism types is not exhaustive.

Constitutionalism, whether liberal or otherwise, shapes the context for addressing national and international issues like terrorism and migration. Key issues such as property rights, human rights violations, and accountability often reach the courts. If courts lack independence, public trust erodes, leading some groups to take the law into their own hands. This undermines the rule of law, fosters terrorism, and

---

[10] Melton and Ginsburg (2014).

[11] Ibid.

[12] Holgado and Urribarri (2023).

[13] Langa (2006).

[14] Tushnet (2016).

[15] Ibid.

discourages economic investment, slowing economic growth and prompting migration to more stable economies. Migration burdens host countries economically, socially, and politically, often dividing public opinion and influencing policies, as seen in Brexit.

Clearly, constitutionalism is not just a national concern. It has significant global implications. However, it is increasingly crucial in countries sharing legal concerns such as gross violation of human rights and deteriorating law and order situation; political issues such as unfair, non-transparent, and non-independent elections and unstable political regimes; economic problems such as high rate of unemployment, low gross domestic product, and rising inflation; and social issues such as women disempowerment, intolerance, and inequality. If the legal systems of countries with these features are strengthened to ensure judicial independence, protect rights, and hold elites accountable, they can attract investment, create equal opportunities, and reduce the need of citizens living in those countries to migrate to countries which they believe have more employment opportunities and better living conditions. This would ease the burden on countries receiving migrants and financing international security, and reduce societal divisions.

There are different terms used for the countries with aforesaid features including but not limited to "The Third World", "Majority World", "Low-income countries", or "Middle-income countries". These terms and their descriptions depend upon different disciplines and how they approach these terms/concepts. Economists and international organisations classify countries as high-income, middle-income, and low-income. Developmental economists and political scientists use "The Third World"[16] or "The Majority World"[17]. Political scientists also classify countries into new democracies, hybrid democracies, authoritarian countries, countries with competitive authoritarian regimes, etc.[18] These include countries that might not be failed states but are ranked low by data agencies using tools such as the Democracy Index.[19] All these approaches and terms overlap in terms of low-income economies, unstable political regimes, socio-political conflicts, and inequality between rich and poor.

The wider literature on constitutionalism mainly focuses on legal factors of constitutionalism attributing the nature and scope of constitutionalism to laws creating powers of actors such as judges and politicians.[20] If written laws alone were sufficient to guarantee judicial independence, courts in countries with the aforementioned characteristics and codified constitutions would have consistently acted autonomously. The majority of these constitutions establish a separation of powers among government branches and explicitly guarantee judicial independence.

---

[16] Corporate Finance Institute (n.d).

[17] Khan et al (2022).

[18] Levitsky and Way (2010).

[19] Democracy index (2024).

[20] Law (2022), Loughlin (2022).

Therefore, legal factors required for constitutionalism do not provide a complete account of the nature and scope of constitutionalism.

Other studies examine political factors of constitutionalism by focusing on the relationship between regime types and courts' ability to hold the government to account. This suggests that constitutionalism followed democratisation.[21] However, Epperly explains how judicial independence (an aspect of constitutionalism) can develop in jurisdictions lacking substantive democratisation.[22] This suggests that political accounts, on their own, are also insufficient to fully explain constitutionalism and that a more advanced explanation requires analysing a combination of political, legal, and social factors particularly in countries that are politically, socially, or legally unstable.

This book advances the study of constitutionalism by providing an integrated analysis of its social, political, and legal dimensions. To this end, it examines constitutionalism in Africa—a region where many countries broadly share the characteristics outlined above—making it a particularly significant case for deepening our understanding of constitutionalism in such contexts. Africa has 54 countries[23], a population of about 1.2 billion[24], and faces some of the world's toughest governance challenges. These include struggles with democracy, peace, and effective government, alongside major issues like poverty, inequality, and limited access to education, healthcare, and jobs.[25] According to the 2024 Freedom House Report, only 7 percent of Africa's population lives in "Free" countries, while 50 percent resides in "Not Free" countries.[26] Africa holds vast natural wealth, including 30% of global mineral reserves, significant shares of gas (8%) and oil (12%), and the world's largest reserves of cobalt, diamonds, platinum, and uranium.[27] It also possesses 40% of global gold, up to 90% of chromium and platinum, 65% of arable land, and 10% of renewable freshwater resources.[28] Yet, Africa is home to 70% of the world's poorest people[29], with one-third of its population living in poverty. While sub-Saharan Africa has 12% of the world's population, it bears 71% of

[21] Huntington (1991), Choudhry and Tushnet (2020).

[22] Epperly (2017, 2019).

[23] Ibid.

[24] Hamel et al (2019).

[25] Del Rio (2017).

[26] Chávez et al (2011).

[27] Komárek et al. (2025), Hirschl & Roznai (2024), Ginsburg et al. 2025.

[28] Reayat et al (2024); Chávez et al (2011).

[29] Helmke and Rious-Figueroa et al. (2011).

global HIV cases.[30] One of the major reasons behind these issues is the limited constraints on government power, which prevents resources from being used efficiently to generate a trickle-down effect for the population and to address the problems mentioned above. This, in turn, necessitates a closer analysis of constitutionalism in Africa. As this volume explains, constitutional developments in Africa have shifted rapidly over the last decade, requiring regular fresh analysis and offering potentially new lessons for countries outside Africa facing similar challenges. Moreover, as discussed later in this chapter, there is limited scholarship offering interdisciplinary and comparative perspectives on the distinct aspects and drivers of constitutionalism in the African context. This book seeks to fill that gap by examining these dimensions both within Africa and in broader comparative perspective.

The remainder of this introduction is organized into three parts. The first part critically engages with existing scholarship on constitutionalism in politically or legally unstable contexts. The second part reviews existing scholarship on constitutionalism in Africa and beyond. The concluding section outlines the book's structure and thematic progression.

1 Constitutionalism in Countries with Unstable Legal and Political Systems

Given the broad nature and global relevance of constitutionalism, there is no shortage of literature on the subject. Whether it is works on the judicialization of politics, judicial independence, constitutional history, or constitutions, they all directly or indirectly address elements of constitutionalism. However, little is known about the factors that shape constitutionalism in unstable socio-legal and socio-political contexts where election fairness and transparency are questionable, the gap between the rich and poor is significant, access to public services is limited, and the law-and-order situation is precarious.[31] This is because of two main reasons: first, much of the existing scholarship on constitutionalism stems from Western experiences, often overlooking the unstable socio-political and socio-legal environments of non-Western states where developments require context-specific analysis.[32] These works tend to emphasize written law, formal institutions, and constitutional design, while rarely engaging with constitutionalism beyond its legal dimensions. This points to a gap in accounting for how political and social dynamics interact with constitutions in less stable settings. Frequent new developments in these regions necessitate fresh and context-specific analysis.

Second, the socio-political and socio-legal environments in many non-Western countries are often unstable. Frequent new developments in these regions necessitate fresh and context-specific analysis. The wider literature on constitutionalism in

[30] Macdonald and Kong (2012).

[31] Ginsburg (2008).

[32] Cho (2020).

these contexts can be divided into several categories. While not exhaustive, these categories capture the main recurring themes that emerge across these contexts. First, a large portion of the literature focuses on judicial independence as the primary lens for understanding constitutionalism.[33] Helmke and Rious-Figueroa et al. highlight how Latin American courts act independently against elected officials[34], while Macdonald and Kong describe judicial independence as a constitutional virtue.[35] Moustafa and Ginsburg argue that authoritarian governments often empower courts to legitimise their rule but retract this empowerment once courts act against regime interests.[36] Similarly, Cho explores how foreign direct investment influences judicial independence in autocracies[37], while Popova uses the theory of strategic pressure to show how authoritarian regimes erode judicial independence through constitutional changes or institutional weakness.[38]

This strand of literature demonstrates how judicial independence—whether *de jure or de facto—functions as both a shield against executive dominance and a bargaining chip within authoritarian or hybrid regimes. The literature also distinguishes between formal (de jure) guarantees of judicial independence and practical (de facto) autonomy. Vanberg emphasises the politics behind establishing de jure independence*[39], while Hilbink examines the Chilean judiciary's passivity under Pinochet, underscoring the limitations of formal rules in constraining authoritarian power.[40] Epperly advances this distinction by showing how political competition contributes more significantly to *de facto judicial independence in autocracies, building on the "insurance model"*.[41] This demonstrates how judicial power is often contingent on regime survival strategies rather than democratic consolidation.

The second category examines the enforcement of socio-economic rights and the rule of law in transitional democracies. Brinks and Gauri show how courts in countries like Nigeria, Brazil, South Africa, and Indonesia enforce socio-economic rights[42], thereby linking legal constitutionalism with social justice. Chavez similarly illustrates how Argentine courts promoted the rule of law in democratizing contexts.[43] Rosenfeld and Sajo highlight the rule of law and constitution making,

[33] Popova (2010, 2012, 2020).

[34] Vanberg (2008).

[35] Hilbink (2007).

[36] Epperly (2017, 2019). The insurance model posits that an empowered judiciary serves as a safeguard for incumbents anticipating a loss of power. Political actors strengthen the courts when they foresee electoral defeat, ensuring that once out of office, they can rely on the judiciary to protect their interests and to constrain the actions of the new incumbents.

[37] Brinks and Gauri (2008).

[38] Chavez (2004).

[39] Rosenfeld and Sajo (2012).

[40] Ginsburg (2003).

[41] Moustafa (2003, 2007).

[42] Chávez et al. (2011).

[43] Popova (2010); Moustafa & Ginsburg (2008).

straddling both legal and political constitutionalism by focusing on how politicians and judges interact in institutionalising constitutional authority.[44]

The third category explores judicial review and the judicialization of politics as mechanisms of judicial empowerment. Ginsburg analyses judicial review in several East Asian democracies[45], while Moustafa demonstrates how Sadat's Egypt strategically empowered the Constitutional Court to reassure international creditors and institutions.[46] Here, judicial empowerment served political and economic ends rather than democratic principles. These cases highlight how judicialisation in authoritarian contexts may strengthen legal constitutionalism while simultaneously entrenching authoritarian control.

Finally, studies increasingly compare constitutionalism across regime types. These studies have concentrated on constitutionalism in countries with authoritarian regimes (where powers are centralised in an office held by an individual or a group), hybrid regimes (a mix of autocratic and democratic features), transitional democracies (regimes moving from authoritarian rules towards democracy), or developing democracies (not failed states but ranked low by data agencies using tools such as the Democracy Index). While valuable, these works often focus on isolated factors—such as judicial independence[47], rights enforcement, or constitutional design—without fully integrating social, political, and legal dimensions.[48] These studies do not simultaneously explain how a combination of social, political, and legal factors contributes to the distinct components of constitutionalism in various regime types in Africa and beyond, nor how constitutionalism strengthens or weakens in these contexts.

This book does not focus solely on a specific kind of constitutionalism. Instead, it is one of the rare interdisciplinary accounts of constitutionalism that advances this field by explaining the distinct components of different kinds of constitutionalism in a range of regime types, including but not limited to authoritarian regimes, hybrid regimes, and developing democracies in Africa and beyond. Unlike the previously cited studies, this book explains the social, political, and legal factors of constitutionalism simultaneously in different regime types and during the transition from one regime type to another. By doing so, this book offers insights that can be used to examine and evaluate non-African countries in similar political and social contexts.

---

[44] Akiba (2021).

[45] Ibid.

[46] Diala and Rautenbach (2024).

[47] Okoth-Ogendo (1993).

[48] Abebe et al. (2022).

2 Constitutionalism in Africa

Nearly every work on constitutions in Africa, regardless of the region, directly or indirectly addresses some form of constitutionalism. Unsurprisingly, constitutionalism in Africa is not an understudied phenomenon. However, most of these studies focus on a single aspect of constitutionalism. Therefore, this section does not aim to cover every work on constitutionalism across different African jurisdictions. Instead, it highlights a limited number of recent studies that either comparatively analyze African jurisdictions, offer some degree of cross-jurisdictional comparison, or provide an interdisciplinary examination of the distinct components of constitutionalism within African contexts. These studies can be divided into three categories.

The first strand of the literature focuses on the challenges facing constitutionalism in Africa. Akiba explores the challenges facing constitutional democracy in transitional African societies, highlighting persistent inequalities and repression despite constitutional rights and political liberalization.[49] It offers a conceptual framework to understand these obstacles, stresses the importance of sustaining public confidence in democracy, and proposes ways to confront entrenched power structures resisting institutional change.[50]

Diala and Rautenbach question the usual way of looking at how state and indigenous legal systems interact, which often treats them as being in conflict.[51] They put forward the idea of adaptive legal pluralism, which focuses on dialogue and cooperation between the two. By promoting this approach, the authors show how it can better deal with problems created when colonial powers imposed industrial legal systems on Africa's traditional, agriculture-based societies.

Abebe et al note that scholarship on constitutionalism in Africa faces two major challenges: the continent's diversity, with 54 countries shaped by distinct histories, and the persistent problem of "constitutions without constitutionalism".[52,53]Although constitutions are widespread and elections regularly held, authoritarian regimes, political dynasties, and manipulated constitutional amendments remain prevalent. In last decade, military coups in countries such as Burkina Faso, Mali, and Sudan have further underscored these difficulties. Against this backdrop, they explore broad themes including the design, amendment, and interpretation of constitutions; democratic transitions; accountability and diversity management; constitutional values, rights, and traditions; and the supranational dimensions of constitutional law. This book, however, demonstrates that challenges highlighted by Abebe et al

[49] See the next chapter of this book, which compares Pakistan with Egypt, and Chapter 6, which examines circumstances in Cambodia similar to those discussed in the African cases in earlier chapters.

[50] Gebeye (2021).

[51] Fombad and Steytler (2020).

[52] Fombad and Steytlar (2025).

[53] Ellett's (2013).

are not unique to Africa, and discusses similar challenges in Cambodia and Pakistan[54]—an especially valuable contribution.

Gebeye provides a theoretical framework for the study of constitutionalism in Africa.[55] They highlight the need for a theoretical framework to explain constitutionalism in Africa. They historically compare constitutional developments in Ethiopia, Nigeria, and South Africa. However, they do not adequately take distinct social, political, and legal factors of constitutionalism into account to explain distinct aspects of constitutionalism.

Fombad and Steytler highlight corruption as a central obstacle to constitutionalism and democracy in Africa [56]. They argue that despite its pervasive impact on all aspects of governance, the issue has only recently received serious attention, with most past anti-corruption measures proving symbolic and ineffective. They aim to foreground the urgency of tackling corruption, acknowledging its complexity and the need for comprehensive remedial action.

The second strand of the literature explores the various stages of the process leading to constitutionalism, with particular emphasis on constitutional design and constitutional change, which shape the behaviour of politicians, judges, and citizens in ways that can either strengthen or undermine constitutionalism. Fombad and Steytlar explain that, since the 1990s, African states have pursued constitutional reforms to curb coups and instability by embedding democracy and constitutional rule; however, frequent and sometimes arbitrary constitutional changes now risk undermining progress toward constitutionalism, good governance, and the rule of law.[57] They investigate the drivers and processes of these reforms, examine the roles of domestic institutions and international actors, and discuss how constitutional change can occur without weakening democratic consolidation in Africa. However, the crucial question insufficiently addressed in their analysis, and one that this volume seeks to examine, is the specific conditions under which those in power can be effectively held to account.

As the chapters in this edited collection demonstrate, constitutional reforms or institutional design, in isolation, have not proven adequate to advance constitutionalism; were they sufficient, one would expect meaningful improvements to have followed the successive waves of constitutional change. A more comprehensive explanation emerges from an interdisciplinary approach, such as that adopted in several chapters of this volume.

Ellett's work is one of the very few studies that comparatively examine constitutional provisions in Uganda, Tanzania, and Malawi.[58] However, the book attributes increasing judicial power in these countries to the historical construction of judicial power during the colonial period. It explains how this power creates opportunities

[54] Fombad and Steytlar (2016).

[55] Fombad and Steytler (2021).

[56] Fombad and Steytler (2019).

[57] Fombad and Steytler (2021).

[58] Ibid.

for the consolidation of democracy. However, there are two issues with this study. First, the study analyses developments regarding judicial power only in three African jurisdictions. Second, it is mainly a historical account of judicial power in these jurisdictions. This book does not provide an interdisciplinary account of distinct components of constitutionalism in a wide range of African jurisdictions.

Fombad edited a multi-authored book focusing on the separation of powers in African constitutionalism.[59] The book explains the formal legal component of constitutionalism but like Ellet (2013) does not provide an adequate analysis of the social, political, and economic factors that shape the context in which the nature and scope of constitutionalism advance in Africa.

Fombad and Steytler explore how Africa's fragile constitutional foundations can withstand authoritarian resurgence and democratic decline.[60] The volume focuses on the role of elections in strengthening democracy and constitutionalism, raising key questions about how to make elections genuinely competitive, reduce the high stakes of losing, and encourage political actors to accept outcomes within democratic rules. While offering no simple solutions, they stress the urgency of addressing these challenges, as constitutionalism and democracy remain the best available options.

Fombad and Steyler previously examined and evaluated the relationship between decentralisation and constitutionalism in Africa.[61] The book explains how decentralisation is constitutionalised in Africa. It touches on constitutionalism in relation to decentralization, but like Ellett (2013) and their subsequent publications[62], it does not offer an interdisciplinary explanation of the distinct aspects of constitutionalism in Africa and beyond.

Similar to Fombad and Steytler's work[63], Sahle discussed the concept of constitutionalism and its historical relationship with democracy in Africa. The book mostly focuses on historical trajectories of constitutions in different African jurisdiction but do not discuss how politicians and judges hold the government to account and to what extent.

The third strand of the literature examines the relationship between specific aspects of constitutionalism and their effects. Fombad and Steytler discuss that since the 1990s, Africa's constitutional changes have raised debates about whether they reflect a distinct "African constitutional identity." Their work examine this question by exploring the influence of colonial legacies, the gap between constitutional ideals and practice, and the role of traditional authorities. It also considers

---

59 Sahle (2017).

60 Fombad and Steytlar (2024).

61 Fombad and Steytlar (2022).

62 Yusuf (2010).

63 Gloppen et al. (2010).

whether constitutionalism itself should be part of African constitutional identity, drawing on examples from both common and civil law systems as well as indigenous legal traditions.

Another study by Fombad and Steytler explores the link between constitutionalism and economic growth in Africa by examining five key questions: whether 1990s constitutional reforms supported market economies; how constitutions address land and natural resources; the role of the state in economic regulation and social welfare; the influence of globalization on constitution-making and economic governance; and whether constitutionalism has promoted economic prosperity in practice. This study intersects with scholarship (discussed above) examining the relationship between constitutionalism and constitutional design, particularly the contribution of constitutional changes to constitutionalism. However, this volume extends the analysis by incorporating the social and political dimensions of constitutionalism into these explanations.

Yusuf focused on the rule of law in Nigeria and explained how the judiciary's public accountability contributes to the transformation of state institutions in a transitional society like Nigeria. The book is a single case study focusing on one formal element of constitutionalism: judicial accountability. It overlooks distinct aspects of constitutionalism in different African jurisdictions.

Gloppen et al. compare the accountability of elites by judiciaries in Latin America and Africa. They explain how and why courts are overzealous in some jurisdictions and are hesitant to exercise their powers actively against governments in other jurisdictions under similar political circumstances. The book looks at the judiciary's role in Latin America and Africa from the perspective of accountability and attributes judicial activism mainly to powers provided to the judiciary in a constitution. The book's focus on the judiciary's ability to hold elites accountable explains a part of legal constitutionalism. However, it does not explain how and why distinct aspects of constitutionalism strengthens or weakens in different jurisdictions of Africa.

Most of the studies mentioned above focus on only one aspect of constitutionalism and do not provide an interdisciplinary explanation of the distinct components of constitutionalism in Africa and beyond. These studies do not draw on African jurisdictions to offer lessons for constitutionalism in jurisdictions with similar experiences beyond Africa.

On the other hand, this book offers an interdisciplinary and partially comparative analysis of the distinct components of various forms of constitutionalism in Africa and beyond. It explores how these aspects of constitutionalism strengthen or weaken in Africa and beyond by addressing several key questions: How and why does constitutionalism grow or decline in Africa and beyond? Why does constitutionalism endure in some African jurisdictions but falter in others? What diverse challenges does constitutionalism face in Africa and beyond? And what lessons does the African experience of constitutionalism offer to jurisdictions outside the continent?

This book is an interdisciplinary account of constitutionalism and explains how social, legal, and political factors simultaneously shape the nature and scope of constitutionalism. It adopts an interdisciplinary approach and combines empirical and comparative perspectives to draw rich implications from the experiences of countries in Africa and beyond. It employs various methodological strategies, including historical analyses, comparative methods, and qualitative approaches.

The book does not claim to explain distinct aspects of constitutionalism in all of Africa. The African continent has many countries; this book focused on only a few of them. This book does not claim to generalise the analysis to all African jurisdictions other than those discussed in this book. Each has its own unique socio-political, politico-legal, and socio-economic contexts. Five chapters of this book focus on five African countries; one chapter offers a comparative analysis of an African and an Asian jurisdiction, and another chapter focuses on a non-African jurisdiction (Cambodia). Each chapter of this book explains constitutionalism in a unique context and offers new insights into the broader literature by using that context.

The book's second chapter comparatively analyses the relationship between judicial populism and the nature and scope of judicial independence in Pakistan and Egypt. Different socio-economic and socio-political issues, such as rising unemployment and inflation, limit the access of large sections of society in both countries to justice and other basic necessities of life. In addition, antagonism between political incumbents and those out of power gives rise to conflict between heterogeneous groups of society and the ruling elite. Strategic judicial leaders in both countries use this discord by cultivating support for the judiciary. They do so from the bench by favouring the public in their decisions or off the bench by heading groups during demonstrations against the regime and for the judiciary. When the ruling elite attempt to control the judiciary through court-packing or court-curbing actions, heterogeneous societal groups protect the judiciary through agitation and/or litigation against the regime and for the judiciary. In this manner, the judiciary in both countries can make decisions consistently against the regime's interests, thereby increasing *de facto* judicial independence.

The third chapter explains how the emergence of the federations ensures the supremacy of the constitution and addresses such disputes where power remains less institutionalised. Federal systems require an institution that impartially and peacefully decides such disputes. Some federations assign this function to regular supreme courts, while others allocate this task to constitutional courts. Ethiopia has assigned this function to a political organ, the House of Federation, as advised by a quasi-expert body. The empirical investigation of the House of Federation indicates that it has primarily remained subservient to the political party in power, resulting in a centralised federation. It has been ineffective as a guardian of the constitution, has rarely set limits on political power, and largely failed to enforce human rights. This chapter establishes that Ethiopia is a federation without constitutionalism and argues the case for establishing an impartial constitutional court that ensures the supremacy of the constitution, resolves disputes impartially, enforces human rights, and sets limits on power.

The fourth chapter examines and evaluates the effects of the institutional legacy of the Nigerian judiciary on human rights, the rule of law, and democracy. Nigeria has experienced more than two decades of civil rule after nearly 30 years of military authoritarian rule. The political transition proceeded with the judicial institution's baggage of complicity in legitimising authoritarian rule and a record of corruption. In an age of the judiciary's increasing involvement in governance, the Nigerian judiciary has been a strategic actor across diverse and critical aspects of administering the country. While the Nigerian judiciary has made significant contributions to governance in the troubled post-authoritarian state, it remains blighted by an unaccounted institutional legacy. This continues to have serious consequences for the rule of law, human rights, and democracy in the polity.

The fifth chapter explains the protection of judicial independence through judicial service commissions in Cameroon. It examines Cameroon's judicial appointment body, the Higher Judicial Council (HJC). The HJC was initially introduced during colonialism, and post-colonial developments of that institution have retained some of its key features, reflecting aspects of the civil law judicial tradition. The chapter critically analyses vital features such as its composition, mandate, and powers. It queries the extent to which the independence of the judiciary can be secured, taking into consideration those key features and their operation within the legal and political culture of Cameroon. The chapter contends that the current configuration of the HJC obviates the potential to secure the independence of the judiciary. Drawing on experiences from other jurisdictions (both civil law and common law) and the standards embedded in the newly developed Commonwealth Model Law on Judicial Service Commissions, the chapter offers alternative perspectives on enhancing the potential for the HJC to better secure the independence of the judiciary in Cameroon.

The sixth chapter focuses on the rule of law and its effects on judicial independence in Madagascar. It argues that rule-of-law building can be potentially successful if there is less emphasis on the orthodox rule of law—depicted by the prioritisation of state-based institutional and procedural systems bent on facilitating economic outcomes—and more emphasis on the substantive rule of law, which is relevant to positive human development. However, a substantive approach is inadequate for transcending the limitations of the Western-centric rule of law. The chapter illustrates this by highlighting the limits of building the rule of law in the plural, post-crisis/conflict states with weak state institutions without prioritising approaches to governance or justice that can comprehend, embrace, and, or navigate the influence of social norms. Specifically, it analyses the concept of *Fihavanana* and its implications for justice and governance by illustrating how the relationship between arms of government (judiciary and executive) is traversed through it and its consequence for perceptions of judicial independence and the fair dispensation of justice. It further argues for embracing and co-opting contextualised notions of the rule of law that embrace the Malagasy worldview and value of *Fihavanana* without orientalising it. Consequently, it recommends the re-appropriation, de-politicisation and rejuvenation of *Fihavanana*, deploying its flexibility, authority, and legitimacy to support building a culture of justice and accountability in governance.

Building upon the discussion on judicial independence in Africa, the seventh chapter discusses judicial independence in Cambodia. This country experienced a tragic past before re-establishing itself as a constitutional democracy following the 1993 elections (the first of its modern era). Its progress towards the plural multiparty democracy foreseen by its modern constitution remains intensely monitored by the international community. It is of considerable interest to many protagonists, particularly Western and European states. The country's developing judiciary has long been tainted with allegations of corruption and a lack of actual independence. Increasingly, the ruling party has engaged the courts to destroy viable opposition parties and legitimise constitutional and legal changes which strengthen the ruling party's position—it secured all the National Assembly seats in 2018 and all but five in 2023.

The eighth chapter provides a South African perspective on how courts act as sites of political contestation. In South Africa, a nascent constitutional democracy, politics have migrated to the courtroom, and courts, especially the South African Constitutional Court, have adjudicated political controversies under the guise of vindicating the Constitution, the rule of law, and fostering a culture of accountability. The supremacy of the Constitution, the notion of transformative constitutionalism, and the courts' extensive remedial powers create an ideal framework for the judicialisation of politics. This chapter critically examines the effects of the judicialisation of politics and contends that this phenomenon threatens the legitimacy of the judiciary. The chapter argues that the courts' outcome-oriented approach to adjudication has led to a notable decline in the quality of their jurisprudence, which itself has adverse implications for the rule of law. The final chapter presents the conclusion. It discusses various challenges facing the distinct aspects of constitutionalism examined in this book and offers recommendations for addressing them. It also highlights potential avenues for future inquiry in the next volume of this collection.

References

Akiba, O (2021) Political Change and Constitutionalism in Africa: Emerging Trends. Routledge.

Bhatti H, Mehtab U, Zehri A, Bilal R, Tanoli I, Hakeem A (2024) "https://www.dawn.com/news/1824079" Calls for probe into letter by 6 IHC judges on 'brazen meddling' in judicial affairs,' *Dawn, 27 March, https://www.dawn.com/news/1824079, accessed 28 August 2025.*

Chávez RB (2004) The rule of law in nascent democracies: Judicial politics in Argentina. Stanford University Press, Palo Alto, CA

Chávez RB, Ferejohn J, Weingast B (2011) A theory of the politically independent judiciary: a comparative study of the United States and Argentina. In: Helmke G, Ríos-Figueroa J (eds) *Courts in Latin America.* Cambridge University Press, pp 219–247

Cho M (2020) Rethinking Judicial Independence in Democracy and Autocracy. Dissertation, Duke University. Retrieved from https://hdl.handle.net/10161/21523.

Choudhry S, Tushnet M (2020) Participatory constitution-making: introduction. Int J Const Law 18(1):173–178. https://doi.org/10.1093/icon/moaa014
Corporate Finance Institute. (n.d.) Third World: Countries that are generally classified poor or developing. https://corporatefinanceinstitute.com/resources/economics/third-world/#:~:text=What%20is%20%E2%80%9CThird%20World%E2%80%9D%3F,(3)%20 high%20mortality%20rates
Cross FB (2008) Judicial independence. In: Whittington KE, Daniel Kelemen R, Caldeira GA (eds) The Oxford handbook of law and politics 557. Oxford University Press, Oxford
Democracy Index (2024). Economic Intelligence. n.d. https://www.eiu.com/n/campaigns/democracy-index-2024/
Diala AC, Rautenbach C (Eds.) (2024) Reimagining Legal Pluralism in Africa. Leiden, The Netherlands: Brill | Nijhoff. https://doi.org/10.1163/9789004696747
Ellett R (2013) Pathways to judicial power in transitional states: perspectives from African Courts, 1st edn. Routledge. https://doi.org/10.4324/9780203539163
Epperly B (2017) 'Political competition and de facto judicial independence in non-democracies,' European Journal of Political Research, 56(2):279–300, https://doi.org/10.1111/1475-6765.12186
Epperly B (2019) The political foundations of judicial independence in dictatorship and democracy. Oxford University Press
Ewokor C, Chibelushi W (2023) Nigeria Supreme Court dismisses election challenges BBC News. 26 October https://www.bbc.co.uk/news/world-africa-67227814
Fombad CF (ed) (2016) Separation of powers in African constitutionalism. Oxford University Press, Oxford
Fombad CF, Steyler N (eds) (2019) Decentralization and constitutionalism in Africa. Oxford University Press, Oxford
Fombad CM, Steytler N (eds) (2020) Corruption and Constitutionalism in Africa. Oxford University Press
Fombad CM, Steytler N (eds) (2021) Democracy, Elections and Constitutionalism in Africa. Oxford University Press
Fombad CM, Steytler N (eds) (2022) Constitutionalism and the Economy in Africa. Oxford University Press
Fombad CM, Steytler N (eds.) (2024) Constitutional Identity and Constitutionalism in Africa. Oxford University Press
Fombad CM, Steytler N (eds.) (2025) Constitutional Change and Constitutionalism in Africa. Oxford University Press
Freedom House (2024) 'NEW REPORT: Africa Marks a Decade of Decline in Freedom, with 2023 Being Marred by Electoral Violence and Civil Conflict,' https://freedomhouse.org/article/new-report-africa-marks-decade-decline-freedom-2023-being-marred-electoral-violence-and,Accessed 19 August 2025
Gauri V, Brinks DM (eds) (2008) Courting social justice: judicial enforcement of social and economic rights in the developing world. Cambridge University Press, Cambridge
Gebeye BA (2021) A theory of African constitutionalism. Oxford University Press, Oxford
Ginsburg T (2003) Judicial review in new democracies: constitutional courts in Asian cases. Cambridge University Press, Cambridge
Ginsburg T, Moustafa T (eds) (2008) Rule by law: the politics of courts in authoritarian regimes. Cambridge University Press, Cambridge
Ginsburg T, Huq AZ, Khaitan T (eds) (2024) The entrenchment of democracy: the comparative constitutional design of elections, parties and voting. Cambridge University Press, Cambridge
Gloppen S, Wilson BM, Gargarella R, Skaar E, Kinander M (2010) Courts and power in Latin America and Africa. Palgrave Macmillan, New York
Gozzi L (2025) "https://www.bbc.co.uk/news/articles/clyrlvwx9rgo" Ukraine's borders must not be changed by force, EU leaders say,' BBC News, 12 August https://www.bbc.co.uk/news/articles/clyrlvwx9rgo, Accessed 23 August 2025

Hamel K, Tong B, Hofer, M (2019) "https://www.brookings.edu/articles/poverty-in-africa-is-now-falling-but-not-fast-enough/" Poverty in Africa is now falling—but not fast enough, Brookings Institution, https://www.brookings.edu/articles/poverty-in-africa-is-now-falling-but-not-fast-enough/, Accessed 12 August 2025
Helmke G, Rios-Figueroa J (2011) Courts in Latin America. Cambridge University Press, Cambridge
Hilbink L (2007) Judges beyond politics in democracy and dictatorship: lessons from Chile. Cambridge University Press, Cambridge
Hirschl R, Roznai Y (eds) (2024) Deciphering the genome of constitutionalism: the foundations and future of constitutional identity. Cambridge University Press, Cambridge
Holgado BG, Urribarri, RS (2023) 'Court-packing and democratic decay'. Global Constitutionalism 12(2):350–377
Huntington SP (1991) The Third Wave: Democratization in the Late Twentieth Century. University of Oklahoma Press, Oklahoma
Hutcheson D, McAllister I (2018) Putin versus the turnout? Mapping the Kremlin's 2018 presidential election support. Russian Polit *3*(3):333–358. https://doi.org/10.1163/2451-8921-00303002
Khan T, Abimbola S, Kyobutungi C, Pai M (2022) How we classify countries and people-and why it matters. BMJ Glob Health 7(6):e009704. https://doi.org/10.1136/bmjgh-2022-009704. PMID: 35672117; PMCID: PMC9185389
Komárek J, Aasa B, Bán M, Krajewski M (eds) (2025) European constitutionalism the other way round: from the periphery to the centre. Cambridge University Press, Cambridge
Langa P (2006) Transformative Constitutionalism. Lecture delivered at Stellenbosch University on 9 October 2006. https://vula.uct.ac.za/access/content/group/43c49dc1-22c9-4c39-9f21-0f588f5182e3/Reading%20Material/Introduction%20to%20Constitutional%20Law/Prescribed%20reading/Pius%20Langa%20-%20Transformative%20Constitutionalism.pdf
Law DS (ed) (2022) Constitutionalism in context. Cambridge University Press, Cambridge
Levitsky S, Way, Luncan.A. (2010) Competitive authoritarianism: hybrid regimes after the cold war. Cambridge University Press, Cambridge
Loughlin M (2022) Against constitutionalism. Harvard University Press, Cambridge
Lowell H, Gedeon J (2025) Chief Justice rebukes Trump for call to impeach judge hearing deportation case. The Guardian. 18 March https://www.theguardian.com/us-news/2025/mar/18/trump-judge-impeachment-venezuelan-deportations
Macdonald RA, Kong HL (2012) Judicial independence as a constitutional virtue. In: Rosenfeld M, Sajó A (eds) The Oxford handbook of comparative constitutional law, online edn. Oxford Academic. https://doi.org/10.1093/oxfordhb/9780199578610.013.0041
Melton J, Ginsburg T (2014) Does De Jure Judicial independence really matter? A reevaluation of explanations for judicial independence. J Law Courts 2:187
Moustafa T (2003) Law versus the state: the Judicialization of politics in Egypt. Law Soc Inq 28(4):883–930
Moustafa T (2007) The struggle for constitutional power: law, politics, and economic development in Egypt. Cambridge University Press, Cambridge, UK
Ndulo M, Emeziem C (2021) Routledge Handbook of African Law. Routledge
Okechukwu N (2023) The fragility of the African governance agenda: A crisis of legitimacy, ECDPM Brief, https://ecdpm.org/work/fragility-african-governance-agenda-crisis-legitimacy, 30 October, Accessed 14 August 2025
Okoth-Ogendo HWO (1993) "Constitutions Without Constitutionalism: Reflections on an African Political Paradox." In: Greenberg D, Katz SN, Oliviero MB, Wheatley SC (eds) Constitutionalism and Democracy: Transitions in the Contemporary World, New York and Oxford: Oxford University Press, pp 65–82
Popova M (2010) Political competition as an obstacle to judicial independence: evidence from Russia and Ukraine. Comp Polit Stud 43(10):1202–1229
Popova M (2012) Politicized justice in emerging democracies: a case study of courts in Russia and Ukraine. Cambridge University Press

Popova M (2020) The post communist judiciary: one step forward, two steps back. In: Engelbrekt K, Kostadinova P (eds) Bulgaria's democratic institutions at thirty: a balance sheet. Lexington Book, pp 241–261

Reayat N, Smith RKM, Cho M (Eds.) (2024). Judicial Independence in Transitional Democracies (1st ed.). Routledge. https://doi.org/10.4324/9781003458296

R (on the application of AAA (Syria) and others) (Respondents/Cross Appellants) v Secretary of State for the Home Department (Appellant/Cross Respondent) [2023] UKSC 42 https://supremecourt.uk/uploads/uksc_2023_0093_etc_judgment_636270e30e.pdf

Rosenfeld M, Sajo A (2012) The Oxford handbook of comparative constitutional law. Oxford University Press, Oxford

Sahle EN (ed) (2017) Democracy, constitutionalism, and politics in Africa: historical contexts, developments, and dilemma. Palgrave Macmillan, New York

Shetreet S, Chodosh H, Eric H (eds) (2021) Challenged justice: In pursuit of judicial independence. Brill | Nijhoff, Leiden, The Netherlands. https://doi.org/10.1163/9789004421554

Soto Barrientos, F., Suárez, O., & Alemparte, B. (2025). The Citizen Initiative in Chile's constitution-making (2021–2023): Lessons from a participatory and digital mechanism in comparative perspective. Global Constitutionalism, 1–29. doi:10.1017/S2045381725100038

Tushnet M, Bugarič B (2022) What is constitutionalism? Power to the people: constitutionalism in the age of populism, online edn. Oxford Academic, New York, 20 https://doi.org/10.1093/oso/9780197606711.003.0002

Tushnet M (2016) Editorial. Int J Const Law 14(1):1–5. https://doi.org/10.1093/icon/mow021

UN Environment Programme (n.d.) https://www.unep.org/regions/africa/our-work-africa, accessed 16 August 2025

Vanberg G (2008) Establishing and maintaining judicial independence. In: Whittington K, Kelemen RD, Caldeira G (eds) The Oxford handbook of law and politics. Oxford Univ. Press, Oxford, UK, pp 99–118

Wasuna B (2025) Chief Justice Maartha Koome's security detail withdrawn, Judiciary Police Unit Trimmed. Nation. 24 January 2025 https://nation.africa/kenya/news/cj-koome-security-withdrawn%2D%2D4899584#story

Yusuf HO (2010) Transitional justice, judicial accountability and the rule of law. Routledge, Oxon

Judicial Populism and Judicial Independence in Developing Democracies: A Comparative Analysis of Egypt and Pakistan

Nauman Reayat

Abstract Judicial developments in Pakistan between 2005 and 2013 and in Egypt between 1979 and 2001 suggest that judicial populism, manifested in the contestation between heterogeneous groups of society (such as civil society organizations, lawyers, and opposition political parties) and ruling elites, alongside the emergence of active and strategic judicial leadership shaped the context in which judicial independence increased. These groups expressed their contestation through anti-regime and pro-judges demonstrations and anti-regime litigation. These actions signaled the emergence of judicial populism and provided the judiciary with protection against state-led court-packing and court-curbing measures, while also enabling an increase in rulings issued against government interests in both countries. How and why does judicial populism shape the context in which judicial independence increases in developing democracies? Little is written about judicial populism, and studies touching upon this subject do not adequately examine the relationship between judicial independence and judicial populism, especially in developing democracies. These studies suggest that judicial populism undermines certain aspects of judicial independence. Comparing Egypt and Pakistan, this chapter argues that judicial populism consists of the contestation between ruling elites and people and the emergence of active and strategic judicial leadership that leverages this contestation to advance judicial independence. These features of judicial populism shaped the context in which the judiciary increased its power against other branches of state between 2005 and 2013 in Pakistan, and between 1979 and 2001 in Egypt. When these elements ceased to exist, judicial independence could not be maintained. This chapter provides the first interdisciplinary comparative analysisof

---

This chapter is based on the research conducted during Economic Social Research Council Postdoctoral Fellowship (ES/W007223/1 Judicial independence in authoritarian and hybrid regimes) of the author at the School of Law and Politics, Cardiff University.

N. Reayat (✉)
Leicester Law School, University of Leicester, Leicester, UK
e-mail: nr210@leicester.ac.uk

N. Reayat, H. O. Yusuf (eds.), *Constitutionalism in Africa and Beyond*, Ius Gentium: Comparative Perspectives on Law and Justice 127,
https://doi.org/10.1007/978-3-032-01180-0_2

judicial populism and judicial independence in Pakistan and Egypt. It advances the study of judicial independence and judicial populism by offering the insight that judicial populism can strengthen judicial independence only when two conditions coexist: sustained contestation between the people and ruling elites, and a strategic judicial leader able to leverage that contestation to enhance judicial independence.

1 Introduction

Judicial independence is a globally important phenomenon. In July 2025, in one of the world's most established democracies—the United States (U.S.), whose judicial developments significantly influence the wider literature on constitutional law and politics—Justice Department announced that it had filed a misconduct complaint against Judge James Boasberg, Chief Judge of the U.S. District Court for the District of Columbia.[1] This move appeared to undermine judicial independence, seemingly in retaliation for Judge Boasberg's April 2025 decision, in which he held that the Trump administration had acted "in bad faith" by hastily arranging deportation flights of Venezuelans to El Salvador while court proceedings on their legality were still ongoing in March 2025.[2] On 4 July 2025, the Chief Justice of Ghana, Justice Gertrude Torkornoo instituted proceedings before the Economic Community of West African States Court of Justice, contesting the constitutionality of her suspension from office in April 2025.[3] This international challenge follows earlier domestic proceedings in which the Chief Justice questioned the procedural propriety of the suspension, raised concerns regarding threats to judicial independence, and underscored the need for compliance with constitutional safeguards. In 2023, forty-nine magistrates, including judges and prosecutors, were dismissed by the Tunisian government, leading to protests across the country.[4] In 2022, the UK Parliament's All-Party Parliamentary Group on Democracy and the Constitution found that ministers had acted improperly by questioning the legitimacy of judges when rulings were deemed unfavourable.[5] The process of transitional justice in Ethiopia is currently at the centre of public discussion, and the success of the process requires an independent judiciary.[6] Judicial independence has never been as important as it is today, being required for the protection of human rights, democracy, and the rule of law.

[1] Raymond and Wolfe (2025).

[2] Ibid.

[3] Naadi (2025).

[4] Human Rights Watch (2023).

[5] Siddique (2022). APPG aims 'to disseminate knowledge, generate debate, and facilitate engagement on democratic and constitutional issues amongst members of both houses of Parliament and the public'.

[6] Adem & Ibrahim (2023).

The wider literature on constitutional law and politics attributes judicial independence to different factors, including (but not limited to) legal systems,[7] democratisation,[8] public support,[9] and federalism,[10] as well as strategies by outgoing regimes to voluntarily empower the judiciary to use it against incoming regimes,[11] and the government's commitment to international organisations or other governments.[12] However, the process of judicial independence in two developing democracies, specifically Pakistan and Egypt, provides a novel explanation of judicial independence. These countries have different societies, political and legal systems, and histories.[13] Egypt's legal system is based on civil law traditions, whereas the legal system of Pakistan is based on common law. However, judicial populism, resulting from the contestation between the people and the ruling elite, and the emergence of strategic judicial leaders, shaped the context of *de facto* judicial independence in both countries. Judicial independence[14] increased in Pakistan between 2005 and 2013 and in Egypt between 1979 and 2001, as evidenced by the ability of the court to protect itself against court-packing[15] or court-curbing actions,[16] as well as the court's decisions against the regime's interests during these periods.

How and why do judicial populism, which arises from a confrontation between the people and the ruling elite, shape the context in which judicial independence increases in developing democracies? The wider literature on comparative constitutional law and politics does not adequately address this question.[17] These studies overlook the role that judicial populism can play in strengthening judicial independence, especially in developing democracies where regimes are in transition between democracy and authoritarianism, elections are perceived as unfair and non-transparent, political equality in terms of equal opportunity to participate in politics

[7] Ramseyer and Rasmusen (1997).

[8] Larkin (1996) and Abraham (1998).

[9] Caldeira & Gibson (1992), Gibson et al. (1998).

[10] Aydin (2013), Epperly (2017, 2018, 2019), Randazzo et al. (2016), Tridimas (2010).

[11] Epperly (2017, 2019). Federal states such as India, US, or Canada provide the higher judiciaries with powers to make decisions on disputes amongst and between the federal government and states government. These powers are usually not available to the higher judiciaries in unitary states (e.g. United Kingdom).

[12] Moustafa (2003).

[13] Discussed below.

[14] As will be explained later in detail *de facto*judicial independence refers to judicial power that is usually visible in courts' exercise of their powers against the interests of ruling elites.

[15] Court-packing involves appointing judges who are affiliated with, or loyal to, the appointing authority.

[16] Court-curbing involves undermining courts' powers.

[17] Arato and Cohen (2021), Çelenk (2016), Bencze (2020, 2021), Bernstein and Staszewski (2020), Blokker (2019), Chavez (2008), de la Torre and Lemos (2016), Hilbink and Ingram (2019), Krygier et al. (2022), Kureshi (2019, 2022), Lacey (2019), Landau (2018), Popova (2020), Tushnet and Bugaric (2021), Kureshi (2024), Hilbink (2024), Waseem (2012, 2015).

is minimal, the gap between the haves and have-nots is high, and the public often finds itself in opposition to the ruling elite.[18]

Comparing Pakistan and Egypt, I argue that different socio-economic and socio-political issues, such as rising unemployment and inflation, limit the access of large section of society to justice and other basic necessities of life. In addition, antagonism between political incumbents and those out of power gives rise to conflict between heterogeneous groups of society and the ruling elite. Strategic judicial leaders use this discord by cultivating support for the judiciary. They do so from the bench by delivering rulings that support these groups, and off the bench by leading them in demonstrations against the regime and in defence of the judiciary. When the ruling elite attempts to control the judiciary through court-packing or court-curbing actions, heterogeneous societal groups protect the judiciary through agitation and/or litigation against the regime and for the judiciary. In this manner, the judiciary is encouraged to make consistent decisions against the regime's interests, thereby leading to a certain increase in *de facto* judicial independence. This argument is explained in more detail in the subsequent sections.

This chapter makes three contributions to the literature on comparative constitutional law and politics. First, it fully unpacks the concept of judicial populism by identifying two main features: the contestation between the people and the ruling elites and the emergence of strategic judicial leaders who are able to leverage this contestation to enhance de facto judicial independence.[19] Second, it advances the field of judicial independence by explaining that the *de facto* component of judicial independence increases when nurtured by judicial populism. Third, it clarifies the role of judicial leaders by explaining how these leaders play an important part in judicial populism, and in turn, contribute to judicial independence. This chapter is the first ever study comparing judicial independence and judicial populism in Pakistan and Egypt.

The rest of the chapter is divided into four parts. The second part conceptualises judicial populism and judicial independence. The third part provides the background on legal and political systems in Pakistan and Egypt. The fourth part analyses how different indicators of judicial populism, such as the contestation between the elites in power and the people (i.e. heterogeneous societal groups) and the emergence of popular strategic judicial leaders, have shaped the context in which judicial independence increased in the two countries. The final part presents the conclusion.

---

[18] These features of developing democracies are not exhaustive. Different scholars used different terms to explain similar phenomenon. For example, Nelson (2025), Wigell (2008), Morlino (2009), Adeney (2017), Samad (2017), and Oldenburg (2017) used the term hybrid regimes where elected regimes come into power through non-transparent and unfair elections and powerful groups such as the military control politics and policy-making from behind the scenes.

[19] The concepts of judicial independence and 'the people' are discussed later in this chapter.

2 Understanding Judicial Independence and Judicial Populism

2.1 *Judicial Populism*

What is judicial populism? This question has not been addressed adequately in the wider literature on comparative constitutional law and judicial politics. Studies on judicial populism view it in terms of the decision-making process of judges according to popular sentiments and legal principles.[20] Kureshi argues that a populist judge seeks to appear closer to the people by making courts more accessible, allowing citizens to approach judges directly rather than strictly through lawyers, and encouraging media coverage of their speeches and rulings to speak openly to the public.[21] They interpret the Constitution as an expression of the people's will rather than merely a framework for dividing power between institutions and use plain, everyday language that resonates with the public instead of relying on complex legal jargon or precedent.[22] This chapter challenges this view, arguing that the above arguments do not fully explain judicial populism. Constitutional provisions such as Article 184(3) of the Pakistani Constitution,[23] Article 86 of the Colombian Constitution,[24] Article 24(C) of the Constitution of Indonesia,[25] and similar provisions in many other jurisdictions encourage citizens to approach constitutional courts established to examine the constitutionality of laws. These provisions enhance public access to courts and encourage citizens to approach judges directly rather than exclusively through lawyers. Thus, the connection between courts and citizens is not solely

[20] Kureshi (2024), Kalhan (2013a, b), Krygier et al. (2022), Popova (2020), Riaz (2021), Jácome (2017). Kalhan and Riaz used decisions of the higher judiciary of Pakistan that benefitted masses to illustrate judicial populism. Popova used similar approach in the context of Bulgaria. The edited collection of Krygier et al. used similar approach to explain constitution-making processes influenced by public sentiments across the world.

[21] Kureshi (2024).

[22] Ibid.

[23] Article 184(3) provides that the Supreme Court has the power to issue orders on matters of public importance related to enforcing Fundamental Rights, but it cannot act entirely on its own initiative (suo motu) and may only decide within the scope of an application filed under this clause.

[24] Article 86 of the Colombian Constitution establishes a mechanism, known as the tutela, that allows any individual to seek immediate judicial protection of their fundamental constitutional rights when threatened by the action or omission of public authorities. Judges may order others to act or refrain from acting, with such orders implemented immediately and subject to review by higher courts, including the Constitutional Court. The action is available only when no other judicial remedies exist, unless used temporarily to prevent irreversible harm, and must be resolved within 10 days. The law also extends its applicability to private actors providing public services or exercising power that directly affects collective interests or vulnerable individuals.

[25] Article 24(c) of the Indonesian Constitution grants the Constitutional Court of Indonesia final authority to review laws for constitutionality, resolve disputes between state institutions, decide on dissolving political parties, settle election result disputes, and rule on parliamentary allegations of constitutional violations by the President or Vice-President.

facilitated by judges themselves. Instead, it emerges from a combination of constitutional provisions that create space for judicial engagement, the strategic approach adopted by judges in applying those provisions, and the broader socio-political or socio-economic context (discussed below) in which they operate—all of which collectively shape the nature and scope of the court–citizen relationship and judicial independence. I further argue that in postcolonial contexts such as Pakistan, Kenya, and India—formerly under British rule—or in countries once colonised by non-English-speaking powers such as France or the Soviet Union, the majority of the population cannot read or understand language (usually English in countries previously ruled by Britain) in which judgments are delivered. This linguistic barrier limits the extent to which judicial decisions delivered in a language other than that spoken by the majority of the population in most of these countries, even when partially simplified, can be directly understood by the broader public, let alone generate their support. It was reported in 2023 that, according to World Bank indicators, Pakistan's adult literacy rate—the percentage of individuals aged 15 and above who can read and write with understanding a simple statement—had increased only marginally over the past 15 years, rising from 54 per cent to 58 per cent.[26] Moreover, Pakistan's level of learning poverty[27] is 18.3 per cent higher than the average for the South Asian region and 16.6 per cent higher than that of lower middle-income countries.[28]

In delivering rulings, judges necessarily rely on precedents, legal provisions, and established doctrines. They cannot rely on everyday language more than on legal language grounded in precedents and statutory provisions. Many rulings employ a combination of accessible language that resonates with the public and technical legal reasoning. This approach acknowledges the primary audience of judicial rulings, litigants and lawyers, while also making judgments intelligible to secondary audiences such as the media, civil society organisations (CSOs), and professionals who can read and understand English. Initially, Baum and later Ginsburg and Garoupa identified different groups of society as potential audiences of judges.[29] Baum explained how judges engage with different groups, while Ginsburg and Garoupa focused on how judges cultivate a positive reputation among them.

Furthermore, media coverage plays an important role in strengthening the relationship between courts and citizens; however, public opinion polls suggest that citizens show limited interest in news, including the reporting and coverage of judicial developments in countries such as Pakistan and Egypt. According to a Gallup Pakistan public opinion poll conducted in October 2022, 88% of respondents reported that they did not read newspapers.[30] In a poll conducted by the same organ-

---

[26] Hasan (2023).

[27] The inability to read and understand basic text in English. See World Bank (2021) for detailed discussion on the concept of learning poverty.

[28] Ibid.

[29] Baum (2008), Ginsburg and Garoupa (2009).

[30] Gallup Pakistan (2022).

isation in 2019, only 19% of respondents claimed that they read newspapers regularly.[31] In the same year, another survey by the organisation found that only 39% of respondents used the internet.[32] In a subsequent survey conducted in 2020, 56% of internet users reported using the internet primarily for entertainment,[33] indicating a limited interest in other content, including news—and by extension, coverage of judicial developments. Another public opinion survey by the same organisation in 2019 found that two in five (40%) internet users in Pakistan rely on Facebook and YouTube as sources of news.[34] These findings suggest that a significant portion of society shows little interest in news, including judicial developments. Therefore, the media is not a very important factor shaping the context in which populist judges emerge or judicial populism more broadly arises.

I argue that judicial populism is analogous to populism but goes beyond popular decision-making by judges. The contestation between the people and the ruling elite is at the core of populism.[35] Like populism in general, judicial populism involves contestation between the people and the elite in power, popular leadership, and the use of societal protests. However, when such contestation expresses itself in demonstrations for the judiciary and against the regimes, or anti-regime litigation for the judiciary and against the elites in power, it points to judicial populism. In judicial populism, popular leadership is provided by judges, not politicians, and judges exercise their legal powers to make decisions in line with the interests of the public at large. I will explain this concept by using the examples of Pakistan and Egypt later in this chapter.

However, the question is: who are the people and the ruling elite? Recent studies on judicial populism[36] frequently use the term people without adequately unpacking its meaning. Clarifying this concept is essential for understanding judicial behaviour, particularly in highly diverse socio-political and socio-economic contexts where societies are deeply divided along lines of class, ideology, ethnicity, and politics. The term 'people' does not necessarily refer to the population at large. While actions or ideas accepted or rejected by the population as a whole may serve as useful indicators of what is broadly popular or unpopular, it is practically impossible to collect data on the opinions of every individual within a society. The wider literature on populism suggests that 'people' refers to heterogenous groups from different socio-economic and socio-political backgrounds.[37] These groups may include opposition political parties, CSOs, rights activists, etc and represent people in relation to court. They do not necessarily need to include groups that are illiterate

---

[31] Gallup Pakistan (2019a).

[32] Gallup Pakistan (2019b).

[33] Gallup Pakistan (2020).

[34] Gallup Pakistan (2019c).

[35] Canovan (1981), Müller (2016), Stockemer (2018), Taggart (2000). These studies suggest that populism is basically anti-elites in nature. Popular politics targets the elites in society.

[36] Kureshi (2024), Hilbink (2024).

[37] Mudde & Kaltwasser (2012), Collier (2002), Conniff (2012), Oxhorn (1998).

or unable to read or understand English, the language in which rulings are delivered in most postcolonial countries formerly colonized by Britain.

Conversely, the classical definition of the ruling elite, or the 'elites', is those who own the means of production.[38] However, the composition of the elites has become complicated with the emergence of the modern state and consistent changes in the composition of the state and society. Therefore, there are different kinds of elites, including, but not limited to political, judicial, and economic elites.[39] This paper focuses on political and judicial elites, who are usually divided into two groups with respect to the contestation between them and the people: those who are in power or support those in power, and those who are out of power or support the people (i.e. other groups of society) against the elites in power. The latter is more representative of the 'people', as heterogeneous groups of society—discussed above—are a standard indicator.

2.2 *Judicial Independence*

Like judicial populism, the concept of judicial independence is also debated, but scholars largely agree on its two main components: *de jure* and *de facto*.[40] The former is not particularly controversial, as it involves the written constitutional guarantees that separate the power between different branches of the government and provides the judiciary with constitutional guarantees against other branches of the state. These guarantees generally include tenure, the process of judicial appointments without undue influence of other branches of the state, salary, powers of the judiciary, jurisdiction of the judiciary, and the removal of judges on reasonable grounds and without political reasons.[41] These guarantees can be assessed by observing the constitutional provisions.

De facto judicial independence refers to the behavioural independence of judges, and it is this component that is highly contested and very difficult to assess. Some scholars use data on the protection of human rights to measure *de facto* judicial independence[42] while others use expert opinions,[43] but judicial independence can

[38] Gatto and Power (2016), Armytage (2015), Halliday (1999), Shoukat & Gomez (2018).

[39] Armytage (2015), Lorch (2021), Tahyar (2012).

[40] Carrubba et al. (2015), Castro-Montero & Dijck (2017), Epperly (2019), Epperly & Sievert (2019), Hayo & Voigt (2007, 2014), Voigt et al. (2015), Hilbink & Ingram (2019), Melton & Ginsburg (2014).

[41] Melton & Ginsburg (2014).

[42] Linzer and Staton (2015) developed quantitative measurement of judicial independence by using Human Rights Country Reports issued by the US State Department or from expert surveys. Cingranelli and Richards (2010) relied upon experts' opinion to develop human rights database coding manual.

[43] Feld and Voigt (2007) used expert surveys on judicial independence to examine the relationship between economic growth and judicial independence. Howard and Carey (2004) relied upon experts'

also be treated as a contextual phenomenon, as some other studies propose.[44] Consequently, I use examples that show the successful protection of the judiciary against court-packing and court-curbing actions[45] by the regimes in Egypt and Pakistan,[46] the decisions of the Supreme Court of Pakistan (SCP) and the Supreme Constitutional Court (SCC) of Egypt against the interests of other branches of the state in politically important cases,[47] and the implementation of those decisions. While these do not constitute an exhaustive list of indicators of *de facto* judicial independence, they arguably provide a better understanding of judicial independence in the context of developing democracies where the judiciary faces significant challenges from dictators or where certain areas of public policy are influenced by powerful organisations such as the military.

What does it mean for a case to be politically important? According to Kapiszewski, cases before the high courts of Brazil and Argentina were deemed politically important if they directly challenged the authority of the government.[48] Similarly, VonDoepp's work in African countries viewed cases as politically important when they involved a challenge to the government's authority.[49] Mate added a further step by confirming the political importance of cases before the Supreme Court of India with experts.[50] A similar criterion is applied in this research: politically important cases herein mean those cases before the SCP under Article 184(3) of the Constitution of Pakistan 1973 and the SCC that involve the fate of political leaders, or directly challenge the authority of the regimes in power and have been discussed in the existing studies on judicial politics in Pakistan[51] and Egypt.[52] These courts are the last resort for determining the constitutionality of laws in the two countries. Other tiers of the legal systems are also important, but they do not have final authority to determine the constitutionality of laws. Accurate and complete data on the number of cases decided by these courts are not available, mainly because the governments of the two countries have no systematically managed data on court cases to date. Rough estimates provided in some studies put the number of

opinions to explain the importance of judicial independence for democracy. Tate and Keith (2009) relied upon experts' opinions on the independence of the judiciary to conceptualise and operationalise judicial independence.

44 Gee at al (2015) while explaining judicial independence in the UK argued that judicial independence is a contextual phenomenon.

45 Landau (2014). Landau assessed judicial power by examining protections against court-packing and court-curbing.

46 Chávez et al. (2011), Landau (2014), Lawlor (1986).

47 Finkel (2005); Ríos-Figueroa (2007). These studies viewed cases before the Supreme Court of Mexico that involve a direct challenge to the regimes in Mexico as politically important cases.

48 Kapiszewski (2007, 2012).

49 VonDoepp (2006, 2009).

50 Mate (2010).

51 Khan (2017), Shafqat (2018), Siddique (2006, 2015).

52 Al Hajjaji (2017, 2018a), Al Hajjaji (2016), Brown (1995, 2012), Brown & Dunne (2013), Hamad (2018), Moustafa (2003).

annual cases received by these courts in the thousands.[53] Due to these challenges and constraints, my focus is on cases discussed in the existing studies on judicial politics in Pakistan and Egypt.

3 Background

3.1 De Jure *Judicial Independence*

Pakistan and Egypt have two different legal systems, but *de jure* judicial independence exists in both countries through written guarantees provided to the judiciary against other branches of the government. These systems and the nature and scope of *de jure* judicial independence in the two countries are discussed in the next two sections.

3.1.1 Pakistan

Unlike in Egypt,[54] different constitutions in Pakistan detail the powers of different branches of the state. The legal system of Pakistan has three main components: the SCP, the provincial high courts, and the lower judiciary (district judiciary). The SCP is the highest court of authority in the judicial hierarchy, while the provincial high courts are the highest authority in the four provinces of the federal state of Pakistan: Punjab, Khyber Pakhtunkhwa, Sindh, and Baluchistan. The capital of Pakistan, Islamabad, has its own high court. Gilgit Baltistan and Azad Kashmir are autonomous administrative regions and have their own supreme courts.

The three constitutions of Pakistan contain schedules that protect the terms and conditions for services, as well as the remuneration for judges of the provincial high courts and the SCP.[55] The constitutions provide that the president shall appoint the judges of the SCP and the provincial high courts after consulting with the Chief Justice of Pakistan (CJP).[56] However, the process of judicial appointments changed in 2011 after the Nineteenth Constitutional Amendment, which established two appointment bodies: the Judicial Commission of Pakistan (JCP) and the Parliamentary Committee (PC). The process is discussed in detail in the subsequent sections.

---

[53] Moustafa (2003), Khan (2014).

[54] Discussed in the next section.

[55] Second schedule of the 1962 Constitution; Fifth schedule of the 1973 Constitution; Fourth schedule part I of the 1956 Constitution.

[56] Article 149 of the 1956 Constitution, Article 50 of the Constitution of Pakistan 1962, and Article 177 of the Constitution of Pakistan 1973.

All three constitutions provide the SCP with original jurisdiction,[57] appellate jurisdiction,[58] advisory jurisdiction,[59] review jurisdiction, and contempt jurisdiction. The original jurisdiction empowers the SCP to make decisions in disputes between the federal government and a provincial government or between two or more provincial governments. The appellate jurisdiction empowers the SCP to decide on appeals against the decisions of provincial high courts and other subordinate courts. The advisory jurisdiction empowers the SCP to advise on matters sent to it by the executive. However, Article 184(3) of the 1973 Constitution also empowers the SCP to issue orders in matters it considers to involve a question of public importance relating to the enforcement of any fundamental right. The 26th Constitutional Amendment to the 1973 Constitution, enacted in 2024, introduced a limitation by providing that the SCP shall not issue an order, direction, or declaration on its own initiative beyond the contents of any application filed under Article 184(3).

These constitutions also protect the process of removing judges from undue influence by other branches of the state. Removal on the grounds of mental or physical infirmity and/or misconduct used to require a two-thirds majority of the National Assembly under the 1956 Constitution,[60] but this procedure changed with the 1962 and 1973 constitutional revisions.[61] Under the new constitutions, the president can direct the Supreme Judicial Council (SJC) to inquire (or the SJC can inquire on its own) in matters regarding the incapability or misconduct of judges. The SJC consists of the CJP, the two most-senior judges of the SCP, and the two-most senior chief justices of the provincial high courts. The president shall notify to the government and the SCP about the removal based on the recommendation of the SJC.

All provinces are divided into different districts, and the lower judiciary operates in these districts. The court of the District and Session Judge (DSJ) is the highest court of authority. Courts of additional district and session judges, senior civil judges, civil judges, and judicial magistrates operate under the court of the DSJ. Courts of civil judges deal with civil matters, such as torts, damages, and land disputes. Courts of judicial magistrates deal with criminal matters, while the courts of district and session judges deal with criminal and civil matters.

57 Article 156 of the 1956 Constitution, Article 57 of the 1962 Constitution, and Article 184 of the 1973 Constitution.

58 Article 157 of the 1956 Constitution, Article 58 of the 1962 Constitution, and Article 185 of the 1973 Constitution.

59 Article 162 of the 1956 Constitution, Article 59 of the 1962 Constitution, and Article 186 of the 1973 Constitution.

60 Article 151 of the 1956 Constitution.

61 Article 128 of the 1962 Constitution and Article 209 of the 1973 Constitution.

3.1.2 Egypt

Unlike the Pakistani constitutions, Egyptian constitutions do not provide details. The original Egyptian constitution, which is written in Arabic, only provides a general overview of the legal system and its various tiers, and the current form of the constitution is vague about guarantees for the judiciary against other branches of the state. However, details of different powers, jurisdictions, and the process of appointments and removals are provided in separate laws.[62]

Egypt's legal system has three parts: the SCC,[63] the ordinary judiciary, and the administrative court.[64] The SCC, in turn, also has three parts, consisting of the Chief Justice of the Court,[65] the People's Assembly,[66] and the Commissioner Authority.[67] The assembly is empowered to deal with administrative affairs of the court,[68] while the Commissioner Authority consists of advisors, judges, and assistant advisors.[69] The authority is empowered in the role of the investigator.[70] It produces a report for the SCC, which consists of constitutional and legal issues and offers a legal opinion on the cases before it.

The ordinary judiciary consists of the Public Prosecution Office[71] and three different types of courts: the Court of Cassation, the Court of Appeal, and the Court of First Instance (primary courts and partial courts).[72] The highest court of authority of the ordinary judiciary is the Court of Cassation.[73] It determines the correct understanding and application of the law by the lower Court of Appeal and determines general legal rules.[74] These rules provide a uniform understanding of the laws to be followed by the lower judiciary. There are 33 circuit courts, of which 16 process criminal cases and 17 process civil, commercial, family, and labour law cases.[75] The fourth part is the Court of Cassation Technical Office,[76] which handles the administrative affairs of the court.

The Court of Appeal deals with civil and criminal cases. Prior to 2006, Egypt had six courts of appeal, which operated in Cairo, Alexandria, Tanta, Mansoura, Bani

---

[62] E.g. Judicial Authority Law discussed below.

[63] Law No. 48 of 1979. See also Supreme Standing Committee for Human Rights (n.d.).

[64] Abolueleid (2019).

[65] Al Hajjaji (2018).

[66] Dupret & Bernard-Maugiron (2002).

[67] Comparative Constitutions Project, n.d.

[68] Ibid.

[69] Ibid.

[70] Al Hajjaji (2018).

[71] OHCHR: LAW 150 of 1950 (n.d.).

[72] Abolueleid (2019).

[73] Dupret & Bernard-Maugiron (2002).

[74] EGYPT JUSTICE (n.d.).

[75] Ibid, Article 4 of Law No. 46 of 1972.

[76] Article 5 of Law No. 46 of 1972.

Swaif, and Assiut governorates.[77] In addition, Qena and Ismalia were introduced in 2006.

There are two divisions for the Court of First Instance: the primary courts and the partial courts.[78] The former is the upper part of the Court of First Instance. It deals with civil law cases worth more than 40,000 Egyptian pounds and appeals in misdemeanour cases.[79] The latter has jurisdiction over civil and criminal matters.

The administrative court consists of the State Council and the Administrative Prosecution Office. The State Council consists of three different branches: judicial, legislative, and advisory. The judicial branch deals exclusively with administrative disputes and has three parts: the Supreme Administrative Court, the Disciplinary Courts, and the State Commission Board.[80] The legislative branch is empowered to revise and pass any proposed law, legal amendment, or regulation that the president or the cabinet issues.[81] The advisory branch provides legal advice to the cabinet, the president, ministers, and public institutions. Moreover, the validation or acceptance of any governmental agency's contract, reconciliation, or arbitration award is subject to the acceptance of the advisory branch of the State Council.[82]

3.2 *Limited* de Facto *Judicial Independence*

The above analysis demonstrates that, while Pakistan and Egypt have different legal systems, *de jure* judicial independence nevertheless exists both, reflected in reasonable degree of separation of powers or in written guarantees for the judiciaries to protect against other branches of the states. However, *de facto* judicial independence in these countries has been limited, except between 1979 and 2001 in Egypt and 2005 and 2013 in Pakistan.

The limited degree of de facto judicial independence was evident in the inability of the judiciaries in the two countries to protect themselves against the court-packing or court-curbing actions of the executive. Three constitutions have been enacted in Pakistan since independence from British colonial rule in 1947. The first constitution was enacted in 1956 by the Constituent Assembly of Pakistan, but the assembly was not elected.[83] Subsequently, the then-army chief, General Ayub Khan, abrogated the 1956 constitution through direct military intervention in 1958[84] and enacted the second constitution of Pakistan in 1962. It, in turn, was abrogated by

[77] Article 10 of Law No. 46 of 1972 (Judicial Authority Law).

[78] Dupret and Bernard-Maugiron (2002).

[79] Al Hajjaji (2018a, 2018b).

[80] Al-khudayri (2009). Also see Supreme Standing Committee for Human Rights (n.d.).

[81] Sherif (1998).

[82] Al Hajjaji (2018a, 2018b).

[83] Khan (2016).

[84] Ibid.

General Yahya in 1969.[85] Yahya supervised the first general elections of Pakistan in 1970, which resulted in the first elected parliament in 1972.

The newly elected parliament enacted the current constitution of Pakistan in 1973. However, General Zia ul Haq suspended this constitution on 5 July 1977, when he toppled the elected government of the Pakistan People Party (PPP). Similarly, General Musharraf suspended this constitution twice, first when he overthrew the elected government of the Pakistan Muslim League Nawaz Group (PML-N) on 12 October 1999, and second when he proclaimed an emergency on 3 November 2007.[86] Both dictators packed the SCP and other provincial courts with judges loyal to regimes and effected many changes in the constitution.[87] The judiciary could not protect itself against these court-packing actions, and consequently, it could not make decisions in politically important cases that ran counter to the interests of the regimes.[88]

Like the military regimes, civilian regimes in Pakistan that came to power through general elections have also controlled the process of judicial appointments. Until 2005, these regimes attempted to appoint judges who could make decisions in their favour and retaliated when judicial decisions ran against their interests.[89] For example, when the SCP conducted the contempt-of-court proceedings against the then-Prime Minister Nawaz Sharif, his political supporters stormed the SCP, interrupting the court proceedings.[90] Storming the judiciary was a court-curbing action that demonstrated the inability of the judiciary to protect itself against such actions. Similarly, Prime Minister Benazir Bhutto appointed judges to the SCP and provincial high courts who would serve her regime. As a result, the judiciary could not make decisions consistently against the ruling elite.[91]

Constitutionalism has been similarly unstable in Egypt. The history of *de jure* judicial independence in Egypt dates to 1923 when the first constitution was enacted. Following the military's Free Officers Revolution in 1952, Egypt's constitutional monarchy was transformed into a republic. However, like the regimes in Pakistan, the authoritarian regime of Gamal Abdel Nasser undermined the powers of the

---

[85] Ibid.

[86] Qureshi (2010).

[87] Both dictators administered oath to loyal judges under provisional constitutions during the suspension of the 1973 Constitution. See Khan (2016) for details.

[88] In The State v. Dosso (1958), the Supreme Court of Pakistan (SCP) ratified General Ayub Khan's military intervention of October 1958. In *Begum Nusrat Bhutto v. Chief of Army Staff* ((1977), the Court upheld General Zia-ul-Haq's military coup of July 1977. Similarly, in *Zafar Ali Shah v. General Pervez Musharraf* (2000), the SCP legitimised General Musharraf's coup of 12 October 1999, and in *Tikka Iqbal Muhammad Khan v. General Pervez Musharraf* (2008), it validated Musharraf's proclamation of emergency issued on 3 November 2007. The only instance in which the judiciary declared a military takeover void was after the fall of General Yahya Khan's regime, when he was no longer in power. See *Asma Jilani v Government of Punjab*, PLD 1972 SC 139, for details on how the Supreme Court addressed the ratification of General Yahya Khan's military takeover following the end of his regime.

[89] See insider accounts of previous chief justices Mian (2004) and Shah (2001).

[90] Muhammad Ikram Chaudhry v. Muhammad Nawaz Sharif (1998).

[91] Shah (2001), Mian (2004).

higher judiciary by forcibly retiring or transferring twenty judges of the Supreme Administrative Court to non-judicial positions and by establishing different courts with sweeping powers.[92] For example, the regime established the Court of Treason in 1952, the Court of the Revolution in 1953, and the People's Court in 1954.[93] These courts were assigned powers to make decisions on issues related to the revolution, treason, and the public interest, and were packed with judges loyal to the regime. Nasser ruled Egypt between 1952 and 1971, during which three constitutions were enacted, in 1956, in 1958, and in 1964.[94] During this period, the Supreme Court of Egypt was granted powers to examine issues pertaining to the constitutionality of laws.

After Egypt's defeat in the war of 1967, different legal organisations, such as the Judges' Club and the Lawyers' Syndicate, demanded political and legal reforms.[95] Viewing these demands as a threat to his government, Nasser issued an executive decree to remove 200 judicial officers, including members of the Judges' Club, judges of the Court of Cassation, and prosecutors from different parts of the Egyptian legal system.[96] The 1964 Constitution remained in force until the enactment of the 1971 Constitution,[97] which, after substantive amendments in 1998, 2005, and 2007, was dissolved in February 2011, following the Arab Spring.[98] Two new constitutions were enacted in 2012 and 2014. Since then, the incumbent regime of Abdel Fattah Al-Sisi has brought about changes, but the 2014 Constitution is still in force.[99] Like the judiciary in Pakistan, the Egyptian judiciary could not protect itself against the court-packing actions of the regimes. Its limited ability to make consistent decisions that ran counter to the regimes' interests indicates limited *de facto* judicial independence.

Such limited *de facto* judicial independence has existed in the two countries during different regime types and political systems. While Pakistan has oscillated between presidential and Westminster-style parliamentary system since it gained independence from Britain in 1947, political systems in Egypt have shifted from kingship to a presidential system, and from presidential to the current, semi-presidential system.[100] Both countries have multi-party systems. While Pakistan is currently a federal parliamentary state, Egypt has always been a unitary state. The central legislature in Pakistan and the parliament in Egypt are both bicameral, with an upper house (the Senate) and a lower house (the House of Representatives).

---

[92] Abdalla (1984), El Bora'i (n.d.), Rubinstein, (1977).

[93] Aziz (2013), Bernard-Maugiron (2009), Hamad (2018).

[94] El Bora'i (n.d.).

[95] Moustafa (2003).

[96] Abdalla (1984).

[97] Rubinstein (1977).

[98] Brown (2012).

[99] Supreme Standing Committee for Human Rights (n.d.).

[100] Bernard-Maugiron (2016).

The fact that *de facto* judicial independence was limited and could not increase significantly in the face of changing political systems and regime types suggests that an increase in such independence lies beyond regime types and legal and political systems. I argue that the key indicators of judicial populism—specifically, contestation between heterogeneous groups of society and the elite, and the emergence of strategic judicial leaders capable of harnessing this contestation to strengthen de facto judicial independence and empower the judiciary—shaped the context in which de facto judicial independence increased in Egypt between 1979 and 2001 and in Pakistan between 2005 and 2013. These indicators are explained in the next section.

4 Judicial Populism's Contribution to Judicial Independence

Existing studies suggest that judicial populism undermines judicial independence.[101] Comparing Egypt and Pakistan, this chapter contends against the foregoing view and argues that judicial populism shapes the context in which *de facto* judicial independence increases in developing democracies. The contestation between the people and the elites, as expressed in anti-regime demonstrations, anti-regime strategic litigation, and the emergence of popular strategic judicial leadership has contributed to the increase in *de facto* judicial independence in the two countries. This argument is explained in the next two sections.

4.1 Contestation Between the People and the Ruling Elite

There is always a certain degree of conflict between the people and the ruling elite in low-income and politically unstable countries such as Egypt and Pakistan. The contestation mainly involves grievances by heterogeneous societal groups, such as journalists, lawyers, opposition political parties, and CSOs against the ruling elite. Such grievances can include corruption, inequality, poor governance, non-independent and non-transparent elections, and limited access to justice. The media has faced censorship in Pakistan since the country's independence in 1947 under various military and civilian regimes.[102] The situation has been similar in Egypt for many decades[103]; consequently, censorship is the media's main grievance against the ruling elite in these countries. Similarly, various military or civilian regimes in

[101] Bencze (2021), Bernstein and Staszewski (2020), Blokker (2019), Granata-Menghini (2022), Kureshi (2019), Lacey (2019), Tushnet and Bugaric (2021).

[102] Jabbar and Isa (1997), Sial and Marco (2011), and Michaelsen (2011).

[103] Amin and Napoli (2000).

Egypt and Pakistan[104] have controlled opposition political parties through rigged elections, the politicised process of accountability, or through laws restricting political gatherings. As a result, restrictions imposed on political activities are the main grievance of opposition political parties in Egypt and Pakistan.

Civil society works for the protection of civil rights, but since the ruling elites in both countries control the activities of CSOs, the lack of autonomy from the regime, as well as continuing violations of civil rights are the main grievances of civil society in Egypt[105] and Pakistan.[106] People in the two countries have expressed their grievances against the ruling elite in different ways over time, through demonstrations, general elections (by voting against incumbents), and/or strategic litigation. However, anti-government sentiments have generally not been expressed by holding large-scale demonstrations or through consistent litigation for the judiciary and against the regime. As a result, other branches of the two states did not face any resistance when they controlled the judiciary on different occasions (before 2005 and after 2013 in Pakistan; before 1979 and after 2001 in Egypt), leading to limited *de facto* judicial independence.

Kureshi identified corruption and dissonant institutionalization as two key factors underpinning the emergence of populist judges in Pakistan.[107] However, I argue that the nature of the contestation between the people and the ruling elites during the 2000s in Pakistan and during the authoritarian regimes of Anwar Sadaat (1970–1981) and Hosni Mubarak (1981–2011) was distinct from contestations centred on corruption and dissonant institutionalization, or from the more general contestation between heterogeneous groups of society and ruling elites, which exists in some form almost everywhere in the world. In both contexts, these conflicts manifested as resistance against the ruling elites and support for the judiciary under specific socio-political conditions, coinciding with the emergence of strategic judicial leadership (discussed in the next section) capable of leveraging such contestation to enhance de facto judicial independence.

In the 2000s, Pakistan received substantial economic aid from the US and other international actors to fight the War on Terror. This aid, coupled with massive privatisation efforts, spurred the enormous growth of the middle-class,[108] the rise of private media,[109] and an increased demand for employment, accountability, and good governance. Different public opinion surveys conducted by Gallup Pakistan suggested that the population in general had grievances against the authoritarian regime of General Musharraf. According to a public opinion survey conducted on 20 December 2002, 67% of the respondents indicated that economic concerns were the

[104] Afzal (1998), Afzal (2000), and Afzal (2002) for details on restrictions over political activities in Pakistan.

[105] Al-Sayyid Sa'id (2005) for civil society activities in Egypt.

[106] Rizvi (1994) and Zaidi (2011) for details on civil society activities in Pakistan.

[107] Kureshi (2024).

[108] Nayab (2011), Maqsood (2017), Rafiq (2017), Rohde (2007).

[109] Ahmed (2012), Bajwa (2016), Mezzera and Sial (2010).

most important issue in their personal lives.[110] According to another survey, conducted on 26 July 2007, 43% of those surveyed believed that corruption would increase sharply over the subsequent 3 years, while 15% believed that it would increase a little, and 23% believed it would remain unchanged.[111] According to a survey conducted in September 2010, 48% of the respondents believed that *sifarish* (a recommendation to get a job) was linked to unemployment.[112]

Furthermore, the exiled leaders of opposition political parties, such as the PPP and the PML-N, were looking for a transition from the authoritarian regime of General Musharraf to democracy.[113] Thus, when the interests of the opposition political parties and the middle class converged, it resulted in the ousting of General Musharraf.[114] The general elections of 2008 marked a successful transition to democracy, leading to the formation of a PPP-led government.[115] The middle class and the opposition political elites represented heterogeneous societal groups, underscoring the division of society into the elites and the people.

Like Pakistan during the 2000s, the population of Egypt was rapidly growing during the 1970s, as was unemployment, inflation, illiteracy, and inefficient bureaucracy.[116] Natural resources, cultivatable land, and investment funds became scarce, and basic life necessities, such as fresh water, were not widely available.[117] The transportation system in Cairo was overburdened, pollution and congestion were widespread, and Cairo's sewage system was overtaxed.[118] As a result of these issues, a large portion of Egyptian society had grievances against the elites.

The next section discusses how strategic judicial leadership was willing and able to exploit this discontent in favour of the judiciary, and how this strategy contributed to an increase in *de facto* judicial independence.

4.2 Strategic Judicial Leadership

I argue that the contestation between the ruling elite and the people is by itself, insufficient to give rise to judicial populism or to enable judicial populism to contribute meaningfully to the enhancement of judicial independence. If it were enough, judicial independence would have increased in other countries with similar political and social landscapes. Some degree of contestation between the ruling elite and the

---

[110] Gallup Pakistan (2002).

[111] Gallup Pakistan (2007).

[112] Gallup Pakistan (2010).

[113] Akbar (1999), Dawn 16 May 2006, https://www.dawn.com/news/192460. accessed 1 June 2023

[114] Zakaria (2008), Zia (2008).

[115] Mehdi (2013).

[116] Bruton (1983) for details on social, political, and economic problems of Egypt during 1970s.

[117] Abdalla (1984), Bruton (1983), Moustafa (2003), Rubinstein (1977).

[118] Moustafa (2003).

people exists in almost every country at all times. The emergence of a popular judicial leader, who is aware of the issues and who can exploit this division to garner the support of societal groups for the judiciary, is equally essential for judicial populism. These factors shape the context in which *de facto* judicial independence increases. This phenomenon is overlooked by the extant literature on judicial leaders[119] and judicial populism,[120] discussing only how individual judges become prominent because of their bold decisions and how they engage with the public. How strategic judicial leadership contributed to judicial populism and judicial independence in Pakistan between 2005 and 2013 and in Egypt between 1979 and 2001 is discussed next.

4.2.1 Pakistan

The grievances of heterogeneous groups of society in Pakistan during the 2000s coincided with the appointment of Iftikhar Muhammad Chaudhry as the CJP on 30 June 2005.[121] CJP Chaudhry was strategic, because he remained loyal to the authoritarian regime of General Musharraf until he became the CJP. This loyalty was evidenced by his elevation from the Baluchistan High Court to the SCP by the military regime of General Musharraf, as well as his participation in the bench that endorsed the direct military intervention and suspension of the constitution by General Musharraf on 12 October 1999.[122] However, his loyalties changed after his appointment as the CJP in June 2005, and during his term, he led heterogeneous societal groups both from the bench and off the bench. In a recent YouTube interview held in 2025 with prominent journalist Irshad Bhatti, CJP Chaudhry framed his actions as part of a broader strategy aimed at advancing the larger goal of democratization.[123]

I argue that CJP Chaudhry was the only judge in the history of Pakistan who was not only aware of the new context in which he had to lead the judiciary but also successfully used the contestation between the people and the ruling elite to contribute to increased judicial independence. His awareness and intention to use these contexts were clear in his first speech after his appointment, when he referenced the concerns about an inefficient justice system voiced by the vibrant civil society and the media.[124]

[119] Appleby and Lynch (2021), Ryder and Hardy (2019), Abeyratne and Porat (2021), Tushnet (2011).

[120] Bernstein and Staszewski (2020), Jacomé (2017), Riaz (2021), Tushnet and Bugaric (2021), Kureshi (2024), Hilbink (2024).

[121] Ghias (2010), Khan (2014).

[122] Qureshi (2010).

[123] https://www.youtube.com/watch?v=TAE1pMqZBwA accessed 17 August 2025.

[124] Cheema and Gilani (2015).

4.2.1.1 Leading People off the Bench

Justice Chaudhry led CSOs, lawyers, journalists, and opposition political parties off the bench on two occasions. During the first occasion, the benches of the SCP (led by CJP Chaudhry) directly challenged the regime's authority by striking down the privatisation of Pakistan Steel Mills[125] and directing the regime to locate persons missing in connection with the War on Terror.[126] General Musharraf reacted to Chaudhry's independent decisions by suspending him on the charges of corruption on 9 March 2007.[127] The suspension was a court-packing action by the Musharraf regime, which was aimed at replacing an independently acting chief justice with one who would make decisions in favour of the regime. The suspension sparked country-wide protests by lawyers, CSOs, journalists, and opposition political parties.[128]

The contestation between the people and the ruling elite expressed itself in these demonstrations. CJP Chaudhry led diverse groups during the demonstrations for the judiciary and against the regime.[129] In addition, he, along with CSOs and lawyers, challenged the suspension directly before the SCP under Article 184(3) of the constitution, demonstrating that the contestation also expressed itself in anti-regime and pro-judiciary litigation.[130] As a result of the mass demonstrations, followed by the anti-regime litigation, CJP Chaudhry was restored on 20 July 2007.[131] This example shows how strategic judicial leadership was able to use contestation in favour of the judiciary to protect it against the regime's court-packing actions.

In a second example, General Musharraf sacked more than sixty judges of the SCP and provincial high courts, including CJP Chaudhry, on 3 November 2007[132] to avoid a probable adverse decision by the SCP against Musharraf's election as president for the next five years. Musharraf also introduced a provisional constitution, promulgated emergency measures throughout the country, and had the judges who were perceived as loyal under the provisional constitution swear an oath.[133] The removal of the judges and the administration of the oath was a court-packing action by the executive.

---

[125] Watan Party v. Federation of Pakistan 2006.

[126] Amina Masood Janjua and others v. the Government of Pakistan and others 2005.

[127] Ghias (2010).

[128] Chesser (2007), Javed (2007), *Suspended chief justice continues his tour - YouTube*. (n.d.). Retrieved February 21, 2020, from https://www.youtube.com/watch?v=-i0AkJaL-6g, Anthony (n.d.), Missing people's relatives criticise action against CJ. Dawn 12 March 2007.

[129] Ibid. See also CJ for dispensation of justice on equal basis: Thousands brave rain, wait all night. Dawn 18 June 2007.

[130] *The Chief Justice Iftikhar Muhammad Chaudhary v the President of Pakistan*, 2007.

[131] Ibid.

[132] Qureshi (2010).

[133] Ibid.

The authoritarian regime of General Musharraf grew increasingly unpopular,[134] intensifying both national and international pressure on him to hold general elections,[135] which were conducted in 2008 and resulted in the formation of a PPP-led government. Lawyers, journalists, students, and judges deposed on 3 November 2007, as well as opposition political elites organised a march in June 2008 to call for the restoration of the judges.[136] These demonstrations showcased the struggle between the people and the ruling elite (the PPP-led government). Notably, the heterogeneous groups with differing worldviews were led by CJP Chaudhry.[137] As a result of this march, many of the judges who had been removed were reappointed by the PPP-led government, thereby demonstrating successful protection of the judiciary against the previous regime's court-packing action and indicating an increase in *de facto* judicial independence.[138]

During this phase, CJP Chaudhry further cultivated the support of the aforesaid social, legal, and political groups, while also receiving different awards from national and international bodies.[139] The American Bar Association even conferred the Rule of Law award on CJP Chaudhry.[140] He even became so popular that a day was named after him (Justice Iftikhar Day), a first for any Pakistani judge.[141] However, he and other likeminded judges who had been removed in 2007 were not restored; consequently, the same groups held the second long march in March 2009, calling for the restoration of the remaining judges. CJP Chaudhry led the protesters once again, and the demonstrations were successful.[142] On 16 March 2009, the PPP-led government restored the remaining judges, including CJP Chaudhry.[143]

These restorations demonstrate that the judiciary was able to protect itself against the court-packing action of different regimes and point to an increase in *de facto* judicial independence, since judges who had been removed prior to 2007 were never restored. This increased independence resulted directly from two coinciding factors: the emergence of CJP Chaudhry as a strategic judicial leader with broad public support, able to harness the contestation between the people and the ruling elite, and the contestation itself, manifested through anti-regime demonstrations

---

[134] Zakaria (2008), Zia (2008).

[135] Witte (2007).

[136] Borka (2008), Iqbal (2008a), Lawyers warm up for long march. Dawn 5 June 2008, Long march gets off the ground. The News International 10 June 2008, Long march stops short of sit-in The News International. 15 June 2008, Preparations for long march in full swing. Dawn 10 June 2008.

[137] Ibid.

[138] Four LHC judges take fresh oath. Dawn 30 August 2008, Iqbal (2008b), Shah, (2008), Borka (2008).

[139] Chief Justice to get International Jurist Award, Pakistan Today 29 April 2012.

[140] US bar confers 'Rule of Law Award' on deposed CJ. The News International 10 August 2008.

[141] Iftikhar Day instils hope in lawyers.Dawn 24 September 2008, Lawyers call for judges' restoration: Justice Iftikhar Day. Dawn 1 February 2008.

[142] Islamabad sit-in till restoration of judges. Dawn 26 January 2009, Malik (2008), Nation celebrates judges' restoration. The News International 17 March 2009, Phelps (2009), Munir (2009).

[143] Ibid.

and litigation. These events suggest that judicial populism shaped the increase in *de facto* judicial independence.

4.2.1.2 Leading People from the Bench

CJP Chaudhry also led people from the bench by using the powers of the SCP. Article 184(3) does not explicitly give powers to the SCP to take suo motu notices and activate a human rights cell (HRC) within the SCP. However, soon after his appointment on 30 June 2005, CJP Chaudhry expanded the scope of human rights enforcement and the public interest under Article 184(3) by reactivating the HRC, and taking suo motu notices, and hearing different issues brought forward by petitioners. By doing so, he justified the intervention of the SCP in different areas of public policy and politics. He increased the engagement with newly privatised media by creating space for media reporters in court rooms and taking notices of malpractices reported in media under Article 184(3).[144] This expanded the space for the media's influence over cases before the SCP under Article 184(3).[145] These actions show that he was aware of the nature and scope of the contestation during the 2000s, and that he strategically chose the time after his appointment as the CJP (and not before) to garner public support for the judiciary.

As a result of CJP Chaudhry's actions, any citizen could submit their complaint directly to the SCP, and human rights petitions and suo motu notices increased exponentially. For example, the number of human rights petitions went from just a few to several hundred between the time of his appointment on 30 June 2005 and his second suspension on 3 November 2007. The number dropped to 81 in 2008, when the SCP was packed with judges loyal to the regime and shot back up to 9879 in 2009, when the SCP was again led by CJP Chaudhry.[146] The SCP became a focal point for the public at large, with CSOs, lawyers, and opposition political groups as petitioners and the regime as the respondent.[147] The contestation between the people and the ruling elite became highly visible in politically important cases before the SCP, particularly since the increased engagement with the media brought the SCP and CJP Chaudhry into limelight and shaped a favourable public opinion.

These developments shaped the context of the SCP's decisions, which ran against the interests of the ruling elite in most cases. Instead, the SCP ruled in favour of petitioners, who were mostly opposition political groups, civil society at large, and individuals with a middle-class background. For example, CSOs and opposition political parties worked together to challenge the privatisation of Pakistan Steel Mills before the SCP, and the court struck down the privatisation in 2006,[148] on the

---

[144] Khan (2014).

[145] Bajwa (2016), Ghias (2010), Khan (2014), Shafqat (2018).

[146] Annual Report of the Supreme Court of Pakistan 2019–20.

[147] Khan (2014).

[148] Watan Party v. Federation of Pakistan, 2006.

grounds that it had not been conducted in accordance with the law. Similarly, CSOs challenged the disappearances of various persons by security agencies, and the SCP, led by CJP Chaudhry, began directing the executive to trace and find persons missing in connection with the War on Terror. The above actions and decisions cultivated the support of heterogeneous societal groups, such as lawyers, CSOs, and opposition political parties,[149] but, as discussed above, this behaviour was not viewed favourably by Musharraf. He first suspended CJP Chaudhry on 9 March 2007, and later, on 3 November 2007, suspended CJP Chaudhry along with other judges of the SCP and the provincial high courts.

After the restoration of the judges in March 2009, the SCP, under the leadership of CJP Chaudhry, reversed all actions of the executive that had been taken between 3 November 2007 and the restoration of the judges in March 2009, except those deemed necessary for the function of the state.[150] This reversal revived the most important cases under the National Reconciliation Ordinance (NRO), as this ordinance had previously quashed criminal proceedings against any members of the ruling party and allies of General Musharraf. The court ultimately deemed the ordinance unconstitutional, and all criminal proceedings that had been closed as the result of the NRO were resumed.[151] The decision went against the interests of Musharraf and the PPP, but the fact that it was nevertheless implemented demonstrates the increase in *de facto* independence of the SCP.

One of the directives issued by the SCP in its decision on the NRO was to request that the Swiss courts reopen the corruption cases against then-President Asif Zardari. When the government refused to obey the court's decision, the SCP held the then-Prime Minister Yusuf Raza Gilani in contempt of court for his disobedience of the SCP's decision. The opposition political parties and CSOs petitioned the SCP under Article 184(3) for the prime minister's disqualification, reflecting the contestation between the people and the ruling elite. In an unprecedented move, the SCP disqualified Prime Minister Yusuf Raza Gilani in 2012.[152] Gilani was replaced with Raja Pervaiz Ashraf against whom the SCP had also initiated contempt proceedings. To avoid conviction, the new prime minister implemented the SCP's directive regarding the NRO and requested that the Swiss courts reopen the cases against the president. The above series of decisions, which were clearly against the government's interest but were nevertheless implemented, indicate how contestation, expressed in anti-regime litigation in politically important cases, contributed to the increase in *de facto* judicial independence.

The PPP-led government made an attempt to pave the way for court-packing by enacting the Eighteenth Constitutional Amendment in 2010. As discussed above, the amendment established the JCP and PC for the appointments of judges in provincial high courts and the Supreme Court. The JCP consisted of the CJP as the

[149] Opposition leaders stand by CJ. Dawn 14 March 2007.

[150] Sindh High Court Bar Association v. Federation of Pakistan 2009 PLD SC 879.

[151] Dr Mobashir Hassan and others v the Federation of Pakistan 2010.

[152] *Mohammad Azhar Siddique and Others v. the Federation of Pakistan and others* 2012.

chair, the three most senior judges of the SCP, a former chief justice or justice of the SCP, nominated by the CJP in consultation with four other justices, the Attorney General of Pakistan, a senior advocate nominated by the Pakistan Bar Council, and the Minister for Law and Justice. The PC consisted of eight members with equal membership from the treasury and the opposition benches of the parliament.[153] The JCP was required to forward the names of the judges to be appointed to the PC, which could convey any reservations about the nominations and send the names back for reconsideration. If deemed suitable, the JCP had the authority to address the PC's reservations; otherwise, it could resubmit the same names to the PC, and these names could not be sent back to the JCP, once submitted. The president would then notify the appointees of the PC's recommendations.

The amendment provided the PC with the final say over the appointments, which was a court-curbing action that limited the court's influence over judicial appointments. If left unchallenged, it would have empowered the regime to pack the judiciary with loyal judges in the future. However, lawyers, opposition political parties, and CSOs challenged the process of judicial appointments in the amendment under Article 184(3) of the constitution. The SCP did not strike down the whole amendment but issued a directive to parliament to increase the number of judges in the JCP from three to five and provide the JCP with the final say over the appointments. While the PC could send the proposed appointments back to the JCP for reconsideration, if the JCP maintained their recommendations for the second time, the PC could not reject them, and the appointments would be forwarded to the president for notification.[154] Even though the SCP did not pass an order or declaration, and the directions issued to parliament were not binding, they were nevertheless implemented through the Nineteenth Constitutional Amendment in 2011, thereby increasing *de facto* judicial power once again.

In another example of the contestation between heterogeneous groups of society and the ruling elite, the PPP-led regime enacted the Contempt of Court Act (COCA) 2012. The objective was to narrow down the definition of contempt of court, shifting it from being solely about judges' contempt to encompassing contempt directed at the court as an institution. This move curbed the powers of judges to notice contempt of court when dealing with threatening statements or non-implementation of decisions. CSOs and lawyers challenged the act, and the government responded. Within this setting, the SCP struck down COCA 2012,[155] and the decision was implemented, despite going against the government's interests.

[153] The JCP, previously dominated by judges, was restructured by the 26th Constitutional Amendment to include members of parliament, the Senate, and a woman or non-Muslim member nominated by the Speaker. Alongside the Law Minister, Attorney General, and a Bar representative, this shift reduced judges to a minority, thereby opening the JCP to direct political influence. For Supreme Court appointments, only five of the 13 members are now judges. See for details on the 26th Constitutional Amendment International Commission of Jurists (2024).

[154] Nadeem Ahmed and others v. the Federation of Pakistan, 2010.

[155] *Baz Muhammad Kakar and others v Federation of Pakistan,* 2012.

The SCP also struck down the illegal appointment of Fasih Bokhari as the chairman of the National Accountability Bureau,[156] it made security agencies accountable for missing persons in connection with the War on Terror, and it held certain elites accountable for large-scale embezzlements in the National Insurance Corporation Limited[157] and the Old-Age Employees Benefits Insurance.[158]

Meanwhile, the contestation between the people and the ruling elite, and public support for CJP Chaudhry and the SCP continued to express themselves in public opinion surveys. According to a PEW public opinion report dated 21 June 2011, CJP Chaudhry was the third most popular figure in Pakistan.[159] According to a public opinion poll conducted by Gallup Pakistan on 18 November 2013, 53% of the respondents believed that CJP Chaudhry was performing well and 25% said that his performance was suitable.[160]

The contestation between the people and the ruling elite continued to exist beyond 2013, but CJP Chaudhry's strategic leadership ceased when he retired in December 2013 and with it went the SCP's consistency in independent decision making. Chaudhry's successors (e.g. CJP Tassaduq Hussain Jillani, CJP Nasirul Mulk, CJP Anwar Zaheer Jamali, and CJP Asif Saeed Khosa) could not cultivate the same support with the various groups, and they were not able to use the contestation between the people and the ruling elite as frequently as CJP Chaudhry had done. As a result, the number of human rights petitions instituted in the SCP decreased from 48738 in 2013 to 29372 in 2014, and then to 27843 in 2015.[161] After 2013, the rise of cricketer-turned-politician Chairman PTI Imran Khan reduced the opportunities for any chief justice to cultivate support, as the Chairman emerged as one of the most popular leaders in the country.

Thus, *de facto* judicial independence in Pakistan faced renewed challenges. These challenges to the higher judiciary can be highlighted with several examples, such as the audio leaks of the former CJP Mian Saqib Nisar, in which he allegedly referred indirectly to the military's influence on the decision-making power of judges.[162] Other examples include the removal of a judge of the Islamabad High Court for speaking out against the interference of security agencies in judicial affairs,[163] and the government-initiated proceedings against Justice Qazi Faez Isa, who directed the military to hold its officers accountable for their involvement in political negotiations with protesters.[164] In 2023, a coalition of the PPP, the PML-N and

156 Iqbal (2013).

157 Suo Motu Case No 18 of 2010 (National Insurance Co. Ltd Scam), 2010.

158 Syed Mubashir Raza Jaffary and another v Employees Old Age Benefits Institutions, 2013.

159 Kohut et al. (2009).

160 Gallup Pakistan (2013).

161 Annual Report of the Supreme Court of Pakistan 2020-22.

162 Naseer (2021).

163 The speech at "ISI Is Involved in Manipulating Judicial Proceedings" - Justice Shaukat Aziz Siddiqui - YouTube (n.d.) https://www.youtube.com/watch?v=_wKx8N8lZ30.

164 Iqbal (2019), Malik (2019).

other political parties initiated a series of political cases against Chairman PTI Imran Khan, and his supporters. The SCP and the provincial high courts provided temporary relief in most of the cases, but the government simply initiated new cases.[165] These examples show that *de facto* independence of the SCP has been limited since the retirement of CJP Chaudhry in 2013.

In addition, the SCP has been selective in making decisions against the interest of the ruling elite. For example, in 2017, the SCP disqualified the Prime Minister Nawaz Sharif for his undeclared assets, which were revealed during the Panama Papers scandal.[166] However, the SCP did not strike down the extension of General Qamar Javed Bajwa's tenure as Chief of Army Staff when it was challenged, even though the government had informed the SCP that there were no laws under which it could grant an extension to the general. Instead of striking it down, the SCP approved a six-month extension and directed the parliament to enact legislation providing a legal basis for granting extensions.[167]

4.2.2 Egypt

Like CJP Chaudhry, a few chief justices of Egypt's SCC behaved strategically by exploiting the contestation between the people and the country's ruling elite. For example, the nature of the cases decided during the tenures of Mamdouh Attia (1979–1982), Awad Al-Morr (1991–1998) and Muhammad Wali al-Din Galal (1998–2001) indicates that the court was able to take advantage of changing socio-economic circumstances to favour the judiciary.

4.2.2.1 Chief Justice Mamdouh Attia (1979–1982)

As was the case in Pakistan between 2005 and 2013, the contestation between the elites in power and the people shaped the context in which Sadaat's regime established the SCC in 1971 and made it functional in 1979.[168] The court was empowered to interpret laws that were disputed for their multiple interpretations, resolve conflict between different parts of the judiciary, and review legislation, if issues of constitutionality arose. It was specified that only cases from the Court of Merit would be transferred to the SCC, and citizens could make an application to the court.[169] However, judges could transfer a case to the SCC if they believed that the issue involved a question of constitutionality.

---

165 Shirazi (2024).

166 *Imran Ahmed Khan Niazi v. Mian Muhammad Nawaz Sharif* PLD 2017 SC 692.

167 Constitutional Petition No 39 of 2019.

168 Hamad (2018), Moustafa (2003).

169 Moustafa (2003, 2009).

Mamdouh Attia was appointed as the first chief justice of the SCC. Justice Attia adopted a strategic approach — guiding the court to issue decisions that opposed the regime's interest in certain policy and political areas, while simultaneously signalling loyalty to the regime by avoiding rulings that threatened the regime's survival. For example, Hamad noted:

> Attia, a former senior judge, used his authority to advance an interest in building a robust constitutional court. He had served on the SCC's predecessor court, the Supreme Court, in the early, 1970s, and was frustrated by its lack of independence. Attia was eager to transform it into a capable institution for advancing the rule of law.[170]

Perhaps owing to his strategic approach, Attia managed to serve as Minister of Justice under Sadaat from 1976–1977 and under Mubarak from 1982–1986.

Using the court's powers, Attia (like Chaudhry) connected the problems of different societal groups to the issue of constitutionality and led the SCC to make decisions against the regime's interests in politically important cases.

Like General Musharraf's approach of exiling PPP and PML-N leaders in the early 2000s, the authoritarian regime of Anwar Sadaat also forced opposition members into exile. However, like the SCP's decision to allow opposition political parties to return from exile in 2007, the SCC enabled prominent opposition activists, such as Fuad Serag Eddin, the Wafd Party leader, to return to political life.[171] Similarly, in a case involving the legality of the Nasserist Party—an opposition party that had the support of anti-regime groups—the SCC legalised the party despite government objections. Attia's tenure was brief but active enough to trigger the process of decision-making by the SCC against the regime's interest, clearly demonstrating an increase in *de facto* judicial independence.

Like the cases involving the political parties, the SCC declared national election laws unconstitutional in 1987 and 1990, a decision that resulted in the dissolution of the People's Assembly and led to early elections. These rulings did not undermine the regime's grip on power, but they nevertheless pointed to an increase in *de facto* judicial independence.

Sadaat's regime had previously introduced Law 35 of 1976 that governed trade unions and contained provisions that limited the freedom of these unions.[172] The Centre for Human Rights and Legal Aid (CHRLA) challenged several provisions of the law before the administrative and civil courts through 50 cases, with the permission to challenge the law's constitutionality before the SCC.[173] These courts ruled in favour of the CHRLA in ten out of the 50 cases, and these ten cases were transferred to the SCC. Going against the interests of the authoritarian regime of Anwar Sadaat, the court exhibited a degree of independent behaviour and declared Article 36 of the law unconstitutional.[174] Similarly, when the CHRLA challenged different provisions

---

[170] Hamad (2018).

[171] Moustafa (2003).

[172] Bishara (2018), Abdalla (2014).

[173] Moustafa (2003).

[174] The Supreme Constitutional Court, Case No 77 of 19th Judicial year cited in Ezzat (2019).

of the penal code, the SCC ruled in their favour on provisions involving newspaper publication offenses that seemed to limit the freedom of the press. These examples further demonstrate an increase in *de facto* judicial independence.

The contestation between the people and the ruling elite continued to express itself in strategic litigation during the authoritarian regime of Hosni Mubarak, shaping the independent behaviour of the SCC. For example, opposition political parties challenged the denial of political rights to politicians of the pre-1952 regime under Article 4 of the Protection of the Internal Front and Social Peace Law.[175] Mubarak's regime was the respondent in this case.[176] The SCC struck down the provision in Case No. 56 that was decided in June 1986.[177] In another example, the regime had restricted the legal right of citizens to participate in elections as independent candidates. When citizens interested in contesting the elections as independents brought forward the constitutionality of this restriction, the SCC removed it in Case No. 131, decided in April 1987, and in Case No. 37, decided in May 1990.

4.2.2.2 Chief Justice Awad Al-Morr (1991–1998)

Unlike Attia, Chief Justice Awad Al-Morr was very active in the 1990s, leading the SCC to make decisions that ran counter to the interests of the executive. Under one provision of the Code of Criminal Procedure, defendants in libel cases were required to submit evidence supporting their published statements within five days of receiving notice from the prosecutor.[178] This provision undermined the freedom of journalists to report on government practices, as 5 days were not reasonable to collect, organise, and submit admissible evidence. The provision empowered the government to control media, but it was challenged before the SCC and struck down in February 1993.[179] The decision was clearly against the interest of the ruling elite and, hence, demonstrated the independent behaviour of the judges.

The authoritarian regime introduced Law No. 40/1977 to apply vicarious criminal liability to statements and speeches of opposition political parties in the media.[180] The law was aimed at controlling opposition political parties and the press. However, the Labour Party challenged the law before the SCC, serving as an example of the contestation between the opposition political parties, the press, and the ruling elite. The SCC did not strike down the law altogether; however, in 1995, it declared that applying the law to heads of political parties was unconstitutional. In 1997, it also

[175] Abu-Odeh (2011).

[176] Case No 56 of 6th Judicial Year cited in Abu-Odeh (2011).

[177] Ibid.

[178] SCC, 6 Feb. 1993, al-Mahkama, vol. 5, pt. 2, 183. cited in Moustafa (2003), Also see Sherif (1997).

[179] Case No 37th for 11th Judicial year, Decided February 6, 1993 cited in Hamad (2018).

[180] Human Rights Watch. (n.d.). Also see Ace The Electoral Knowledge Network (n.d.) for English Translation of the Law.

banned the application of the law to editors-in-chief of newspapers.[181] The court behaved strategically by first cultivating the support of opposition political parties and subsequently securing the support of the press. The decisions indicate independent behaviour on the part of the SCC, since they were against the interest of the ruling elite. The dissension between opposition political parties on one side, and the ruling elite on the other, shaped this independent behaviour.

4.2.2.3 Chief Justice Muhammad Wali Al-Din Galal (1998–2001)

Unlike Attia, Chief Justice Muhammad Wali Al-Din Galal did not serve under different regimes and in different capacities, but, like Attia, he also made decisions against the regime's interest[182] without undermining it. Therefore, both judges could not fully exploit the contestation against the regime and for the judiciary as Chaudhry had done after he became the CJP in 2005. However, like Chaudhry, Galal seemed to be aware of the contestation between the people and the ruling elite and was able to use it to carve out space for the SCC to make decisions that ran counter to the regime's interests. His efforts were evident in the cases that came before the SCC. For example, Article 24 of the Law of Political Participation (73/1956) empowered state and public sector employees to head local election committees, thereby allowing the government to influence the elections.[183] However, in 2000, the SCC struck down the provision and ruled that the judiciary would keep full oversight, thereby reducing opportunities for the ruling elite to rig the elections.[184] As a result, the ruling party of Hosni Mubarak lost its majority but managed to remain in power by securing the support of independent candidates.[185]

Neither Attia nor Galal nor Al-Morr ever achieved the same level of popularity or enjoyed the degree of public support attained by CJP Chaudhry. While they were prominent, they lacked the skill of leading heterogeneous groups of people from and off the bench. They were similarly unable to get the SCC to consistently challenge the regime's legitimacy and interests in different areas of politics and policy. Unlike CJP Chaudhry, they also did not receive recognition at the national or international level.

Just as contestations continued in Pakistan after the retirement of CJP Chaudhry in 2013, contestation between the people and the ruling elite continued to exist in Egypt, but strategic judicial leadership ceased after the tenures of Chief Justices Morr and Galal in 1998 and 2001, respectively. As a result, Mubarak's regime successfully undermined the judicial powers. Unlike General Musharraf, who reacted to the independent behaviour of CJP Chaudhry by suspending him, Mubarak waited

[181] Moustafa (2009).

[182] These decisions are separately discussed later in the chapter.

[183] Aziz (2013), Hamad (2018). Article 24 concerns monitoring of parliamentary elections.

[184] Hamad (2018).

[185] Perthes (2005).

for the opportunity to control the behaviour of the judiciary. When SCC Chief Justice Galal retired in August 2001, Mubarak saw an opportunity to pack the judiciary with loyal judges. In a clear court-packing action, the authoritarian regime appointed Fathi Naguib, a well-known pro-regime figure, as the Chief Justice of the SCC.[186]

With Galal's replacement by Naguib, a strategic judicial leader who could use contestation to challenge the regime ceased to exist. Justice Naguib used his constitutional role to help the regime pack the SCC with loyal judges. He also increased the number of SCC judges from nine to 15 and appointed new judges from the Court of Cassation and the Appeals Courts who were mostly loyal to the regime.[187] Under Naguib's leadership, the SCC accepted the government's proposal of abstract review, which reduced the SCC's power in the judicial review to an advisory role.

When Naguib died in 2003, the regime replaced him with another loyal judge, Mamdouh Marra.[188] Justice Marra helped the regime to strengthen its rule by directing the SCC to involve government authorities in the supervision of parliamentary elections and to endorse the constitutional amendments introduced by Mubarak's regime in 2005.[189] The amendments empowered President Mubarak to appoint six judges of the SCC, including the chief justice and five public figures, to the Supreme Presidential Election Commission (SPEC). SPEC introduced stringent qualification requirements for presidential elections for which only members of Mubarak's party could qualify. The regime presented these amendments to the SCC for abstract review, and the court, packed with judges loyal to the regime, endorsed the amendments.[190] This approach helped Mubarak to get re-elected for a subsequent term.

Justice Marra retired in 2006 and was replaced by Maher Abd Al-Wahid, who previously served as a public prosecutor, and, like his predecessors, had a reputation of being loyal to the regime.[191] When Justice Wahid retired in 2009, the regime replaced him with another loyal judge by the name of Farouk Sultan. Like his predecessor, Judge Sultan kept the SCC on a pro-regime path, and the court did not make decisions consistently against the regime's interest.[192]

On certain occasions, individual judges became prominent for challenging the government's authority, and occasionally, some members of the Judges' Club led heterogeneous groups against the regime by holding country-wide demonstrations against court-packing actions. However, the impact of these events on *de facto* judicial independence was limited, since the club lacked the strategic approach and public support, comparable to that of CJP Chaudhry, to lead diverse groups both from the bench and beyond. In addition, the Judges' Club did not head the judiciary,

[186] Aziz (2014).

[187] Aziz (2016).

[188] Moustafa (2009).

[189] Hamad (2018).

[190] Stilt (2010).

[191] Ibid.

[192] Lombardi (2009).

and, consequently, the judges of the SCC could not fully exploit the mass mobilisation triggered by the club outside the courtrooms in favour of the judiciary.

When Mubarak stepped down, he handed over the power to the Supreme Council of Armed Forces. The government held elections in 2011, in which the Freedom and Justice Party secured a majority, and Mohammed Mursi came into power as the country's new president. President Mursi restored the People's Assembly with the aim, among others, of weakening the judiciary–military alliance; however, the SCC quickly struck down the restoration.[193] Mursi's regime enacted a new constitution in 2012, in which the regime reduced the number of the SCC judges from 18 to 11 and removed the power of the SCC to dissolve elected national or local assemblies and to review presidential decrees endorsed in a referendum.[194] These decisions were all court-curbing actions that undermined the SCC's powers to make decisions against the interests of other branches of the government. These actions widened the gulf between Mursi and the military establishment and the judiciary, in reaction to which anti-regime groups continued to protest against the regime.

In reaction, the SCC struck down the establishment of the Constituent Assembly (CA) in June 2012, as well as the criteria for selecting members of the CA. It also questioned the legitimacy of the legislature (Shura Council) and the 2012 Constitution.[195] Additionally, the Ismailia Misdemeanour Court asserted that the leadership of the Muslim Brotherhood, including President Mursi, had conspired with Hamas, Hezbollah, and local militants during the January 2011 uprisings.[196] These allegations further weakened the legitimacy of Mursi's regime, and anti-Mursi forces united. These events, coupled with continued anti-regime protests, created the right conditions for military intervention. The Egyptian military, led by General Abdel Fattah El-Sisi, toppled the government, and removed Mursi's regime with little resistance on 3 July 2013.

Like the current limitations on *de facto* judicial independence in Pakistan, which were discussed above, judicial independence in Egypt is also currently facing challenges. The military regime of General Sisi had been using courts to repress the regime's critics since July 2013 by holding trials and interrogations that fall short of minimum required standards and are held in locations controlled by the Ministry of Interior.[197] In 2017, the regime also attempted to control the independent behaviour of the judicial bodies by changing the mechanism by which the heads of the Administrative Prosecution Authority, the Court of Cassation, and the State Council are appointed.[198] Also in 2017, the Egyptian parliament introduced a court-curbing law by providing President Sisi with the powers to select the heads of these judicial

[193] Hamad (2018).

[194] Amnesty International Report, 30 November 2012, See Beaumont (2012).

[195] Aljazeera 14 June 2012.

[196] Masr (2013).

[197] International Bar Association Human Rights Institute (2014).

[198] Hamad (2018), Rutherford (2018).

bodies from a pool of three senior judges who are nominated by their peers.[199] These peers are the seven most-senior members in each judicial body. Law No. 137 of 2021 amended the SCC Law No. 48 of 1979 to empower the Supreme Constitutional Court—upon a request from the prime minister—to review the constitutionality of decisions issued by international organisations and foreign court judgments whose enforcement is sought against the Egyptian state. This move can arguably be seen as using the Court as a shield against adverse international rulings and further tying its jurisdiction to regime interests.[200]

The above analysis suggests that judicial populism has two main features: contestation between the people—heterogeneous groups of society such as CSOs, opposition political parties, and journalists—and the ruling elite; and the emergence of judicial leaders who are willing and able to exploit the contestation in favour of the judiciary. Both features shaped the context in which *de facto* judicial independence increased in Pakistan and Egypt. Currently, contestation exists in the two countries, but a strategic judicial leader does not. Therefore, *de facto* judicial independence is limited and will continue to be as long as either of the two factors (specifically the contestation between the people and the ruling elite and the judicial leadership) is absent. However, once these two factors coincide, *de facto* judicial independence could increase once again.

5 Conclusion

Judicial populism does not simply mean that judges make decisions in accordance with public sentiments. It also involves the division between the people and the ruling elite and the emergence of strategic judicial leaders. While contestation has always existed in Egypt and Pakistan, Pakistan did not witness the emergence of a strategic judicial leader capable of leveraging the contestation between the people and the ruling elite to strengthen judicial power and safeguard against court-packing or court-curbing measures by other branches of the state until the appointment of Iftikhar Muhammad Chaudhry as CJP in June 2005. Such leadership was again absent following his retirement in 2013. The SCP was not able to protect itself against the regime's court-packing and court-curbing actions and could not make consistent decisions against the interests of the different regimes before 2005 or after 2013.

The examples of contestation manifested through demonstrations or strategic litigation in support of the judiciary and against the ruling elite between 2005 and 2013. The contestations coincided with the emergence of CJP Chaudhry as a strategic judicial leader who was willing and able to use the dissent to secure public support for the judiciary. This support contributed to the successful protection of the

[199] Amnesty International (2017), Saad (2017).

[200] Benany and Nouman (n.d.).

judiciary against the court-packing and court-curbing actions of the regimes in Pakistan between March 2007 and March 2009. The SCP was able to make decisions counter to the interests of the PPP-led regime from March 2009 to December 2013. When one of the above features (i.e. a strategic judicial leader) ceased to exist with the retirement of CJP Chaudhry in December 2013, *de facto* judicial independence in Pakistan faced renewed limitations.

In Egypt, like in Pakistan, the contestation between the elites in power and the people expressed itself in anti-regime demonstrations and politically important cases before the SCC, and shaped the context in which the SCC was established. These events contributed to independent decision-making by the SCC against the interests of the authoritarian regime of Anwar Sadaat, and, for a time, during Mubarak's regime.

Like Pakistan before 2005 or after 2013, the contestation between the people and the ruling elite in Egypt did not manifest in anti-regime and pro-judiciary strategic litigation or public demonstrations prior to 1979 or after 2001. Consequently, judicial independence in Egypt could not be sustained, resulting in only a limited degree of judicial independence during these periods. The second factor—judicial leadership capable of leveraging the contestation between the people and the ruling elite to strengthen judicial empowerment—did not exist before 1979 and ceased to exist after the retirement of Justice Galal in the 2000s. As a result, the SCC was not able to protect itself against the court-packing or court-curbing actions of the regime. The court could not continue to make consistent decisions against the interests of the authoritarian regimes of Mubarak, Mursi, and Sisi.

The comparative analysis of judicial populism and judicial independence in Pakistan and Egypt offers an important insight into the wider literature on judicial independence and judicial populism in developing democracies. Both the contestation between the people and the ruling elite and the presence of a strategic judicial leader willing and able to use the contestation are essential for judicial populism and its contribution to the increase in judicial independence in developing democracies. When any of these features of judicial populism are absent, judicial independence in countries like Pakistan and Egypt faces limitations.

References

Abdalla N (1984) Egypt's absorptive capacity during 1960-1972. Int J Middle East Stud 6(2):177–198

Abdalla N (2014) Egyptian Labor and the State https://www.mei.edu/publications/egyptian-labor-and-state, accessed 14 May 2025

Abeyratne R, Porat I (Eds.) (2021) Towering Judges: A Comparative Study of Constitutional Judges. Cambridge University Press. https://doi.org/10.1017/9781108879194

Aboulueleid T (2019) Legal system in Egypt, https://d1wqtxts1xzle7.cloudfront.net/58285578/Legal_system_in_Egypt_-_Taher_Aboueleid-libre.pdf?1548772753=&response-content-disposition=inline%3B+filename%3DLegal_system_in_Egypt_Taher_Aboueleid_pd.pdf&Expires=1756212133&Signature=AoWrt1k2O0dEupDU2-LezhsFALHSjD~

YIx4bPpCe9Cgp4V3HCaLQsM1hpLQCjWxydnpyPJ-2IHPz2zr~~wEta8sxq8fBiSa8mttNfrfje6HfXdEpH1sMTMIjCgZLsDQy4kYMiICR6v-fqxvFskJ5s90eOAuw~RY1EBQgPo1Vw~p7nl2HLjXgCgE7WLoe4gxWgn0YV-epCU4~KVLWGP2z5QORxD-xcggZ7ttkSz0TxTJHuyu-3AAJ5vtmzZjWzQb6kpgz-jNhrMxXNMjk~p5HHDEryNht36y8ZeYWYUQKHqEzHzGCwxfSmp~1hK8Uh16t60ABS8D95m9QeBj6279pkw&Key-Pair-Id=APKAJLOHF5GGSLRBV4ZA, accessed 14 August 2025

Abraham HJ (1998) The Judicial Process: An Introductory Analysis of the Courts of the United States, England, and France. Oxford University Press

Abu-Odeh L (2011) The Supreme Constitutional Court of Egypt: The Limits of Liberal Political Science and CLS Analysis of Law Elsewhere. Georgetown Law Faculty Publications and Other Works. 1636. https://scholarship.law.georgetown.edu/facpub/1636

Ace The Electoral Knowledge Network (n.d.) "Egypt: Law No. 40 of 1977 concerning the Political Party System", https://aceproject.org/ero-en/regions/mideast/EG/Law%20No.%2040%20of%201977%20-%20english.pdf/view, accessed 25 October 2025

Adem S, Ibrahim AM (2023) Ethiopia is not ready for transitional justice. Foreign Policy. 14 March https://foreignpolicy.com/2023/03/14/ethiopia-tigray-war-crimes-transitional-justice-human-rights/, accessed 17 August 2025

Adeney K (2017) How to understand Pakistan's hybrid regime: the importance of a multidimensional continuum. Democratization 24(1):119–137. https://doi.org/10.1080/13510347.2015.1110574

Afzal MR (1998) Political parties in Pakistan 1969–1971. Islamabad: National Institute of Historical and Cultural Research

Afzal MR (2000) Political parties in Pakistan 1958–1969 (3rd ed.). Islamabad: National Institute of Historical and Cultural Research

Afzal MR (2002) Political parties in Pakistan 1947–1958 (4th ed.). Islamabad: National Institute of Historical and Cultural Research

Al Hajjaji SADAS (2017) A call for judicial reform in Egypt. ICL J Vienna Journal on International Constitutional Law 11(2):257–283

Al Hajjaji SADAS (2018a) The dilemma of judicial appointment in Egypt questions of gender equality, elimination of political opposition and underprivileged citizens. DePaul J Soc Just 11:1–32

Al Hajjaji SADAS (2018b) The reform of judicial appointment process in the ordinary judiciary in Egypt. Middle East Law Gov 10(1):1–24

Al Hajjaji SADAS (2016) Form of reform: judicial reform in Egypt lessons from the developed countries. Doctor of Juridical Sciences Dissertation. University of California UC Berkeley https://escholarship.org/content/qt84q1g0bg/qt84q1g0bg_noSplash_49cd02a19d78e943c65124184cdcacae.pdf?t=pdymjq accessed 29 July 2025.

Asma Jilani v the Government of Punjab PLD 1972 SC 139

Al-khudayri M (2009) The law on judicial authority and judicial Independence. In: Bernard-Maugiron N (ed) Judges and political reform in Egypt. American University in Cairo Press. https://doi.org/10.5743/cairo/9789774162015.003.0004

Al-Sayyid Sa'id M (2005). 'Human Rights in the Arab World', in Sarah Ben Nefissa, Nabil Abd al-Fattah, Sari Hanafi and Carlos Milani (eds), NGOs and Governance in the Arab World (Cairo & New York: AUC), pp. 131–147

Amin H, Napoli J (2000) Media and Power in Egypt in Curran, J., & Park, M.-J. (Eds.) De-Westernizing Media Studies (1st ed.). Routledge. p157-167 https://doi.org/10.4324/9780203981764

Amnesty International (2017) 'New legislation threatens judicial independence in Egypt,' 27 April. https://www.amnesty.org/en/latest/press-release/2017/04/new-legislation-threatens-judicial-independence-in-egypt/, accessed 13 June 2025

Annual Report of the Supreme Court of Pakistan 2020–22

Anthony A (n.d.) Supporters hold rally for suspended Pakistani judge - Reuters. https://uk.reuters.com/article/uk-pakistan-judge/supporters-hold-rally-for-suspended-pakistani-judge-idUKISL19665420070526, accessed 29 March 2025

Appleby G, Lynch A (2021) Sir Anthony Mason: towering over the high court of Australia. In: Abeyratne R, Porat I (eds) Towering judges: a comparative study of constitutional judges. Cambridge University Press, pp 56–88.

Arato A, Cohen JL (2021) Populism and Civil Society: The Challenge to Constitutional Democracy. New York: Oxford University Press, https://doi.org/10.1093/oso/9780197526583.001.0001, accessed 18 Aug. 2025

Armytage R (2015) The social lives of the elite: friendship and Power in Pakistan. Asia Pac J Anthropol 16(5):448–463. https://doi.org/10.1080/14442213.2015.1076887

Aydin A (2013) Judicial independence across democratic regimes: understanding the varying impact of political competition. Law Soc Rev 47(1):105–134. https://doi.org/10.1111/lasr.12003

Aziz SF (2013) Revolution without reform: a critique of Egypt's election laws. Geo Wash Int Law Rev 45:1

Aziz, SF (2014) Egypt's Judiciary, Coopted. Carnegie Endowment for International Peace. 20 August, https://carnegieendowment.org/sada/2014/08/egypts-judiciary-coopted?lang=en, accessed 13 June 2025

Aziz, SF (2016) "Independence Without Accountability: The Judicial Paradox of Egypt's Failed Transition to Democracy," Penn State Law Review: Vol. 120: Iss. 3, Article 1. https://insight.dickinsonlaw.psu.edu/pslr/vol120/iss3/1, accessed 19 July 2025

Bajwa HK (2016) Pakistani media, public opinion, and the downfall of Pervez Musharraf: news attribute agenda-setting, and cognitive liberation in the lawyers ' movement. The University of Texas

Baum L (2008) Judges and their audiences: A perspective on judicial behaviour. Princeton University Press

Baz Muhammad Kakar v. Federation of Pakistan PLD 2012 SC 870

Begum Nusrat Bhutto v Chief of Army Staff PLD 1977 SC 657

Baz Muhammad Kakar and others v Federation of Pakistan (2012)

Benany T and Nouman E. (n.d.) "Amendments to the Supreme Constitutional Court's Law" https://shalakany.com/amendments-to-the-supreme-constitutional-courts-law/ accessed 15 October 2025

Bencze M (2020) Explaining judicial populism in Hungary—a legal realist approach. Iuris Dictio 14. https://doi.org/10.18272/iu.v25i25.1635

Bencze M (2021) Judicial populism and the Weberian judge—the strength of judicial resistance against governmental influence in Hungary. Germ Law J 22(7):1282–1297. https://doi.org/10.1017/glj.2021.67

Bernard-Maugiron N. (ed) (2009) Judges and Political Reform in Egypt. American University in Cairo Press

Bernard-Maugiron N (2016) A clash of institutions: judiciary vs. executive in Egypt. In: Bellin E. (ed.), Lane H.E. (ed.). Building rule of law in the Arab world: Tunisia, Egypt, and beyond. Boulder (USA); Londres: L. Rienner, p. 29-49

Bernstein A, Staszewski G (2020) Judicial Populism. SSRN Electron J 2020. https://doi.org/10.2139/ssrn.3694132

Beaumont P (2012) Mohamed Morsi signs Egypt's new constitution into law. The Guadian, https://www.theguardian.com/world/2012/dec/26/mohamed-morsi-egypt-constitution-law, accessed 12 July 2025

Bishara D (2018) The 2011 Uprising and Beyond: The Struggle for a New Interest Regime in Post-Mubarak Egypt. In Contesting Authoritarianism: Labor Challenges to the State in Egypt. Cambridge: Cambridge University Press. pp. 129–146

Blokker P (2019) Populism as a constitutional project. Int J Const Law 17(2):536–553. https://doi.org/10.1093/icon/moz028

Borka A (2008) Pakistani lawyers gather for "Long March" protest. Reuters. https://www.reuters.com/article/us-pakistan-protest/pakistani-lawyers-gather-for-long-march-protest-idUSISL26530020080609, accessed 16 June 2025

Brown NJ (1995) Law and imperialism: Egypt in comparative perspective. Law and Society Review, 29(1):103–126
Brown NJ (2012) Egypt's judges in a revolutionary age. The Carneigie Papers. https://carnegieendowment.org/research/2012/02/egypts-judges-in-a-revolutionary-age?lang=en accessed 12 August 2025
Brown NJ, Dunne M (2013) Egypt's draft constitution rewards the military and judiciary. Carnegie Endowmentfor International Peace, https://carnegieendowment.org/research/2013/12/egypts-draft-constitution-rewards-the-military-and-judiciary?lang=en accessed 21 August 2025
Bruton HJ (1983) Egypt's development in the seventies. Econ Dev Cult Chang 31(4):679–704
Caldeira GA, Gibson JL (1992) The Etiology of public support for the supreme court. Am J Polit Sci 36(3):635–664
Canovan M (1981) Populism. New York: Harcourt Brace Jovanovich. https://books.google.co.uk/books?id=mh9mAAAAIAAJ
Carrubba CJ, Helmke G, Gabel M, Martin AD, Staton JK (2015) When parchment barriers matter: De jure judicial independence and the concentration of power, https://www.gretchenhelmke.com/uploads/7/0/3/2/70329843/parchment.pdf accessed 14 June 2025
Castro-Montero JL, van Dijck G (2017) Judicial politics in unconsolidated democracies: an empirical analysis of the Ecuadorian constitutional court (2008–2016). Just Syst J 38(4):380–398. https://doi.org/10.1080/0098261X.2017.1327336
Çelenk AA (2016) The myth of 'independent judiciary': the evolution of judiciary-executive relations in Turkish politics. Contemporary Politics. 22(2): 232–247. https://doi.org/10.1080/13569775.2016.1153283
Chavez RB (2008) The rule of law and courts in democratizing regimes. In: Caldeira GA, Kelemen RD, Whittington KE.(eds). The Oxford handbook of law and politics. Oxford: Oxford University Press, pp 63–80. https://doi.org/10.1093/OXFORDHB/9780199208425.003.0005
Chávez RB, Ferejohn JA, Weingast BR (2011) A theory of the politically independent judiciary. In: Helmke G, Rios-Figueroa J (eds) Courts in Latin America. Cambridge University Press, pp 219–247. https://doi.org/10.1017/CBO9780511976520.009
Cheema MH, Gilani IS (eds) (2015) The politics and jurisprudence of the Chaudhry court 2005–2013. Oxford University Press
Chesser SG (2007) Pakistan: Significant Recent Events March 26 - June 21, 2007' CRS Report for Congress. https://sgp.fas.org/crs/row/RL34075.pdf accessed 14 August 2025
Chief Justice to get International Jurist Award (2012) Pakistan Today. 29 April https://www.pakistantoday.com.pk/2012/04/28/cj-iftikhar-chaudhry-to-get-international-jurist-award/, accessed 14 August 2025
Cingranelli DL, Richards, DL (2010) The Cingranelli and Richards (CIRI) Human Rights Data Project. Human Rights Quarterly, 32(2):401–424. http://www.jstor.org/stable/40783984
CJ for dispensation of justice on equal basis: Thousands brave rain, wait all night (2007) Dawn 18 June https://www.dawn.com/news/252290/cj-for-dispensation-of-justice-on-equal-basis-thousands-brave-rain-wait-all-night,accessed 19 June 2025
Comparative Constitutions Project (n.d.) Comparing Three Versions of the Egyptian Constitution, https://comparativeconstitutionsproject.org/comparing-the-egyptian-constitution/
Conniff ML (Ed.) (2012) Populism in Latin America: Second Edition. University of Alabama Press. https://doi.org/10.2307/jj.30346775
Constitutional Petition No 39 of 2019
de la Torre C, Ortiz Lemos A (2016) Populist polarization and the slow death of democracy in Ecuador. Democratization 23(2):221–241 https://doi.org/10.1080/13510347.2015.1058784
Dr. Mobashir Hassan v Federation of Pakistan PLD 2010 SC 265
Dupret B, Bernard-Maugiron N (2002) Egypt and its laws: a general presentation of law and judicial bodies. https://hal.science/hal-02614267v1/document accessed 13 May 2025
EGYPT JUSTICE (n.d.) Court of Cassation: The Supreme Court of Egypt's Common Court System, https://egyptjustice.com/court-of-cassation/, accessed 5 June 2023

El Bora'i N (n.d.) The Independence of the judiciary: the truth as it is! University of Minnesota. http://hrlibrary.umn.edu/research/Egypt/independence-of-the-judiciary-in-egypt-en.pdf accesed 13 August 2025
Epperly B (2017) Political competition and de facto judicial independence in non-democracies. Eur J Polit Res 56(2):279–300. https://doi.org/10.1111/1475-6765.12186
Epperly B (2018) (Re)examining the insurance model of judicial Independence across democracies. J Law Courts 6(2):405–419. https://doi.org/10.1086/698534
Epperly B (2019) The political foundations of judicial Independence in dictatorship and democracy. Oxford University Press. https://doi.org/10.1093/oso/9780198845027.001.0001
Epperly B, Sievert J (2019) Conflict and courts: civil war and judicial Independence across democracies. Polit Res Q 72(3):700–713. https://doi.org/10.1177/1065912918803200
Ex Chief Justice Iftikhar Muhammad Chaudhry Exclusive Interview | Podcast with Irshad Bhatti, https://www.youtube.com/watch?v=TAE1pMqZBwA, accessed 21 August 2025
Ezzat A (2019) "Challenging the Legal Ideology of the State: Cause Lawyering and Social Movements in Egypt," 24 May 2019. Arab Reform Initiative
Feld LP, Voigt S (2003) "Economic growth and judicial independence: cross-country evidence using a new set of indicators" European Journal of Political Economy 19(3):497-527. https://doi.org/10.1016/S0176-2680(03)00017-X
Finkel J (2005) Judicial reform as insurance policy: Mexico in the 1990s. Latin Am Polit Soc 47(1):87–113. https://doi.org/10.1111/j.1548-2456.2005.tb00302.x
Four LHC judges take fresh oath (2008) Dawn 30 August https://www.dawn.com/news/319098/four-lhc-judges-take-fresh-oath, accessed 13 August 2025
Gallup Pakistan (2022) (88) DO NOT READ THE NEWSPAPER: GALLUP AND GILLANI PAKISTAN. 20 October https://gallup.com.pk/wp/wp-content/uploads/2022/10/20-oct_merged-1.pdf, Accessed 20 August 2025
Gallup Pakistan (2019a) 'Despite rise in literacy in Pakistan, only 1 in 5 (19%) Pakistanis claim they read newspaper', 9 December https://gallup.com.pk/wp/wp-content/uploads/2019/12/9th-December-2019-English.pdf Accessed 24 August 2025
Gallup Pakistan (2019b) ONLY 2 IN 5 (39%) PAKISTANIS CLAIM TO USE THE INTERNET, 10 December, https://gallup.com.pk/wp/wp-content/uploads/2019/12/10th-December-2019-English.pdf, Accessed 20 August 2025
Gallup Pakistan (2019c) 2 in 5 (40%) internet users in Pakistan say they visit Facebook and YouTube for news, 19 December, https://gallup.com.pk/wp/wp-content/uploads/2019/12/19th-December-2019-Poll.pdf accessed 20 August 2025
Gallup Pakistan. (2020) Almost 3 in 5 (56%) internet users in Pakistan say they use the internet for entertainment, 1 January, https://gallup.com.pk/wp/wp-content/uploads/2020/01/01st-January-2020-English.pdf accessed at 20 August 2025
Gallup Pakistan (2013) '53% Pakistanis believe that Chief Justice Iftikhar Muhammad Chaudhry is performing well,' 18 November, https://gallup.com.pk/wp/wp-content/uploads/2016/02/1811131.pdf Accessed 14 August 2025
Gallup Pakistan (2002) 'ECONOMIC ISSUES AS THE FIRST WORRY FOR MAJORITY PAKISTANIS' https://gallup.com.pk/wp/wp-content/uploads/2016/06/20-12-20021.pdf Accessed 14 August 2025
Gallup Pakistan (2007) '43% of the urbanites believe that 'corruption' will increase in the next 3 years: Gallup Pakistan Survey,' 26 July, https://gallup.com.pk/wp/wp-content/uploads/2016/06/2707071.pdf Accessed 19 August 2025
Gallup Pakistan (2010) 'Lack of 'Sifarish' seen as main reason for unemployment' https://gallup.com.pk/post/11632 Accessed 21 August 2025
Gatto MAC, Power TJ (2016) Postmaterialism and political elites: the value priorities of Brazilian federal legislators. J Polit Latin Am 8(1):33–68. http://nbn-resolving.org/urn/resolver.pl?urn:nbn:de:gbv:18-4-9394
Gee G, Hazell R, Malleson K, O'Brien P (2015) The Politics of Judicial Independence in the UK's Changing Constitution. Cambridge: Cambridge University Press

Ghias SA (2010) Miscarriage of chief justice: judicial Power and the legal complex in Pakistan under Musharraf. Law Soc Inq 35(4):985–1022. http://www.jstor.org/stable/40926291

Gibson JL, Caldeira GA, Baird VA (1998) On the legitimacy of National High Courts. Am Polit Sci Rev 92(2):343–358. https://doi.org/10.2307/2585668

Ginsburg T, Garoupa N (2009) “Judicial Audiences and Reputation: Perspectives from Comparative Law,” 47 Columbia Journal of Transnational Law 451

Granata-Menghini S (2022) In: Castellà Andreu JM, Simonelli MA (eds) Populism and constitutional courts: a perspective from the Venice commission BT-populism and contemporary democracy in Europe: old problems and new challenges. Springer International Publishing, pp 91–111. https://doi.org/10.1007/978-3-030-92884-1_5

Halliday TC (1999) Politics and civic professionalism: legal elites and cause lawyers. Law Soc Inq 24(04):1013–1060. https://doi.org/10.1111/j.1747-4469.1999.tb00417.x

Hamad M (2018) Judges and generals in the making of modern Egypt: how institutions sustain and undermine authoritarian regimes. Cambridge University Press. https://doi.org/10.1017/9781108559393

Hasan S (2023) ’77 percent children aged 10 unable to comprehend basic English text, report says’. Dawn 9 September https://www.dawn.com/news/1774845 accessed 23 Auugust 2025.

Hayo B, Voigt S (2007) Explaining de facto judicial independence. Int Rev Law Econ 27(3):269–290. https://doi.org/10.1016/j.irle.2007.07.004

Hayo B, Voigt S (2014) Mapping constitutionally safeguarded judicial independence-a global survey. J Empir Leg Stud 11(1):159–195. https://doi.org/10.1111/jels.12038

Hilbink L, Ingram MC (2019) Courts and rule of law in developing countries. Oxford University Press. https://doi.org/10.1093/acrefore/9780190228637.013.110

Hilbink L (2024) Judicial Populism: A Conceptual and Normative Inquiry. Law & Social Inquiry, 1–33. https://doi.org/10.1017/lsi.2024.47

Howard R, Carey HA (2004) Courts and Political Freedom: A Measure of Judicial Independence, 87 JUDICATURE 285

Human Rights Watch (2023) Tunisia: President: Intensifies Attacks on Judicial Independence Ignoring Court Order to Reinstate Fired Judges, Prosecuting Them Instead https://www.hrw.org/news/2023/02/27/tunisia-president-intensifies-attacks-judicial-independence, accessed 13 October 2025

Human Rights Watch (n.d.) “The Political Parties Law”, https://www.hrw.org/legacy/backgrounder/mena/egypt0107/2.htm#_ftnref10 accessed 14 October 2025

International Commission of Jurists (2024) Pakistan: 26th Constitutional Amendment is a blow to the independence of the judiciary. https://www.icj.org/pakistan-26th-constitutional-amendment-is-a-blow-to-the-independence-of-the-judiciary/, 21 October, accessed 12 June 2025

International Bar Association Human Rights Institute (2014) Separating law and politics: challenges to the Independence of judges and prosecutors in Egypt. https://upr-info.org/sites/default/files/documents/2014-10/ibahri_upr20_egy_e_annexe1.pdf accessed 23 June 2025

Iftikhar Day instils hope in lawyers (2008) Dawn. 24 September https://www.dawn.com/news/322586/iftikhar-day-instils-hope-in-lawyers, accessed 29 June 2025

Iqbal N (2008a) Caravans set off for lawyers’ long march. Dawn. 10 June https://www.dawn.com/news/306793/caravans-set-off-for-lawyers-long-march, accessed 15 June 2025

Iqbal N (2008b) Eight deposed SHC judges may take oath today. Dawn. 27 August https://www.dawn.com/news/318516/eight-deposed-shc-judges-may-take-oath-today, accessed 28 June 2025

Iqbal N (2013) SC removes NAB chief Fasih Bokhari. Dawn. 29 May https://www.dawn.com/news/1014659/sc-removes-nab-chief-fasih-bokhari, accessed 14 June 2025

Iqbal N (2019) Govt wants subservient judiciary, says Faez Isa. Dawn. 14 October https://www.dawn.com/news/1510721, accessed 23 June 2025

Islamabad sit-in till restoration of judges (2009) Dawn. 26 January https://www.dawn.com/news/340433/islamabad-sit-in-till-restoration-of-judges, accessed 25 June 2025

ISI is Involved in Manipulating Judicial Proceedings - Justice Shaukat Aziz Siddiqui - *YouTube*. (n.d.). Retrieved July 14, 2021, from https://www.youtube.com/watch?v=_wKx8N8lZ30
Jácome, JG (2017) In Defense of Judicial Populism: Lessons from Colombia, VerfBlog, 3 May, https://verfassungsblog.de/in-defense-of-judicial-populism-lessons-from-colombia/, accessed 14 August 2025
Jabbar J and Isa QF (1997) Mass Media Laws and Regulations in Pakistan, and a Commentary from a Historical Perspective. Asian Media Information and Communication Centre
Javed R (2007) CJ gets rousing welcome: 14-hour drive from Islamabad to Abbottabad. Dawn. 3 June https://www.dawn.com/news/250098/cj-gets-rousing-welcome-14-hour-drive-from-islamabad-to-abbottabad
Kalhan A (2013a) Gray zone' constitutionalism and the dilemma of judicial Independence in Pakistan. Vanderbilt J Transnatl Law 46(1): 1-96 https://scholarship.law.vanderbilt.edu/vjtl/vol46/iss1/1/, accessed 13 May 2025
Kalhan A (2013b) Beyond judicial populism. The Express Tribune. 23 December https://tribune.com.pk/story/649601/beyond-judicial-populism
Kapiszewski D (2007) Challenging decisions: high courts and economic governance in Argentina and Brazil. University of California, Berkeley
Kapiszewski D (2012) High courts and economic governance in Argentina and Brazil. Cambridge University Press. https://doi.org/10.1017/CBO9781139017664
Khan H (2016) A history of the judiciary in Pakistan (first). Oxford University Press
Khan H (2017) Constitutional and political history of Pakistan, 3rd edn. Oxford University Press
Khan M (2014) Genesis and evolution of public interest litigation in the supreme court of Pakistan: toward a dynamic theory of Judicialization. Temple Int Comp Law J 28(2):285-359
Kohut A, Wike R., Carriere-kretschmer E., Researcher S., Horowitz JM, Holzwart K, Poushter J (2009) Pakistani public opinion: growing concerns about extremism, Continuing Discontent With U.S. Pew Research Center13 August, https://www.pewresearch.org/wp-content/uploads/sites/2/2009/08/Pew-Global-Attitudes-Pakistan-Report-August-13-2009.pdf, accessed 14 August 2025
Krygier M, Czarnota A, Sadurski W (2022) Anti-constitutional populism. Cambriadge University Press. https://doi.org/10.1017/9781009031103
Kureshi Y (2019) What is judicial populism and how does it work in Pakistan? DAWN. 1 February https://www.dawn.com/authors/8287/yasser-kureshi, accessed 13 July 2025
Kureshi Y (2022) Seeking supremacy: the pursuit of judicial Power in Pakistan. In: Cambridge studies in law and society. Cambridge University Press
Kureshi Y (2024) The People's Court: Dissonant Institutionalization and Judicial Populism in Pakistan. Law & Social Inquiry, 1–32. https://doi.org/10.1017/lsi.2024.49
Lacey N (2019) Populism and the rule of law. Ann Rev Law Soc Sci 15(1):79–96. https://doi.org/10.1146/annurev-lawsocsci-101518-042919
Landau D (2018) Populist constitutions. Univ Chicago Law Rev 85(2):521–543
Landau DE (2014) Beyond judicial Independence: the construction of judicial Power in Colombia. Harvard University Cambridge, Massachusetts. http://nrs.harvard.edu/urn-3:HUL.InstRepos:14226088, accessed 16 June 2025
Lawlor JM (1986) Court packing revisited: a proposal for rationalizing the timing of appointments to the supreme court. Univ Pa Law Rev 134:967–1000. https://scholarship.law.upenn.edu/cgi/viewcontent.cgi?article=4000&context=penn_law_review
Lawyers call for judges' restoration: Justice Iftikhar Day (2008) Dawn. 1 February, https://www.dawn.com/news/287361/lawyers-call-for-judges-restoration-justice-iftikhar-day accessed 14 October 2025
Lawyers warm up for long march (2008) Dawn 5 June https://www.dawn.com/news/413822/lawyers-gather-for-long-march, accessed 27 July 2025
Linzer DA, Staton JK (2015) A Global Measure of Judicial Independence, 1948–2012. Journal of Law and Courts, 3(2): 223–256. https://doi.org/10.1086/682150
Lombardi C (2009) 'Egypt's New Chief Justice,' Blog of the International Journal of Constitutional Law. https://www.iconnectblog.com/egypts-new-chief-justice/, accessed 18 August 2025

Long march gets off the ground (2008) The News International. 10 June, https://www.thenews.com.pk/archive/print/657593-long-march-gets-off-the-ground, accessed 18 August 2025
Long march stops short of sit-in (2008) The News International. 15 June https://www.thenews.com.pk/archive/print/657700-long-march-stops-short-of-sit-in, accessed 18 May 2025
Lorch J (2021) Elite capture, civil society and democratic backsliding in Bangladesh, Thailand and the Philippines. Democratization 28(1):81–102. https://doi.org/10.1080/13510347.2020.1842360
Malik H (2019) ISI challenges SC's Faizabad sit-in verdict. The Express Tribune. 15 April, https://tribune.com.pk/story/1951538/1-isi-challenges-scs-faizabad-sit-verdict, accessed 17 May 2025
Maqsood A. (2017). Meet Pakistan's Modern Middle Class. The New York Times. 24 September, https://www.nytimes.com/2017/09/24/opinion/pakistan-modern-middle-class.html accessed 14 May 2025
Masr M (2013) Morsi detained for another 15 days.12 August, https://www.madamasr.com/en/2013/08/12/news/u/morsi-detained-for-another-15-days/ accessed 15 May 2025
Malik MA (2008) The Pakistan lawyers' Movement: An Unfinished Agenda. Pakistan Law House
Mate MS (2010) The variable Power of courts: the expansion of the Power of the supreme court of India in fundamental rights and governance decisions, University of California, Berkeley, https://escholarship.org/uc/item/3f1640wm, accessed 13 June 2025
Mehdi T (2013) An overview of 2008 general elections. Dawn. 16 April, https://www.dawn.com/news/802815, accessed 13 August 2025
Mezzera M and Sial S (2010) "Media and Governance in Pakistan: A Controversial yet Essential relationship." Dingendael Organization. https://www.clingendael.org/sites/default/files/pdfs/20101109_CRU_publicatie_mmezzera.pdf accessed 14 August 2025
Melton J, Ginsburg T (2014) Does De jure judicial Independence really matter? J Law Courts 2(2):187–217. https://doi.org/10.1086/676999
Missing people's relatives criticise action against CJ (2007) Dawn. 12 March https://www.dawn.com/news/237065/missing-people-s-relatives-criticise-action-against-cj, accessed 14 May 2025
Mian A (2004) A Judge Speaks Out. Karachi: Oxford University Press
Michaelsen M (2011) 'New Media Vs. Old Politics: The Internet, Social Media, and Democratisation in Pakistan'. fesmedia Asia Series. https://library.fes.de/pdf-files/iez/08748.pdf accessed 19 August 2025.
Morlino L (2009) "Are There Hybrid Regimes? Or are They Just an Optical Illusion?" European Political Science Review 1 (2):273–296. https://doi.org/10.1017/S1755773909000198
Moustafa T (2003) Law versus the state: the judicialization of politics in Egypt. Law Soc Inq 28(4):883–930. http://www.jstor.org/stable/1215790
Moustafa T (2009) The struggle for constitutional power: law, politics, and economic development in Egypt. Cambridge: Cambridge University Press
Mudde C, Rovira KC (2012) Populism in Europe and the Americas: threat or corrective for democracy? Cambridge University Press http://ebookcentral.proquest.com/lib/york-ebooks/detail.action?docID=907174
Muhammad Azhar Siddique and others v. Federation of Pakistan and others PLD 2012 SC
Muhammad Ikram Chaudhry v. Muhammad Nawaz Sharif, 1998 SCMR 176 (1998)
Müller J-W (2016) *What Is Populism?*, Philadelphia: University of Pennsylvania Press. https://doi.org/10.9783/9780812293784
Munir D (2009) The Pakistani lawyers' movement and the popular currency of judicial Power. Harv Law Rev 123:1705–1726
Naadi T (2025) "Ghana president suspends chief justice in unprecedented move" BBC News 22 April https://www.bbc.co.uk/news/articles/cp8v28q8y5po Accessed 14 August 2025
Nadeem Ahmed v Federation of Pakistan PLD 2010 SC 1165
Naseer T (2021) Dawn. 8 December, Saqib Nisar audio leak: Why should court take action when involved parties have not pursued it, asks IHC CJ. https://www.dawn.com/news/1662627, accessed 13 August 2025

Nation celebrates judges' restoration (2009) The News International. 17 March, https://www.thenews.com.pk/archive/print/663287-nation-celebrates-judges'-restoration
Nayab D (2011) 'Estimating the Middle Class in Pakistan,' The Pakistan Development Review, 50(1):1–28. https://www.jstor.org/stable/pdf/23617431.pdf, accessed: 14 August 2025
Nelson MJ (2025) Pakistan in 2024: Reconstituting a Hybrid Regime. Asian Survey 65 (2): 202–213. https://doi.org/10.1525/as.2025.65.2.202
OHCHR: LAW 150 OF 1950 (n.d.). https://www.google.com/url?sa=t&rct=j&q=&esrc=s&source=web&cd=&ved=2ahUKEwjV8rWN0aiPAxUIV0EAHU--FwwQFnoECBcQAQ&url=https%3A%2F%2Fwww.ohchr.org%2Fsites%2Fdefault%2Ffiles%2FEgypt_EN.docx&usg=AOvVaw1EVv0ClAzVhg2ev_3O93E5&opi=89978449 accessed 13 August
Oldenburg P (2017) Loyalty, disloyalty, and semi-loyalty in Pakistan's hybrid regime. Commonwealth Comp Polit 55(1):82–103. https://doi.org/10.1080/14662043.2017.1261650
Opposition leaders stand by CJ (2007) Dawn. 14 March, https://www.dawn.com/news/237377/opposition-leaders-stand-by-cj accessed 15 July 2025
Oxhorn P (1998) 'The Social Foundations of Latin America's Recurrent Populism: Problems of Popular Sector Class Formation and Collective Action.' Sociology Lens.11(2): 212-246
Perthes V (2005) Pharaoh Relected: Egypt on the Road to Political Pluralism. German Institute for International and Security Affairs, https://www.swp-berlin.org/publications/products/comments/comments2005_39_prt_ks.pdf accessed 19 August 2025
Phelps J (2009) Pakistan's Lawyers Movement (2007–2009) | ICNC. https://www.nonviolent--conflict.org/pakistans-lawyers-movement-2007-2009/, accessed 11 July 2025
Popova M (2020) The Postcommunist judiciary: one step forward, two steps Back. In: Engelbrekt K, Kostadinova P (eds) Bulgaria's democratic institutions at thirty a balance sheet. Lexington Book, pp 241–261
Preparations for long march in full swing (2008) Dawn. 10 June, https://www.dawn.com/news/306760/preparations-for-long-march-in-full-swing accessed 21 August 2025
Qureshi TA (2010) State of emergency: general Pervez Musharraf's executive assault on judicial Independence in Pakistan. North Carolina J Int Law Commer Regul 35:485
Ramseyer JM, Rasmusen EB (1997) Judicial Independence in a Civil Law Regime: The Evidence from Japan, The Journal of Law, Economics, and Organization, Oxford University Press, 13(2), 259-286
Randazzo KA, Gibler DM, Reid R (2016) Examining the development of judicial independence. Polit Res Q 69(3):583–593. https://doi.org/10.1177/1065912916656277
Raymond N and Wolfe J (2025) 'Trump Administration files misconduct complaint against prominent judge Boasberg' Reuters 29 July https://www.reuters.com/legal/government/trump-administration-files-misconduct-complaint-against-prominent-judge-boasberg-2025-07-28/ accessed 16 August 2025
Riaz A (2021) Judicial populism and its impact on the quality of democracy in Pakistan. In: Populism in Asian democracies: features, structures, and impacts. Brill, pp 80–94. https://doi.org/10.1163/9789004444461_006
Ríos-Figueroa J (2007) Fragmentation of Power and the emergence of an effective judiciary in Mexico, 1994–2002. Latin Am Polit Soc. 49: 31–57
Rizvi G (1994) Democracy, Governance and Civil Society in South Asia. The Pakistan Development Review. 33(4). 593–624
Rohde D (2007) "Pakistani Middle Class, Beneficiary of Musharraf, Begins to Question Rule", The New York Times, 25 November https://www.nytimes.com/2007/11/25/world/asia/25class.html. accessed 13 June 2025
Rubinstein AZ (1977) The Egypt of Anwar Sadat. Curr Hist 72(423):19–38. http://www.jstor.org/stable/45314314
Rutherford BK (2018) Egypt's new authoritarianism under Sisi. Middle East J 72(2):185–208
Ryder E, Hardy ST (2019) Judicial leadership: a new strategic approach. Oxford University Press
Saad R (2017) Snapshot - All the President's MPs: The Egyptian Parliament's Role In Burying Human Rights and Silencing Dissent - MEDC, 12 June, https://mideastdc.org/publication/

snapshot-all-the-presidents-mps-the-egyptian-parliaments-role-in-burying-human-rights-and-silencing-dissent/, accessed 19 May 2025
Samad Y (2017) Elections and democratic transition in Pakistan: one step forward and two steps backwards. Commonwealth Comp Polit 55(4):509–530. https://doi.org/10.1080/14662043.2017.1323399
Shafqat S (2018) Civil society and the lawyers' movement of Pakistan. Law Soc Inq 43(3):889–914. https://doi.org/10.1111/lsi.12283
Shah SA (2001) Law Courts in a Glass House. Oxford University Press
Shah WA (2008) Three PHC judges to take fresh oath. Dawn. 5 September, https://www.dawn.com/news/319861/three-phc-judges-to-take-fresh-oath accessed 19 June 2025
Sherif AO (1997) " The Supreme Constitutional Court of Egypt and Vicarious Criminal Liability". In The Role of the Judiciary in the Protection of Human Rights. Leiden, The Netherlands: Brill. https://doi.org/10.1163/9789004635005_007
Sherif AO (1998) An overview of the Egyptian judicial system, and its history. Yearb Islamic Middle Eastern Law Online 5(1):xix–28. https://doi.org/10.1163/221129899X00034
Shirazi Q (2024) 'Eight PTI workers rearrested after release on bail,' The Express Tribune, 28 March. https://tribune.com.pk/story/2460858/eight-pti-workers-rearrested-after-release-on-bail accessed 12 March 2025
Shoukat A, Gomez ET (2018) Transformation of political elite as regime changes in Pakistan. Asian J Polit Sci 26(1):35–52. https://doi.org/10.1080/02185377.2017.1356738
Siddique H (2022) Judicial independence tainted by ministers, Commons inquiry finds. The Guardian 8 June, https://www.theguardian.com/uk-news/2022/jun/08/judicial-independence-tainted-by-ministers-commons-inquiry-finds accessed 21 July 2025
Siddique O (2006) The jurisprudence of dissolutions: presidential Power to dissolve assemblies under the Pakistani constitution and its discontents. Arizona J Int Comp Law 23(3):622–711
Siddique O (2015) The Judicialization of politics in Pakistan: the supreme court after the lawyers' movement. In: Unstable constitutionalism: law and politics in South Asia. Cambridge University Press, pp 159–191. https://doi.org/10.1017/CBO9781107706446.006
Stockemer D (2018) Populism around the world: a comparative perspective. Springer International Publishing. https://books.google.co.uk/books?id=Q3hvDwAAQBAJ https://link.springer.com/book/10.1007/978-3-319-96758-5
Stilt K (2010) The End of "One Hand": The Egyptian Constitutional Declaration and the Rift between the "People" and the Supreme Council of the Armed Forces. Yearbook of Islamic and Middle Eastern Law Online 16(1): 43–52. https://doi.org/10.1163/22112987-91000238
Suo Motu Case No 18 of 2010(National Insurance Co. Ltd Scam) (2010)
Supreme Standing Committee for Human Rights (n.d.) "The Egyptian Constitution" https://sschr.gov.eg/en/the-egyptian-constitution, accessed 5 June 2023
Suspended chief justice continues his tour - YouTube(n.d.) https://www.youtube.com/watch?v=-i0AkJaL-6g accessed 21 February 2022
Syed Mubashir Raza Jaffary and another v Employees Old Age Benefits Institutions 2014 SCMR 949
Taggart PA (2000) Populism. Buckingham: Open University Press. https://books.google.co.uk/books?id=suIUAQAAIAAJ
Tahyar BH (2012). Patrimonialism, power and the politics of judicial reform in post-Soeharto Indonesia: an institutional analysis. PhD thesis. SOAS, University of London. DOI: https://doi.org/10.25501/SOAS.00015945
Tate CN and Keith LC (2009) "Conceptualizing and Operationalizing Judicial Independence Globally." Working Paper cited in Randazzo KA, Gibler DM, Reid R (2016). Examining the Development of Judicial Independence. Political Research Quarterly, 69(3): 583–593 https://doi.org/10.1177/1065912916656277
The Chief Justice Iftikhar Muhammad Chaudhary v the President of Pakistan PLD 2007 SC 578
The State v. Dosso and the other PLD 1958 SC 533
Tikka Iqbal Muhammad Khan v. General Pervez Musharraf, PLD 2008 SC 6

Tridimas G (2010) Constitutional judicial review and political insurance. Eur J Law Econ 29(1):81–101. https://doi.org/10.1007/s10657-009-9112-z

Tushnet M (2011) Judicial leadership. In: Kane J, Patapan H, Hart P (eds) Dispersed democratic leadership: origins, dynamics, and implications. Oxford University Press. https://doi.org/10.1093/ACPROF:OSO/9780199562992.003.0008

Tushnet M, Bugaric B (2021) Power to the people: constitutionalism in the age of populism. Oxford University Press. https://books.google.co.uk/books?id=gfhQEAAAQBAJ

US bar confers 'Rule of Law Award' on deposed CJ (2008) The News International. 10 August https://www.thenews.com.pk/archive/print/128061-us-bar-confers-'rule-of-law-award'-on-deposed-cj, accessed 11 August 2025

Voigt S, Gutmann J, Feld LP (2015) Economic growth and judicial independence, a dozen years on: Cross-country evidence using an updated Set of indicators. European Journal of Political Economy, 38(1).197–211

VonDoepp P (2006) Politics and judicial assertiveness in emerging democracies: high court behavior in Malawi and Zambia. Polit Res Q. 59(3): 389-399 https://doi.org/10.1177/106591290605900306

VonDoepp P (2009) Judicial politics in new democracies: cases from southern Africa. Lynne Rienner

Waseem M (2012) Judging democracy in Pakistan: conflict between the executive and judiciary. Contemp South Asia 20(1):19–31. https://doi.org/10.1080/09584935.2011.646077

Waseem M (2015) Constitutionalism and extra-constitutionalism in Pakistan. In: Unstable constitutionalism: law and politics in South Asia. Cambridge University Press, pp 124–158. https://doi.org/10.1017/CBO9781107706446.005

Watan Party v. Federation of Pakistan PLD 2006 S.C. 697

Wigell M (2008) Mapping 'Hybrid Regimes': Regime Types and Concepts in Comparative Politics. Democratization 15(2). 230–250. https://doi.org/10.1080/13510340701846319

Witte G (2007) Musharraf ends 6-week emergency rule. The Washington Post. 15 December, https://www.washingtonpost.com/archive/national/2007/12/16/musharraf-ends-6week-emergency-rule/b0c31a79-99b3-473d-8875-7a3b9de31785/, accessed 11 August 2025

World Bank (2021) 'What is Learning Poverty'. 28 April, https://www.worldbank.org/en/topic/education/brief/what-is-learning-poverty#:~:text=Learning%20poverty%20means%20being%20unable,simple%20text%20by%20age%2010. accessed 21 August 2025

Zafar Ali Shah v. General Pervez Musharraf PLD 2000 SC 869

Zakaria F (2008) 'Musharraf's Last Stand' International Republican Institute, 21 January, https://www.iri.org/news/newsweeks-fareed-zakaria-cites-iri-pakistan-poll/ Accessed 18 August 2025

Zaidi SA (2011) Military, Civil Society and Democratization in Pakistan. Lahore: Vanguard Press

Zia S (2008)'Musharraf most unpopular leader' Nation, 18 July, https://www.nation.com.pk/18-Jul-2008/musharraf-most-unpopular-leader?version=amp accessed 14 July 2025

Ethiopia: Federalism Without Constitutionalism?

Assefa Fiseha

Abstract Disputes among branches and levels of governments are bound to arise in federations. How do emerging federations ensure the supremacy of the constitution and address such dispute where power remains less institutionalized? Federal systems require an institution that impartially and peacefully umpires such disputes. Some federations assign this function to regular supreme courts while others allocate this task to constitutional courts. Ethiopia has assigned this function to a political organ, the House Federation as advised by quasi expert body. The empirical investigation over the House of Federation indicates that it has largely remained subservient to the political party in power resulting in centralized federation. It has failed to serve as guardian of the constitution, has rarely set limits on political power and largely failed to enforce human rights. This chapter establishes that Ethiopia's case is a federation without constitutionalism and argues the case for establishing an impartial constitutional court that ensures supremacy of the constitution, resolves disputes impartially, enforces human rights and sets limits on power.

1 Introduction

Despite its abysmal human rights record, Ethiopia experienced significant stability for almost 30 years after adopting the 1995 Constitution and the federal system it put in place. It has held six elections, even though they were regarded as being below international standards, and has managed a promising economic growth for

A. Fiseha (✉)
Professor of Law and Governance, Center for Federalism and Governance, Addis Ababa University, Addis Ababa, Ethiopia
e-mail: assefa.fiseha@aau.edu.et

N. Reayat, H. O. Yusuf (eds.), *Constitutionalism in Africa and Beyond*, Ius Gentium: Comparative Perspectives on Law and Justice 127,
https://doi.org/10.1007/978-3-032-01180-0_3

more than 10 years.[1] For a long time, the country was considered a bulwark of stability in the region. However, it has faced major instability in recent times. The federal government is engaged in what it calls a 'law enforcement operation' in Tigray, though at later stages, it became clear it is one of the most devastating civil wars Ethiopia had in recent history between the federal government, and the Tigray People's Liberation Front (TPLF).[2] Inter-communal conflicts have also flared up across the country, resulting in thousands of deaths, and the displacement of millions of people.[3] A large part of the country is now under a state of emergency. Political institutions are proving unable to provide solutions, while the special police (and other informal forces) of regional states are emerging as key actors and competing with the federal armed forces for influence. This chapter argues that among the factors behind the crisis of governance in Ethiopia is the failure to institutionalise political power and a lack of constitutionalism, with the latter reflecting the absence of a functioning mechanism for resolving constitutional disputes.

The chapter begins by explaining the relevance of constitutional adjudication to constitutional governance. It then examines the constitutional adjudication systems of Ethiopia. This is followed by a discussion of different cases brought before the interpreter, mapping some general trends. The last section draws some conclusions.

2 Linking Constitutional Adjudication and Governance

Understanding the major role played by constitutional interpretation (particularly in its links to constitutional governance, and the rule of law) is critical for understanding the Ethiopian context.[4] As will be shown later, those engaged in constitutional interpretation often fail to grasp the importance of their role and end up becoming subservient to people in power. Among the essential roles of the interpreter is to ensure that power is exercised for public purposes and thereby safeguard constitutional governance. This means ensuring that the public institutions established by the constitution exercise their mandate for public purposes as defined in the constitution. It also means ensuring respect for the limits of power as expressed in the form of vertical and horizontal division of powers, enforceable human rights, maintain checks and balances, and the rule of law.

In this chapter, 'constitutional governance' refers to the attempt to institutionalise power and assert the limits through constitutional adjudication. One of the

[1] See Prunier and Ficquet (2015).

[2] At the time of writing, the armed conflict that began in November 2020 has dragged on for more than a year and half, with a few lulls in between but no end to the war in sight.

[3] Ethiopia: IDP Population Movement - Emergency Plan of Action Final Report DREF n° MDRET019 <https://reliefweb.int/report/ethiopia/ethiopia-idp-population-movement-emergency-plan-action-final-report-dref-n-mdret019>.

[4] Roux (2013), pp. 33–73.

most daunting challenges to achieving this goal is to find a way to shift the exercise of power away from personal rule and into institutions through the enforcement of the supreme law. Federalism or devolution is a rule-based system. The constitution defines the competence of the different branches, and levels of government and thereby determines the limits of power. Ways must be found to handle the issues that arise when there are violations of the limits of power.

The link between constitutional adjudication and governance (in particular, the exercise of power) is understood to be a significant problem. Max Weber examined the transition in Europe from patrimonial regimes to the modern state in terms of respect for the rule of law, and the exercise of checks and balances between the branches of government to ensure that power is used for public purposes.[5] The modern state is an impersonal state in which the relationship between the ruler and the citizen is based not on any personal ties, but on merit and technical knowledge. In patrimonial regimes, by contrast, the polity remains the personal property of the ruler (the 'big man' or the single party). Here, according to Fukuyama, 'the state administration is essentially an extension of the ruler's household'.[6] As such, there is little or no distinction between private and public spheres.

In today's globalised world, few African states are likely to refer to themselves as patrimonial. States make formal pretensions to adopt constitutions that include at least some element of the separation of powers and rule of law. Yet behind these pretensions, the use of public power for private benefit, and the exercise of public power based on personal, party, or ethnic ties is pervasive. Hence, the product of this uneven mixture of formal pretence with patrimonial practice is often referred to as the 'neo-patrimonial regime' or extractive state.[7]

In the neo-patrimonial state, the political elite in power comes to control state institutions; with the massive resources that are then made available, it can create and command patronage at the many different levels of the state. The country's public assets become in effect the ruler's private property, and with the resources at his disposal, he is able to bring about the conditions necessary for winning elections.[8] Behind the scenes of the formal institutions, the ruling party (epitomised by the imperial president or 'big man') distributes the spoils of office to its supporters and punishes dissenters.[9] In these situations, and despite constitutional principles, neo-patrimonial regimes determine who may engage in politics and what spaces are available for such engagement. The old principle of 'divide and rule' is used to weaken any opposition. Meanwhile, informal networks are used to weaken formal institutions and undermine their ability to deliver supposedly impersonal levels of public service.[10]

---

[5] Weber (1946).

[6] Fukuyama (2014).

[7] Acemoglu and Robinson (2012).

[8] Hyden (2006), p. 95.

[9] Bratton (2008), pp. 621–632.

[10] Chabal and Daloz (1999).

If political power is to be used for public purposes, the locus of power needs to move from the personal or party level to that of the impersonal institution. In this way, it can be better regulated by the rule of law and through the agreed-upon system of checks and balances. Constitutional adjudication (either through a Supreme Court or Constitutional Court) has been proven to provide some institutional guarantee against the use of power for personal use. The role of the interpreter in shaping and regulating the political process and serving as guardian of the constitution is thus of paramount importance since most constitutions declare themselves as the supreme arbiter. Constitutions are higher laws that establish the main public institutions and define their mandates and also work to set limits on power by binding elected legislators and ensuring the basic rights of citizens and minorities. The supremacy of constitutions reflects their status as the embodiment of the will of the people: constitutions are authored not by the majority or minority but by the people and ought to bind both the ruler and the ruled.

The Ethiopian constitution continues to face legitimacy crises. This is arguably due to a crucial omission: declaring the supremacy of the constitution is meaningless unless there are the institutional means to enforce it. The primary function of supreme courts or constitutional courts is to decide when governments contravene the constitution through the promulgation of laws or implementation of decisions. Supreme courts act as the guardians of the constitution. Where this function is lacking (as is the case in Ethiopia), any constitution becomes a dead letter and no more than an instrument of factional interests: a 'constitution without constitutionalism'.[11] It must be noted, though, that constitutional courts are themselves subordinate to the constitution. Thus, they cannot legitimately assume the constituent power (which belongs to the people) to make changes or modifications to the constitution under the pretext of interpretation.[12]

Constitutions are often assumed to stand for generations, and express eternal principles. However, constitutions should be open to amendment and able to adapt to new situations, even though this can be difficult. Similarly, constitutional interpreters can find new ways of adapting the understanding of the existing constitution to the current context. Two hundred years ago, the principle of equality was understood in the West to mean equality for rich white men, and did not extend to apply to women, the poor, blacks, and other minorities.[13] But without amending the provisions of the constitution, constitutional interpreters have shifted the meaning of equality such that it applies to women, blacks, and all human beings.[14] Similarly federal government mandates regarding defence might not have envisaged nuclear

---

[11] Okoth-Ogendo (1993), pp. 65–84.

[12] Brewer-Carías (2011), pp. 16, 20. In countries where constitutional courts ensure supremacy of international treaties (dealing with human rights such as European Human Rights Treaty), these courts also have the mandate over conventions and treaties.

[13] *Ibid.* p. 52.

[14] *Brown v Board of Education* of Topeka, 347 US 483 (1954) ended segregation and the separate-but-equal doctrine.

weapons or the use of drones, air forces, space technology, and other modern means of warfare, but they apply to all of these. Freedom of expression did not envisage the internet, social media, and other means of communication but continues to cover them. In Germany, for instance, the Federal Constitutional Court (FCC) extended the right to confidentiality, previously only applicable to human beings, to apply to computers and information technology systems.[15] In short, interpreters, continue to find ways of adapting constitutions to meet the demands of the day. It is in this sense that some argue the constitution is not an archaic fossil, but a living document. Adhering to the text of the constitution is vital, but the text of the constitution is meant to be read in such a way that it makes sense today, rather than be limited to the meaning assigned to it centuries ago. Adapting the constitution to meet the demands of the current generation is a vital function of the interpreter.

However distinguishing between an active interpretation of the existing constitution and the setting of new constitutional norms by a 'juristocracy' is a controversial matter. Stone explained the risk well, writing in the *New York Times* of 'our Fill-in-the-Blank constitution' and suggesting that the content of the constitution is written by judges as they decide cases, as if the constitution contained no pre-set principles whatsoever.[16] Constitutional courts play a crucial role in the process of constitutional adjudication in a messy situation in which the realms of law and politics are in a state of constant interaction and friction. In the academic debate on interpretation, considerable divergences exist. There are originalists (who insist the interpreter should stick to the historically discoverable meaning of the constitution); those who advocate interpretation based on strict principles of teleology and harmony[17]; and those who consider the constitution as a 'living tree' and advocate that the role of the interpreter is to adapt the constitution to changing circumstances.[18]

Another role for the interpreter is focused on constitutional courts and their role in shaping and safeguarding the democratic political order in order to ensure a polity governed by the rule of law.[19] This focus is not a claim to establish courts as 'democracy builders'.[20] To be sure, democracy is not born in the courts: democracy is about rule by the people, much of which happens outside the judicial backyard. But once the political process sets the direction for democratic rule, courts play a role in reinforcing it. Thus, alongside the institutions that administer elections,

---

[15] See BVerfG, Reference 1 BvR 370/07 (27 February 2008) www.bverfg.de/entscheidungen/rs20080227_1bvr037007.html.

[16] See Stone (2010).

[17] Decision of the German Constitutional Court, Southwest State case, 1 bverf GE 14, 32 (1951), in Kommers and Miller (2012), pp. 62–66. The Court stated that, on the need for the internal coherence of the Basic Law, 'no single constitutional provision may be taken out of its context and interpreted by itself but must be interpreted in such a way as to render it compatible with the fundamental principles of the Constitution and the intentions of its authors'.

[18] See Scalia (1998); Waluchow (2007).

[19] See Kommers (2006), pp. 114–116.

[20] Ginsburg (2013).

courts can work to ensure that the electoral process remains inclusive, free, and fair. Courts seek to guarantee that political rights are respected and enforced; that state authority is subject to constraints; and that power is dispersed between different actors as framed by the constitution.[21] Here we have the example of the German FCC. It has made key decisions regarding elections;[22] the role and status of political parties; issues relating to the dissolution of parliament;[23] foreign affairs (and notably the overseas deployment of armed forces which requires legislative approval);[24] the monitoring of party finance; as well as overseeing internal democracy within Parliament and ensuring the role of small parties. It also demarcates mandates among branches and levels of government. Article 21 of the Basic Law establishes political parties as the major agencies of political representation, and thus they enjoy constitutional status. Consequently, the FCC protects its role in the political process,[25] but can also declare them unconstitutional if and when political parties seek to threaten the democratic order.[26] Given fears of any return to fascism, articles 18 and 24 stipulate that individuals and political parties which threaten the democratic order face the threat of forfeiting their rights. The Court has an express mandate to defend democracy from anyone that threatens it as an arm of a militant democracy.[27]

The FCC resolves wide-ranging, politically delicate issues and, as the guardian of the Basic Law, it ensures that the political system is governed by law. The courts can perform important functions in the consolidation and maintenance of democratic government. Many constitutional courts make invaluable contributions to the establishment and maintenance of democratic institutions.[28] They provide a site for the enforcement of human rights and for the delineation of the powers of governmental bodies (vertical and horizontal). By adjudicating constitutional questions and enforcing constitutional provisions, constitutional courts make the constitution a living document that shapes the exercise of political power rather than an aspirational collection of fine phrases. They can contribute, in other words, to making a new regime not merely a democracy in name but a state governed in practice by law.

---

[21] Daly (2017), p. 58.

[22] See Hessian Election Review Case (103 BVerfGE 111: 2001). The case according to Kommers is comparable to *Bush v Gore* (531U.S. 98 [2000]). While *Bush v Gore* remains contested, the FCC decision on a related matter is less contested in Germany.

[23] Dissolution Case II www.bverfg.de/entscheidungen/es20050825_2bve000405.html.

[24] See AWACS-Urteil BVferG, 12 July 1994, BVeffGE 90, 585–603. The FCC required the legislative body to approve the deployment.

[25] 4 BVerfGE 27: 1954.

[26] See Communist Party case 5BVerfGE85, 139: 1956. In accordance with the doctrine of militant democracy, the FCC can disqualify political parties when it thinks they are opposed democracy: in this fashion, democracy defends itself from extremists.

[27] Collings (2015), p 38.

[28] Horowitz (2006), p. 127.

In many developing countries, the idea of the peaceful resolution of disputes and the institutionalisation of power (including the idea of resolving vertical and horizontal disputes through independent and impartial bodies) are aspirations rather than reality. The formal institutions that exist are often side-lined in practice by the informal and patrimonial networks of the ruling party. As Roux suggests, 'constitutional courts in new or otherwise fragile democracies can play [a role] in preventing elected majorities from using their democratic mandate permanently to entrench themselves in power'[29] and thereby reduce the risks of authoritarianism; or, as Issacharoff puts it, they can serve as 'hedges' against majority authoritarianism.[30]

The risks presented by extending presidential terms beyond their original constitutional limits are all too familiar in Africa. Ethiopia experienced considerable political turmoil precisely because ruling elites decided to extend their terms of office beyond the constitutional limits without obtaining consensus on this. In situations like these, the interpreter can play a pivotal role in warding off such efforts by enforcing the term limits stipulated by the constitution. As will be seen below, the Ethiopian House of Federation (HoF) gave permission for such an extension, including its own term, became a judge on its own case and part of the problem rather than part of the solution.

The key challenge in most parts of Africa is both the conception of the law in general, and specifically, the rule of law. In many cases, the rule of law is generally understood as an instrument of power, a simple means through which emperors or elected leaders impose their will on the people. This is well illustrated by the long history of the consolidation of power in Ethiopia. Emperor Haile Selassie (1931–1974) oversaw two constitutions that legitimised his power, and sought to consolidate his dynasty. Similarly, the military junta (1974–1991) instrumentalised the rule of law for building 'socialism', while, for the purposes of Ethiopia's post-developmental state, it was subordinated to the acceleration of economic growth under the hegemonic party. But these are perhaps better understood as examples of rule by law rather than the rule of law.

The rule of law is best understood not as an instrument of power and oppression, but as a means of setting limits on public institutions and thus regulating, even shaping, power. After the Second World War (WWII), the rule of law has been understood—for those countries with firm constitutions in place—as placing a substantive limit on the agency of political actors and public institutions.[31] The law, in the first place, must reflect the wishes of the people and, more importantly, it must guarantee their rights and freedoms. The rule of law was transformed from merely formal legality (which did not set firm limits on the legislature), to substantive legality; one that actively restrains the power vested in political institutions. In other words, the rule of law, as it is conceived today, puts a limit on the power of public institutions and ensures freedom for the citizen.

---

[29] Roux (2013), p. 35.

[30] Issacharoff (2011), p. 965.

[31] Tamanaha (2004), pp. 108–109.

The inclusion of human rights in post-WWII constitutions, the establishment of constitutional courts that enforce the will of the people (that is, the constitution) to ensure that these rights are not violated by the political branches, and the imposition of rigid procedures for amending constitutions, were high points in understandings of the rule of law. As Tom Ginsburg notes, 'Post-war constitutional drafting efforts focused on two concerns'

> First the enunciation of basic rights to delimit a zone of autonomy for individuals, which the state should not be allowed to abridge; and second, the establishment of special constitutional courts to safeguard and protect these rights. These courts were seen as protecting democracy from its own excesses and were adopted precisely because they could be countermajoritarian, able to protect the substantive values of democracy from procedurally legitimate elected bodies.[32]

There are strong links between constitutional adjudication and governance. Governance in the form of federalism or devolution without the institutional backup to oversee and maintain the constitutional balance is prone to political manipulation. Strong institutions that regulate political power in the form of supreme or constitutional courts are critical in shaping the behaviour of political institutions, and so giving life to constitutionalism and the rule of law.[33] However, as the next section illustrates, adjudication and institutionalization of power remain major challenges in Ethiopia.

3 Constitutional Adjudication and Governance

3.1 Political and Institutional Context

Ethiopia is the second most populous country in Africa next to Nigeria. It relishes its status as the only African country never to have been colonised. With a population of more than 120 million, it is both the most populous country in the region and the most diverse, inhabited as it is by over 80 distinct ethno-linguistic communities. Most of its population (80%) live in rural areas, making it one of the least urbanised countries in the world in spite of its fast rate of urbanisation (4.6% per annum).

Ethiopia adopted a federal system with the promulgation of the 1995 Constitution. The principal objective of this system is to help manage ethnic diversity and respond to the age-old demand for self-government by ethno-national groups. The federal system is thus based on the recognition of the right of the country's ethnic communities to self-determination,[34] and is a product of more than 50 years of political contestation. A unitary state for over a century, Ethiopia gradually became a

[32] Ginsburg (2003), p. 2.

[33] Horowitz (2015), p. 126.

[34] Preamble, FDRE Constitution (1995).

centralised state. While this was taking place, the country became increasingly unable to accommodate the ethno-cultural diversity of its people. The situation was exacerbated by the fact that centralisation decreased the prospects of good governance, given its absence of democratic participation. All these factors together led to public protests, and rebellion in different parts of the country.[35]

It was the Ethiopian Student Movement of the 1970s that brought what had been a taboo topic fully centre-stage: the accommodation of diversity, under the rubric of 'the question of nationalities'.[36] The movement placed this issue on the same footing as other key political demands such as those for multi-party democracy, and land redistribution (promoted under the slogan 'land to the tiller').[37] Successive governments sought to suppress the demands for diversity, but this led only to the emergence of ethnic liberation movements across the country, each of which vowed to 'liberate' the communities whose cause they championed. The strongest of these was the Ethiopian Peoples' Revolutionary Democratic Front (EPRDF), a coalition of four rebel groups the most influential of which was the TPLF. The latter waged a 17-year civil war against Mengistu Haile-Mariam's military government and defeated it in May 1991.

The EPRDF began the process that led to its federalisation of the country immediately upon its seizure of control of Addis Ababa. In June 1991, it convened a conference which adopted the Transitional Period Charter that was to serve as a draft constitutional document for 4 years. The Charter recognised each ethnonational group's right to self-determination, which included the right to dissociate from the country.[38] The Charter also established the Representative Council. This was a transitional legislative body which enacted a proclamation re-organising the subnational units of the country along ethnic lines.[39] The country was divided into 14 regions mainly along ethno-lingustic lines with its capital in Addis Ababa. The number of these subnational units was later slimmed down to nine when five of the regions came together to form what is known as the Southern Nation, Nationalities and Peoples' (SNNP) state. In 1995, the current constitution was adopted, and Ethiopia formally became a federal state with nine states and a federal city.[40] Between June 2020 and 2022, additional regional states, the Sidama, Southern state, Central Ethiopia and the South West, were recognised following the fragmentation of the former Southern regional State. Ethiopia consequently has 12 states.

---

[35] Teffera (2012), pp. 67–72; Tiruneh (1994), p. 37.

[36] Balsvik (2005).

[37] *Ibid.*

[38] Negarit Gazeta, Peaceful and Democratic Transitional Conference of Ethiopia: Transitional Period Charter of Ethiopia: Proclamation No. 1 (1991).

[39] Negarit Gazeta of the Ethiopian Transitional Government: A Proclamation to Provide for the Establishment of National Regional Self-Governments No. 7 (1992).

[40] Another federal city, Dire Dawa, does not enjoy constitutional recognition but was instead federalised by an act of Parliament. The Oromia and Somali states claim ownership of it.

3.2 *Institutional Structure of the Federation*

Ethiopia has a federal system with two constitutionally recognised levels of government: the federal and state governments.[41] The system is that of a 'dual federalism' where each level of government has its own legislature, executive, and judiciary. The federal government has a bicameral legislature—the House of Peoples' Representatives (HPR) and the HoF.[42] The HPR, the Lower House, is composed of directly elected representatives and enjoys exclusive legislative power on federal matters.[43] The Upper House is not involved in the legislative process as such, but is empowered to resolve constitutional disputes, decide on the allocation of subsidies to the subunits, and deal with ethnic-identity claims for recognition and self-government. Ethiopia has a parliamentary system of government. The Prime Minister, who heads the Council of Ministers, is elected by and from the members of the HPR.[44] The federal government has its own judiciary, which is structured at three levels: first instance court, high court, and Supreme Court. The Supreme Court is established for the whole of the federation and has no mandate to interpret the constitution. Federal first instance and high courts are established in the two federal cities and in several other states.[45]

3.3 *Institution of Constitutional Adjudication*

Unlike many other countries, Ethiopia assigns its second chamber, the HoF, the power to resolve constitutional disputes and have oversight over Ethiopian federalism. What was the reasoning behind the decision to vest the power of interpreting the constitution in the HoF rather than in the regular judiciary or in a constitutional court? Analysis of the minutes of the Constitutional Assembly suggests the decision was grounded in the views of the initial framers on the nature of the Constitution in general and the role and status of the nationalities in particular. The framers saw the new federal dispensation as the outcome of the 'coming together' of the nationalities.[46] Thus, it is clearly stipulated in the Constitution that the 'nations, nationalities and peoples are sovereign'. The Constitution is considered the expression of the 'free will and consent' of the nationalities. It is, in the words of the framers, 'a political contract', and therefore the power of interpreting the Constitution should

[41] Federal Democratic Republic Ethiopia Constitution (1995), article 46.

[42] Constitution, article 53.

[43] Constitution, article 55.

[44] Constitution, articles 72–77.

[45] Constitution, article 78.

[46] See the preamble to the Constitution, which begins: 'We the nations, nationalities and peoples ... adopted this constitution.' See also article 8, which grants sovereignty to the nations, nationalities and peoples.

be vested in the nationalities.[47] Since the HoF is composed of representatives of various nationalities, it is expressly granted the power to review the constitutionality of laws and resolve disputes between the federal and state governments.[48] This means Ethiopia has a distinctive practice for constitutional interpretation.

The HoF currently has 153 members who represent 76 nationalities and are indirectly elected by the states. The HoF is not part of the federal law-making process: a federal bill does not need the consent of the HoF to become a law. With regard to composition, article 61(2) of the Constitution stipulates that 'each Nation, Nationality and People shall be represented in the HoF by at least one member. Each Nation or Nationality shall be represented by one additional representative for each one million of its population.' As a result, the nationality with the largest number of people has as many seats as its size will allow in the HoF. As of 2005, state governors, the highest political figures in the states, have been among the key members sent to represent the states and nationalities in the HoF and to decide on crucial issues such as constitutional interpretation and the size of the federal subsidy to be allocated to each state.

The foregoing distinctive constitutional design is due to the nature of a political reality established by ethno-nationalist mobilisation and ideological commitment.[49] The country's distinctive arrangement for constitutional adjudication and the way in which it impacts governance needs some brief clarification. The design is the product of a constitution-making process that took place under the influence of a dominant party. The restructuring of the previous, centrist state—a process that began during the transition and continued during the formation of the federation—was dominated by the 'national liberation movements' that ousted the military junta and ended its project of forcibly integrating the country through the adoption of socialism. The movements remained dominant in the ruling party until it too fell into internal crisis due to renewed protests. They began in Oromia in 2015 and soon spread to other places, resulting in the coming to power in 2018 of new leadership under Abiy Ahmed, which has altered the course of Ethiopian politics.

It is essential to understand the effects that the domination of one party has on both the political system in general and constitutional interpretation in particular. With the exception of the early period of the transition in 1991–1992 and the 2005–2010 period (when various opposition groups shared parliamentary seats and political institutions at federal as well as state levels), the federation has been dominated since 1991 by the same ruling party. As the cases discussed below will

[47] See *Ye Ethiopia Hige Mengist Gubae Kale Gubae* v. 4 *Hidar* 14–20, 1987 E.C. (Minutes of the Constitutional Assembly, November 1994) for its discussion of articles 59, 61, and 62.

[48] Article 62(1).

[49] Apart from the fact that it was a long-held view of the current ruling party, its inclusion in the Constitution was justified as a means of bringing liberation movements with secessionists inclinations—among them the Oromo and the Ogaden National Liberation Fronts—to the negotiation table. It would have been difficult to persuade them to join the Transitional Government of Ethiopia without the rights mentioned in article 39.

demonstrate, an effective system of checks and balances between the key institutions has never been in place. Thus, for instance, a majoritarian political organ such as the HoF is supposed to play a counter-majoritarian role in the enforcement of human rights, limiting power and adjudicating impartially on inter-governmental disputes, but is controlled by key political figures from the ruling party.

What caused the HoF to have such a compromised role? In part, it is the simple fact that the same party has been in control of political institutions (including the HoF). Less simply, it is the fact that the constitution-making process was dominated by one party, rather than entailing an inclusive procedure in which competing forces were allowed some equality of voice. As Ginsburg notes in regard to the experience of East Asia,

> Where a single party dominates the process, it has little incentive to set up a neutral arbiter to resolve disputes about the constitutional meanings … Explicit constitutional power of and access to judicial review will be greater where political forces are diffused than where a single dominant party exists at the time of constitutional design … Where political forces are… scattered, no party can confidently predict that it will be able to win post-constitutional elections. Because of such uncertainty to win, all parties will prefer to limit the majority and institutionalize judicial review. The structure of the party system and configuration of political forces remain key factors.[50]

Ginsburg suggests that when political pluralism is the norm, parties prefer to institute an 'insurance model of judicial review' involving a Supreme Court or Constitutional Court. Given that a dominant party could lose control of political institutions through free and fair elections, it seems prudent for an impartial and autonomous court to ensure its rights as a political minority until the time comes when a free and fair election can return it as a political majority. The new political minority will rely on the same institutional guarantee.[51] The institution therefore serves as a form of insurance for when political losses occur in democracies. Such an arrangement is a key institutional safeguard for any constitution that advocates multi-party democracy, and thus seeks to promote political pluralism. As we see below, this provision helps one understand the HoF's reluctance to mediate constitutional disputes impartially.

Ethiopia's distinctive institutional design has resulted in a centralised federation that lacks judicial review. This leaves the system open to political manipulation by the dominant party despite the Constitution's conception of the federation as a compact between nations. Logically, such a compact would entail a more decentralised federation, one that could accommodate the demands of sub-state nations for greater political autonomy and self-government. It is these demands for autonomy and self-government that are at the core of Ethiopia's age-old political crisis and the ongoing civil war, particularly in Tigray and Oromia.

[50] Ginsburg (2003), pp. 24–25.

[51] See also Tushnet (2014), p. 44.

3.4 Constitutional Adjudication in Practice

Since its establishment in 1995, the CCI/HoF has received close to 6000 applications demanding its intervention in matters of constitutional interpretation. The majority of these arose (more than 90%) from court litigation and thus making the HoF look more of an appellate court contrary to its original design of presiding over delicate political and constitutional issues of the highest nature, but some requested constitutional opinion regarding the federal government, including on the question of the postponement of the general elections in 2020. Close to 3000 of the applications were rejected on the grounds of not involving constitutional issues. About 110 cases were deemed to be about constitutional issues and were therefore examined by the CCI.[52] In these, the CCI/HoF was asked to decide on matters related to the smooth running of the federation; the protection of individual and minority rights; access to land related rights; questions of the abuse of power by the political branches of the federal government, and a variety of issues related to the state of democracy in the country.

3.4.1 The HoF on Ethiopian Federalism

The HoF is supposed to deal with inter-jurisdictional disputes between the federal and state government in two ways: either by inhibiting the emergence of such disputes or by resolving them when they do arise.[53] The Ethiopian federal system has functioned suspiciously smoothly in the past 27 years, with very few intergovernmental disputes presented to the HoF. This apparent lack of conflict is probably attributable to the fact that the various levels of government were controlled by a single party operating on the basis of democratic centralism and enforcing strict party discipline. Any inter-jurisdictional disputes were settled within the party, with the result that the only jurisdictional issues brought before the HoF were constitutional issues that arose in court litigation between individuals (for example *Biyadglegn Meles* et al. *v the Amhara Regional State*,[54] in which an individual plaintiff unsuccessfully challenged a proclamation regulating land usage).

The HoF was called upon several times to provide opinions on jurisdictional issues. The HPR requested its advice when provisions in a draft proclamation on urban land registration were challenged when tabled for debate in the federal parliament. It also dealt with a number of identity claims and demands linked to the right to self-determination of ethnic groups (the foundational principle of the Ethiopian federal system) stemming from petitions that communities made to it for recognition and local self-rule as distinct ethnic communities. Take for instance, the Silte

[52] This data was obtained via email from Yadeta Gizaw, a researcher at the CCI.

[53] Constitution, article 62.

[54] *Biyadglegn Meles* et al. *v the Amhara Regional State* petition *Miazia* 301,989 EC (unpublished).

case.[55] Here, a certain community that had been perceived to be part of the Guraghe ethnic group claimed a separate identity from the latter, and set up a local government in the Southern state. As required by articles 39 and 47 of the Constitution, such a process has to involve the local population, the regional state parliament (itself constituted by diverse groups), and the HoF. But the precise roles of these different actors in the political process were never clear. The matter was eventually resolved in 2001 in a referendum held by the HoF. Thereafter, a large majority of the Silte chose to separate themselves from the Guraghe and form a local government within the constituent unit. Meanwhile, in November 2019, the Sidama in the South voted overwhelmingly in favour of forming a new regional state, which joined the federation as its tenth member in June 2020. The fact that the process was resolved through the National Electoral Board rather than the HoF testifies to significant procedural inconsistencies and the political pressures inherent in the system.

Several other demands (from the Kimante of the Amhara region, the Menja and Wellene of the South) for the establishment of local governments remain in play. The HoF has been reluctant to provide any direct response to these demands, and has focused instead on the need to address 'issues of governance'. Here, the new thinking is that demands by sub-state minorities for recognition and self-rule express political and resource marginalisation at the local level, and that addressing those issues directly might reduce the repeated demands for recognition and self-rule. Importantly, in the case of the Kimante (who form a minority within the Amhara regional state), a less-than-accommodating response from the regional state, combined with the HoF's failure to mediate the conflict without delay, cost lives in 2015 and 2016. With the exception of the Silte and later the new states established following the fragmentation of the former Southern state, the HoF thus failed to deliver even on its crucial mandate: issues related to local self-governance which is considered as corner stone and foundation of the constitution.

3.4.2 The HoF on Human Rights

Another area the HoF is concerned with is human rights. At the centre of many human rights disputes is the question of whether an ethnic community's right to self-rule should take precedence over an individual's right to equality and non-discrimination. A case in point was brought before HoF in 2000. The issue arose in the regional state of Benishangul-Gumuz, where the Berta, Gumuz, Shinasha, Komo, and Mao peoples are considered indigenous, and the Amhara, Oromo, and Tigray peoples (often referred to as 'the highlanders'), non-indigenous. Most of the highlanders were forcibly transferred to the regional state during the military junta's resettlement programme, but they now comprise some 47% of the region's population. Several wanted to run as candidates in the state and federal elections; however, the Election Board prevented them from registering on the ground that they were

[55] See the opinion of the CCI written on 25 January 2000 (unpublished).

unable to speak any of the indigenous vernaculars. The highlanders asked the HoF to intervene in the Board's decision, arguing that it violated their constitutional rights to non-discrimination and electability as it contravened the equality and supremacy clauses of the Constitution.[56]

The CCI proved to be divided on the issue. The majority viewed the case in terms of the Constitution's bill of rights, which guarantees the rights to equality, citizenship, and self-rule.[57] Utilising 'clause-bound' interpretation, they concluded that the Board's decision violated the Constitution.[58] But a minority insisted on a 'purposive interpretation'. From this perspective (one that insists on keeping to the fundamental normative assumptions of the Constitution), it is the right to self-rule of ethnonationalist groups which is primary, and they consequently endorsed the original decision of the Board, denying the highlanders the right to run as candidates.[59]

The HoF duly considered both opinions from the CCI and came to a decision closer to that of the minority opinion.[60] It emphasised there could be no doubt that a candidate should be required to speak the working language of the state he or she represents (in this case, Amharic). It is necessary for candidates both to communicate their aims to the electorate and to speak for the people they represent in Parliament. By virtue of proclamation 111/1995, the candidate is required to know the working language of the regional state and to that extent that the proclamation does not contradict the principles of the Constitution. Nevertheless, the HoF found the Board's interpretation of the proclamation to mean a candidate should be versed in any of the indigenous languages unconstitutional, declared it null and void with prospective effect, and allowed the highlanders to participate as candidates in future elections. The decision enjoyed wide support, as it sought to balance conflicting interests between the right to self-rule and the right of citizenship and yet its implementation remained weak and the marginalisation of minorities in several regional states remained a major concern and source of conflict.[61]

---

[56] Constitution, article 9.

[57] See the opinion of the CCI (unpublished).

[58] Clause-bound interpretation is not usually a preferred method as it focuses on a specific clause of the Constitution without looking at the text as a whole. Purposive (or teleological or functional) interpretation attempts to resolve issues by grasping the spirit of the Constitution. See Barak (2006).

[59] See article 38(1) of the Constitution, article 38 of Proclamation 111/1995, and Article 45 of Proclamation 532/2007.

[60] See the decision of the HoF of *Megabit* 5, 1995 EC (12 March 2003).

[61] Yet one could pose a question: What would the decision of the HoF be if the regional state adopted one of the local languages as working language instead of Amharic? The case goes beyond the debate between group and individual rights. It raises the core issue of carefully balancing the right of citizenship—which includes the right to participate in public affairs throughout the country and which is the mandate of the federal government—and the right to self-rule, which remains within the mandate of the states. This fundamental issue is unresolved. Given that the Ethiopian federal system is strongly in favour of the right to self-rule of ethno-national groups, it remains critical for the HoF to strike some balance between the mandates of either level of governments. Whether this role be discharged impartially and effectively by the HoF, given that it is the institution of the 'nations, nationalities and peoples', is something that time will tell.

The CCI/HoF also examined several other cases involving human rights violations. While citizens are provided, as a last resort, with the possibility of applying to the CCI about violations of their human rights, the CCI has proved reluctant to enforce these rights, with the result that political institutions have few restrictions on their powers. An exemplary case is *Heirs of Wasihun v Agency*. After exhausting the available judicial remedies, the heirs in question applied to the CCI for relief, but their case was rejected by the CCI on the grounds that no constitutional interpretation was involved. The decision of the Cassation Court was therefore endorsed. However, when the case came to the HoF for interpretation, it was remanded to the Supreme Court to address the violation of the right of the heirs to due process.[62] It is ironic that the Supreme Court was instructed by the HoF to address the right to due process of the applicants violated in the case. The Supreme Court and the CCI adopting a very positivist understanding of the rule of law, failed to address the violation of due process right despite a clear appeal to that effect by the applicants. Nor was the court interested to assert an implicit mandate given to it under Article 13 of the constitution that requires courts and other institutions to 'respect and enforce' the list of rights enshrined in chapter three of the constitution. Chapter three was meant to be a minimum standard human rights guarantee applicable throughout the country, and the courts to be its guardian with the implicit mandate mentioned above. Yet, as indicated in this case and many other cases the Court simply abdicated one of its core functions, instead of asserting it. Thus constitutional design that denies the judiciary the mandate to interpret the constitution and the courts own timidity and failure to assert an implicit mandate on chapter three made human rights without a guardian.[63]

The new government led by Abiy Ahmed has introduced some reforms including laws that aim to ensure judicial independence and a more transparent judicial appointment process. The new laws ensure judicial autonomy, empower the court to administer its own budget, hire and fire its own support staff. However, like all reforms, it has lost vigour and promises were never taken seriously.[64] The Prime Minister, on assuming power in 2018 said '*Sanatara Anasrim*', meaning we will not arrest citizens without having evidence (blaming his former allies for doing so), yet the regime soon began to arrest people in large numbers, putting civilians in different concentration camps.[65] Thousands continue to languish in concentration camps without being brought to court. Journalists, prominent figures, political party leaders are sent to jail, and often the regime fails to bring suspects before court as

---

[62] Based on the instructions of the HoF, the Federal Supreme Court reversed its own decision after addressing the violation of due process to the heirs of Wassihun et al. See *Heirs of Wassihun* et al. *v Agency for Government Houses*, decision of the Cassation division of the Supreme Court file number 43511 v.14 P.211.

[63] For details on the Ethiopian Judiciary see Fiseha (2011), pp. 702–715.

[64] See Proclamation number 1234/2021 Federal Courts Proclamation, Federal *Negait Gasetta*, Addis Ababa 27th year No. 26, April 2021.

[65] See Human Rights Watch and Amnesty International Reports for 2020 and 2021.

required by law.[66] In some cases, courts order the release of prisoners because the prosecutor failed to submit enough evidence, but police and security officers often fail to comply with court orders, and suspects continue to suffer in jail indefinitely.[67]

Judicial autonomy among others implies that judges and courts' autonomy is respected; judicial decisions are respected and complied with by other organs.[68] While there is some progress from the side of courts in adjudicating criminal cases independently, they still suffer from intimidation in politically motivated charges that the regime filed in high profile cases.[69] The police, security forces and the executive continue to disregard judicial decisions, particularly in criminal cases.[70] On November 3, Oromia Supreme Court judges (Adama branch) were rounded up and taken to jail from their offices by regime security disregarding their immunity. This is the most outrageous violation of the rule of law and judicial autonomy and demonstrates the situation in the country. The rule of law index shows Ethiopia ranks one of the lowest in the world (123 out of 140 countries) and continues to regress.[71]

3.4.3 Prevention of Abuse of Power

The CCI/HoF has also been called upon to prevent the abuse of power by declaring certain decisions made by the executive branch of government unconstitutional. A good example is *Asehanfi Amare* et al. *v Ethiopian Revenue and Customs Authority*.

In 2008, Proclamation 587 established the Ethiopian Revenue and Customs Authority (ERCA), authorising the Council of Ministers (CoM) to regulate the hiring and firing of ERCA staff. Staff could be dismissed if the director-general (DG) lost confidence in them or suspected them of being involved in corruption. Dismissal

---

[66] According to an expert in this field who is also a practicing lawyer based in Oromia, thousands of suspects continue to suffer in jail without bring brought to court of law. And when courts make orders for release of suspects on bail, court orders are not complied with. In his opinion, there is dismal failure in the area of criminal justice in Ethiopia at the moment. Interview 15 August 2022, Addis Ababa; see also Abraham Hailemeskel, Yehualashet Tegegn, 'When Politics Undermines the Judiciary' https://www.ethiopia-insight.com/2021/01/14/when-politics-undermines-the-judiciary-the-case-of-mulugeta-tesfakiros/.

[67] International Human Rights Organizations such as Human Rights Watch and Amnesty International have released detail reports in 2020, 2021 and 2022 disclosing the horrific human right situation in Ethiopia.

[68] News: Outcry over arrest of three Oromia Supreme Court judges after allowing bail to Jawar Mohammed's security detail, *Addis Standard*, https://addisstandard.com/news-outcry-over-arrest-of-three-oromia-supreme-court-judges-after-allowing-bail-to-jawar-mohammeds-security-detail/#:~:text=The%20Judges%20Dessaleny%20Lammii%2C%20Mohamed,the%20matter%20told%20Addis%20Standard.

[69] Leul Estifanos, *Judicial Reform in Ethiopia: Inching Towards Justice* https://www.ethiopia-insight.com/2021/09/05/judicial-reform-in-ethiopia-inching-towards-justice/.

[70] Fiseha (2011), pp. 702–715.

[71] See 'Ethiopia' at https://worldjusticeproject.org/rule-of-law-index/country/2022/Ethiopia/.

could take place 'without adhering to the formal disciplinary procedures.' The regulation further provides that no judicial organ can order the reinstatement of an employee so dismissed. Note also that the DG is not required to provide any proof of corruption, mere suspicion is enough for dismissal. In addition, the DG has his or her own legal expert on the panel of CCI arbiters.

The DG chose to dismiss several employees from ERCA. One of these, Asehanfi Amare, sued the DG for not ensuring due process of law, and for denying him access to justice as provided for under article 37 of the Constitution, but the DG's decision was apparently non-reviewable according to the proclamation. The Court, without considering the merits of the case, referred the matter directly to the CCI/HoF, noting that the decision of the authority seemed to conflict with article 37 (1) of the Constitution, which promises access to justice. The CCI ruled that in a parliamentary system of government, the legislature has the discretion to define which cases need to come before courts and which do not. Thus, the regulation falls into this discretion and does not violate the right of access to justice. With this stance of refusing to review the DG's decision, both the CCI/HoF and the Cassation Court suggest that the rule of law is no more than an instrument of power. By twist of events the DG was himself sent to jail suspected of corruption and a new proclamation placed the mandate to try higher officials on the Supreme Court. The DG applied to the CCI/HoF alleging that his right to appeal will be meaning less as it denies access to justice, if tried by the Supreme Court challenging the proclamation's constitutionality. The HoF consulted several experts in closed sessions disregarding the CCI's proposal and declared the particular article in the law as unconstitutional.

3.4.4 Constitutional Adjudication and Democratic Order

On 31 March 2020, the newly appointed National Election Board of Ethiopia (NEBE) announced that the elections scheduled for 29 August 2020 could not take place in view of the Covid-19 pandemic. The announcement triggered a country-wide debate around two issues: how to manage the health crisis, and how to address the deadlocked election. The ruling party issued an emergency decree that was followed by detailed regulations addressing the pandemic. The postponement of the election was a major issue given that the mandate of the federal government and the then nine regional states was to come to an end in October 2020.

The HPR requested constitutional advice from the HoF, which in turn referred the matter to the CCI. It can be hazarded that the government selected this route because it has sufficient votes in these bodies to secure whatever constitutional opinion it desires. The CCI, after holding a 'public' hearing (which excluded all voices that might be critical of the government's position), decided the elections should be postponed until Parliament declared that Covid-19 was no longer a threat to the public health. It also extended the terms of both Parliament and the regional state councils until after the sixth general elections. The decisions were fully endorsed by the HoF. Although a clause in the Constitution expressly sets a five-year term for Parliament, there is no consensus among legal scholars as to whether the Constitution can be interpreted to allow for the postponement of elections, and a consequent extension of the term of Parliament. There is, however, general agreement that both the CCI/HoF decision and the process by which it was reached were deeply flawed: the public hearing lacked diversity, while the decision itself suffered from at least four major flaws.

First, the CCI failed to recommend any limits on the powers that the government could exercise during its extended period of office. Thus, the government is allowed to act as if it is within its proper term limit. Second, the CCI recommended that the government decide the timing (if any) of the sixth national elections. Third, the CCI did not see fit to require inclusivity in the government. It did not enjoin the government to consult with other political parties or stakeholders on public matters during the extended period (including on the key question of how and when the next elections would be held). Finally, the CCI recommended that the term of the state councils also be extended but provided no justification for doing so. States exist as autonomous levels of government, and are intended to have a say on certain matters, such as elections for state councils, and determining the term of state councils through their constitutions. In its one-page decision, the CCI simply ignored the question of autonomy. Meanwhile, although endorsing the CCI's decision, the HoF took the opportunity to extend its own term, ignoring the very real possibility of a conflict of interest in this regard.

A further issue concerns the election held in September 2020 in Tigray while the country-wide elections were postponed. Here, the ruling TPLF in Tigray state insisted on holding elections before the expiry of the terms of Parliament as part of its political tit-for-tat with the federal government and the Prosperity Party. It argued that the federal government's postponement of the elections was unconstitutional and would lead to a power vacuum, since (according to the TPLF) the mandate of the current Parliament would end on 10 October 2020. It therefore resolved to hold state-wide elections in Tigray should the national elections be postponed and followed through on this in September. Its central claim was that holding regional state elections is an essential part of the mandate of self-government. In turn, the Tigray Democratic Party challenged the constitutionality of the measures taken by the TPLF in establishing an electoral board and in holding elections. The CCI decided in favour of the Tigray Democratic Party, ruling that the action of the Tigray state government was unconstitutional.[72] One cannot help but suspect that this decision (regardless of its strictly legal rationale) was influenced by political considerations. One should note, among other factors, it was this decision that triggered the imposition of martial law on the regional state and subsequent war that broke out in November 2020. Empirical evidences show except on issues related to rights of the child, women, access to land; many of the cases submitted to the CCI/HoF related

[72] የትግራይ ዴሞክራሲያዊ ፓርቲ እና የትግራይ ክልላዊ መንግስት የኢ.ፌ.ዴ.ሪ ፌደሬሽን ምክር ቤት 5ኛ የፓርላማ ዘመን፣ 5ኛ አመት አንደኛ አስቸኳይ ስብሰባ (ነሐሴ 30/2012) (*Tigray Democratic Party v Tigray Regional State FDRE House of Federation*, fifth Year of Parliament, fifth extra-ordinary meeting August 2020.

to vertical and horizontal separation of powers (power politics) and individuals challenging the authority of the state for a violation of rights were decided in favor of the government in power. Since the new government assumed power in 2018, the army and security has heavily been engaged in the affairs of regional states through countless 'command posts' whose constitutional status remained disputed. Civilian institutions have been suspended and the country is slowly entering into a system of martial law with the army and security heads taking over routine administration of some regional states (Amhara, parts of Oromia and Tigray during the war). Following the dissolution of the EPRDF and the formation of Prosperity Party, the four coalitions and other affiliate parties have been dissolved. As there is merger between party and state, PP from its headquarters in Addis Ababa can now hire and fire regional state heads as they are branches of Addis Ababa, not anymore autonomous units, as has partly been the case during the EPRDF era. None of these controversial measures that compromise self-rule and made the federation a farce are challenged for their constitutionality and the very few efforts that were brought before the CCI/HoF as in the Tigray election case never succeeded.

The HoF has revealed itself to be a weak institution in terms of safeguarding constitutionalism in Ethiopia. It has a record of inconsistent decisions and even made decisions—based on political considerations—that are clearly unconstitutional (as its decision regarding *Asehanfi Amare* et al. shows), while its support for the postponement of the sixth general election was also problematic. This decision in particular has been the source of considerable unrest and instability in some parts of the country. The HoF has consistently failed in its central task of mediating constitutional debates in an impartial fashion. This has resulted in a centralised federation that lacks judicial review and leaves human rights unprotected, meaning the governance system is open to manipulation by the dominant and centralised party. The situation in Ethiopia is a textbook example of what Landau and Dixon call 'abusive constitutional review', a situation in which the interpreting body acts as a tool of power rather than a guardian of the constitution.[73]

4 Conclusion

Ethiopia presents the case of a federation that does not enjoy the judicial review and which has generous human rights but no guardian to oversee them. Ethiopia's constitution is like a garden full of nice fruits but can not be eaten. Ethiopia's age-old problem—leaving power unregulated by not subjecting it to the rule of law—remains unaddressed. As a leading expert in constitutional law, Mark Tushnet, remarks, 'Courts in nations where a single political party dominates the system for an extended period rarely find national legislation unconstitutional.'[74] It is naïve to

[73] Landau and Dixon (2020), pp. 1313–1387.

[74] Tushnet (2014).

expect the HoF to serve as a guardian of the Constitution, enforce human rights, and impartially demarcate the mandates of the federal and state governments—it is a political organ through and through, controlled by the same party at federal and state levels.

As a political institution, the HoF remains a pawn under the thumb of those who wield power from the centre. This explains its consistent pro-centre position on key federalist problems, its failure to set limits on power or properly enforce human rights, and, of course, its failings around the extension of the government's term of office. All of these things, along with other issues (such as questions around concurrent power and the demarcation of the mandates of federal and state governments in relation to self-rule and citizenship rights), reveal the substantial difficulties that emerge when a political organ is selected to oversee and referee the workings of a federation. The HoF's record in the protection and enforcement of human rights and setting limits on power is worrisome. So far, it has nullified only two laws for their unconstitutionality, even though several applications were made to that effect.

All in all, federalism appears to be operating without the institutional safeguards necessary for dealing with inter-governmental disputes. Ethiopia's political institution for constitutional adjudication is open to political manipulation. Federalism is, above all, about the need for bargaining and the division of power in politics. For it to function well, it requires a delicate institutional balance. If the subunits are too powerful, the federation may face the threat of secession or dissolution; if the central government is too strong, it may impose too much on the subunits, rendering federalism a fiction, and ultimately giving way to a unitary system. Studies have shown the central role played by the institutions that are meant to act as impartial umpires in federal and devolved systems. It is essential that these are self-enforcing and stable. Supreme or constitutional courts can act to check the efforts of either the subunits to resist the federal government or federal governments to encroach on the mandate and authority of the states.

Ethiopia's case shows some of the outcomes of efforts to federalise power without putting in place the necessary judicial institutions for checking political power. Federalism without active constitutionalism is open either to authoritarian centralisation or for subversion, depending on the political dynamics of the particular context.

Cases

Biyadglegn Meles & et al v the Amhara Regional State petition Miazia 30 1989 EC (unpublished).

BVerf G, Reference 1 BvR 370/07 (27 February 2008) www.bverfg.de/entscheidungen/rs20080227_1bvr037007.html.

Communist Party case 5BVerfGE85, 139: 1956.

Dissolution Case II www.bverfg.de/entscheidungen/es20050825_2bve000405.html.

Federal Democratic Republic Ethiopia Constitution (1995).

Heirs of Wassihun et al. v Agency for Government Houses, Decision of the Cassation Division of the Supreme Court File Number 43511 v.14 P.211.

Justice Malek Mathiang Malek v Minister of Justice the Republic of South Sudan & the Secretary General of the East African Community East African Court of Justice, Reference No. 9 of 2017 (3 September 2017).

References

Books

Acemoglu D, Robinson JA (2012) Why nations fail: the origins of power, prosperity and poverty. Crown, New York

Balsvik R (2005) Haile Sellassie's students: the intellectual and social background to revolution, 1952–1974. Addis Ababa University Press, Addis Ababa

Barak A (2006) The judge in a democracy. Princeton University Press, Princeton

Brewer-Carías AR (2011) Constitutional courts as positive legislators: a comparative law. Cambridge University Press, Cambridge

Chabal P, Daloz J-P (1999) Africa works: disorder as political instrument. James Currey, Oxford

Collings J (2015) Democracy's guardians: the history of the German Federal Constitutional Court 1951–2001. Oxford University Press, Oxford

Daly TG (2017) Questioning our faith in courts as democracy builders. Cambridge University Press, Cambridge

Fukuyama F (2014) Political order and political decay: from the industrial revolution to the globalization of democracy. Farrar, New York

Ginsburg T (2003) Judicial review in new democracies: constitutional courts in Asian cases. Cambridge University Press, Cambridge

Hyden G (2006) African politics in comparative perspective. Cambridge University Press, Cambridge

Kommers D, Miller R (2012) The constitutional jurisprudence of the Federal Republic of Germany, 3rd edn. Duke University Press, Durham

Scalia A (1998) A matter of interpretation: Federal Courts and the law. Princeton University Press, Princeton

Tamanaha B (2004) On the rule of law: history, politics, theory. Cambridge University Press, Cambridge

Teffera H (2012) Tower in the sky. Addis Ababa University Press, Addis Ababa

Tiruneh A (1994) The Ethiopian revolution 1974–1987: a transformation from an aristocratic to a totalitarian autocracy. Cambridge University Press, Cambridge

Tushnet M (2014) Comparative constitutional law. Edward Elgar, Cheltenham

Waluchow WJ (2007) A common law theory of judicial review: the living tree. Cambridge University Press, Cambridge

Weber M (1946) Essays in sociology. Oxford University Press, New York

Journal Articles

Bratton M (2008) Vote buying and violence in Nigerian election campaigns. Elect Stud 27(4):621–632

Fiseha A (2011) Separation of powers and its implications for the Judiciary in Ethiopia. J Eastern Afr Stud 5(4):702–715
Horowitz D (2006) Constitutional courts: a primer for decision makers. J Democr 17(4):125–137
Issacharoff S (2011) Constitutional courts and democratic hedging. Georgetown Law J 99:961–1012
Kommers D (2006) The Federal Constitutional Court: Guardian of the basic law. Ann Am Acad Polit Soc Sci 603:114–116
Landau D, Dixon R (2020) Abusive judicial review: courts against democracy. UC Davis Law Rev 53(3):1313–1387
Prunier G, Ficquet E (eds) (2015) Understanding Ethiopia: Monarchy, revolution and the legacy of Meles Zenawi. Hurst and Company, London
Roux T (2013) The South African constitutional court's democratic rights jurisprudence. Const Court Rev 5(1):33–73

Other

ACHPR (n.d.) Background. https://inquiry.achpr.org/elementor-536/
Ginsburg T (2013) The politics of courts in democratization: four junctures in Asia. In: Kapiszewski D, Silverstein G, Kagan R (eds) Consequential courts: judicial roles in global perspective. Cambridge University Press, Cambridge, pp 45–66
Negarit Gazeta (1991) Peaceful and Democratic Transitional Conference of Ethiopia: Transitional Period Charter of Ethiopia: Proclamation No 1
Negarit Gazeta of the Ethiopian Transitional Government, A Proclamation to Provide for the Establishment of National Regional Self-Governments No. 7 (1992)
Okoth-Ogendo HWO (1993) Constitutions without constitutionalism: reflections on an African political paradox. In: Greenberg D et al (eds) Constitutionalism and democracy: transitions in the contemporary world. Oxford University Press, New York, pp 65–84
Stone GR (14 April 2010) Our fill-in-the-blank constitution. The New York Times
Ye Ethiopia Hige Mengist Gubae Kale Gubae v. 4 Hidar 14–20, 1987 E.C. (Minutes of the Constitutional Assembly, November 1994)

The Past Has Not Passed Away: Burdens of an Unreformed Judiciary

Hakeem O. Yusuf and Abdul-Wahab Egbewole

Abstract Nigeria has now experienced more than two and half decades of civil rule after nearly 30 years of military authoritarian rule. The judicial record in governance during the authoritarian period was virtually unaddressed, despite widespread public concerns about the role of the judiciary during the period. The political transition proceeded with the judicial institution's baggage of complicity for legitimising authoritarian rule and a record of corruption. In an age of increasing involvement of the judiciary in governance, the Nigerian judiciary has been a strategic actor across diverse and critical aspects of governance in the country. While the Nigerian judiciary has made significant contributions to governance in the troubled post-authoritarian state, the judiciary remains blighted from an unaccounted institutional legacy. This continues to have serious consequences for the rule of law, human rights, and democracy in the polity. This chapter examines and evaluates the effects of the institutional legacy of the Nigerian judiciary on human rights, rule of law, and democracy.

1 Introduction

All has not been well with the Nigerian judiciary lately. After more than two and half decades of the country's post-authoritarian transition to civil rule, the judiciary has all but come into disrepute. A number of related factors, mostly structural, carried over from the authoritarian period and the transition arrangements have been

H. O. Yusuf (✉)
Centre for Justice, Law, and Society, University of Derby, Derby, UK
e-mail: h.yusuf@derby.ac.uk

A.-W. Egbewole
Department of Jurisprudence and International Law, Faculty of Law,
University of Ilorin/Vice Chancellor University of Ilorin, Ilorin, Nigeria
e-mail: eabdulwahab@unilorin.edu.ng

N. Reayat, H. O. Yusuf (eds.), *Constitutionalism in Africa and Beyond*, Ius Gentium: Comparative Perspectives on Law and Justice 127,
https://doi.org/10.1007/978-3-032-01180-0_4

instrumental to the growth of the judiciary, and principally, the Supreme Court effectively into a truly 'political court' within less than a decade of the political transition to civil rule. An un-negotiated political transition which bequeathed an imposed constitution, a continued legitimacy deficit of the political branches, a lop-sided, often conflictual federalism, inordinate ambition for power, and wrangling among hegemonic elite, are some of the most prominent factors in Nigeria's political transition. They have culminated in thrusting power on the judiciary in a country coming to grips with years of military misrule. It is within the foregoing context that the judiciary has found its way into, and remained for years now, 'in the eye of a storm.'[1]

Stakeholders within and outside of the judiciary have been advocating for an institutional reset in the interest of the society. In a speech at the valedictory court session held in his honour on his retirement from the bench in late 2023, Justice Musa Dattijo Muhammad, a retiring justice of the Supreme Court, who had risen to the position of the second most senior Justice of the apex court, rather uncharacteristically, lashed out at the judiciary.[2] He asserted that the office of the Chief Justice had become too powerful, contending that 'such enormous powers are effortlessly abused'.[3] Justice Muhammad also decried corruption in the Nigerian judiciary and influence-peddling in judicial appointments.[4] He noted that public perception of the judiciary in recent times has become 'witheringly scornful and monstrously critical'.[5]

On 26 June 2022, then Chief Justice of Nigeria, Justice Mohammed Tanko, and head of the Supreme Court, resigned amid allegations of maladministration levelled

---

[1] 'Judiciary: A third arm still in the eye of the storm' *Punch Newspaper* Online (21st December 2023) available at: https://punchng.com/judiciary-a-third-arm-still-in-the-eye-of-the-storm/, Evelyn Okakwu 'Nigerian judiciary not as corrupt as NBS report shows – NJC' *Premium Times* (10 August 2017) available at: https://www.premiumtimesng.com/news/headlines/240878-nigerian-judiciary-not-corrupt-nbs-report-shows-njc.html; Ameh Ejekwonyilo 'Supreme Court Justice laments corruption, inequity in Nigeria's judiciary' available at: https://www.premiumtimesng.com/news/headlines/531981-supreme-court-justice-laments-corruption-inequity-in-nigerias-judiciary.html (May 23 2022); Evelyn Okakwu 'Nigerian judiciary was too silent on corruption among members – Senior Advocates' (10 November 2016) available at: https://www.premiumtimesng.com/news/top-news/214981-nigerian-judiciary-silent-corruption-among-members-senior-advocates.html; Premium Times 'The Rot in The Judiciary, By Femi Falana' *Premium Times* (27 May 2013) available at: https://www.premiumtimesng.com/opinion/136274-by-femi-falana.html; 'Nigeria's Judiciary is my main headache in corruption war – Buhari' *Premium Times* (30 January 2016) available at: https://www.premiumtimesng.com/news/headlines/197761-nigerias-judiciary-main-headache-corruption-war-buhari.html.

[2] Channels Television 'Full Text Of Justice Dattijo's Speech On CJN's Powers, State Of The Judiciary, Other Matters' *Channels Television* (27 October 2023) available at: https://www.channelstv.com/2023/10/27/full-text-of-justice-dattijos-speech-on-cjns-powers-state-of-the-judiciary-other-matters/.

[3] Ibid. at 10.

[4] Ibid at 22.

[5] Ibid at 20.

against him by all the other (14) of the justices of the Supreme Court.[6] The letter from his colleagues alleged among others that the conduct of the Chief Justice was 'clear evidence of the absence of probity and moral rectitude'.[7] The allegations and the subsequent resignation of the Chief Justice were unprecedented developments in the annals of the country's legal history and over 60 years existence of the Supreme Court of Nigeria. Then President of Nigeria, Muhammadu Buhari, accepted the resignation of the Chief Justice Muhammed who predicated his action not on the allegations which had been denied by his spokesman, but on failing health.[8] Justice Muhammad thus departed office under controversial circumstances, but he had also assumed office as Chief Justice under controversial circumstances.

Moreover, in February 2019, shortly before a general election in the country, President Buhari had suspended Chief Justice Muhammed's predecessor, Chief Justice Walter Onnoghen from office. The action was based on a controversial order of the Code of Conduct Tribunal on allegations of breaching the Code of Conduct for Public Officers. This led to an uproar within and outside the country with some taking the view that the president's action was mostly driven by political considerations.[9] Chief Justice Onnoghen later retired from office and was convicted for non-declaration of assets and banned from holding public office for 10 years.[10] The resignations of the two successive Chief Justices in turn, were subject of intense discourse among a divided public, including members of the legal profession. In all events, both incidents demonstrate the fraught position of the judiciary as a major player in post-authoritarian governance in the country.

Remarkably, in the first decade of Nigeria's post-authoritarian transition to civil rule, the Nigerian judiciary was largely viewed as the main stay of the country's 'democracy.'[11] The judiciary was even declared 'The Man of the Year' in 2007 and 2008 and was hailed as 'the last hope of the common man'.[12] At that time, the Nigerian Supreme Court was commended from home and even unusual quarters abroad. On the home front, the profile of Supreme Court in governance in the coun-

---

[6] Ise-Oluwa Ige 'CJN, Tanko Mohammad resigns' *Vanguard Newspaper* (Abuja 27 June 2022); Dennis Eseni 'CJN Tanko Muhammad Resigns' *Guardian Newspaper* (Lagos 27 June 2023).

[7] John Chuks Azu and Adelanwa Bamgboye 'How Tanko Muhammad was 'forced' to resign as CJN' *Daily Trust* (Abuja 28 June 2022).

[8] Al Jazeera 'Nigeria's chief justice resigns on health grounds' (27 June 2022) available at: https://www.aljazeera.com/news/2022/6/27/chief-of-justice-of-nigeria-tank-muhammad-is-set-to-resign; Reuben Abati 'Exit of Justice Ibrahim Tanko Muhammad, CJN' *Premium Times* (27 June 2022).

[9] Al Jazeera 'UN: Suspension of Nigeria's Top Judge Breaches Human Rights' (11 February 2019) available at: available at: Evelyn Okakwu 'Onnoghen pleads not guilty to false asset charges' *Premium Times* (11 February 2019).

[10] 'CCT Finds Onnoghen Guilty, Bars Him from Public Office for 10 Years' *The Cable* Online Edition (Abuja 18 April 2019) available at: https://www.thecable.ng/breaking-cct-finds-onnoghen-guilty-bans-him-from-public-office-for-10-years.

[11] I share the view that civil rule 'Civil rule' or 'civil governance' better captures what the political transition has achieved as against 'democracy' or 'democratic rule'.

[12] Onyema Omenuwa '2007: The Year of the Supreme Court' *Daily Independent* Online Edition (Lagos Thursday 27 December 2007).

try became visible in the public square like never before.[13] As one respected commentator stated, the Court had made it clear that it was the 'sentinel…guard for democracy and good governance.'[14] On the international front, observers including the United States Congress[15] and influential media, like *The Economist* hailed its demonstration of independence, redirecting the country's democracy away from the precipice and upholding human rights.[16] However, the situation has changed, with some now accusing the courts of not only a lack of independence, but an institution enlisted to subvert democracy by legalising 'electoral kleptocracy'.[17] The question is, how did things come to such a pass that the wheels seem to have turned full circle against the judiciary in the country? In the light of the importance of judicial independence,[18] this chapter critically examines this question, and the consequences for the rule of law and democracy in the country.

This chapter advances the view that the developments in the judicial branch were predictable though not inevitable. This chapter proceeds as follows. The next part examines the context of the judicial role in the country. The section sets out the historical and socio-political, and constitutional context of the judicial function in Nigeria. The next section examines the judicial role during the period of authoritarian rule in the country, setting out its complicity in legitimising military rule. The analysis then turns to the burdens of Nigeria's judiciary in performing its role in post-authoritarian governance as where the political branches are struggling with little or no institutional memory. The penultimate section examines the vagaries of judicial governance in a post-authoritarian society. The judiciary plays a critical role in the post-authoritarian society with the magnification of the judicial role in an era of judicialisation of politics. It faces a herculean task with its accountability gap haunting its critical role and the politicisation of the judiciary rebounding to challenge its already shaky credibility.

[13] See 'Belgore, Oputa, Sagay, Others Hail Supreme Court' *The Guardian* Online Edition (Lagos Sunday 24 June 2007).

[14] Charles Adingupu 'Obi's Judgement is Warning to Political Gangsters' *The Guardian* Online Edition (Lagos Sunday 24 June 2007).

[15] Constance Ikokwu 'Nigerian Judiciary Strong, Independent, Says US Congress' *This Day* Online Edition (Abuja Thursday 19 July 2007).

[16] 'Nigeria - Democracy by Court Order' *The Economist* (London Thursday 24 January 2008).

[17] Chidi Anselm Odinkalu 'Concerning Court of Electoral Kleptocracy' *The Cable* Online Edition (12 November 2023).

[18] Smith (2023), pp. 1–3; van Dijk and Vos (2019), pp. 2–4; Moliterno and Čuroš (2021), pp. 1159, 1163–1164.

2 The Context

2.1 *Historical and Socio-Political Context*

Nigeria, the most populous black nation in the world, is a federation. The country gained political independence from Britain on 1 October 1966 and became a republic on 1 October 1963. The country's operative written republican constitution, the 1999 Constitution (as amended) allocates the powers of the federal state among the branches of government—the executive, legislature and the judiciary. The country operates a presidential system and a two-tier legislature at the federal level, the National Assembly consisting of the Senate (upper chamber) and the House of Representatives (lower chamber). The 36 states each have a House of Assembly, a unicameral legislature.

Less than 6 years after independence, the military took over the reins of power in a bloody *coup de'tat* in January 1966. There was a counter-coup 6 months later, culminating in a civil-war a year after. The military ruled the country continuously between 1966 and 1999 with a four-year interregnum of civil rule. The military imposed its hierarchical command structure on fundamental principles of federalism in its nearly three decades of ruling the country. In principle, successive military regimes maintained the federal political system. However, in practice, the command-structure style of governance did not accommodate agitations for political restructuring of the country.

The military rulers suspended parts of the constitution and declared their decrees supreme over the constitution.[19] Successive military regimes followed the path of colonial legislation to impose their rule.[20] Their 'laws' either prohibited courts from questioning the legality of military actions or limited their ability to do so. Military authoritarianism virtually destroyed the fabric of state and society. The economic and social well-being of the people took a downward spiral. Like the colonialists who had established the institution, the army ruled the country like captured territory. Institutions of civil governance suffered and deteriorated with the military authorities ruling with decrees that undermined fundamental parts of the constitution. Rather than carry through the promise to curb corruption, the military institutionalized it, even as the country's economic fortunes nose-dived.

Gross violations of human rights were rampant all over the country. Security agencies, including the armed forces, and police were notorious for deploying lethal force against the civil populace and particularly those who were actively involved in opposing authoritarianism. Student groups, the Nigerian Bar Association, political associations, labour unions, human rights activists and organizations, journalists, market associations, regularly bore the brunt of state violence. Government measures against these and similar groups included proscription, illegal arrests, detention, seizure of property and arson, mysterious disappearances and in some cases,

[19]Yusuf (2008), pp. 194–226, 207–219.

[20]For an in-depth socio-political evaluation of military rule in Nigeria see Osaghae (1998).

state-sponsored murder through assassination, death in detention and other measures, including allegedly in at least one case, a letter-bomb.[21]

In some cases, the military sought to compromise, and factionalise civil society groups during the authoritarian period. The military regimes adopted a carrot and stick approach in its dealings with these groups to divide them or at the least, weaken their ability to mobilise the public against them. In the context of their multiple and expensive failed touted political transition programmes, this tactic was extensively applied by the military regimes of General Ibrahim Babangida and General Sani Abacha in the late 1980s to the mid-1990s.[22]

After many failed promises to reinstate democratic governance, the military eventually handed over power to an elected government on 29 May 1999 with the promulgation of a hurriedly produced and imposed Constitution. The transition to civil rule followed a period of strong and sometimes violent agitation. The eventual political transition to civil rule was accidental at best with no negotiation of its form and content between the civil populace and the military rulers. As a result, some have argued that the political transition programme lacked a valid legal foundation.[23] The military left a legacy of distortions and dysfunctions across economic, social, political, constitutional and legal dimensions. This led to gross dissatisfaction among interest groups who felt disempowered by military authoritarianism to challenge the situation. It remains a problematic legacy of military rule despite constitutional reviews in the last two decades and a continuing source of tensions and violence in the country.

2.2 Constitutional Context

As a result of the homogenising approach of successive military governments, when the country returned to civil rule, governance had become a distorted federal system, with an over over-centralized political system. Over time, the federal government accumulated so many powers that it dominates virtually every aspect of governance in the country including vital aspects of land matters within States, commerce and trade, weight and measures, social security, police and policing, arms and ammunition and labour. This is reflected in the statement of competencies of the levels of government in the legislative lists contained in the Constitution. The 1999 Constitution assigns at least 66 broadly worded exclusive powers to the federal authorities. The exclusive powers are in addition to a concurrent (in practice,

[21] Dimeji Kayode-Adedeji 'Dele Giwa's Murder: Soyinka replies ex-Police DIG, Omeben' *Premium Times* (29 October 2015) available at:https://www.premiumtimesng.com/news/headlines/192320-dele-giwas-murder-soyinka-replies-ex-police-dig-omeben.html.

[22] Hakeem Yusuf *African Transitional Justice Research Project: Case Study on Transitional Justice in Nigeria* (Centre for the Study of Violence and Reconciliation, Pretoria, 2018) 27-28 available at: https://www.csvr.org.za/comparative-study-of-transitional-justice-in-africa/.

[23] Ogowewo (2000), pp. 135, 140–141.

overriding) powers, over 30 other items, with the states. This is a far cry from the position at independence.[24] It is instructive in this regard for instance that the final act of British constitutional legislation in the country, the Nigerian (Constitution) Order in Council, 1960 enacted separate constitutions for the federal government and three regions.

Nigerian superior courts have exercised the powers of judicial review since the country gained independence from Britain in 1960, dating back to the post-independent constitutional arrangements and through the heady days of military rule. The operative 1999 Constitution confers powers of judicial review on the superior courts of record; the high courts (state and federal), the Court of Appeal and the Supreme Court, but there is no constitutional court. The operation of judicial review in the legal system in the country is similar to the American system but is best described as a 'hybrid.' Like the American system of judicial review, there is a diffusion of the power of judicial review that runs across the hierarchy of federal and state courts. Sections 6 and 46 of 1999 Constitution and judicial practice support *ex ante* and *ex post facto* judicial review on concrete as against abstract issues. This is a feature the Nigerian courts share with constitutional courts in some European jurisdictions.[25] Furthermore, Section 315 (3) of the Constitution confers wide powers of judicial review of legislation on the courts. It provides that nothing in the Constitution shall be construed as affecting the power of a court of law or any tribunal established by law to declare invalid any existing law in the country. More importantly, this power extends to any provisions of the Constitution.

However, in practice, the courts created restrictive rules of *locus standi*; right or capacity to institute a legal action in court, in the case of *Abraham Adesanya v President of the Federal Republic of Nigeria & Another* (*Adesanya*).[26] The Supreme Court stated that on the construction of Section 6(6) of the 1979 Constitution based on the interpretation Sections 6(6) (b),[27] 'it is only when the civil rights and obligations of the person who invokes the jurisdiction of the court are in issue for determination that the judicial powers of the courts may be invoked. In other words, standing will only be accorded to a plaintiff who shows that his civil rights have been or are in danger of being violated or adversely affected by the act complained of.'[28]

Significantly, the dominant restrictive approach to *locus standi* is a remarkable instance of judge-made law formulated by Supreme Court during the country's interlude of civil rule (within an otherwise undisturbed stretch of nearly three decades of military authoritarianism). The dominant judicial attitude to the capacity

---

[24] Elaigwu (2002), p. 73, 76–77.

[25] Epstein et al. (2001), p. 117, 121.

[26] SC (1981) ANLR 1.

[27] It provides that 'The judicial powers vested in accordance with the foregoing provisions of this section (b) shall extend to all matters between person, or between government or authority and any person in Nigeria, and to all actions and proceedings relating thereto, for the determination of any question as to the civil rights and obligations of that person'. The provision has remained the same in Section 6(6), of the1999 Constitution.

[28] Per Justice Bello in *Adesanya* note 26 supra at 39.

or right to institute legal action remains largely the same today. Public interest litigants are treated as meddlesome interlopers wasting the time of the court.[29] This has left a legacy of a challenging environment for public interest litigation in the post-authoritarian transition to civil rule.[30]

It is noteworthy that previously, the position had been in conformity with the liberal, common-law position on locus standi which accorded standing based on the nature of the cause.[31] However in recent times, some judges have tended towards a liberal interpretation of the standing to sue based on the application of the Fundamental Human Rights (Enforcement Procedure) Rules 2009 (Rights Enforcement Rules)made by then Chief Justice Kutigi for the enforcement of human rights in the country based on the provisions of Section 46 (3) of the 1999 Constitution.[32] One of the 'overriding objectives' set out in the preamble of the Rights Enforcement Rules is to entrench a liberal approach to the practice and procedure for enforcement of human rights in the country.[33]

3 Legitimising Authoritarianism

Judicial review of legislation is commonly conceived of in terms of its restraint on legislative and executive action. However, there is also the way in which the mechanism of judicial review legitimates laws, and decisions of the political branches of government. Put in another way, where the judiciary does not declare legislative or executive actions unconstitutional in cases of legal challenges to them, judicial review invests constitutionality on legislation and the legislative process and, or executive action pursuant to them.[34] In that respect, judicial review is potentially a double-edged sword, and interestingly so in troubled societies.

---

[29] Ekeke (2022), pp. 339, 340–341.

[30] See for instance the Supreme Court decision in *Nworika v Ononeze-Madu and Others* LER [2019]SC.307/2008.

[31] Ogowewo (1995), p. 1, 2.

[32] Ekeke note 29 supra at 341–342.

[33] For instance paragraph 3 (e) provides that: 'The Court shall encourage and welcome public interest litigations in the human rights field and no human rights case may be dismissed or struck out for want of locus standi. In particular, human rights activists, advocates, or groups as well as any non-governmental organizations, may institute human rights application on behalf of any potential applicant. In human rights litigation, the applicant may include any of the following:

(i) Anyone acting in his own interest;
(ii) Anyone acting on behalf of another person;
(iii) Anyone acting as a member of, or in the interest of a group or class of persons;
(iv) Anyone acting in the public interest, and
(v) Association acting in the interest of its members or other individuals or Groups'.

[34] Kwasi Prempeh (2007), pp. 469, 504–505.

From the onset of military intervention in governance in Nigeria, the judiciary, and notably, the Supreme Court, demonstrated an ambivalent attitude to the legitimacy of military rule. Remarkably, the claim of the military interventionists to legality was challenged within 6 months of military rule in *Isaac Boro v Republic*.[35] Furthermore, in *Council of the University of Ibadan v Adamolekun*,[36] the Supreme Court decided *inter alia* that the mutiny that resulted in the military usurpation of executive and legislative powers was a 'military takeover of the Government of Nigeria.' Significantly, it went further to hold that the military takeover was of a nature that kept 'the Constitution of the Federation alive *subject to the suspensions and modifications made by the Decree.*'[37] In this way, the judiciary at the highest level legitimised the unconstitutional, purported 'transfer' of power by the Council of Ministers to the mutinous soldiers who had murdered some key political figures in the country, including then Prime Minister, Abubakar Tafawa Balewa.

Nonetheless, it is the Court's decision in *E O Lakanmi and Kikelomo Ola v The Attorney –General (Western State), The Secretary to the Tribunal (Investigation of Assets Tribunal) and the Counsel to the Tribunal* (*Lakanmi*) that irretrievably established the foundations of judicial obeisance to authoritarian military rule in the country. From then on, this became an imprimatur of most judicial decisions bearing on the constitutionality and legitimacy of military rule in the country.[38] The main issue of contention in *Lakanmi* was the constitutionality of the Decree No. 45 of 1968- Forfeiture of Assets Validation Decree- promulgated by the Federal Military Government (FMG) directed specifically to declare the forfeiture of the assets of the Plaintiffs/Appellants for alleged corruption while in public office. The Plaintiffs argued that the decree was of no legal effect as it constituted a violation of their property rights guaranteed by the 1963 Republican Constitution.

The FMG government argued that the decree had legal force as the events of 16 January 1966 that brought the FMG was a revolution of the Kelsenian type that destroyed the previous legal order. Upon the successful coup *de'tat* the FMG, argued, it had become the supreme legislative authority in the country based on the provisions of Decree No.1 of 1966- Constitution Suspension and Modification Decree, that provided inter alia that 'the Federal Military Government shall have powers to make laws for the peace, order and good government of Nigeria or any part thereof with respect to any matter whatsoever.' The FMG also relied on section 1(1) of the latter decree which modified the 1963 Republican Constitution to the effect that the Constitution shall have force and prevail over any other law throughout the country, but not over any decree promulgated by the military.

The Supreme Court reiterated that it had the power to review executive action thereby rejecting the proclaimed ouster of its jurisdiction by the decree. It held that the decree is a piece of legislative judgement. Nonetheless, the Court accorded

[35] (1967) Nigerian Monthly Law Reports 163.

[36] (1967) S.C 378.

[37] Italics for emphasis.

[38] (1971) University of Ife Law Reports 201.

recognition to the FMG as a legitimate government based on the principle of 'necessity' and one which is a 'constitutional government', in line with the purview of the 1963 Republican Constitution. The Court further held that the FMG was 'the Supreme Legislative body' in the country.

The Court went even further to legitimise the military government in *Adejumo v Johnson* (*Adejumo*).[39] In *Adejumo* the Court declared an unqualified acknowledgement of the events of January 16, 1966, as a revolution. The decision in the *Adejumo* case was sequel to the promulgation by the FMG of the Federal Military Government (Supremacy and Enforcement of Powers) Decree No.28 of 1970,[40] barely 2 weeks after the decision in the *Lakanmi* case. The Court adopted, and went on to retain the plain-fact jurisprudence in the interpretation of military decrees. The decision in the *Adejumo* case gave effect to the provisions of not only Decree No.28, but that of Section 1(1) of Decree No.1 of 1966 that it had partly hitherto partly rejected in the *Lakanmi* case. Based on the application of the common law principle of precedent, lower courts, and indeed, the highest court itself, proceeded to apply the plain-fact jurisprudential approach when interpreting an array of military legislation during the authoritarian period.

4 Post-Authoritarian Transition and the Courts: Burdens of An Unaccounted Judiciary

As mentioned above, the Nigerian judiciary, and particularly, the Supreme Court received accolades from various quarters in the early period of the country's political transition for the most part. A major factor for the acclaim of the judiciary at that point was the adoption of a purposive jurisprudence towards the resolution of the popular branches of government namely the executive and legislature expressed in intergovernmental disputes and election disputes among political parties and politicians. However, before examining how the judiciary came into the crucial role of mediating politics, inter-, and intra-governmental disputes in the last two decades, it is important to first advert to a critical issue in the Nigerian experience; the lax approach to the accountability of the judiciary for its role in governance during the period of authoritarianism, a praxis gap that remains prominent in accountability paradigms in troubled societies during transitions to democratic governance.[41]

---

39 (1972) 1 All Nigeria Law Reports 159.

40 This set the pattern which subsequent military usurpers adopted in the country. Every other coup *d'etat* in the country was declared along with the passage of not only a Constitution Suspension and Modification Decree but also a (Military) Supremacy and Enforcement of Powers Decree.

41 For a comprehensive analysis see, Yusuf (2014).

4.1 The Past Does Not Pass Away

The default approach to accountability for the past during periods of political transition in societies from a troubled past for the gross violations of human rights is to focus on the (in)actions of the political institutions; those who exercised executive and legislative powers. There has been a neglect of the role of the judiciary in governance in such contexts.[42] The default approach to accountability for the past played out in Nigeria during the political transition in 1999 to 'democratic' civil rule. This was in a context where even the attempt at extracting accountability and securing justice for victims of human rights violations during the period of authoritarian military rule was half-hearted, and questionable.[43]

The default approach dominates the accountability for the past paradigm despite the crucial nature of the judicial role in all political settings, including post-authoritarian societies.[44] An approach in post-authoritarian, democratising societies, that does not include judicial accountability, implicitly undermines the basic understanding that the judiciary is the third branch of government. This is the case considering the judiciary has a critical role in mediating the power of the political branches and ensuring the rule of law.[45] As Graver similar pointed out, 'many authoritarian rulers actively employ law and legal institutions in their oppression and go to great pains to maintain a working legal order with independent courts.'[46]

In any event, accountability for the judicial role in authoritarian regimes provides a comprehensive *dealing* with the past.[47] This is particularly important, as examining the institutional role of courts in authoritarian regimes 'provide[s] a useful lens through which to examine a variety of political dynamics in an environment that is otherwise distinguished by a lack of transparency.'[48] As 'the public nature of judicial process and the paper trail that courts provide opens a point of access into internal regime dynamics and state-society contention',[49] that may otherwise not be available for assessing and understanding what transpired during such periods in a society's history.

While there was a recourse to lustration, this was deliberately circumscribed, and limited in scope, and impact.[50] The main mechanism for dealing with the past was the truth-seeking process in the form of the Human Rights Violations Investigation Panel, otherwise known as the Oputa Panel.[51] Significantly, the Oputa Panel did not

[42] Ibid.

[43] Yusuf (2007), p. 268.

[44] Moustafa (2007); Dyzenhaus (2010b).

[45] Dyzenhaus (2010a), p. 61.

[46] Petter Graver (2015), p. 19.

[47] Yusuf note 43 supra at 14–15.

[48] Ginsburg and Moustafa (2008), p. 3.

[49] Ibid.

[50] Yusuf (2023a), pp. 437, 438–439.

[51] Yusuf (2023b), p. 232.

examine the judiciary as an institution. This was despite the fact that it had a respected retired Justice of the Supreme Court as its chairperson and despite holding institutional hearings for the police, the security agencies, and the prisons services.[52] It recommended various measures for institutional transformation of these agencies.[53]

That the Oputa Panel did not hold a hearing about the judicial role in governance during the authoritarian period remains a major *faux pax* of the truth-seeking process in the country and a major gap in the accountability process. This is even more telling in the light of institutional recognition that the rule of law was compromised during the period, and that there were corrupt elements in the temples of justice. Indeed, Justice Oputa had himself noted during the authoritarian period that 'the solemn, sacred and beautiful image of justice and the judiciary' was being tarnished and desecrated by the 'stark and naked reality that some judicial officers are corrupt.'[54] It thus remains an irony that the Oputa Panel did not seize on the opportunity of the truth-seeking process to hold special hearings on the judicial function in the authoritarian past.

A retired Justice of the Supreme Court and then head of the National Judicial Institute responsible for the training of judges had stated at an annual conference of Nigerian judges that law in the authoritarian period had become weakened due to 'ouster and suspensions of the constitution and existing laws which gave us liberty and freedom. The constitutional duty to protect the liberty and freedom of the citizens by the state was regularly breached by those entrusted with that sacred duty'.[55] The judiciary was one of those 'entrusted' with the 'sacred duty' of upholding the rights of citizens. Comprehensive accountability at the least, but also institutional reform, and repositioning of the judiciary for its critical role in post-authoritarian governance commended extending the focus on its role in past governance.

Other institutional performance features commended extending scrutiny of the role of the judiciary in authoritarian governance in the transitional justice processes in the country. It was a notorious fact that criminal and civil trials (and appeals) went on in many cases for years and sometimes decades, a fact that was readily acknowledged by the judiciary. Moreover, as the special hearings for other key players in the criminal justice system, disclosed, the system was essentially in shambles. The judiciary is a major component of the criminal justice system and there were references to its role and functioning by the other key players like the prisons services and the police. This was only logical as it is not possible to examine the work

---

[52] Hakeem Yusuf *African Transitional Justice Research Project: Case Study on Transitional Justice in Nigeria* (Centre for the Study of Violence and Reconciliation, Pretoria, 2018) 47-49 available at: https://www.csvr.org.za/comparative-study-of-transitional-justice-in-africa/.

[53] Yusuf note 51 supra at 234.

[54] Oputa (1981) at 9.

[55] Justice Olajide Olatawura, retired Justice of the Supreme Court of Nigeria and erstwhile administrator of the National Judicial Institute, Welcome Address at the 1999 All Nigeria Conference of /Judges' Conference (1 November 1999) in National Judicial Institute, 1999 All Judges Conference xxv (2000) quoted in Oko (2006), p. 9, 11.

of these other key players without reference to the role of the judiciary. To cite one example, there was (and there remains) a major problem of prison congestion during the period of authoritarian rule in the country due in part to delays in the criminal trial process.

Judges signed thousands of remand warrants that sent and kept thousands in prison as 'Awaiting Trial' persons for years in prison. At the time, this category of detainees far outnumbered convicted persons (and they still do till date).[56] The story was no better in civil cases as delays in trials led to many dying waiting to have their day in court, or for judgments to be delivered at the end of trials. There is also the fact that the courts upheld military legislation made in violation of due process and human rights. All these, in addition to judicial acquiescence to, and legitimation of military usurpation of power, constitutional distortions, gross mis-governance and violation of human rights.

Not only was the judiciary left out in the transitional justice process, but it also ended up lending itself to truncating the implementation of the report of the Oputa Panel. The Supreme Court deferred yet again to the caprices of three erstwhile military heads of state in litigation they instituted to defy summons to appear before the Oputa Panel.[57] Suffice it to say in this regard that the Supreme Court held in the litigation that the President lacked constitutional powers to set up a body like the Oputa Panel, with a remit to enquire into human rights violations in the whole country.[58] Consequent upon the judgment, the government which set up the Oputa Panel refused to implement the white paper of its report premising its position on the Supreme Court decision.

4.2 *Reforming without Accountability?: The National Judicial Council*

Nonetheless, at the critical point of political transition in 1998–1999, it was evident that there was a need to reform, if not transform, the judiciary and ensure its independence in the post-authoritarian period. The exiting military government demonstrated this awareness in its provisions for the establishment of the National Judicial Council (NJC) under section 153 of the 1999 Constitution of the Federal Republic of Nigeria which it promulgated as part of the political transition arrangements. The

[56] The situation remains largely the same despite some initiatives by the government to ameliorate the situation. See for instance UNODC Nigeria 'Strengthening the Capacity of the Nigerian Correctional Service in the North-Eastern States' (8 June 2023) available at: https://www.unodc.org/nigeria/en/strengthening-the-capacity-of-the-nigerian-correctional-service-in-the-north-eastern-states.html.

[57] For a full account, see Yusuf note 2 43 supra at 276–281.

[58] See *Gani Fawehinmi, Justice Chukwudifu Oputa (Rtd.) and Human Rights Violations Investigation Commission v. General Ibrahim Babangida, Brigadier Halilu Akilu and Brigadier Kunle Togun* [2003] M.J.S.C 63.

NJC itself has declared, that it was established to 'insulate the Judiciary from the whims and caprices of the Executive; hence guarantee the independence of this Arm of Government, which is a sine qua non for any democratic Government.'[59]

The NJC, headed by the Chief Justice of Nigeria, recommends judicial officers for appointment across the spectrum of the superior courts of records in Nigeria. It also has powers to 'deal with all other matters relating to broad issues of policy and administration'[60] of the judiciary. The NJC has powers to discipline judicial officers, and this has a bearing on the issue of judicial accountability however, the exercise of that power has been controversial. Sixteen of its twenty-three members are judicial officers of the superior courts.[61] The other seven are legal practitioners of high professional standing, five of whom are nominated by the Nigerian Bar Association. These five members only participate in the deliberations regarding the recommendation of persons for judicial appointment.[62] The other two members are nominated by the CJN. Thus, the pre-eminent body is essentially a judicial affair. The NJC has been active in investigating complaints (petitions) of judicial misfeasance and recommending appropriate action. Its recommendations have led to the sacking, suspension or dismissal of such judges. Only justices of the Supreme Court have not been touched by the disciplinary actions of the NJC.

The NJC has sometimes been criticised for high-handedness, failure to observe fair-hearing and selectivity in its recommendations. In some cases, its decisions have been challenged for eroding, rather than affirming judicial independence.[63] Apprehensions of unchanged ways, foreshadows the workings of the NJC. Critics have also identified inconsistencies in its operational procedures as well as a lack of courage in its approach to some cases.[64] Moreover despite its role in sanitising the judiciary, leading members of the NJC, including the highest echelons of the judiciary, have themselves sometimes been mired in allegations of bribery and corruption, including at least three Chief Justices of Nigeria as mentioned earlier. It is important to recall in this regard that most, if not all the judges who are members of the NJC (all of whom are there by various statutory permutations, notably their specific headship of levels of courts), were appointed to the bench by one or the other previous military administration in the first place. Thus, since its establishment in 1999, the NJC has by default been largely constituted and led by the 'old guard' in the judiciary. All of these have cast a shadow on the institutional accountability measure which the NJC represents (as far as its disciplinary powers are concerned) in the post-authoritarian period.

---

[59] National Judicial Council 'NJC Profile' available at: https://njc.gov.ng/profile-of-NJC.

[60] Paragraph 21. (a-i).

[61] Paragraph 20 (a-h). Schedule 3, Constitution of the Federal Republic of Nigeria, 1999.

[62] Paragraph 20 (i-j).

[63] Editorial "NJC and Oyo Judiciary Saga" *Daily Independent* Online Edition (Lagos Thursday 13 2008).

[64] Badejogbin (2005).

The NJC's 'goals' include ensuring the judiciary is 'committed to the rule of law'.[65] However, the NJC was not established to deal with the past record of the judiciary but only to change the superstructure of the judicial bureaucracy. At best, the operations of the NJC and its continued struggle to sanitise the judicial institution (a task which has continued to prove Herculean), has served as a constant reminder of the judicial accountability gap in the post-authoritarian period in which the judiciary has been saddled with great expectations.[66] The NJC has some success, though limited in curbing the level of judicial misfeasance. The making of the National Judicial Policy[67] as a reference for the operations of the judiciary and some others,[68] is a major development and commendable achievement in this regard. However, the implementation of the laudable provisions of this document has been benign, including notably, the appointment of judges through a merit-based system. The judiciary and its functioning in the post-authoritarian period remain haunted by its unaccounted past. More than that, the accountability deficit has arguably negatively impacted its salient role in post-authoritarian governance, at a time when real and perceived institutional integrity and independence are critical for the rule of law and the democratic process.

Dealing with the role of the judiciary during the period of authoritarian rule would have provided a forum for establishing the NJC (or any such similar body), in a way that would have better secure the reformation and transformation of the judiciary. Such a process has better potential to deliver a more representative body cognisant of the society's aspirations for social reconstruction. Such a body would arguably assist in better fortifying the judicial institution against the vagaries of judicialised politics which potentially challenges any judiciary, drawn as the Nigerian courts are, into mediating highly contested political choices and questions.

5 Judicial Governance in an Age of Rights

There is a consensus in the comparative constitutional law scholarship that the last three and a half decades has witnessed a substantial and concrete growth in judicial governance in both developed and developing countries.[69] Courts are continually

[65] Ibid.

[66] Ikechukwu Amaechi "Judiciary and the Burden of Expectation" *Daily Independent* Online Edition (Lagos Tuesday 25 March 2008).

[67] The National Judicial Council 'The National Judicial Policy' April 2016 available at: https://www.njc.gov.ng/assets/press-release/NationalJudicialCouncil-15.pdf.

[68] These are the Judicial Discipline Regulations of 9th March, 2017; Revised Code of Conduct for Judicial Officers of the Federal Republic of Nigeria of February, 2016; Revised NJC Guidelines and Procedural Rules for the appointment of Judicial Officers of all Superior Courts of Record in Nigeria of 3rd November, 2014.

[69] See for example, Prempeh (2006), p. 1239; Sadurski (2005); Hirschl (2006), p. 721, Hirschl (2004); Epstein et al. (2001), p. 117; Ginsburg (2003); Gloppen et al. (2010).

being drawn into adjudicating matters arising from political differences or politically charged situations and are sometimes wary of the implications of adjudicating political issues. Consider for example the pivotal role the judiciary played in resolving the appropriate legal approach for issuing the required notice of withdrawal of the United Kingdom from the European Union. The matter had raised some tension across the country. The close call in the referendum led to divisions that were virtually unprecedented in the contemporary political history of the UK. A consolidated appeal involving litigation commenced on the issue in England, Northern Ireland, and Scotland came before the UK Supreme Court in the case of *R (on the application of Miller and another) (Respondents) v Secretary of State for Exiting the European Union Supreme Court* (*Brexit Case*).[70]

Following the referendum for exiting the EU, there was a dispute between the executive and parliament as to the steps which are required to be taken as a matter of UK domestic law, before the process of leaving the European Union can be initiated. The specific issue is whether a formal notice of withdrawal can lawfully be given by ministers (the executive) without prior legislation passed in both Houses of Parliament (Parliament) and assented to by the Queen. The government (executive) was intent on by-passing Parliament in issuing the required notice to the EU on the basis of the application of the prerogative powers of the Crown. However, Parliament maintained that there was a need to secure parliamentary approval for the notice.

The UK Supreme Court upheld the decision of the High Court that the prerogative powers to make and unmake treaties, which operated in the international sphere, was inapplicable on the facts. The government required appropriate legislation made by Parliament for the notification of withdrawal from the EU. Nonetheless, the UK Supreme Court was at pains to have it known that it was only concerned with the constitutional, rather than the sundry political decisions that had to be made by the political branches of government.[71] Examples abound in other jurisdictions, developed and developing alike on the recourse to the judiciary for resolving thorny issues of high politics crafted as constitutional issues for judicial resolution even in developed democracies.

Thus, it is particularly important that the judiciary in transitional societies be positioned to take on a critical role that is typically required of it in such societies. The role of the judiciary in governance rises to a further level of acuity in transitional societies. Teitel provides a useful insight on the critical role of law, and the judicial function in transitional societies.[72] In the context of political change in transitional societies, the judiciary, due in part to institutional fragility of the executive and the legislature, is usually faced with deciding important but difficult, time-bound cases. This will include cases that relate to arrangements and processes of the political transition. In such situations, the judiciary has to contend with the

---

[70] [2017] UKSC 5; [2017] WLR (D) 53.

[71] Ibid. at paragraph 3.

[72] Teitel (1996–1997), p. 2009.

'ambivalent directionality of law.'[73] Teitel's analysis of transitional jurisprudence as being a distinctive and legitimate conceptualisation of law in society is relevant to this study of the judiciary, particularly the Supreme Court in the context of the political transition in Nigeria.

The judiciary in Nigeria has played a pivotal, if not strategic role post-authoritarian governance in Nigeria in era of 'new constitutionalism.'[74] The judiciary has been involved in adjudicating what Hirschl has described as 'core executive prerogatives', 'foundational "nation-building" processes', 'fundamental restorative justice dilemmas' and 'political transformation, regime change, and electoral disputes'.[75] Specifically, like many courts in other parts of the world in recent decades, the Nigerian courts of record (higher courts) have become entangled in the web of the judicialisation[76] of politics. Hirschl defines the phenomenon as 'the reliance on courts and judicial means for addressing core moral predicaments, public policy questions and political controversies.'[77]

Furthermore, in societies in political transition, particularly formerly authoritarian ones, the judiciary is usually the only one of the three branches of government that has a record of institutional continuity throughout the period of distortion in the exercise of state powers. The political branches suffer either suspension or abrogation at some points and only remerge as democratic institutions in the post-authoritarian period. They are thus usually, as in the Nigerian experience, fragile partly due to their chequered institutional existence. The judiciary thus emerge as a critical player in governance building on the privilege of institutional continuity and function as a mediator.

5.1 *Bungling Politicians, Powerful Courts?—The Judicialisation of Politics in a Post-Authoritarian Context*

As stated earlier, the combination of dysfunctional institutions, inordinate power contestations among the political elite, glaring deficit in the political and democratic legitimacy of the transition process promoted the judicialisation of politics into a major feature in governance in the last two decades in the country. The first decade of the post-authoritarian period in particular witnessed disputes arising from the legacy of dysfunctional constitutional, economic, social and political arrangements of authoritarian rule. The deficient, or even lack of institutional memory of the

[73] Ibid. at 2033.

[74] Hirschl (2004).

[75] Hirschl (2002), p. 191; Hirschl (2006), p. 721; see also Shapiro and Sweet (2002); Sweet (2004), Tate and Vallinder (1995).

[76] Especially in the American scholarship, the judicialisation of politics is usually referred to as the 'constitutionalization of democratic politics'. See for instance Prempeh (2006), p. 1239; Ackerman (1997), p. 771; Pildes (2004), p. 28; Isaacharoff (2004), p. 1861.

[77] Hirschl (2010), p. 119; Hirschl (2008), p. 93, 94.

executive and legislature, compounded by an imperial president (a former military head of state), engendered serial litigation among the national (federal) and subnational (states) branches of government. This line of litigation has not abated more than 20 years on.

In addition, disputes within and among political parties, and politicians on election matters have become a perennial staple of the higher courts. The judiciary has had to deal with a large number of disputes on the right to participation, disqualification of candidates and sanctioning of election results in the post-authoritarian period. While courts have been playing an important role in electoral contests elsewhere,[78] the situation in Nigeria has become notorious. Nigerian politicians remain perhaps the sorest losers, ready to challenge results of elections even at party primaries in many instances, all the way to the Supreme Court. The situation is so pervasive that the judiciary has been admonishing politicians and political parties to put their houses in order internally, in line with their constitutions rather than congesting the dockets of the courts with their electoral wranglings.[79] Testimony to this feature of Nigerian politics as well as the implications for magnifying the role of the judiciary in electioneering and who holds elected political office is demonstrated by media reports in January 2024. Newspapers reports stated that the Supreme Court was billed to hear 21 appeals from the gubernatorial elections in the country in the week beginning 8 January 2024.[80]

In plain terms, the reports meant the tenure of the governors in this instance, literally laid in the hands of the judges, not in the hands of the electorate. Bear in mind that the appeals had gone through the Governorship Election Petition Tribunals, then the Court of Appeal before further appeal to the Supreme Court. Indeed, election petitions and appeals had gone all the way to the Supreme Court regarding all the 31 governorship elections conducted in the country. The number would easily have been 36 appeals (that is all the states in the country) but for the fact that there are out of season elections in five states across the country due to previous decisions of the courts declaring void, the governorship elections in those states in previous election cycles. Nor is the situation unique, but rather a repetition of the practice in previous general elections since the political transition to civil rule in 1999; a reflection of a winner takes all, 'do or die' political climate.[81] It serves to examine a few

---

[78] Hirschl note 75 supra at 722.

[79] 'Allow judiciary to function, CJN tells politicians' *Vanguard Online* (22 October 2022) available at: https://www.vanguardngr.com/2022/10/allow-judiciary-to-function-cjn-tells-politicians/.

[80] Bolanle Olabimtan 'Ebonyi, Benue, Plateau…Supreme Court to Hear 21 Governorship Appeals this Week' *The Cable* Online (8 January 2024) available at: https://www.thecable.ng/ebonyi-benue-plateau-supreme-court-to-hear-21-governorship-appeals-this-week; Eric Ikhilae '21 Governorship Appeals for Hearing at S'Court this Week' *The Nation* (8 January 2024) available at: https://thenationonlineng.net/21-governorship-appeals-for-hearing-at-scourt-this-week/; Godwin Tsa 'Governorship poll: Supreme Court begins hearing in over 21 appeals' *The Sun* (9 January 2023) available at: https://sunnewsonline.com/governorship-poll-supreme-court-begins-hearing-in-over-21-appeals/.

[81] Bunmi Makinwa 'Judges Should rebuild the Temples of Justice' *The Cable Online* (11 April 2019) available at: https://www.thecable.ng/judges-should-rebuild-the-temple-of-justice.

cases on the wranglings of the political elite for power as well as those involving the disputes between the federal and state governments in the post-authoritarian period.

5.1.1 Thwarting Presidential Vendetta: AC v INEC

Elite power-wrangling has become a defining feature of the current civil transition and democratisation process in Nigeria and the judiciary has been continually drawn into resolving this. A prime example is the case, *Action Congress (AC) and Alhaji Atiku Abubakar v Independent National Electoral Commission* (*AC v INEC*),[82] where judicial intervention was enlisted by prominent political actors to settle the ground rules on the contentious issue of individual participation and exclusion in the political process. This was specifically with regard to the position of president in the 2007 presidential elections in Nigeria. The incumbent President Olusegun Obasanjo wanted to secure a third term through a constitutional amendment. The 'Third Term Project,'[83] as it was known in Nigerian political circles, created a lot of acrimony on the socio-political landscape.[84]

President Obasanjo's third-term project elicited serious opposition from the public and was frustrated by the Nigerian Parliament.[85] The opposition to President Obasanjo's third-term project was openly led by Vice-President, Abubakar Atiku, a long-standing presidential hopeful himself. In retaliation, President Obasanjo removed Vice-President Atiku's aides and also pushed for the latter to be impeached by the legislature, but without success. However, the People's Democratic Party (PDP) which they both belonged to, expelled the Vice-President at the behest of the President. Vice-President Atiku then joined the main opposition party, the Action Congress (AC) to pursue his presidential ambition.

The AC and Vice-President Atiku intsituted this case to challenge the decision of the Independent National Electoral Commission (INEC) to disqualify the Vice-President and exclude him from contesting in the presidential poll. INEC had based its decision on the purported indictment of Vice-President Atiku for abuse of office by an Administrative Panel of Inquiry (Panel) set up by the President following his investigation by the Economic and Financial Crimes Commission (EFCC). The trial court held that INEC has no power to disqualify a candidate presented to it by a political party from contesting the 2007 elections. Dissatisfied, INEC appealed. The Court of Appeal allowed the appeal and AC and the Vice-President appealed to the Supreme Court.

---

[82] (2007) 6 S.C Pt. II 212 (-314).

[83] Gilbert da Costa 'Nigerian Senate Denies Obasanjo Third Term' *Voice of America* available at: http://www.voanews.com/english/archive/2006-05/2006-05-16-voa68.cfm?CFID=269274608&CFTOKEN=30412515.

[84] For an account of the project which Chief Olusegun Obasanjo has always denied, see Chidi Odinkalu and Osori (2008).

[85] Editorial 'Triumph of The National Assembly' *This Day* (Abuja Wednesday 17 May 2006). See also Posner and Young (2007), p. 126, 127.

The court was expected to determine whether INEC, the electoral umpire but a non-judicial agency, could enforce or invoke the exclusionary provisions in view of constitutional provisions on judicial powers in Section 6 and the fundamental right to fair hearing contained in Section 36 (1), (4)-(12) of the Constitution of the Federal Republic of Nigeria, 1999 (the Constitution). These questions were all to be determined in 'the context of the system of constitutional democracy established for the country by the Constitution.'[86] In its unanimous decision allowing the appeal, the Supreme Court held that the Defendant lacked constitutional or statutory powers to disqualify any candidate in the 2007 elections. It stated further that only a conviction by a court of law was sufficient to constitute a bar to eligibility to contest for public office, as according to the court 'convictions for offences and imposition of penalties and punishments are matters appertaining exclusively to judicial power.'[87]

It is relevant to note that the power to disqualify candidates from elections was formerly vested in INEC. At that time, the courts generally declined jurisdiction on such matters. This remained the situation of the law in the immediate period of the transition to civil rule and the first two elections of 1999 and 2003. However, the power was taken away with the passing of the Electoral Act 2006 and vested in the judiciary. This was a deliberate act of the legislature following the abuse in the application of the power by INEC in the 2003 general elections, in which some segments of the public and the political class felt short-changed.[88] Indeed, the decision facts in *AC v INEC* is a poignant reflection of situational context of the legislative preference. The courts have a critical role to play in confronting the designs of political incumbents to circumvent democratic competition through artful control of electoral bodies like INEC.[89] This is perhaps most critical in the global south.

The federal dominance mentioned earlier, secured for it a disproportionate share of the country's resources.[90] It is then no surprise that claims on federalism and the need to restructure the polity has been a major source of conflict in intergovernmental relations between the federal (central), and the state (subnational) governments in the post-authoritarian period. The Supreme Court has original jurisdiction in such matters and has remained a mediator in the recurring contestations on the principle. It serves to examine two representative cases on the issue.

5.1.2 The Resource Control Case

Oil is the main foreign exchange earner for the country and, along with other natural resources, is controlled by the Federal government. However, agitations by the oil producing areas in the Niger Delta for 'resource control' (as it came to be known),

---

[86] *AC v INEC* note 81 supra at 222.

[87] Ibid. at 230. Emphasis mine.

[88] *AC v INEC* note 81 supra at 265.

[89] Isaacharoff (2008), p. 231, 264.

[90] Adamolekun (2005), p. 383, 390.

had gained momentum before the exit of the military from power. In an unexpected move, the federal government approached the Supreme Court for resolution of the claims in *Attorney-General of the Federation v Attorney-General of Abia State & 35 Ors* (*Resource Control Case*).[91] The central issue was the determination of what constituted the boundaries of a state to qualify it under section 162 (2) of the Constitution to be paid 'not less than thirteen percent' of revenue accruing to the federation account from natural resources exploited in the state (derivation principle).

The federal government challenged the claim of eight littoral states (which included two not in the Niger Delta) as to the limits of the seaward boundary of each of the states. The position of the federal government was that the low-water mark of the land surface or where applicable, the seawards limits of the inland waterways, constituted the boundaries of the littoral states. Thus, it argued further that natural resources within the continental shelf of Nigeria were not attributable to any of the 36 states. By implication revenue from natural resources from such areas (invariably including all offshore oil and gas) paid into the federation account, were not subject to the principle of derivation.

The littoral states on the other hand contended otherwise. They claimed onshore and offshore natural resources were appurtenant to their respective territories and formed part of them. The federal government could not lay claim to offshore waters, as it constitutionally had no territory beyond the Federal Capital Territory.[92] Based on that position, natural resources offshore belonged to the respective littoral states and were subject to the principle of derivation.[93] All the other states joined the suit as interested parties.

The Supreme Court upheld the position of the federal government basing its decision essentially on the fact that the low water mark constituted not only the boundaries of the eight littoral states, but also the country itself. The country was only entitled to the seaward limits and the continental shelf (and the resources therein) by virtue of certain international laws, treaties, and conventions, most important of which is the 1958 Convention on the Territorial Sea and the Contiguous Zone and the 1982 United Nations Conventions on the Law of the Sea. All such instruments conferred certain limited benefits on the sovereign, the Federal Republic of Nigeria, rather than the littoral states or any other state of the federation for that matter.[94]

The Supreme Court also upheld some of the counter claims made by some of the states. It declared illegal, the 'first line charges' made from the federation account for certain expenditure before disbursement of the net to the constitutional beneficiaries; itself, the states and the local governments. They included deductions from the federation account to service external federal debts. The Court upheld the claim,

---

[91] [2002] 4 S.C. (Pt.I) 1.

[92] Ibid. at 198–199.

[93] Ibid. at 10–11.

[94] *Resource Control Case* note 90 supra at 21–30.

stating that such debts should be paid from the revenue and assets of the Federal Government and not the federation account.[95] Thus the judgment was a marginal victory to the states and the federal government also lost some grounds with regards to the deductions it had made under the so called 'first line charges,' now declared illegal by the Court.

5.1.3 Tackling Corruption: A Matter of Urgent Concern

Another critical issue of national and international concern in Nigeria at the dawn of the political transition in 1999 (till date), is the unenviable record of corruption in the country. The military had institutionalised corruption and misappropriation of public funds in the country by the time it handed over power in 1999.[96] Corruption had, and continues to affect socio-economic development and a major factor in growing rate of poverty in a country with immense human and natural resources. Indeed, it has been observed that combating corruption in the polity was clearly a policy imperative for the incoming administration, if it was intent on halting the downward spiral in the nation's economic and social development.

As part of anti-corruption measures, the federal government under President Olusegun Obasanjo established the Independent Corrupt Practices Commission (ICPC)[97] and the Economic and Financial Crimes Commission (EFCC).[98] However, the move soon ran into rough weather when the ICPC was challenged by a state government, Ondo, for being in violation of federal principles in as much it sought to investigate and prosecute state officials in state high courts.

The Ondo State government took its challenge to the Supreme Court in *Attorney-General of Ondo State v Attorney-General of the Federation & 35 Ors* (the *ICPC* Case).[99] The Plaintiffs argued with the support of many of the states, that it was not within the powers of the National Assembly to make laws for the creation of a body with such an all-encompassing reach as the ICPC or the offences (of corruption) for the whole country. It was argued that the offence of corruption was a residual matter, and thus within the exclusive competence of the states by virtue of the legislative lists in the Constitution.

The Supreme Court disagreed. It held, as argued by the federal government, that the National Assembly could enact the legislation for the whole country by virtue of

---

[95] Ibid. at 47–49.

[96] Nigeria ranked fifth most corrupt country in a worldwide survey of 85 countries in 1998 during the last few months of military rule. See, Transparency International, *Transparency International Corruption Index 1998* (Berlin, 1999).

[97] Established under the Corrupt Practices and Other Related Offences Act 2000, No. 5 of 2000 as amended.

[98] Established under the Economic and Financial Crimes (Establishment) Act 2002, No. 5 of 2002. It has been repealed by the Economic and Financial Crimes (Establishment) Act 2004 of 23rd March 2004.

[99] (2002) 6 S.C. (Pt I) 1 (-196).

the (non-justiciable) provisions of the 'Fundamental Objectives and Principles of State Policy' of the constitution which provided in part that the state had a duty to 'abolish all corrupt practices and abuse of power.'[100] It similarly held that the National Assembly was empowered to pass the ICPC Act by virtue of the provisions of section 4 of the Constitution which conferred on it the power to 'make laws for the peace, order and good governance of the federation.'[101] Corruption the Court noted, threatened the peace, order and good government of the country.[102]

Justice Uwaifo stated that the issue of corruption and abuse of power has become a matter of international concern. Where it has been declared state policy to combat it in the country, it assumes the character of a 'national issue of high priority' to be legislated on by the National Assembly an addressed through a central agency like the ICPC.[103] With the unanimity of the highest judicial panel in the country behind it, the Federal Government proceeded with an anti-corruption drive that has been quite controversial in its operations and results till date.

5.2 *What Goes Round: Politicisation of the Judiciary*

Judicialisation of politics can rebound in politicisation of judiciary and the problematic nature of this has been evident in various ways in the Nigerian experience. In Nigeria, this has manifested in the judiciary losing public trust to the point that some now view it as a pliable and corrupt institution. Despite the fact that the country has always had a crop of credible, hardworking, and incorruptible judges,[104] the institutional credibility and perceptions of the independence of the Nigerian judiciary has incrementally nose-dived in recent years.

Perhaps the most topical concern about the judiciary is the continued incidence of corruption and attendant questionable adjudication, especially in the high courts, and sometimes, the Court of Appeal. Even the Supreme Court has eroded public confidence in a few cases. Electoral matters in particular has all but brought the judiciary into disrepute. There are more than a few instances of questionable judgments been delivered by different branches of the Court of Appeal on the same issue, sometimes on issues that have long been settled by the apex court. The imputation, even where this may have been due to jurisprudential preferences, is that the judges have received bribes from a party in the litigation. There continue to be confirmed incidents of corruption on the part of some judges who adjudicated at the various elections petitions tribunals all over the country in the aftermath of general elections sometimes leading to dismissal of some judges. Conscious of the damage

[100] Section 15 of the Constitution of the Federal Republic of Nigeria, 1999.

[101] *ICPC* Case note 100 supra at 116.

[102] Per Ogwuegbu JSC, *ICPC* Case ibid. at 59.

[103] *ICPC* Case note 98 supra at 116.

[104] Many will still argue these outnumber those with questionable integrity.

this has done to the image of the judiciary, successive heads of the various branches of the judiciary warn judges at the point of appointment as judges or to *ad hoc* election matters, to be wary of politicians and not run afoul of their judicial oaths. However, allegations of judicial turpitude in the adjudication of such matters have only increased over the years, including in the last 2023 general elections.

One of the ways the judicialisation of politics and the magnification of the judicial role in governance across the spectrum of economic, social, and political matters, in Nigeria has rebound into politicisation of the judiciary is the keen interest of politicians in the appointment of judges. The last 20 years has witnessed an overt and overly practice of executive and legislative office holders securing the appointment of their preferred candidates, usually family members as judicial officers across all levels of courts in the country from the magistrate to the Supreme Court. Simultaneously, there has also been a notable increase in the appointment of family members of senior judges to the bench. Observers have decried this politicisation of judicial appointments.

An observer has decried the development as an 'Executive-Judiciary tag team', which is eroding the separation of powers and independence of the judiciary.[105] In this regard, it has been pointed out that in a recent appointment round of 34 nominees to the Federal High Court in 2023, 23 were 'sons, daughters, mistresses and acquaintances of the top-ranking politicians.'[106] Also, the son-in-law of the President of the Court of Appeal (a member of the NJC) had been promoted (from the National Industrial Court) to the Court of Appeal in 2023 while the daughter, who is the wife of the promoted judge, was also appointed a judge of the High Court of her state by the state governor 2 years previously. In 2022, 'the wife of the Judge President of the NICN [National Industrial Court] was similarly appointed a judge of the High Court of the Federal Capital Territory. Her brother, like her husband, was also a member of the NJC.'[107] Another governor appointed his wife a judge of the high court in his state in 2022.[108] In an earlier appointment round by the NJC, the now erstwhile Chairman of the Presidential Advisory Committee Against Corruption alleged that the 'sons and daughters of retired and serving Judges and Justices are being nominated for appointment into sensitive judicial positions at the expense of more qualified candidates without privileged support and backing.'[109]

[105] Lawyard 'Odinkalu Exposes Politicization of Judiciary Appointments, Calls for Reform' available: https://www.lawyard.org/news/odinkalu-exposes-politicization-of-judiciary-appointments-calls-for-reform/.

[106] Ibid.

[107] Chidi Anselm Odinkalu 'A captured temple of justice, By Chidi Anselm Odinkalu' *Premium Times* (2 October 2023) available at: https://www.premiumtimesng.com/opinion/631725-a-captured-temple-of-justice-by-chidi-anselm-odinkalu.html.

[108] Ibid.

[109] John Chuks Azu and Muideen Olaniyi 'Controversy trails appointment of new judges' *Daily Trust* Online (15 May 2020) available at: https://dailytrust.com/controversy-trails-appointment-of-new-judges/.

Questionable appointments to the bench are fast becoming the order of the day across the country. It has been noted that the objective is to inoculate the political elite against electoral misadventures given the critical role the judiciary plays in the process and validation of outcomes from sundry litigation that follows every round of elections in the country to date. This approach to judicial appointments is a violation of international principles on judicial appointment like the United Nations Basic Principles on the Independence of the Judiciary, (the Bangalore Principles) as well as the NJC's policies and rules on the matter.[110] For instance Rule 8.3 of the Judicial Code of Conduct provides that: 'a Judge who takes advantage of the judicial office for personal gain or for gain by his or her relative or relation abuses power.' There is thus a cause for concern on the independence and integrity of the judgments of judges appointed in violation of national and international principles on the appointment of judges.

Institutional transformation, and strengthening of the judiciary, in view of its potential to foster development and the rule of law, are key aspirations in a democratising polity. On the obverse, weakening the judicial function through politicisation of the judiciary in such societies is detrimental to its functioning. This is particularly so in the Nigerian context where the political branches suffer from democratic legitimacy deficit,and the judiciary is usually temporally, the viable public option for deepening the democratic culture and instituting accountability in governance.

6 Conclusion

The judiciary is a critical institution for social transformation from authoritarian pasts. Widespread judicialisation of politics all over the world has dispelled any hitherto existing doubts as to the ramifications of the judicial function in society and its direct implications for governance in contemporary times. Especially in transitional contexts, the political branches in their contestations for hegemony and domination, provide ample opportunity for the ascendance of the judiciary as a principal force in governance. The judiciary is requested to intervene in setting the ground rules for political competition within the democratic space opened up after years of authoritarian rule. The judiciary also at the vanguard of preserving the rule of law assailed almost continuously by a largely self-serving political elite with suspect legitimacy credentials.

While the foray of the judiciary into the arena of resolving a myriad of political contestations couched as constitutional disputes by the political elites can potentially erode some of its institutional integrity in developed democracies, the interventions are particularly fraught for the third branch of government in transitional societies. Thus, the judiciary in transitional societies need to be prepared for taking

[110] Odinkalu note 107 supra.

on the challenges of post-authoritarian governance. It is important to ensure that deliberate measures are instituted as part of the transitional justice process to address the judicial role in past authoritarian rule. This is with a view to ensuring accountability and institutional reforms to prepare the judiciary for its near-inevitable role as the mediator and stabilizer of the new democracy and protector of the rule of law. As it is, the accountability gap on the institutional role of the judiciary in Nigeria during the country's troubled period haunts the judicial function. It has continued to challenge its attempts at self-transformation and regulation constituted by the establishment of the NJC. This predictably, will be the case in any society that fails to include judicial accountability in governance during a period of authoritarian rule.

References

Ackerman B (1997) The rise of world constitutionalism. Va Law Rev 83:771

Adamolekun L (2005) Nigerian federation at the crossroads: the way forward. Publius: J Federalism 35:383–405

Dyzenhaus D (2010a) The idea of the judge. Univ Toronto Law J 60:61

Dyzenhaus D (2010b) Hard cases in wicked legal systems: pathologies of legality. Oxford University Press, Oxford

Ekeke AC (2022) Liberalization of the rule on locus standi before Nigerian Courts: lessons from India. J Afr Law 66(2):339

Elaigwu JI (2002) Federalism in Nigeria's new democratic polity. Publius: J Federalism 32(2):73

Epstein L et al (2001) The role of constitutional courts in the establishment and maintenance of democratic systems of government. Law Soc Rev 35(1):117

Ginsburg T (2003) Judicial review in new democracies. Cambridge University Press, New York

Ginsburg T, Moustafa T (2008) Rule by law. Cambridge University Press, New York

Gloppen S, Wilson BM, Gagarella R, Kinander M, Skar E (2010) Courts and power in Latin America and Africa. Palgrave Macmillan, New York

Graver HP (2015) Judges against justice: on judges when the rule of law is under attack. Springer, Berlin

Hirschl R (2002) Resituating the judicialisation of politics: Bush v Gore as a global trend. Can J Law Jurisprud 15(2):191

Hirschl R (2004) Towards juristocracy: the origins and consequences of the new constitutionalism. Harvard University Press, Cambridge

Hirschl R (2006) The new constitutionalism and the judicialization of pure politics worldwide. Fordham Law Rev 75(2):721

Hirschl R (2008) The judicialization of politics and the rise of political courts. Annu Rev Polit Sci 11:93–118

Hirschl R (2010) The judicialization of politics. In: Caldeira GA, Daniel Kelemen R, Whittington KE (eds) The Oxford handbook of law and politics. Oxford University Press, Oxford, p 119

Isaacharoff S (2004) Constitutionalizing democracy in fractured societies. Tex Law Rev 82:1861

Isaacharoff S (2008) Democracy and collective decision making. Int J Const Law 6(2):231–266

Moliterno JE, Čuroš P (2021) Recent Attacks on Judicial Independence: the vulgar, the systemic, and the insidious. Germ Law J 22:1159

Moustafa T (2007) The struggle for constitutional power: law, politics and economic development in Egypt. Cambridge University Press, New York

Ogowewo T (1995) The problem with standing to sue in Nigeria. J Afr Law 39(1):1–18

Ogowewo TI (2000) Why the Judicial Annulment of the Constitution of 1999 is Imperative to the Survival of Nigeria's Democracy. J Afr Law 44:135–166

Oko O (2006) Seeking justice in transitional societies: an analysis of the problems and failures of the judiciary in Nigeria. Brooklyn J Int Law 9:9
Oputa C (1981) The law and the twin pillars of justice. Government Printer Owerri
Osaghae E (1998) Crippled Giant: Nigeria since independence. Hurst and Co. Publishers Ltd, London
Pildes RH (2004) The Supreme Court 2003-foreword: the constitutionalization of democratic politics. Harv Law Rev 118(1):28
Posner DK, Young DJ (2007) The institutionalization of political power in Africa. J Democr 18(3):126, 127
Prempeh K (2007) Africa's "Constitutional Revival": false start or new dawn. Int J Const Law 5(3):469
Prempeh KH (2006) Marbury in Africa: judicial review and the challenge of constitutionalism in contemporary Africa. Tulane Law Rev 80:1239
Sadurski W (2005) Rights before courts: a study of constitutional courts in postcommunist states of Central and Eastern Europe. Springer, Dordrecht
Shapiro M, Sweet AS (2002) On law, politics, and judicialization. Oxford University Press, Oxford
Smith BC (2023) Judges and democratization: judicial independence in new democracies, 2nd edn. Routledge, Abingdon
Sweet AS (2004) Governing with Judges: constitutional politics in Europe. Clarendon, Oxford
Tate NC, Vallinder T (1995) The global expansion of judicial power. New York University Press, New York
Teitel RG (1996–1997, 2009) Transitional jurisprudence: the role of law in political transformation. Yale Law J 106(7)
van Dijk F, Vos G (2019) Method for Assessment of the independence and accountability of the judiciary. Int J Court Adm 9(3):2
Yusuf H (2007) Travails of truth: achieving justice for victims of impunity in Nigeria. Int J Transitional Just 1(2):268
Yusuf H (2008) Calling the judiciary to account for the past: transitional justice and judicial accountability in Nigeria. Law Policy 30(2):194
Yusuf H (2014) Transitional justice, judicial accountability, and the rule of law. Routledge, Abingdon
Yusuf H (2023a) Country studies—Nigeria. In: Stan L, Nedelsky N (eds) *Encyclopedia of Transitional Justice Volume 2*, vol 437, 2nd edn. Cambridge University Press, Cambridge, pp 438–439
Yusuf H (2023b) Human rights violations investigation commission, the Oputa Panel (Nigeria). In: Stan L, Nedelsky N (eds) Encyclopedia of transitional justice, vol 3, 2nd edn. Cambridge University Press, Cambridge, p 232
Badejogbin O (2005) The national judicial council: weaving a patchwork of praiseworthy accomplishments and ruinous shortfalls. Judicial Observ J 3

Path Dependency and the Politics of Judicial Governance by the Higher Judicial Council in Cameroon

Laura-Stella Enonchong

Abstract This chapter offers a critique of the institutional design of Cameroon's judicial appointment body, the Higher Judicial Council (HJC). It critically interrogates the extent to which the HJC can enhance or protect judicial independence in Cameroon. It is contended that the institutional design of the HJC, which has largely remained unaltered since its establishment, obviates the potentials to secure the independence of the judiciary. The author adopts institutional theory to argue that lack of progressive change to the structure and functioning of the HJC can be attributed to a path dependent approach to institutional evolution which is intrinsically linked to a political culture of executive dominance. The persistence of this institutional design in its original configuration, is part of a self-reinforcing process necessary to achieve the coordination effect—to ensure that the other institutions within the political system complement each other in maintaining a system of executive dominance. To consider the prospects for reforming the HJC, the author offers some reflections on the potentials for institutional transformations in political systems where institutional interdependence is deeply entrenched and underpinned by an established political culture.

1 Introduction

The independence of the judiciary is an essential feature of a democratic society, and this partly explains why its protection is vital. Increasingly, the task of securing the independence of the judiciary is falling on judicial appointment bodies, referred to variously as judicial councils, judicial appointment committees or judicial service commissions. However, the focus has often been on the processes through which judicial independence can be secured in the appointment and discipline of

L.-S. Enonchong (✉)
College of Law, SOAS, University of London, London, UK
e-mail: le14@soas.ac.uk

N. Reayat, H. O. Yusuf (eds.), *Constitutionalism in Africa and Beyond*, Ius Gentium: Comparative Perspectives on Law and Justice 127,
https://doi.org/10.1007/978-3-032-01180-0_5

judicial officers, with a lesser focus on the characteristics of the institutions through which these processes are deployed. In addition, despite the growing relevance of these institutions, scholarship is still divided on the extent to which they can actually contribute to the development and entrenchment of an independent judiciary.[1] Moreover, it is unclear under what circumstances judicial councils can effectively contribute to the independence of the judiciary. Yet, judicial councils are being adopted widely as an international 'best practice' for judicial independence. It has become almost fashionable for the judicial architecture of states to include a judicial council, even in circumstances where the institution has played little or no role in protecting judicial independence. Whilst reforms have occurred in some countries to enhance the potential of judicial councils to support the development of an independent judiciary,[2] in others, for instance in Francophone African countries, reforms in the judiciary have not significantly transformed the judicial councils despite their less than perfect performance.[3] This raises the wider question of how or why such institutions persist despite their unsatisfactory performance?

It is against this backdrop that this chapter examines the Higher Judicial Council in Cameroon and its role in enhancing the independence of the judiciary. The analysis is undertaken within the framework of the path dependence theory of historical institutionalism to proffer a theoretical explanation for its persistence, despite its inability to make meaningful contributions to the independence of the judiciary. It is argued that lack of progressive change to the institutional design - composition and competence of the HJC can be attributed to a path dependent approach to institutional evolution which is intrinsically linked to a political culture of executive dominance. The persistence of this institutional choice contributes significantly to its inability to effectively support the development of an independent judiciary. In the early 1990s when the country witnessed a purportedly democratic wind of change which saw the elevation of the constitutional status of the judiciary, the key political actors responsible for change viewed that critical juncture as an opportunity to appear to embrace popular demand for democratic reforms whilst surreptitiously reinforcing the status quo. The change in the status of the judiciary was not accompanied by concomitant change to the factors that are supportive of an independent judiciary. The HJC in particular, continued to exist within a constrained framework that is dependent on the executive with little institutional autonomy to meaningfully contribute to judicial independence.[4] The persistence of this institutional structure in its original configuration is part of a self-reinforcing process necessary to achieve the coordination effect - to ensure that the other institutions within the political system complement each other in maintaining a system of executive dominance.

[1] Šipulová et al. (2022), p. 1.

[2] Liwanga (2012), p. 194; Thuki, (2013), p. 45.

[3] Nonnou (2018), p. 715.

[4] Mbaku (2014), pp. 381–382.

The aims of this chapter are twofold. First is to examine the HJC in Cameroon and evaluate the extent to which it is adequately structured to secure judicial independence. Second, to the extent that the HJC falls short of its responsibilities to support judicial independence, the chapter attempts to proffer an explanation for its institutional inertia by drawing on path dependence theory to explain how Cameroon's history influences the evolution of its institutions. Although research on judicial independence in Cameroon is developing, academic scholarship on the nexus with the HJC is scant. This chapter endeavours to fill that gap by resorting to an analytical focus that captures the intricacies between law, history and politics in Cameroon. Ultimately, the broader objective of the chapter is to explore how the failure to adopt a new path to reform the HJC can inform our understanding of power asymmetry and political culture.

To develop these arguments, the chapter first discusses the role and merits of judicial councils in relation to judicial independence. Next, it examines the HJC within the context of its institutional design before exploring the theory of path dependence. It then applies the theoretical framework to explain the HJC's persistence despite its failure to support judicial independence. Drawing on comparative examples, the chapter proceeds to explore potential alternatives to a path dependent approach to institutional reform of the HJC. The conclusion highlights the difficulties in developing a coherent theory of institutional change in political contexts like Cameroon where institutional interdependence is deeply entrenched and underpinned by an established political culture.

2 Judicial Councils and Judicial Independence

Judicial councils like other institutions assume an influential role in society. Douglas North states that, institutions 'are humanly devised constraints that shape human interaction'.[5] Judicial councils can also be understood from that perspective as they shape the interaction between the judiciary and the executive and other institutions that possess the capacity or potential to influence the independence of judges. This is implicit in their diverse roles as typically, they are responsible for the appointment, promotion and discipline of judges.[6] Judicial councils matter due to their impact on judicial incentives such as independence. They are generally perceived as institutions designed to insulate the judicial career from political influence while also ensuring the accountability of judges.[7] The Council of Europe's Committee of

[5] North (1990), p. 3.

[6] Garoupa and Ginsburg (2009a), p. 119.

[7] Garoupa and Ginsburg (2009b), p. 57. See also Garoupa and Ginsburg (2009a), p. 106.

Ministers describes judicial councils as 'independent bodies … that seek to safeguard the independence of the judiciary and of individual judges'.[8]

In recognition of their potential influence on judicial independence, many countries have established judicial councils.[9] The UN Special Rapporteur on the Independence of Judges and Lawyers specifically recommends the establishment of judicial councils in countries undergoing a political transition as a measure of strengthening judicial independence. Nuno Garoupa and Tom Ginsburg have argued conversely that there is little evidence of the capacity of judicial councils to promote independence.[10] Nevertheless, in line with assertions in the literature, they affirm that judicial councils provide a space for the diversification of judicial governance,[11] an aspect which intuitively has a bearing on the insulation of the judiciary from undue influences. Moreover, in view of their role in regulating the judicial career, it is implausible that they have no influence on judicial independence, when the appointment, promotion and discipline of judges is at the heart of judicial independence. Perhaps the objection of Garoupa and Ginsburg is more in relation to the simplistic view that judicial councils necessarily enhance judicial independence without looking into the specific determinants and conditions under which judicial councils can effectively constitute a 'best practice' to support judicial independence. It is imperative to highlight therefore that one important determinant is institutional design and, in that respect, two specific elements are worthy of further examination. These are, composition and competence.

The composition of judicial councils can influence judicial independence and the considerable variety of approaches adopted by states in respect of composition might be suggestive of that potential. Some judicial councils are composed of judges in the majority while others have a more plural composition including professionals from outside the legal or judicial corps. In many civil law-oriented countries, the institution is headed by a member of the executive and in particular, the president of the republic. It should be noted that there is no consensus on the specific composition of judicial councils, for instance on the question of whether they should be composed of judges in the majority[12] or whether some other form of plurality would be more beneficial.[13] Yet, it is generally agreed that the presence of political

---

[8] Council of Europe recommendation on judicial independence Recommendation CM/Rec(2010)12 of the Committee of Ministers to member states on judges: independence, efficiency and responsibilities *(Adopted by the Committee of Ministers on 17 November 2010* para 26. https://search.coe.int/cm/Pages/result_details.aspx?ObjectId=09000016805afb78.

[9] Garoupa et al. estimate that over 60% of countries have established judicial councils. Garoupa and Ginsburg (2009a), p. 105.

[10] Garoupa and Ginsburg (2009a), p. 130.

[11] Garoupa and Ginsburg (2009a), p. 131.

[12] There is however considerable support for this approach. See Dublin Declaration on Standards for the Recruitment and Appointment of Members of the Judiciary; IBA Minimum Standards. See also Garoupa and Ginsburg (2009a), p. 120.

[13] Bingham Centre for the Rule of Law, *The Appointment of Judges by Independent Commissions in the Commonwealth* (Bingham Centre for the Rule of Law) 33–34 Available at https://binghamcentre.biicl.org/projects/theappointment-of-judges-by-independent-commissions-in-the-commonwealth.

representatives like the executive or the legislature is inherently inimical to the very notion of independence. These concerns are intensified where the judicial council is headed by the executive. As the UN Special Rapporteur on the Independence of Judges and Lawyers noted, these institutions are required to act in an objective, fair and independent manner and this would be undermined where the composition significantly reflects political representatives.[14] In which case, the purportedly independent institutions 'might become merely formal or legal rubber-stamping organs behind which the government exerts its influence indirectly'.[15]

With regard to competence, the potential for judicial councils to safeguard judicial independence may be influenced by the specific contours of their substantive powers. As noted earlier, they are responsible (in varying degrees) for appointments, promotions and the discipline of judges. These roles are sometimes given jurisdictional contexts to reflect specific needs or political or judicial traditions. Some countries limit their functions to nomination of candidates for appointments or promotions while the ultimate decision is taken by another institution. In terms of discipline, some judicial councils act as ad hoc tribunals that undertake hearings of disciplinary complaints and either make the decision to discipline a judge or make recommendations to the executive or legislature. Whatever approach is adopted, one of the main issues is to ensure that the judicial council is not simply given a titular function. The specific institutional design should seek to ensure that their role is decisive. For instance, where they make recommendations on appointments or promotions or discipline, the implementing authority such as the executive or legislature should be bound by that recommendation. Alternatively, the implementing body should be subjected to an independent process of review, should they wish to disregard the recommendation of the judicial council. These safeguards are intended to ensure that the judicial council is not simply a window dressing institution with no authority to insulate the judicial career from improper political interference.

By and large, the institutional design of a judicial council is relevant to safeguarding judicial independence. In addition, the political context in which this operates must be considered when assessing the extent to which the judicial councils can effectively safeguard the independence of the judiciary. As suggested by Garoupa and Ginsburg, there is a complex relationship between institutional design and political incentives of the various actors at the time of adoption.[16] In view of the importance of institutional design in the realm of judicial independence, it is imperative that the design continues to safeguard judicial independence amidst political or social developments in the society. Institutional design can remain stable for long periods which may or may not reflect changing societal dynamics and judiciaries

[14] United Nations Special Rapporteur. Report on the independence of judges and lawyers, Leandro Despouy (2009). UN Doc A/HRC/11/41 (2009), para 28.

[15] United Nations Special Rapporteur. Report on the independence of judges and lawyers, Leandro Despouy (2009). UN Doc A/HRC/11/41 para 28.

[16] Garoupa and Ginsburg (2009a), p. 129.

need to 'shift their location in the framework'.[17] Periodic reforms are necessary to correct perceived or emergent deficiencies in the system.[18]

The next section will examine the judicial council in Cameroon in the light of the preceding discussion on the relevance of judicial councils to judicial independence and the role of institutional design.

3 The Higher Judicial Council in Cameroon and Judicial Independence

To provide a better contextual appreciation of the judicial council in Cameroon, it is deemed necessary to delve briefly into its composition and competence before assessing the adequacy of its institutional design.

3.1 Composition and Competence

The HJC is composed of nine members, including the President of the Republic as chair of the institution and the Minister of Justice as deputy/vice chair.[19] The president may however appoint an alternative vice chairperson.[20] Other members include, three members of parliament (MP) nominated by the National Assembly, an independent personality nominated by the President of the Republic, and three senior judges (at least of the fourth grade) nominated by the Full Bench of the Supreme Court.[21] The President appoints all nominees and the length of their mandate is 5 years.[22]

The normative function of the HJC is to assist the President of the Republic in discharging his duty to secure the independence of the judiciary and in particular, his responsibility in the appointment, promotion and discipline of judges. In that respect, article 37(3) of the Constitution states that;

> The President of the Republic shall guarantee the independence of judicial power. He shall appoint members of the bench and of the legal department. He shall be assisted in this task by the Higher Judicial Council which shall give him its opinion on all nominations for the bench and on disciplinary action against judicial and legal officers.[23]

---

[17] Garoupa and Ginsburg (2009b), p. 61.

[18] Garoupa and Ginsburg (2009b), p. 61.

[19] Law No. 82/014 of 26 November 1982 on the Organisation and Functioning of the Higher Judicial Council (as amended by Law No. 89/16 of 28 July 1989), hereafter HJC Law, s. 1(1)(2).

[20] HJC Law, s. 1(2).

[21] HJC Law, s. 3.

[22] HJC Law, s. 4(1).

[23] That provision is restated in the HJC Law, s. 10.

The HJC gives it opinion on proposals relating to the appointment, transfer, promotion, secondment or discipline of judges.[24] In relation to promotions, it is responsible for drawing up a list of proposed nominees and in disciplinary matters, it acts as the disciplinary body.[25] In addition, the HJC advices the President in his exercise of the prerogative of mercy.[26] Although this latter role is important, it will not be discussed here given that this paper is focused on the HJC's role in promoting the independence of the judiciary.

3.2 A Flawed Institutional Design?

The institutional design of the HJC appears problematic in terms of its ability to meaningfully enhance the independence of the judiciary by insulating it from political influence. Its composition is evidently counterintuitive. It is inconceivable that the HJC can act independently to protect judges from political influences when the institution is effectively led by members of the executive. The government of Cameroon has previously attempted to counter aspersions of lack of independence of the judiciary, exacerbated by the composition of the HJC. In that regard, it stated that the HJC was part of a balancing mechanism to enhance judicial independence and that it was composed of distinguished personalities and characterised by a broad and balanced representation.[27] It argued that those were unique qualities that provided the necessary balance to pre-empt exclusive executive control of the judiciary.[28] A more substantive examination of the dynamics of that composition can conveniently rebut that view.

The President of the Republic chairs the HJC which is meant to advise him on the important issues relating to a judge's career. In the deliberations and decision-making process of the HJC, the President is present and acts as chair. This is compounded by the presence of the Minister of Justice. These two officials have a significant influence on the career of judges, the minister being head of the Ministry of Justice under which the judiciary is placed. He is the hierarchical superior of the judges, and so is the President in terms of his role as chief executive of the state and guarantor of the independence of the judiciary. Their presence inevitably acts as a constrain on the objectivity or assertiveness of the judicial members of the HJC. For similar reasons, the independent personality appointed by the President is unlikely

[24] HJC Law, s. 11(2).

[25] Constitution of Cameroon, art. 37(3); HJC Law, s. 12 and 13 respectively.

[26] HJC Law, s. 11(1).

[27] United Nations Human Rights Committee, 'Consideration of Reports Submitted by States Parties under Article 40 of the Covenant on Civil and Political Rights: Fourth Periodic Report of Cameroon' (19 - 20 July 2010) CCPR/C/CMR/Q/4/Add.1 para. 176-177.

[28] United Nations Human Rights Committee, 'Consideration of Reports Submitted by States Parties under Article 40 of the Covenant on Civil and Political Rights: Fourth Periodic Report of Cameroon' (19 - 20 July 2010) CCPR/C/CMR/Q/4/Add.1 para. 177.

to exhibit objectivity or assertiveness in expressing any opinion which deviates from that of the President or the Minister of Justice. With regard to the MPs, again, it is no secret that Parliament is significantly influenced by the President.[29] As such, MPs may be under similar constrains to act in consonance with the views of the President, chair of the HJC. This position is supported by the African Commission on Human and Peoples' Rights as gleaned from a view expressed in *Kevin Mgwanga Gunme et al v Cameroon*[30] in which the independence of the judiciary in Cameroon was called into question with respect to its compliance with article 26 of the African Charter on Human and Peoples' Rights. The Commission stated that the presence of the President as chair of the HJC and the Minister of Justice as vice chair, was 'manifest proof' of the lack of judicial independence in Cameroon.[31] It went further to emphasise that the presence of the non-judicial members of the HJC was 'not likely to provide the necessary "checks and balance" against the Chairperson, who happens to be the President of the Republic'.[32]

It may be argued further that the minority judicial representation is an issue with regard to the extent to which the judicial members of the HJC can effectively influence judicial independence. It has been asserted that, having a majority of judges in a judicial council is advisable. The Venice Commission affirms that, 'a basic rule appears to be that a large proportion of its membership should be made up of members of the judiciary and that a fair balance should be struck between members of the judiciary and other ex officio or elected members'.[33] Admittedly, it is not exactly clear that a majority judicial membership necessarily enhances the potential of the judicial council to significantly influence judicial independence. A conceivable weakness of such an institutional design may be the development of a 'corporatist management'[34] style which may be averse to judicial accountability. While the proportion of judicial membership remains debatable, the issue of the executive's control of the institution and the potential effect on the HJC's objectivity and assertiveness cannot be easily discounted. These concerns are not alleviated by the presence of MPs. The involvement of the legislature is not objectionable as a matter of principle. Even the Venice Commission notes that '[i]n a system guided by democratic principles, it seems reasonable that the Council of Justice should be linked to the representation of the will of the people, as expressed by Parliament.'[35] Nevertheless, it advises that the legislature can elect some of

---

[29] Mbaku (2014), pp. 383–386.

[30] *Kevin Mgwanga Gunme et al v Cameroon*, Communication No. 266/2003 ACHPR (05/2009), Ex.CL/529(XV) Annex 4.

[31] *Kevin Mgwanga Gunme et al v Cameroon*, Communication No. 266/2003 ACHPR (05/2009), Ex.CL/529(XV) Annex 4, para. 211.

[32] *Kevin Mgwanga Gunme et al v Cameroon*, Communication No. 266/2003 ACHPR (05/2009), Ex.CL/529(XV) Annex 4, p. 212.

[33] European Commission for Democracy through Law (Venice Commission), 'Opinion on Recent Amendments to the Law on Major Constitutional provisions of the Republic of Albania' CDL-INF (1998)009, para. 12.

[34] European Commission for Democracy through Law (Venice Commission), 'Judicial Appointments – Opinion No. 406/2006; CDL-AD(2007)028' Report adopted by the Venice Commission at its 70th Plenary Session (Venice, 16-17 March 2007)para 30. Available at https://rm.coe.int/0900001680700a62.

[35] European Commission for Democracy through Law (Venice Commission), 'Opinion on Recent Amendments to the Law on Major Constitutional provisions of the Republic of Albania' CDL-INF

the membership of the judicial council, but in order to insulate it from politics, those members should not be active members of parliament.

In relation to the HJC's competence, in particular, its role in assisting the President to guarantee the independence of the judiciary, it may be argued that the role is rather limited in two specific ways. First, the President *may*[36] consult the HJC in relation to any question or issues concerning the independence of the judiciary. The use of 'may' rather than the mandatory 'shall' indicates that the President is not obliged to consult the HJC. Second, the HJC only provides its opinion on the related matters rather than assume a decisive role. For instance, the law states that the HJC shall provide its opinion on all nominations to the bench and on disciplinary sanctions to be imposed on judicial officers.[37] Concerning promotions and appointments, identifying potential candidates for either event is the responsibility of the presidents of the relevant courts,[38] but for the senior judges in the Supreme Court and the Courts of Appeal, responsibility lies with the Minister of Justice acting on the advice of the Secretary General and directors at the Ministry of Justice.[39] The jurisdiction of the HJC is only invoked at the point of presentation of a list of candidates nominated for promotion. At that point, the HJC compiles a consolidated final list based on votes obtained by each proposed candidate voted by members of the HJC.[40] This list which forms the basis of the opinion or recommendation of the HJC is presented to the President of the Republic who ultimately makes the final decision on appointments and promotions.[41] Despite the apparently elaborate process, political considerations have been known to influence appointment decisions, in which case, the HJC's views will simply align with the wishes of the chair person.[42] In fact given the President is chair of the HJC, in such politically motivated appointments, his view will necessary supersede that of the HJC's membership.

The HJC plays a similarly restricted role in terms of discipline. Although it acts as a disciplinary body which conducts disciplinary hearings in alleged cases, its disciplinary dimension can only be invoked by the President after receipt of disciplinary files from the vice chair. Moreover, the HJC is limited to making recommendations to the President following any disciplinary hearing. Again, the President makes the ultimate decision whether or not a judge is disciplined and the decision is

(1998)009, para. 9.

36 Author's emphasis. HJC Law, s.10.

37 Constitution of Cameroon, 1996, article 37(3); HJC Law s. 10.

38 Decree No. 95/048 of 8 March 1995 on the Status of the Magistracy, hereafter SOM, articles 32(2), 34(1). Note however that for the High Courts and Courts of First Instance, the president of the Court of Appeal of the geographical region is primarily responsible although he/she acts on the advice of the presidents of the respective courts. See in that respect, SOM, art 34(1) (2).

39 SOM, article 31 (1)(a)-(f), (2)-(4).

40 SOM, article 42(3)(4).

41 SOM, article 6(1).

42 See below in relation to the appointment of the first ever Anglophone president of the Judicial Bench of the Supreme Court.

not subject to independent review.[43] There have been reported disciplinary outcomes where the President failed to adhere to the recommendations of the HJC to sanction or exculpate judges, without reasons advanced to explain his non-compliance with the recommendations.[44] In 2017, a senior judge of the Supreme Court noted to be a vociferous critic of President Biya's government was abruptly placed on retirement (allegedly against the HJC's recommendations).[45] The judge was initially arrested and placed in prolonged pre-trial detention on charges of terrorism, conspiracy against the security of the state, revolution, secession and insurrection,[46] following the outbreak of civil unrest in the English speaking regions of Cameroon. Due to the political nature of the events surrounding his arrest, and the fact that he was an overt critic of the government, the presidential decree abruptly placing him on retirement was widely perceived as an act of retaliation from the government. In view of its constrained competencies, the HJC was not in a position to protect the independence of the judge despite the suspicious circumstances surrounding his arrest and subsequent retirement.

To further demonstrate the impotence of the HJC, the President can act independently to sanction judges without a formal hearing, or convening of the disciplinary dimension of the HJC. In July 2020, a presidential decree was issued dismissing a judge (without pension rights) for allegedly abandoning his judicial duties.[47] Ironically, no session of the HJC had been convened to hear a disciplinary complaint against the judge and no opportunity offered to the judge to represent himself before a disciplinary panel.[48] This was in contravention of the disciplinary procedure under the applicable law by which the President, upon receipt of a disciplinary file from the Minister of Justice, constitutes a disciplinary panel to commence investigations, and a subsequent hearing to which a judge should be provided the opportunity to present a defence.[49] In fact, a session of the HJC was only convened in August 2020,[50] after the decree sanctioning the judge. Regrettably, the HJC appeared

---

[43] SOM, article 60(1); HJC Law, article 34.

[44] Enonchong (2012), p. 324 esp fn 72.

[45] Enonchong (2021), p. 126. See also Actu Cameroun 'Cameroun: Le président Paul Biya désavoue ses conseillers et envoie à la retraite Ayah Paul Abine, l'opposant et magistrat hors hiérarchie' (June 2017, Journal Actu Cameroun). <Available at https://actucameroun.com/2017/06/08/cameroun-le-president-paul-biya-desavoue-ses-conseillers-et-envoie-a-la-retraite-ayah-paul-abine-lopposant-et-magistrat-hors-hierarchie/>.

[46] *Ayah Paul Abine v The People.* SLR 10(2020) 118.

[47] Decret No.2020/398 du 27 Juillet 2020 Portant révocation d'un Magistrat, s. 1.

[48] Journal du Cameroun, 'Cameroon: Dismissed Anglophone Judge Fires Back at Biya' (28 July 2020 Journal du Cameroun). Available < https://www.journalducameroun.com/en/cameroon-dismissed-anglophone-judge-fires-back-at-biya/>.

[49] HJC Law, ss. 22(3) to 34.

[50] See Presidential Decision No. 001 CAB/PR of 08 July 2020 to Convene the Higher Judicial Council. Section 1 of the Decree states that the HJC is convened on 06 August 2020 at the presidency. See also, Francis, J. 'Le Conseil Supérieur de la Magistrature: réunion ce jour au palais de l'Unité' (Yaoundé, 10 August 2020, *Cameroun Tribune*). Available at https://www.cameroon-tribune.cm/article.html/34168/fr.html/conseil-superieur-de-la-magistrature-reunion-ce-jour-au-palais-de-lunite.

incapable of objecting to the irregularity of the process and by implication, remained silent in the face of political interference with the career of a judge. The law however makes provision for independent action by the President. Sections 23 and 24(1) of the HJC Law provide cumulatively that the President can issue by order, a warning or a reprimand. Nevertheless, the sanction in this case was neither a warning nor a reprimand and was not effected by an order. Instead, it was the most severe sanction (dismissal with forfeiture of pension rights), despite the failure to adhere to the appropriate disciplinary procedure.

Beyond the issue of composition and competence, the HJC is effectively controlled by the President. For instance, as chair he convenes the sessions of the HJC, draws the agenda for the sessions and the HJC meets at the presidency.[51] These organisational issues further restrict the HJC's capacity to act independently. As a practical illustration, the HJC held a session in June 2017 after over 2 years of inertia during which the judiciary witnessed a *de facto* freeze on appointments, promotions and transfers.[52] There were other issues of judicial governance which remained unattended. These include potentially over 100 disciplinary complaints relating to allegations of corruption, and impartiality of specific judges. These unattended issues caused disillusionment within the judiciary, as judges entitled to promotions became dissatisfied with the failure of the HJC to convene. It exacerbated public dissatisfaction with the absence of disciplinary sanctions against the impugned judges.[53] The inertia of the HJC was due to the fact that it could only meet at the instance of the President who had failed to convene a session without any consequences or mechanisms to trigger him to act.[54] Critics related the weaknesses in this system to wider issues of political governance concerning the dominant role of the President to whom other political institutions and processes were subordinate.[55] The inference to be drawn from the situation is that in the absence of presidential action, inertia becomes rife. In addition, the convening of the HJC session in 2017 was rather quite opportune, as it coincided with the abrupt retirement of the senior judge discussed earlier. Moreover, another issue which raised the suspect role of the HJC was the appointment of an Anglophone judge for the first time in Cameroon's judicial history, to head the Judicial Bench of the Supreme Court.[56] Although this

---

[51] HJC Law, s. 38(1)(2).

[52] Nsom, Y.K. 'Higher Judicial Council Sanctions Loom over 100 Magistrates' 02 September 2016, Cameroon Post). Available at https://cameroonpostline.com/higher-judicial-council-sanction-looms-over-100-magistrates/%E2%80%8B.

[53] Nsom, Y.K. 'Higher Judicial Council Sanctions Loom over 100 Magistrates' 02 September 2016, Cameroon Post). Available at https://cameroonpostline.com/higher-judicial-council-sanction-looms-over-100-magistrates/%E2%80%8B.

[54] The next session of the HJC was convened in August 2020.

[55] Nsom, Y.K. 'Higher Judicial Council Sanctions Loom over 100 Magistrates' 02 September 2016, Cameroon Post). Available at https://cameroonpostline.com/higher-judicial-council-sanction-looms-over-100-magistrates/%E2%80%8B.

[56] Décret No. 2017/279 du 07 Juin 2017 Portant nomination de Magistrats au Siege de la Cour Suprême.

intervention was welcomed, it came at the heels of demands by Anglophone lawyers and the general Anglophone population for more equitable representation in a bijural legal system which has historically marginalised the Anglophone populations. That appointment reflected the nature of political interference with the career of judges and the instrumental role of the HJC in facilitating such interference or in other instances, its inability to prevent it.

From the above analysis of the HJC's institutional design, two important implications could be drawn. First, the HJC does not seem to have been established as an institution intended to insulate the judiciary from political interference. In fact, the composition of the HJC suggests otherwise. Second, in terms of the scope of its mandate, it is designed to 'assist' the President, indicating that it only plays a supportive role to the President, rather than a decisive role in enhancing the independence of the judiciary. It is inconceivable that the HJC can play a significant role in enhancing judicial independence when the President acts as its chair, and the institution is supposed to advise him on any action on matters which would have been discussed with the same President in the HJC. Undoubtedly, it is not the sole factor responsible for promoting judicial independence in Cameroon. Yet, as a judicial council, the HJC should do more than play the role of a window dressing institution, assisting the President to assume definitive control of the judiciary.

At this point, it may be necessary to enquire into the reason(s) for the continued existence of the HJC with its flawed institutional design, despite its inertia and inability to effectively support or enhance the independence of the judiciary in Cameroon. The next section attempts to answer that question.

4 Accounting for the Persistence of the HJC

The issue of how an institution's history influences its evolution and contemporary state of being has preoccupied scholars from many disciplines within the social sciences. An influential dimension from which to study the historical evolution of institutions is historical institutionalism, and, from the perspective of path dependence which offers a useful theoretical framework for understanding institutional change overtime. Closely associated with path dependence is the concept of critical juncture which is used as an analytical tool to explain critical moments at which change can occur to initiate or break a cycle of dependence.[57] In the discussion that follows, a theoretical perspective of path dependence is presented as the framework for the subsequent explanation of the continued existence of the HJC in Cameroon. The aim is to demonstrate that the HJC's current configuration is compatible with the linked infrastructure of the political system.[58] It complements other subservient institutions that cumulatively sustain a political culture of executive ascendancy. As

[57] Thelen (1999), pp. 388–392; Collier and Collier (1991).

[58] For more on the general conceptual framework, see Pierson (2000), p. 254.

a result, during critical moments in the political life cycle of Cameroon when change can occur, the dependent approach is not altered to interrupt the benefits of maintaining the status quo.

4.1 A Theory of Path Dependency

Like many other concepts, path dependence has been subjected to diverse interpretation and meanings.[59] From a broad theoretical perspective, path dependence is used to highlight the influence of history on future outcomes.[60] In terms of institutional change, path dependence may explain how initial institutional preferences can become impossible to deviate from due to self-reproduction or self-reinforcing processes. As an institution reproduces itself, overtime it becomes stable (locked-in) and change becomes almost impossible.[61] The 'lock-in' position is what conditions the path of institutional evolution as it constrains the avenues for change leading to institutional inertia. The central idea underpinning path dependence is the self-reinforcing processes within an organisation which condition the dominant path of the organisation's evolution, causing other alternative paths to be less likely options to traverse.[62]

According to path dependency, institutions may persist over time but a critical juncture period may cause actors to select a specific institutional arrangement due to prevailing factors. However, after this period, other factors may lead to reproduction of the institution's patterns in a way that it becomes 'extremely difficult to transform'.[63] James Mahoney notes that a 'defining feature of path dependence is the idea that it is difficult for actors to reverse the effects of choices made during a critical juncture'.[64] The concept of critical juncture has been applied by scholars of regime change in the context of democratic transitions often to identify critical moments at which key political actors can effect change in the social or institutional structures to interrupt the cycle of dependence.[65] Giovanni Capoccia and Daniel Kelemen define critical juncture as 'relatively short periods of time during which there is substantially heightened probability that agents' choice will affect the outcome of interest'.[66] What happens during this period is uncertain as political actors are unsure of the outcome of their decisions even though they may aim for specific outcomes. Moreover, irrespective of the increased potential for change during this

---

[59] Rixen and Viola (2015), p. 302.

[60] Rixen and Viola (2015), p. 302.

[61] Thelen (1999), p. 385.

[62] Mahoney (2001), p. 114.

[63] Mahoney (2001), p. 114.

[64] Mahoney (2001), p. 114.

[65] Thelen (1999), pp. 388–392; Collier and Collier (1991).

[66] Capoccia and Kelemen (2007), p. 348.

period, there is no guarantee that change will necessarily occur. During a critical juncture, there is an expansion of plausible choices which could result in significant political change. This does not however imply that re-equilibration is impossible or improbable.[67] Nevertheless, faced with alternatives that can substantially influence positive development of an institution, actors would prefer to reinstate the status quo.[68] Reinstatement of the status quo prior to the critical juncture may be perceived as a missed opportunity.

Critical junctures may trigger or reinforce path dependent processes, for instance, by political actors choosing to maintain self-reinforcing mechanisms within institutions. Reproduction of institutions can be explained by endogenous increasing returns relating to the benefits that accrue to individuals in positions of power.[69] For instance, 'an institution may persist even when most rational individuals prefer to change it' but change will not occur if powerful individuals benefiting from the existing arrangements receive sufficient incentives from the status quo and have sufficient power to prevent any transformation.[70] This is partly due to the coordination effect which requires that the institutions within the system complement each other.[71] It follows that, from the nature of the laws and policies, actors within the system are intuitively aware of the contours of permissible action and the rewards and penalties associated with specific types of action.[72] They would seek to preserve the status quo through the self-reinforcing processes in order to pre-empt any possible penalties and to reap the rewards flowing from the system. Even where change may purportedly occur, this is rather incremental and tangential, unlikely to destabilise the equilibrium. Any change is more realistically aimed at, or results in reinforcing the established pathway.

4.2 *Path Dependence and the Influence of Political Culture on the HJC's Inertia*

4.2.1 Emergence of the HJC

Cameroon's initial experience with a judicial council can be traced back to the period of French colonialism in the French administered section of Cameroon.[73] As part of the administrative structure established by the French colonial administration between 1922 and 1958, the judicial system fell within the remit of the French

[67] Capoccia and Kelemen (2007), p. 352.

[68] Ibid.

[69] Mahoney (2001), p. 114.

[70] Mahoney (2001), p. 114. See also Bell (2013), pp. 794–795.

[71] Rixen and Viola (2015), pp. 306–307.

[72] Pierson (2004), p. 35.

[73] Portions of Cameroon were administered separately by Great Britain and France.

Ministry of Justice and Ministry of State in Charge of relations with Associate States.[74] At the level of the territories, the judicial system was regulated by the *Conseil Supérieur de la Magistrature* (the Higher Judicial Council—HJC), which was also responsible for the discipline and independence of judges.[75] When French Cameroon gained independence in 1960, it seemed inevitable that a judicial council would be established. The initial conditions of establishment of the current system of the HJC therefore seemed tied to the colonial legacy rather than any specific contingent factors. It was a pre-determined outcome as most former French colonies gaining independence at the time or subsequently, adopted institutions identical to those existing in France.[76]

4.2.2 Entrenchment and Continuity

Inevitably, the 1960 Constitution of the newly independent French Cameroon made provision for the HJC which was presided by the President of the Republic and vested with the responsibility to assist the President in his duty as guarantor of the independence of the judiciary.[77] That provision replicated in identical terms, article 64 of the French Constitution. In fact, the institutional designed of the HJC emulated that of the French *Conseil Supérieur de la Magistrature* (CSM) at the time, which placed the President at the helm of the institution as chair and the Minister of Justice as vice-chair.[78] The French approach to institutional design was predicated partly on the French traditional aversion to an independent judiciary which accounted for the constitutional subordination of the judiciary to the executive.[79] Enagnon Nonnou describes the historical relationship between the executive and the judiciary in France as motivated by the desire of the executive to ensure significant control of the judiciary in order to influence politically sensitive cases.[80] In that respect, asserting control over the method of appointing and promoting judges becomes an essential political issue.[81] Placing the CSM under the control of the executive ensured that the latter kept tight reigns on the judiciary. The approach was consistent with the French Fifth Republic's approach to a strong executive reinforced by the 1958 Constitution.[82] The circumstances of the independence of French Cameroon were dissimilar to the circumstances under which the French Constitution of 1958 was adopted. Yet, the ideological underpinnings of a strong executive and a

[74] Anyangwe (1997), pp. 102–103.

[75] Anyangwe (1997), pp. 102–103.

[76] See generally Nonnou (2018), p. 715.

[77] Constitution de La République du Cameroun 1960, article 41.

[78] Constitution of the Republic of France, article 65.

[79] Garoupa and Ginsburg (2009a), p. 108.

[80] Nonnou (2018), p. 718.

[81] Nonnou (2018), p. 718.

[82] Garoupa and Ginsburg (2009a), p. 108.

subordinate judiciary were transplanted to Cameroon through the 1960 Constitution which was modelled on the French Constitution and incorporated important aspects of the institutional design such as extensive executive control. The continuity of that model was validated by subsequent political developments.

In 1961, when part of the British administered section of Cameroon gained independence by reuniting with the Republic of Cameroon (the former French territory), a federal structure was adopted with a Constitution that preserved the HJC in its original configuration except with the slight modification to its name as the Federal HJC to reflect the federation.[83] There was yet another change to its name in 1972 when the federal form of the state was transformed to a unitary state. The new Constitution of 1972 dropped the federal dimension of the name which reverted to the HJC with the same institutional configuration.[84] The details relating to its organisation and functioning were to be determined by a legislative instrument. Subsequently, Ordinance No. 72/8 of 26 August 1972 was enacted and it consolidated the institutional design of the HJC. The 1972 Ordinance was repealed by the 1982 Law which currently regulates the HJC as described earlier.[85] In 1996, the Constitution of Cameroon was amended substantially, but it retained the provisions relating to the role of the President in guaranteeing judicial independence and the role of the HJC in 'assisting' the President.

At each of the stages described above, changes to the political or constitutional system consolidated the dominance of the executive, and in particular, the powers of the President. Thus, the political culture which developed post-colonialism was characterised by a strong executive President. Institutions such as the legislature and the judiciary remained subordinate to the executive. Constitutionally, the judiciary in particular was referred to as an 'authority' as opposed to a power unlike the executive and the legislature. This formulation was only altered under the current 1996 Constitution. One plausible explanation for this approach is that the need to maintain a strong executive president was motivated by the anxieties arising from the desire to preserve the political and territorial unity of Cameroon. In view of their disparate colonial history, the two parts of Cameroon (the British and French administered sections) had developed unique political, social, cultural, linguistic and judicial identities which naturally posed a threat to national unity. A strong president with unrestrained powers was essential to maintaining territorial and national unity. To achieve that objective, relevant institutions within the system were designed to be subordinate to the executive with the President having significant leverage over these institutions. The subordination of the judiciary to the executive was in line with the requirement to maintain a strong presidency and the institutional design of the HJC served well to achieve that purpose. The fact that it is granted the nominal

[83] Federal Constitution of Cameroon 1961, article 32.

[84] Unitary Constitution of Cameroon 1972, article 31.

[85] Law No. 82/014 of 26 November 1982 on the Organisation and Functioning of the Higher Judicial Council (as amended by Law No. 89/16 of 28 July 1989).

role of 'assisting' the President in guaranteeing judicial independence is evidence of the need to ensure that it maintains a system of executive dominance.[86]

It is necessary to highlight here that the Cameroonian political system developed within the framework of the political system introduced in France under the 1958 French Constitution (Fifth Republic) which established a very strong executive president.[87] The Fifth Republic was a Gaullist construction to deal with prevailing political problems, but it also impacted on the problem of an 'errant judiciary' that developed under France's Third and Fourth Republics.[88] That colonial legacy significantly influenced the political culture of Cameroon. However, like many legal transplants, the political system of Cameroon has developed contextually to consolidate and embed executive dominance in ways that are unique to Cameroon.

In light of the above context, it is implausible to envisage significant changes to the institutional design of the HJC as it must necessarily complement the matrix of subordinate institutions within a system geared at maintaining executive dominance. The relevant actors of change (the government and the legislature) are cognisant of the rewards under the status quo and the penalties that may accrue to them if meaningful reforms are introduced.[89] From a political perspective, the relevant actors are not motivated to introduce change and due to their monopoly on the processes of change, they choose not to break the path of dependence. This was evident in the 1990s democratic revival when substantial reforms were introduced to the political and constitutional landscape of Cameroon.

In discussing path dependence in relation to legal transplants, Jaakko Husa explains that it is important to distinguish between early path dependence and recent path dependence because some legal reforms are not dependent on the entire historical path of a legal institution.[90] Thus, while history matters, it is necessary to pinpoint what periods or what parts in particular matter. Applying Husa's view, the 1990s democratic revival in Cameroon may be considered a recent path dependent period representing a critical juncture at which potential reforms may have been possible. The 1990s were characterised by a sequence of reactive events during which Cameroon witnessed a purported democratic wind of change influenced by events in the continent and within the country. Many African states were undergoing democratic reforms from previously authoritarian governments. Cameroonians embraced that vision to demand for change domestically. Despite initial reluctance from the government, some democratic reforms were introduced, mainly legislative and institutional.[91]

---

[86] This view is also expressed by Nonnou in relation to the judicial councils in Francophone African countries. See Nonnou (2018), p. 726.

[87] Mbaku (2014), p. 30.

[88] Stone (1992), p. 24.

[89] Mbaku (2014), p. 358.

[90] Husa (2018), p. 141.

[91] These reforms have been discussed extensively elsewhere. See Enonchong (2021), esp the introductory section.

Consistent with Mahoney's inferences,[92] the resistance of the Cameroonian people to prevailing institutions is what triggered the sequence of events that led to staggered changes in some aspects of the constitutional and political system. The reforms in some areas were substantial, although overall, they maintained the status quo. For instance, a new Constitutional Council was established but subjected to executive influence. In relation to the judiciary in particular, its constitutional status was elevated from an 'authority' to a 'power' similar to the executive and legislative powers.[93] However, that did not result in significant transformation of the power asymmetry between the executive and the judiciary. The executive continued to dominate the judiciary, remaining the guarantor of its independence, assisted in that regard by the HJC. The HJC itself escaped reform of any kind. So, effectively, the coordination effect was maintained with the HJC retaining its original deficient institutional design. That position defies Mahoney's prediction that the final outcome of reactive sequences is the formation of new institutional patterns.[94] While there was a reactive sequence of events which may have prompted actual reform of the HJC, that did not occur, and within the wider political system, reforms introduced maintained the essential ethos of the system.

The above situation highlights the difficulties inherent in introducing reforms to an institution which is deeply embedded in a system characterised by institutional interdependencies.[95] The solution may be more complex and difficult to explain within the framework of institutional theory alone.

5 Overcoming Path Dependence in Reforming the HJC

A major limitation of the concept of critical juncture is its backward-looking nature. It does not predict when these junctures can occur, but looks to the past to determine when they occurred.[96] The problem is that, without the ability to predict in future when a critical juncture can occur, it becomes almost impossible to determine when opportunities for change can present themselves. Nevertheless, a backward look at critical junctures may provide insights for future determinants of change. What path dependency can shed light on is the conditions under which change may occur. In its strongest version, path dependency presupposes the impossibility of, or unlikelihood of change, except during rare instances characterised by radical ruptures, or reorientations resulting from external shocks.[97] Whereas the 'soft' version permits change and projects various forms of change to established institutional arrange-

[92] Mahoney (2001), p. 115.

[93] Enonchong (2021), pp. 1, 120–121.

[94] Mahoney (2001), p. 115.

[95] Husa (2018), p. 140; Prado et al. (2009), p. 366.

[96] Prado and Trebilcock (2009), pp. 355–357.

[97] Djelic and Quack (2007), p. 162.

ments, for instance a form of hybridization.[98] Both versions ultimately foresee change, although as asserted by John Bell, change is not automatic.[99] This section attempts to analyse path dependence from a broader perspective by considering the circumstances surrounding the critical junctures at which other jurisdictions have attempted to reform their judicial councils to enhance their ability to protect the independence of the judiciary. Two specific examples are selected here, France and Kenya for the invaluable comparative context that they provide in terms of history, contemporary factors and judicial and political traditions.

As already noted, the HJC in Cameroon has its ancestral roots in the historic configurations of the French HJC. Like many French speaking African countries, the judicial councils are modelled on the French Judicial council with the President and the Minister of Justice at the helm and typically 'assist' the president in guaranteeing the independence of the judiciary.[100] In many instances, despite reforms to the inadequate institutional configuration, the judicial councils have largely remained incapable of protecting judicial independence.[101] Nonnou asserts that, although the judicial councils in these countries have been vested with the noble task of 'protecting' judicial independence, they are hemmed in by the executive due to their institutional context. He notes further that the political culture of executive dominance in these countries further compounded by lack of a democratic culture, limits the extent to which the HJC can reflect an independent institution responsible for protecting the independence of the judiciary.[102] The position can be contrasted with that of France which may be characterised as a more open and democratic society. That is not to imply that change comes more easily to France.[103] Nevertheless, it may be argued that the openness of the society and a better democratic culture[104] enable conditions for a more functional lock-in situation where the efficiency of institutions in achieving outcomes may determine the extent to which change in a different direction can be accommodated. Drawing on a softer version of path dependency as an explanatory framework, it would seem that a series of incremental reforms prompted by endogenous and exogenous factors, paved the way for reforms to France's judicial council. Most recently, pursuant to the constitutional amendments

[98] In such a case, the institution is reformed to carry out a different task or to perform specific tasks in a different way without altering its overall ethos or the integrity of the entire system. Djelic and Quack (2007), p. 166.

[99] Bell (2013), p. 795.

[100] Nonnou (2018), pp. 719–720.

[101] Nonnou (2018), pp. 719–720.

[102] Nonnou (2018), p. 719.

[103] In fact, proposed reforms to France's judicial council in the 1990s initially faced opposition from the government which perceived it as dismantling of its hold over the judicial council. See generally, Bancaud (2006), p. 371.

[104] Events such as the phenomenon of cohabitation are said to have enhanced democratic participation and weakened the traditional dominance of the executive vis-à-vis the judiciary. Garoupa and Ginsburg (2009b), pp. 74–75.

under the *Loi Constitutionelle* 2008 -72,[105] one of the key reforms was the removal of the President and the Minister of Justice from the composition of the judicial council. According to Vincent Lamanda the First President of the *Cour de Cassation* in 2011, it was a measure to enhance the independence of the judiciary which had appeared compromised by the presence of these key executive officials.[106] The reforms were undertaken within the framework of broader reform of the political system aimed at modernising the institutions of the Fifth Republic.[107] They were driven by pressure from, and supported by multiple actors from within the judiciary itself, and political and administrative actors, with a goal towards inter alia, enhancing the efficiency and the quality of justice vis-à-vis the ordinary citizen.[108] In addition to these internal forces, there was pressure from external forces such as the European Union and the European Court of Human Rights for France's justice institutions to align with the standards imposed by treaty obligations.[109] It is worth noting that a series of constitutional and legislative reforms in the 1990s gave some teeth to the judicial council which since its establishment had been dominated by the executive and senior judges.[110] These incremental reforms were again driven by political events that empowered the judiciary, a previously subordinate institution, and by the influence of the European Convention on Human Rights, within the domestic system.[111]

In Kenya, a combination of endogenous shocks led to a tipping point at which wide scale institutional transformations were required, and these came in the form of a new constitution voted in a referendum in 2010. One of the key reforms was that of the judicial council, referred to as the Judicial Service Commission (JSC). Prior to 2010, the JSC was seen as an institution in the service of the executive, infused with presidential appointees and therefore perceived as an extension of the executive.[112] This unsatisfactory position contributed to the lack of independence of the judiciary due to the JSC's lack of independence and objective impartiality. The critical juncture at which the old system was overhauled was precipitated by events after the 2007 elections, with the violent political fallouts following the contentious presidential election. Over a thousand Kenyans lost their lives to post-electoral violence, while many others were injured and displaced. The extreme violence and loss of lives following the disputed elections led the government, and other political

105 Loi Constitutionnelle 2008-724 du 23 Juillet 2008 de Modernisation des Institutions de la Ve République.

106 Lamanda, V. 'Discours de M. Vincent Lamanda, Premier Président de la Cour de cassasion' (Audience Solennelle de la Cour de cassation, Paris, 7 January 2011). Available at https://www.courdecassation.fr/files/files/Evenements%20Cour/andience/Discours_Lamanda_audience_solenelle_7jv11(2).pdf.

107 Loi Constitutionnelle 2008-724. See also Neuman (2010), p. 19; Ficet (2011), p. 91.

108 Vigour, (2008), p. 30.

109 For instance, in the case of judicial review. See Neuman (2010), p. 42.

110 Garoupa and Ginsburg (2009b), pp. 73–75; Mbaku (2014), p. 365.

111 Garoupa and Ginsburg (2009b), pp. 73–75; Mbaku (2014), p. 365.

112 Thuki (2013), p. 69.

actors, to seek institutional reforms aimed at preventing a return to such turbulence. Due to the judiciary's critical role, it was earmarked as an institution in need of reform, in particular, the composition and the role of the judicial service commission.[113] The 2010 Constitution was the blueprint for the reforms to the judiciary and JSC and other institutions of the state.[114] Njeri Thuki asserts that, in considering the catalyst for change in the judicial appointment system, political will was an important factor, as well as the support of civil society organisations and the public.[115]

Kenya and France present two distinct political contexts; Kenya a developing democracy and France a more established democracy. Yet, the problem with the judiciary and judicial councils appear parallel. This underscores the struggle with the issue of judicial independence and the important role that judicial councils play in instituting and protecting it. From the brief analysis of the two countries, a number of contingent factors seemed to have been relevant for change to their judicial councils. In both countries, there was political pressure supported domestically by multiples actors, both political and non-governmental and the wider public. In the case of France, there was additional external pressure from supranational institutions. The latter may also have applied to Kenya, to a limited extent (through the role of the African Union). In both countries, the reforms to the judicial councils were not isolated; they were part of a broader package of reforms aimed at reforming aspects of the political system, and state institutions.

Despite the lessons from France and Kenya, they do not necessarily provide a coherent set of responses to the circumstances under which change can occur in a context like Cameroon. However, they provide two distinct indicative possibilities. The first possibility as demonstrated in the case of Kenya is when the inefficiency of the HJC reaches a tipping point, a point at which 'the benefits obtained from preserving a coordinated inefficient system are outweighed by the relative cost of living under such a system'.[116] The situation may prompt the relevant actors to introduce amendments to address the inefficiency, even if it implies departing from the dependent path. As in France and Kenya, this would require a broad scale of reforms affecting the entire political system, not just the HJC. In theory, this is feasible. However, in practice, it may be difficult to conceive given the depth of interdependency of state institutions in Cameroon and the bigger problem of lack of political will.[117] The second possibility as exhibited by France, is the influence of supranational institutions or norms. The caveat here is that success would depend on the extent to which supranational institutions or norms can collide with and disrupt the domestic system, to the point of prompting the relevant actors to introduce change. International norms have not often, in practice, assumed the supra-legislative status

[113] Thuki (2013), p. 60.

[114] Thuki (2013), pp. 57–59.

[115] Ibid pp. 60–62.

[116] For more on that phenomenon see Stewart Wood (2001), p. 368.

[117] Mathieu Tankeu attributes this to the strong 'presidential' system in Cameroon. Tankeu (2019), p. 207.

accorded by the Constitution of Cameroon.[118] The influence has been minimal and courts do not routinely apply it over legislative provisions.[119] Moreover, supranational institutions have an even lesser impressive record of influencing political action in Cameroon. For instance, the recommendation of the ACmHPR in *Gunme* which recognises the problematic composition of the HJC and for which the government was advised to reform the HJC to remove the Minister of Justice and the President. It is yet to be implemented, more than 10 years on.

6 Conclusion

The problem of devising effective measures to secure judicial independence is pervasive. In that connection, judicial councils have come to occupy a pivotal role as institutional best practice to support both the independence and the accountability of judges. Judicial councils have been established in different jurisdictions across the globe, with a diverse institutional configuration. The diversity demonstrates the struggle to establish an institutional mechanism which adequately fulfils the expected duties of judicial councils. As this chapter has demonstrated, Cameroon, like many other jurisdictions established a judicial council following its political independence from colonialism. It is now no secret that the HJC was established not as the guardian of judges but, more because transplantation was the logical option since one existed in France at the time of Cameroon's independence. The HJC's institutional configuration was ideal to fit within a political system hinged on preserving executive power. Whereas, marginal incremental changes have occurred within the wider political system, the judiciary and the HJC have remained under the shadow of the executive. Thus, the HJC continues to play the role of the President's assistant, rather than guardian of the judiciary.

The theory of path dependence has provided a plausible explanatory framework to account for the persistence of the HJC despite its inertia and inefficiency in protecting or enhancing judicial independence. The HJC is part of an institutional matrix which maintains a political system characterised by executive dominance. The belief system underlying that matrix is underpinned by the desire to preserve the benefits accruing to actors within that system and avoiding potential costs from any proposed change. The belief system significantly undermines or deters radical change to any institution within the matrix. As a result, the HJC is bedevilled by a historical continuity which does not assure its independence or that of the judiciary. Yet, as Mathieu Tankeu asserts, in the intervening period since 1960, the judicial council in France has undergone important reforms which paradoxically, Cameroon has remained indifferent to, despite the fact that the HJC was modelled on the

[118] Metou (2009), p. 135; Olinga (2005), p. 63.

[119] Enonchong (2019), pp. 106–109.

judicial council in France.[120] As this chapter has demonstrated, the circumstances under which change occurred in France and Kenya cannot be easily replicated in Cameroon and an enormous political will would be necessary for any radical change to be considered. While path dependence has been useful in explaining the persistence of the HJC, the analysis has also highlighted the logical limits of institutional theory in conceptualising change to the HJC in a political system like Cameroon where over time, institutions have become embedded in a broader matrix of interdependence. Perhaps what the analysis evokes is a sobering awareness that we return full circle to the conclusion that judicial independence and politics will always have a tenuous relationship, and the search for institutional mechanisms to protect judicial independence may inevitably involve political forces, whether the process adopts a historical path or not.

References

Actu Cameroun (2017) Cameroun: Le président Paul Biya désavoue ses conseillers et envoie à la retraite Ayah Paul Abine, l'opposant et magistrat hors hiérarchie. https://actucameroun.com/2017/06/08/cameroun-le-president-paul-biya-desavoue-ses-conseillers-et-envoie-a-la-retraite-ayah-paul-abine-lopposant-et-magistrat-hors-hierarchie/

Anyangwe C (1997) The Cameroonian judicial system. CEPER, Yaoundé

Bancaud A (2006) Normalisation d'une Innovation: Le Conseil Supérieur De La Magistrature Sous La Ive République. Droit et Société 63–64(2):371–391

Bell J (2013) Path dependence and legal development. Tulane Law Rev 87(4):787–810

Bingham Centre for the Rule of Law (2015) The Appointment of Judges by Independent Commissions in the Commonwealth. https://binghamcentre.biicl.org/projects/theappointment-of-judges-by-independent-commissions-in-the-commonwealth

Capoccia G, Kelemen D (2007) The study of critical junctures: theory, narratives and counterfactuals in historical institutionalism. World Polit 59(3):341–369

Collier RB, Collier D (1991) Shaping the political Arena. Princeton University Press, Princeton

Council of Europe (2010) Recommendation on Judicial Independence: Recommendation CM/Rec(2010)12 of the Committee of Ministers to member states on judges: independence, efficiency and responsibilities (Adopted by the Committee of Ministers). https://search.coe.int/cm/Pages/result_details.aspx?ObjectId=09000016805afb78

Djelic M, Quack S (2007) Overcoming path dependency: path generation in open systems. Theory Soc 36(2):161–186

Enonchong L (2012) Judicial independence and accountability in Cameroon: balancing a tenuous relationship. Afr J Legal Stud 5(3):313–337

Enonchong L (2019) International constitutional law and judicial review of domestic human rights legislation. Vienna J Int Const Law 13(2):87–118

Enonchong L (2021) The constitution and governance in Cameroon. Routledge, London

European Commission for Democracy Through Law - Venice Commission (1998) Opinion on Recent Amendments to the Law on Major Constitutional provisions of the Republic of Albania: CDL-INF (1998)009. https://www.venice.coe.int/webforms/documents/?pdf=CDL-INF(1998)009-e

[120] Tankeu (2019), p. 206.

European Commission for Democracy Through Law - Venice Commission (2007) Judicial Appointments – Opinion No. 406/2006; CDL-AD(2007)028. Report adopted by the Venice Commission at its 70th Plenary Session. https://rm.coe.int/0900001680700a62
Ficet J (2011) Trajectoires de Réforme de la Carte Judiciaire et Managérialisation de l'État. Analyse Comparée des Politiques de Territorialisation de la Justice en France et en Belgique. Revue Internationale de Politique Comparée 18(4):91–118
Francis J (2020) Le Conseil Supérieur de la Magistrature: réunion ce jour au palais de l'Unité. https://www.cameroon-tribune.cm/article.html/34168/fr.html/conseil-superieur-de-la-magistrature-reunion-ce-jour-au-palais-de-lunite
Garoupa N, Ginsburg T (2009a) Guarding the guardians: judicial councils and judicial independence. Am J Comp Law 57(1):103–134
Garoupa N, Ginsburg T (2009b) The comparative law and the economics of judicial councils. Berkeley J Int Law 27(1):53–83
Husa J (2018) Developing legal systems, legal transplants and path dependence: reflections on the rule of law. Chinese J Comp Law 6(2):129–150
Journal du Cameroun (2020) Cameroon: Dismissed Anglophone Judge Fires Back at Biya. https://www.journalducameroun.com/en/cameroon-dismissed-anglophone-judge-fires-back-at-biya/
Lamanda V (2022) Discours de M. Vincent Lamanda, Premier Président de la Cour de Cassassion. https://www.courdecassation.fr/files/files/Evenements%20Cour/andience/Discours_Lamanda_audience_solenelle_7jv11(2).pdf
Liwanga R (2012) Judicial independence in the democratic republic of congo: myth or reality? J Afr Law 56(2):194–214
Mahoney J (2001) Path dependent explanations of regime change: Central America in comparative perspective. Stud Comp Int Dev 36(1):111–141
Mbaku JM (2014) Judicial independence, constitutionalism and good governance in Cameroon. Eur J Comp Law Gov 1(4):357–391
Metou B (2009) Le Moyen de Droit International Devant les Juridictions Internes en Afrique: Quelques Exemples d'Afrique Noire Francophone. Revue Québécoise de Droit International 22(1):129–165
Neuman G (2010) Anti-Ashwander: constitutional litigation as a first resort in France. J Int Law Polit 43(1):15–42
Nonnou E (2018) Le Conseil Supérieur de la Magistrature et l'indépendance du Pouvoir Judiciaire dans les États Francophones d'Afrique. Les Cahiers de la Justice 4(4):715–733
North D (1990) Institutions, institutional change and economic performance. Cambridge University Press, Cambridge
Nsom YK (2016) Higher Judicial Council Sanctions Loom over 100 Magistrates 02 September 2016 - Cameroon Post. https://cameroonpostline.com/higher-judicial-council-sanction-looms-over-100magistrates/%E2%80%8B
Olinga AD (2005) Réflexions sur le Droit International, la Hiérarchie des Normes et L'office du Juge Camerounais. Juridis Periodique 63:9
Pierson P (2000) Increasing returns, path dependence, and the study of politics. Am Polit Sci Rev 94(2):251–267
Pierson P (2004) Politics in time. Princeton University Press, Princeton
Prado M, Trebilcock M (2009) Path dependence, development and the dynamics of institutional reform. Univ Toronto Law J 59(3):341–379
Rixen T, Viola LA (2015) Putting path dependence in its place: towards a taxonomy of institutional change. J Theor Polit 27(2):301–323
Šipulová K,Spáč S, Kosař D et al (2022) Judicial Self-Governance Index: Towards better understanding of the role of judges in governing the judiciary. Regulation and Governance. https://doi.org/10.1111/rego.12453
Stone A (1992) The birth of judicial politics in France: The constitutional council in comparative perspective. Oxford University Press, Oxford

Tankeu M (2019) L'Administraton de la Justice au Cameroun: Vers un Dépassement de la Colonialité. L'Harmattan, Paris
Thelen K (1999) Historical institutionalism in comparative politics. Ann Rev Polit Sci 2:369–404
Thuki N (2013) A comparative analysis of judicial councils in the reform of judicial appointments between Kenya and England. Ann Surv Int Comp Law 19(1):45–103
United Nations Human Rights Committee (2010) Consideration of Reports Submitted by States Parties under Article 40 of the Covenant on Civil and Political Rights: Fourth Periodic Report of Cameroon. CCPR/C/CMR/Q/4/Add.1
United Nations Special Rapporteur. Report on the Independence of Judges and Lawyers, Leandro Despouy (2009). UN Doc A/HRC/11/41 (2009)
Vigour C (2008) Politiques et magistrats face aux réformes de la justice en Belgique, France et Italie. Revue Française d'administration Publique 125(1):21–31
Wood S (2001) Labour market regimes under threat? Sources of continuity in Germany, Britain and Sweden. In: Pierson P (ed) The new politics of the welfare state. Oxford University Press, Oxford, pp 368–409

The Paradox of Madagascar's Legal Institutions: Rethinking Law's Rule

Olivia Lwabukuna

Abstract The western liberal institutional approach centers law and legal institutions within the state. Consequently, it is presumed that an ideal, institutional rule of law is essential for dispensing justice and facilitating effective governance. This chapter argues that this state-centred rule of law is ill-suited for attaining justice or effective governance within developing countries with weak state institutions, and strong non-state normative systems like Madagascar. It particularly demonstrates that Madagascar's perceived rule of law deficit is underpinned by the struggle to reconcile its state, and non-state institutions following recurring low and high intensity crises. This presumably stems from the western-centric conceptualisation and practice of rule of law, notably, its failure to acknowledge and embrace the reality, and role of non-state institutions and norms in Madagascar's legal and governance structures.

1 Introduction

The western liberal institutional approach centers law and legal institutions within the state. Consequently, it is presumed that an ideal, institutional rule of law is essential for dispensing justice and facilitating effective governance (Chan 2020). This chapter argues that this state-centred rule of law is ill-suited for attaining justice or effective governance within developing countries with weak state institutions and strong non-state normative systems like Madagascar. It particularly demonstrates that Madagascar's perceived rule of law deficit is underpinned by the

O. Lwabukuna (✉)
Institute of Commonwealth Studies, School of Advanced Study, University of London, London, UK

Free State Center for Human Rights, Faculty of Law, University of the Free State, Bloemfontein, South Africa
e-mail: olivia.lwabukuna@sas.ac.uk

N. Reayat, H. O. Yusuf (eds.), *Constitutionalism in Africa and Beyond*, Ius Gentium: Comparative Perspectives on Law and Justice 127,
https://doi.org/10.1007/978-3-032-01180-0_6

struggle to reconcile its state and non-state institutions following recurring low and high intensity crises (Lwabukuna 2022). This presumably stems from the western-centric conceptualisation and practice of rule of law, notably, its failure to acknowledge and embrace the reality and role of non-state institutions and norms in Madagascar's legal and governance structures.

The chapter's argument is informed by monarchical and colonial remnants implicit in Madagascar's crises. This includes the role of *Merina* cultural influence, power and privilege, as reflected in the origins of the *Fihavanana* norm—central to this chapter.[1] It also includes institutional failures and political mistakes, originating in the French dominated independence government of Madagascar. These protracted governance weaknesses are what catalysed social protests and a mutinous military intervention that led to the 2009 political crisis, precipitating an extended international intervention (Marcus 2016, pp. 10–11; Ratsimbaharison 2017, p. 56).[2] The chapter's argument is further informed by limitations noted within imported governance and legal frames influenced by intervention: It traces Malagasy crises to a difficult and externally managed state-building project after independence, a contested and coerced transition to democracy after prolonged economic crises, and failure to consolidate democratic processes and structures thereafter. Importantly, the said processes and structures seem to have been underpinned by neoliberal transplanted models of legality and governance prescribed by international development programs, and were therefore often uncontextualized and ineffective in Madagascar (Rittich 2016, p. 3; Ratsimbaharison 2016). The chapter illustrates that Madagascar's institutional crises reflect fractures underlying the formation of most African states and therefore raises fundamental questions around the viability of the post-colonial state and its transplanted legal institutions as a tool for development (Ouédraogo 2014, p. 1).

The aim of this chapter is twofold: First, it argues that rule of law building has prospects of success if there is less emphasis on orthodox rule of law—depicted by the prioritisation of state—based institutional and procedural systems, bent on facilitating economic outcomes, and more emphasis on substantive rule of law which is relevant to positive human flourishing (Sen 2000). However, taking a substantive approach is inadequate for transcending limitations of western-centric rule of law. The chapter illustrates this by highlighting the limits of building the rule of law in plural, post crisis/conflict states with weak state institutions, without prioritising approaches to governance or justice that can comprehend, embrace and, or navigate the influence of social norms (Tamanaha 2004; 2008). Specifically, it analyses the concept of *Fihavanana* and its implications for justice and governance by

[1] *Merina* People are a Malagasy ethnic group hailing from the central highlands of Madagascar; *Fihavanana* is a Malagasy social norm underpinning kin-based social relations, of late it has been deployed to reinforce national solidarity.

[2] The crisis evolved around president Marc Ravalomanana being challenged by a young and upcoming Mayor of Antananarivo, Andry Rajoelina. After weeks of violent protests, Ravalomanana was ousted in a constitutional coup, justified by the High Constitutional Court of Madagascar, in support of Rajoelina.

illustrating how the relationship between arms of government (judiciary and executive) is traversed through it, and the consequence of this for perceptions of judicial independence and the fair dispensation of justice.

The chapter then further argues for embracing and co-opting contextualised notions of rule of law that embrace the Malagasy worldview and value of *Fihavanana*, without orientalising it (Said 1978). Consequently, it recommends the re-appropriation, de-politicisation and rejuvenation of *Fihavanana*, deploying its flexibility, authority and legitimacy to support building a culture of justice and accountability in governance. This it is argued, would transform its current co-optation by local elites as a tool for traversing state institutions and pacifying communities, which negatively impacts trust in state institutions, including the justice system. These arguments are premised on the reality of a Malagasy state with a history of centralised monarchical foundations, non-state institutions and normative frames which remain alive and strong, while it struggles with weak state institutions—including a repressed political space and an ill financed and ill staffed legal system (Tamanaha 2011a, p. 211).

This chapter is arranged as follows: after the introductory section, section two engages with conceptual shortcomings of framing the rule of law as a development tool and outcome in pluralised post-crisis countries. Section three introduces the pluralistic prevalence of *Fihavanana*. The complicated nature of legal institutional set-up in Madagascar and its consequences for rule of law follows in section four. In winding up, the paper reiterates the need for a heterodox but contextual rule of law, which, while supporting institutional rebuilding in fragile Madagascar, accounts for fluid and plural realities and prioritises just outcomes for Malagasy people.

2 Rule of Law in Non-Western Contexts

This section analyses the rule of law in order to understand its theoretical essence. In the context of development, this entails the rise, diffusion, transformation and disintegration of ideas, concepts and paradigms on how law can bring about social change. (Rittich 2016). Unfortunately, this rule of law as a theoretical, disciplinary and practice area, is essentially saddled with legal instrumentalism and centralism, where western state law is understood and mis-used as a means for developmental ends in non-western contexts.

2.1 Development

Within this framing, law is at minimal considered a tool for social control (providing order and security). Furthermore, the law in rule of law constitutes formal legality which limits state power-constituting accountability, predictability, and uniformity. This is a step, from the minimalist law for social order, and can include aspects of judicial independence, fair public hearings and judicial oversight. It is still largely procedural, and leaves out substantive issues such as justice, rights, social welfare or equality (Twining 2009). Rule of law can also be conceptualised as a vehicle for free markets, requiring minimal state intervention, favourable rules for investors, protecting property rights, enforcement of contracts and the facilitation of economic activity. Equally, chastened neo-liberalism has reflected a rule of law that promotes economic activity while endorsing some human rights, good governance and democracy—balancing wealth creation and some distributive justice. For purposes of this discussion a substantive rule of law simply refers to 'just law' or 'the rightness of law' in accordance with a pre-existing higher standard (such as human rights), including, but in addition to promulgated legal rules, while the formal or institutional rule of law is only in accordance with promulgated legal rules (Tamanaha 2005, p. 132; Twining 2009).

Formal rule of law iterations are narrow or instrumentalist ways of deploying the rule of law in development—which emphasise conversations about law by lawyers, and focus on pragmatist technical approaches to law building, leaving out local conditions, histories, culture and participation, and forgetting that law is not a neutral tool (Twining 2009). For instance, law can be, and has been deployed to gain, define, and perpetuate the galvanisation of power, advantaging some over others as will be illustrated in Madagascar (Bedford 2020, p. 234). Therefore, analysing the rule of law within a pluralist developing country context, calls for rethinking the idea of law, transcending universalised western approaches, in order to question whether law and legal institutions are the same in all societies, and whether the transplanting, settling and perhaps diffusion of legal concepts and institutions is possible or necessary for purposes of bringing about social change, or redressing a social ordering 'vacuum' that might exist in non-western societies (Tamanaha 2005, p. 131; Twining 2009; Harding 2019).

Notably, the contemporary western approach to rule of law for development has been mainly influenced by legal assistance programmes of international development organisations, but not necessarily local needs or realities of developing countries (Faundez 2011, p. 19). In fact, questions of state law and governance are considered central to development policy. Law is therefore increasingly instrumentally deployed to catalyse social and economic change in developing countries, with legal and judicial reform being conflated with development itself (Faundez 2010, Trubek 2006). Consequently, a 'well governed' or 'legalese' state is considered to have rule of law, which is an essential marker of development (Rittich 2016, p. 821; Sen 2000). However, as the the Malagasy legal institutional set up will illustrate, the insistence on legal and judical reform in the process of institutional building for development, only emphasises an uncontextualised transplanted formulaic approach entailing:

> drafting legal codes; training legal officials (police, prosecutors, and judges); solidifying law schools and the legal profession; and enhancing legal access for citizens. These legal reforms have not taken hold. Corruption and dysfunction continues to plague legal institutions, many transplanted codes lie unused, and substantial proportions of the populace are not served by the legal system (Tamanaha 2011a, p. 213).

In Madagascar, these formulaic approaches have maliciously failed to translate into legal development or economic and social development because they target state legal institutions in isolation from the society within which they are to operate (Siems 2018). They orthodoxly emphasise Diceyan conceptions on how law should limit the power of the state at the instance of the public, without comprehending the Malagasy public, or invoking its participation in the construction of such legalities or legal development. These approaches bypass key Malagasy social norms including *Fihavanana* which underlies daily social interaction (Humphreys 2010, p. xv). Such prescriptive emphasis on formal legality, certainty, equality and uniformity, rooted in western idealism and formalities, lacks concrete 'rule of law in action' interpretations—beyond its institutional emphasis, built within constitutional and administrative law in western societies (Jowell 2019, p. 9; Fombad 2018, p. 216; Okoye 2004). Consequently, failure to comprehend Malagasy society portrays a rule of law deficit because the transplanted legal institutions seem dysfunctional and have failed to serve a substantial portion of the Malagasy public.

For instance, the conception of constitutional supremacy and separation of powers does not account for Malagasy contexts, where *Fihavanana* informally underpins institutional governance as a non-legal pro-social norm that is key for shaping legal phenomena and culture. Despite being a social force that influences law and governance in Malagasy society, the western-centric view of the resulting legality is that it is outmoded in modernity, is defective and reflects institutional corruption which must be cured (Humphreys 2010, pp. xv, xvi, xvii; Mutua 2016, pp. 163–4; Adelman & Paliwala, 2021, p. 5; Tamanaha 2011a, b). Often, state proscription, regulation or disregard of such legal culture is the solution, however, this becomes difficult where the state is itself institutionally weak. Notably, ineffective regulation of the local legal culture can lead to stunting its diversity, destroying useful positive values embedded within its flexibility, or at worst, exposing it to elite capture which is what has transpired in Madagascar (Fung, 2022). Accordingly, *Fihavanana* is currently being deployed by Malagasy elites to navigate legislative, executive and judicial power. This not only erroneously confirms a deficit in rule of law, but also impacts how the local legal culture is viewed, denying it any external legitimacy.

2.2 Pluralism

The argument against the above ineffective legal centralism emphasises that, 'the legal pluralist perspective on the rule of law must seek to decenter the material infrastructure of the state, its institutions and processes as based on constitutional and administrative law' (Zumbasen 2017, p. 7). Such a pluralist approach to the rule of law is expected to expose a complex, constantly shifting and evolving assemblage of actors, norms and processes, including, and beyond the state. It therefore, counteracts focusing exclusively on building state legal systems alone, or in isolation from co-existing non-state systems, under the assumption that law is consolidated only within the state in non-western societies (Tamanaha 2011a, b; Zumbasen 2017).

Key to this argument are normative and legal pluralism which are integral social facts and features of most non-western contexts, including Madagascar (Merry 1988). Normative pluralism has been described as the 'coexistence in the same time—space context of multiple systems of norms or rules or of institutionalized normative orders' (Twining 2010, p. 476). These might be social norms, or otherwise. Social norms can be legal or non-legal, but they are either broadly referred to as norms that govern social relations, or specifically as norms of a given society, community, or group with a normative character geared towards social ordering. Legal pluralism tends to describe social norms with a legal character, co-existing with official law—or 'the coexistence of two or more autonomous or semi-autonomous legal orders in the same time–space context' (Merry 1988). Legal pluralism has therefore been considered a sub-specie of normative pluralism. Consequently, *Fihavanana* is a non-legal social norm of Malagasy society that underpins social ordering (Twining 2010, pp. 481, 489).

A discussion on rule of law naturally evokes mixed reactions, but when pluralism is involved, the complexity is heightened. While multiple normative assertions in relation to rule of law do co-exist uncomfortably, clarity on one particular meaning has remained elusive. However, there is no contestation about the contribution of the concept to the foundations and aspirations of a modern legal system. The term conjures community, and insists on authority whilst emphasising rule-boundedness as well as the promise of enforceability. Nevertheless, it lacks unanimity on its stakeholders and constituents—those who root its legitimacy and are affected by it. This is a gap that can be exploited for purposes of discussing the rule of law in a country like Madagascar with plural non-state systems and fragile state institutions (Zumbasen 2017, pp. 3, 4).

In addressing the rule of law 'gap', it is important to clarify the parameters of engagement, and highlight key factors to consider when engaging with the rule of law and its place in legal development within developing pluralist states. In clarifying this, we can be led by these factors: Whose rule of law are we concerned with? This calls for us to consider the constituents, stakeholders and users who matter in how such rule of law is conceptualised, because they are its source of legitimacy and are affected by, and subjected to it. In developing, pluralist states where the constituents do not necessarily play a part in conceptualisation of state law (due to institutional democratic deficit or ideological alienation), they do not identify with it. This is because it is transplanted into social, economic and political contexts that differ from where it originates, making the establishment of a western institutionalised rule of law culture difficult (Tamanaha 2011a, b). This could be related to values that are enshrined in the rule of law's concrete instantiation in a particular place and time. It seems that the values underpinning western law and the society within which the ideal rule of law emanates, differ from those underpinning non-western law found in non-western societies, where it is transplanted to. This also means that legal and institutional transplants within rule of law reform kits, do not land in a vacuum, but compete with co-exiting normative systems and legal cultures. How this is acknowledged, reconciled and negotiated is imperative for the success of rule of law building programs (Tamanaha 2011a).

Secondly, procedurally, it is important to think about which processes of legitimation and execution are required or presupposed for building the rule of law. How institutions of governance and power and norms underpinning these operate, or interact, or are legitimated would look different depending on society. Additionally, the actors who are considered central or peripheral to the optimal operation of the rule of law are also completely different. While educated elites, the state and formal institutions play a central part in western law that forms a large part of transplanted non-western state legal systems, it is communities, personalised informal institutions and social norms such as *Fihavanana* that play this central role within non-state systems which interact with, or underpin state legal systems, yet they are considered peripheral in the optimal operationalisation of the transplanted rule of law. This is mainly due to them being dispersed or decentralised, communal, flexible, and strongly dependent on social relations and embeddedness (Garth 2002, p. 390). These factors have proved problematic for rule of law-building in countries with weak state and strong non-state institutions like Madagascar.

Thirdly, and notably, rule of law stakeholders, values and legitimation processes underpinning state-based legal development, are conceptualised around benchmarks for bottom-line norms for optimal rule of law (framed in terms of institutional rule of law). Here, legality, certainty, equality and uniformity, plus perhaps political human rights (to justify neoliberal development), are the basic minimum. Within this predominantly procedural rule of law, questions of substantive justice, might not arise, but legal systems must be able to limit state power. This benchmark is important for critiquing how basic rule of law has been erroneously conceptualised for developing countries, with weak state and strong non-state power and institutions. For instance, how would the formal rule of law be effective in limiting state power without considering the non-state institutional realm of power that permeates state power? In Madagascar, failure to comprehend *Fihavanana* which is a social norm influencing social and governance interactions, has had an impact on the effectiveness of rule of law systems, especially its benchmark on formally limiting state power. This and other formal elements of rule of law reflect how the ideal rule of law is out of reach within developing countries with amorphous non-state realms. Clearly, a different approach is necessary, perhaps the promotion of substantive and contextualised social justice can be the basic benchmark for rule of law in plural societies with diverse ways of dealing with state and non-state power. Perhaps, a consideration of rule of law in terms of a spectrum of hierarchies of norms might redress issues raised. This must be accompanied with a reflection on whether the rule of law itself allows for an identification of values for determining and regulating that hierarchy, and whether that is at all necessary (Zumbasen 2017, p. 2)? If these factors are affirmed, this would facilitate the existence of some form of rule of law from below, which is inclusive and substantive, as will be discussed later.

There is obvious need for embracing local norms in rule of law building, but often there is limited reliance on, or interaction with local laws or norms and procedures (Humphreys 2010: xv, xvi, xvii; Zumbasen 2017, p. 3). While acknowledgement of local norms in rule of law programming has been reflected in international development, emphasis has been on modernising and co-opting these systems as opposed to learning from them (Humphreys 2010, p. xvii; Carothers 2006, pp. 26–28). More importantly, this 'orientalist' turn to culture in law and development has been superficial at best, and incomplete at worst. Indeed, acknowledgement that cultural attitudes are imperative for the sustainability of rule of law is good, but inadequate since legal culture is not the sum of legal institution-building, even though the two are mutually co-constitutive. Culture happens to be complex, is difficult to mould, changes incrementally, and is influenced by power dynamics within societies, history, tradition, political and economic systems and institutional alignments as illustrated in Madagascar (Tamanaha 2011a, p. 214; Cohen 2009, p. 514; Brooks 2003, p. 2285). It is therefore important to understand culture and work with it, but transforming it in attempts to modernise it for purposes of legal reform is tricky, misplaced and imperialistic. The next section looks at *Fihavanana*, its cultural relevance in Madagascar and the role it plays in social and governance institutions. This section anticipates limitations of operationalising the rule of law in Madagascar without taking *Fihavanana* into account.

3 *Fihavanana*: Straddling State and Non-State Institutions

Malagasy society is founded on values of solidarity and social harmony. These values may be referred to differently in various parts of the country and even throughout Africa.[3] *Fihavanana* which emanates from pre-colonial Malagasy social systems, reflects these values, and is commonly considered a value of interpersonal relationships. As a kinship norm, it encompasses *Havana* which implies parenthood, affinity and lineage—factors underpinning relationality (Gannon 2014). Basically, Malagasy social relations are rooted in a mode of parenthood where all co-residents are enjoined through scales of relational parenthood. This is reflected in family or religious rites, and social, economic and political relations. Organised at different levels of societal concentric circles, *Fihavanana* first links family members, then the neighbourhood, then territorial communities, then the ethnic group, and eventually by extension, at the national level, *Fihavanana Gasy*, refers to the union of Malagasy people (Razanadrakoto 2020).

Fihavanana is therefore a cultural reference for peaceful social co-existence. Thus, deploying it in rule of law building would emphasise Malagasy human—centric legal development through the recognition and promotion of local social justice ideals, which are incidentally embedded within it. For instance, this could entail the promotion of fundamental rights mapped into *Fihavanana's* normative values of

[3] *Filangoa* among the Bara of Southern Madagascar; see *Utu* or *Ubuntu* which emphasises the importance of community to an individual in East and Southern Africa respectively.

fairness, common sense and social participation, which can abridge the rule of law 'gap'.

Fihavanana already influences interaction and governance in Madagascar, straddling state and non-state domains, while drawing from social and political capital built off systems deeply embedded in past Malagasy kingdom(s). Presumed to be a regional concept with origins in the highlands of central Madagascar, within the dominant Merina, *Fihavanana* has influenced institutional development over the years by regulating national moral identity and development programs (Bonar 1997; Scheidecker 2016, pp. 130–131, 143). Having co-evolved with the Malagasy state, it has been redeployed in post-colonial Madagascar to recover Malagasy values amidst colonization and modernity—considered a threat to authentic Malagasy culture (Kneitz 2022). For instance, a national construction of *Fihavanana* is reflected in the Preamble to the Malagasy Constitution (2010). This state—constructed *Fihavanana* within national discourse, is counterbalanced by a living *Fihavanana* within everyday interaction at local and sub-state level. While the former has been co-opted by political elites to serve their interests, facilitating the capture of state institutions, the latter's cultural relevance has been diluted by economic and social changes over the years (Spath 2016, pp. 106–107). These changes, including recurring state instability and protracted economic crises, have impacted the communal social fabric, where personal needs underpin new individuality, creating opportunities to corrupt or disregard *Fihavanana*.

Accordingly, Malagasy informal and formal institutions operate and are mediated by *Fihavanana* which guides daily interaction, forming both structural (social networks) and attitudinal (principles of trust) social capital (Spath 2016). *Fihavanana* determines the scope and influence of social networks that people belong to within Madagascar. It is also responsible for determining the levels and boundaries of trust between them. This determined *Fihavanana* and its developed levels of trust is what builds the necessary bonds for governance. *Fihavanana* determines who is an insider and who is an outsider, within politics, government, social relations, ethnic groupings and even in business. This determination whilst good and indigenous, is full of fluidity, with possibilities swinging based on adjustment in levels of trust, creating opportunities for positive or negative co-option (Adelman and Paliwala 2020, pp. 3, 4). This explains the paradox of institutions in Madagascar, they are organised around and managed through social relations, social networks and social definitions that are determined and adjusted through community norms or rules (*Dina*) or kinship norms (*Fihavanana*) (Marcus 2016, p. 24; Spath 2016; Scheidecker 2016).

Trust in institutions and organizations is usually first and foremost, built along clan and kinship lines, even though ethnic or "tribal" identities were superficial French constructions and should have less influence in contemporary Madagascar. Nonetheless, where pre-colonial kingdoms flourished (dominant ones being: Sakalava, Betsimisaraka and Merina), these identities are stronger and have persisted. The spread of the Merina kingdom's controversial caste identities as part of its expansion in the nineteenth century is a good example (Randrianja and Ellis 2009, pp. 99–106; 112–118; 124–125). Consequently, in Imerina, classifications of

Andriana (nobles), *Hova* (free commoners) and *Andevo* (descendants of slaves) might not reflect the economic distinctions they once did, but they do figure prominently in social life. Such classifications do influence the formation and distribution of social capital, including how *Fihavanana* is traversed and who wields power in doing so. This eventually influences how legal and governance mechanisms are co-opted by Malagasy nobility descendants and political elites, projecting a rule of law deficit (Randrianja and Ellis 2009, p. 4; Jennings 2017, p. 11).[4]

The implication of this is that in practice, formal Malagasy institutions are not what rule of law formulas presume them to be (Tamanaha 2011a, p. 213). In fact, since the rise of Madagascar's third republic after 1992, high technocracy has met personalisation of power and kin-based social capital to create malleable institutions. Tamanaha has made convincing points on the relationship between culture and elite power dynamics that explain how the Malagasy moral value of *Fihavanana* has been co-opted by opportunistic elites for their own benefit. (Tamanaha 2011a, p. 214; Spath 2016, p. 108). Consequently, Malagasy institutions—the legislature, the executive, the judiciary, civil society, the church, military, police and political parties are devoid of competition within and between themselves and serve elites in power (Marcus 2016, p. 24). Since most institutional participation takes place outside formal institutions, this affects the legitimacy of decisions taken by such institutions, leading to alienation, exclusion, inequality, and discrimination of average Malagasies—further reflecting a rule of law deficit (Mutua 2016, p. 162).

For instance, *Fihavanana* has been deployed to co-opt and capture state justice institutions by Malagasy elites who manipulate personal alliances and build adaptive strategies. This oftentimes facilitates their straddling across various social strictures for political, economic and social survival, illustrating how trust as a concept and trust within institutions or by virtue of institutional positions can be captured, distributed, used to create alliances, or break them (Marcus 2016, p. 25; McLain et al. 2021, p. 17). This has created an imbalance between the strength and set of institutions and it drives interaction mechanisms (Marcus 2016, p. 26). This interaction means that the personalisation and co-option of trust and social goodwill within formal institutions for the benefit of informal institutions, has created a blend of weak formal institutions and strong informal institutions, thus weakening or co-opting enforcement mechanisms (such as courts and criminal justice mechanisms) (Jackson et al. 2011, p. 4; McLain et al. 2021, p. 17).

Because of such system, the Malagasy do not trust their formal institutions, since they have been co-opted into the personal tools of leaders, whose incentive to govern is usually based on their eventual molding of such institutions to serve them and their personal agenda, as well as those of people close to them (Mutua 2016, p. 162; Spath 2016). This makes it very difficult to facilitate successful institutional reforms, including legal and judicial reform as a way of redressing rule of law issues. That would lead to changing formal rules without redressing the underlying social

[4] *Andriana* denotes nobility in most Malagasy ethnic communities; Note how identity based on caste or region-highlander versus coastal people, is also predominant.

context. The consequence of such personalised approach to politics and institutional set up has been recurring institutional crises in Madagascar because it defeats expectations of western types of institutions, including judicial systems, transplanted from different contexts (Spath 2016, p. 107). These factors underpin failures in rule of law building that is strictly hegemonic, institutional, centralist and unrepresentative, thus lacking legitimacy in states like Madagascar (Garth 2002, pp. 385, 396).

4 Malagasy Legal Institutions

This section illustrates how issues attributed to *Fihavanana* in previous sections, are reflected in the transplantation, formation and functioning of Malagasy legal and judicial institutions. It reiterates that elements of judicial institutional practice that are considered defective or corrupt within rule of law terminology, are especially attributed to the personalisation of power influenced by *Fihavanana* which underpins governance practice in Madagascar, but has not been considered in legal and judicial institutional set up. This it is argued, confirms weaknesses inherent in uncontextualized institutional transplantation during legal reform, mostly stemming from international development projects. For instance, the third wave of democratisation in the early 1990s underpinned mass constitutional, legal and judicial reforms on the African continent, but resulted in limited constitutionalism (Ratsimbaharison 2016). In its defence, development policy and praxis has promoted the argument that an effective and independent judiciary is inevitably imperative for promoting constitutionalism, including resolving most crises within judicial institutions (Garth 2002, p. 383; Bulmer 2017). Consequently, legal and judicial reform is specifically considered central to development because it can facilitate procedural factors necessary for effective institutions of rule of law, including the judiciary. However, this section illustrates that this is not a panacea for creating an ideal Malagasy rule of law. Relevant surrounding factors, including Malagasy people's voluntary compliance and trust in Malagasy law and institutions, the effectiveness of the whole Malagasy legal system, and a corresponding efficient justice bureaucracy and legal culture, are all lacking, but necessary (Tamanaha 2011a).

4.1 Constitutional Co-optation

Constitutional co-optation, ambiguity, and the subsequent erosion of separation of powers have resulted in a powerful 'monarchic' presidency and a weak judiciary in Madagascar. A closer look at the Malagasy independence constitution and subsequent versions amended over the years to centralise power in Malagasy presidents, portrays neo-patrimonial networking going back decades, with implications for the rule of law and functioning of the judiciary. It is the combination of this neo-patrimonial networking within organs of government and primordial normative systems (including elite deployment of *Fihavanana*), that has precipitated fluidity, blurring separation of powers within arms of government (Ratsimbaharison 2016).

Madagascar's institutional history shows how Malagasy 'imperial' presidents have over the years changed the constitution, tied up political parties and religious elites as well as civil society within a form of neo-patrimonial and rent-seeking relationship, restricting options for accountability (Marcus 2016, p. 3; Ratsimbaharison 2016). Madagascar's very strong presidency which is dominated by Malagasy monarchic descendants and regional elites is central to this. Since the presidency has limited accountability, with no properly institutionalised checks and balances, the legislature (Senate and the National Assembly) has limited ability to manage and constrain presidential powers. The judiciary has equally struggled to assert independence against the president, and is constantly beset by corruption allegations. These governance and institutional weaknesses have shaped Madagascar's three arms of government, creating impediments in governance reform, projecting bias and a rule of law deficit, and eroding public trust.

Madagascar's first constitution was inherited at independence and based on the French Constitution. It was voted for through the referendum of 28 September 1958 and adopted in October 1958. This constitution and its successors have been extensively amended over the years: the 1958 independence constitution was amended under Philibert Tsiranana in June 1960, institutionalising a strong presidential form of government to secure his reign. The referendum of December 1975 under the newly installed Didier Ratsiraka, introduced a new constitution with more presidential powers, commencing the second Malagasy Republic (Ratsimbaharison 2021). The referendum of 19 August 1992 occasioned the 1992 constitution which was ushered in by pro-democracy protests that also introduced Albert Zafy and the third Republic. This constitution went on to get amended in 1995, 1998, 2002 and 2007, becoming a malleable document, without power to address institutional imbalances or ensure political checks and balances (Ratsimbaharison 2016, p. 2). It also strengthened the presidency at the expense of the National Assembly, the Senate and the High Constitutional Court. During these amendments, Malagasy presidents suspended constitutions, the national assembly and senate at will, devised immunity against impeachment procedures, introduced third presidential terms, controlled all branches of national government and various levels of local government, ruled by decree, and restricted eligibility of candidates for national elections (Ratsimbaharison 2016, p. 2).

The galvanisation of power in successive presidencies contributed to patrimonial relationships between arms of government, and blurred the public and private dichotomy, eventually leading to Madagascar's recurrent political crises (Ratsimbaharison 2016, p. 2). Madagascar's constitutions have been political compromises constantly failing to safeguard political excesses. This has encouraged predation linked to kin-based personal networks underpinned by *Fihavanana*, eventually failing to safeguard healthy political competition, favouring business, nobility and political elites.[5]

An illustration of inherent weaknesses within the constitutions can be seen in the effort put in the post-2009 crisis negotiation for the 2010 constitution, and its results. The debates over this constitution, involved Malagasies from all walks of life—legal, policy experts, judges and judicial experts as well as academics and civil society. Yet, what was eventually unveiled failed to reflect the inclusive and rich debates that had preceded it. It too became a political compromise, blurring roles and jurisdiction, whilst centralising power in the presidency (Marcus 2016, p. xiii).[6] For instance, the constitution's age provisions were specifically amended to facilitate Andry Rajoelina's participation in the post 2009 elections, even though he was eventually barred because he was a key actor in the prevailing political crisis. Separate provisions barred candidates who were domiciled outside Madagascar 6 months prior to the elections, limiting competition from opposition leaders in exile (HCC 2009).

Issues raised above illustrate limitations around the promotion of rule of law through constitutional transplants in weak states. Inadvertently, the constitutional system of Madagascar has had little impact on the development of the kind of constitutionalism reflected within western models from which it was borrowed (Chakrabarty 2007; Ginsburg and Dixon 2011). Instead, it has been co-opted by political elites to the detriment of its intended purpose. Critiques levelled towards such globalisation of western constitutional models abound. Consequently, there has been a push especially from global south scholars, for constitutional and judicial intervention to be steeped in local legal cultures. For instance, key emphasis is placed on the role of extra-judicial actors in the development of legal systems in the global south, by employing localised law and society understandings of rule of law building. There is also emphasis on contextualising judicialization processes and their constitutional underpinnings within local or regional contexts with similar histories of less centralisation (Zumbasen 2017, pp. 8–9). Attempts to compare, assimilate, translate and fit legal development into ideal western legal theoretical moulds, have been criticised for portraying non-western legal systems as lesser, defective, and acontextual when they fail to live up to western-centric standards—Madagascar is a case in point (Rodríguez-Garavito 2016, pp. 3, 4).

[5] Cultural norms and fluid personal networks led to a limitation in who could politically compete, with the most powerful elites getting more opportunities than others.

[6] See art 107 of the 2010 Constitution which links the president's executive power to judicial oversight; Note that a revised Article 54 of the Constitution of the Fourth Republic of Madagascar now establishes a new semi-presidential system.

4.2 Judicial System and Independence

The Malagasy judiciary has tended to survive better than other institutions because the institutional framework of courts has remained unaltered by political changes. However, tenure is problematic due to political appointment and influence over of judges. The Malagasy judicial system is loosely based on the French system. At the top is the High Constitutional Court (HCC) which is considered the judicial branch government. It is responsible for ruling on the constitutionality of treaties, laws, ordinances, organic laws and regulations, in addition to adjudicating jurisdictional conflicts involving state institutions, regional territorial entities and election disputes—where political influence has been noticeable (Constitution 2010, Art 114, 116).[7] This is followed by the Supreme Court which sees to the regular functioning of the jurisdictions of the judicial, administrative and financial order, as well as ruling on conflicts of competence involving two jurisdictions of different orders. These jurisdictional orders include: the Court of Cassation; the Council of the State; and the Court of Accounts (Constitution 2010, Art 121).

The Parliamentary/High Court of Justice (HCJ), which is a new institution, is responsible for helping the Courts of Appeal and the Lower Courts which are regionally stationed, in carrying out their functions (Constitution 2010, Art 131, 133, 106). It has jurisdiction over acts carried out by the President of the Republic in the exercise of his functions in the eventuality of high treason, serious or repeated violations of the constitution or failure to carry out duties, where that failure is manifestly incompatible with the exercise of his mandate. This court also has jurisdiction over the criminal responsibility of presidents of parliamentary assemblies, the Prime Minister, other members of the government, as well as the president of the HCC, for acts committed in connection with the exercise of their functions, and considered to be crimes or offences at the time when they were committed (Constitution 2010, Art 106). The vision of the court is an indication of government's willingness to be subjected to the law, and thus create a rule of law environment (even if donor prompted). Yet, the delay in its establishment and finalisation of appointment of all its members, showed reluctance in senior government officials subjecting themselves to accountability. Incidentally, requirements for parliamentary approval and for impeachment processes to precede prosecution, might also politically frustrate the vision-indicating further reluctance (Madagascar Govt. 2015; Schatz 2019).

At lower court level, the court system is made up of local tribunals. Legally, tribunals receive all petitions including those against the state. However, this is in practice hindered by several factors including: insufficient legal knowledge by the citizenry, particularly in rural areas; court fees that many rural Malagasies cannot afford; and lack of staff and funding. Excessive backlog is another hindering factor, since it results in discrepancies between the types of cases tribunals will hear.

[7] Note that a higher court has been envisioned by the 2010 Constitution: the High Court of Justice which became operational in 2018; See Art 167 of the Constitution of Madagascar.

Typically, low-level corruption becomes a solution to redress the backlog and get one's case heard. Consequently, certain economically privileged groups, including regional elites, have successfully influenced priorities and outcomes within these burdened lower courts (BTI 2020, p. 11).

While the juridical structure of courts in Madagascar seems relatively sound, it is markedly subservient to political and economic pressure. The main struggle for the judiciary and justice mechanisms is related to judicial independence, corruption and poor public image, resulting in loss of trust. For instance, when it comes to judicial independence, the president of the Republic of Madagascar appears to have a strong influence over the judiciary informally, through the personalisation of power underpinned by kin-based networks (*Fihavanana*) and through neo-patrimonialism. Formally, the constitution equally affords him a lot of power over the judiciary by appointing him the guarantor of judicial independence and President of the Superior Council of Magistrature (*Counseil Superieuer de la Magistarure-CSM*) (Constitution 2010, Art 107). Here he is responsible for appointing the CSM's governing magistrate who is charged with upholding judicial independence, overseeing the careers of magistrates (justices) and maintaining disciplinary measures for justice.[8] This means that through the CSM, the president has control over justices of courts that are under the authority of the governing magistrate. In the future, the General Inspection of Justice will be responsible for specifically ensuring compliance with ethical rules for magistrates, as well as the actions and accountability of personnel of justice. Incidentally, it will also be attached to the Presidency, possibly subjecting all ethical compliance issues in the judicial system to the president's control (Constitution 2010, Art 112).[9] In past constitutions, this institution was linked to the Supreme Court, demonstrating how judicial independence has been encroached upon overtime.

Currently, the president indirectly influences the appointment of the First President of the Supreme Court and the Public Prosecutor in the Supreme Court, who are not elected, but appointed by a Decree of the Council of Ministers, incidentally, following the mandatory opinion of the CSM (United Nations 2019, Art 216–232; Constitution 2010, Art 122). Within the Appeal Courts, similar procedures apply to the appointment of the First President and Public Prosecutor (Constitution 2010, Art 130). Higher Court Justices have subsequently noted their misgivings over the president's role within the judiciary, confirming the limitations they feel the role and the CSM place over them (Marcus 2016, p. 60). These misgivings are compounded by the fact that the President is also responsible for appointing three of the nine members of the HCC, which is the highest court in the land, which is not so different from other African jurisdictions (Constitution 2010, Art 114). However, what complicates it is the fact that the President already has a lot of other influence over the judiciary, including influencing the appointment of the other two

[8] Organic Law No 2007-039 on the Supreme Council of the Judiciary (CSM) was passed on 14 January 2008. It was modified and supplemented by Organic Law No 2011-006 of 1 August 2011 and Organic Law No 2014-019 of 12 September 2014.

[9] The General Inspection of Justice is yet to be operationalized.

justices of the HCC who are usually elected by the CSM. The last four HCC justices are elected by the National Assembly and the Senate, which are clearly from above also indirectly controlled or influenced by the president (Constitution 2010, Art 114, 107; Ratsimbaharison 2016).

The naming of the president of the HCC, subject to peer election, still reiterates lack of judicial independence in Madagascar (Constitution 2010, Art 114). In most sub-Saharan African countries, the President nominates the president of the superior court, but he does so with advice and in consultation with the Minister of Justice and the Judicial services commission (JSC). For instance, in South Africa, a JSC made up of representatives from the judiciary, legal profession, academia, and politicians, makes nominations to the President for appointments to the Constitutional Court (Bulmer 2017). Most importantly, the South African president does not have all the other roles and influence on the judiciary referred to above. To be the guarantor of judicial independence, president of the SCM, and appointer of the overseer to the SCM—automatically influences any process of peer election. In naming the head of the superior court, appointing most of the higher court justices, and influencing the appointment of others, the president defeats the theory of separation of powers and completely dilutes the doctrine of judicial independence (Marcus 2016, p. 60). The constitutional safeguard of an independent justice system is actually weakened by the same constitution allocating the president so much power over the judiciary.

4.3 Judicial Corruption

The co-option of judicial institutions is simultaneously formally embedded through constitutional entrenchment and informally influenced by the personalisation of power-underpinned by *Fihavanana*, as is seen in sections above, but there are also instances where it is just a matter of perceptions due to blurred institutional structures. This is associated with perceptions of political interference in the interest of shielding perpetrators from investigation or prosecution.[10] The main premise for this is that the Malagasy judiciary is powerless against people with either political connections or enough wealth to bribe officials (Schatz 2019, p. 1; Ratsimbaharison 2016). Nonetheless, the web of elite litigants versus improperly remunerated civil servants is distinct, and has overtime also fuelled a real noteworthy cycle of corruption resulting from fatalism and public compliance, with even poor litigants feeling obliged to foot the bill in order to access justice (VonDoepp 2015, p. 45). Extreme corruption, especially within lower ranks of the judiciary is more visible and has been linked to economic factors such as inadequate salaries. However, the levels of corruption are the same at higher and lower ranks, yet it is predominantly within lower ranks where petty bribery is reported consistently, and has often been

[10] More than 75 percent of Malagasy believe corruption had increased in Madagascar since 2018, according to the 2019 Afrobarometer Survey; 44 percent of Malagasy believed that police and gendarmes were involved in corruption; 39 percent believed the same of judges and magistrates.

investigated and prosecuted, maintaining the trend of lack of accountability for the powerful (Marcus 2016, p. 61).

The issue of limited or lack of properly trained staff has also led to overworked and undercompensated judicial functionaries (Ravalomanda 2005, pp. 123–124; Ratsimbaharison 2016, p. 19). Lack of proper training and extremely complex judicial procedures that are barely understood by functionaries within lower ranks, increases corruption opportunities.[11] The lack of transparency in the process of recruitment, as well as lack of continuous training, especially in judicial ethics, proper case reasoning and understanding of judicial procedures, has left lower judicial functionaries open to manipulation. Most importantly, the limited transparency on the education, training and qualifications of people who take on judicial roles, as well as limited transparency in procedures of promotion and retainment, affects the conduct and mannerisms of judicial officers within all levels of the judiciary. A systematic, transparent system, with checks and balances, clarifying conditions of employment and promotion, and offering proper security of tenure and salaries would strengthen the judicial system, as noted in the new Anti-Corruption Courts (PACs) (Schatz 2019).

Consequently, International development (rule of law reform) programs targeting to eliminate judicial corruption have been introduced, providing improvements in physical and electronic infrastructure, training for judicial officers, neighbourhood justice initiatives and legal assistance for the poor. This has been coupled with institutionalised anti-corruption efforts, through donor support for setting up anti-corruption bureaus, their staffing, training as well as policy overhaul and legislative toolkits (Ravalomanda 2005, p. 121; VonDoepp 2015, p. 47; Schatz 2019, p. 2). Accordingly, the anti-Corruption Judiciary Unit (CPEAC) *Chaîne Pénale Economique et Anti-Corruption* was established in May 2004.[12] It was a one-stop anti-corruption judicial office with a mandate to prosecute, investigate and make decisions in relation to corruption cases referred by the Independent Anti-Corruption Bureau (*Bureau Indépendant Anti-Corruption*-BIANCO) (Schatz 2019, p. 1).

The CPEAC suffered from lack of independence and ineffectiveness driven by underfunding, understaffing, and incapacity to demand accountability of the most powerful, limiting its conviction rates. It also reviewed very few cases referred, only investigating corruption within local tribunals around Antananarivo (Ravalomanda 2005, p. 123; Schatz 2019, pp. 1–2). It was replaced in 2016 by the donor funded specialized stand-alone Anti-Corruption Poles (PACs), which are courts meant to address its weaknesses, including administrative and jurisdictional difficulties, and

[11] The Malagasy legal system as inherited from the French is complex and outdated. This coupled with outdated court procedures and archaic texts, increases opportunities for corruption. Complex and numerous prerequisites decrease the accessibility of justice and in order to come to a fast resolution of a case, bribes are solicited and offered. The solution would be judicial reforms which would increase public access to legal information and make judicial procedures clearer and less complicated to encourage a speedy resolution of disputes. This is where hybridity through non-state systems would be suitable.

[12] Created through Inter-ministerial Circular No. 001/MJ/MDN/SESP of July 2, 2004.

its weak underpinning legal framework.[13] The PACs have first instance and appellate jurisdiction, with options for final appeal to the Supreme court. Their main limitation is that their corresponding provincial courts are yet to be operationalised, with sessions only taking place around the capital—Antananarivo (CPEAC n.d.), limiting options for regional corruption cases to get heard (Schatz 2019, p. 6).

BIANCO, a key champion of the CPEAC reform, was also established in 2004 with the intention of investigating, regularising institutional oversight and redressing the politics of self-aggrandization (Schatz 2019, pp. 2, 7). Like CPEAC, it has been responsible and effective at routing out low-level corruption, but failed to address complaints involving the powerful, including grande-corruption which is much more concerning. BIANCO has been more effective at redressing low-level cases concentrated around central Madagascar, while the rest of its cases were resolved through judicial review (Marcus 2016, p. 37). Housed in the President's office, it prescribes accountability, yet it lacks the power to exercise mandate over those at higher level who are un-accountable (Marcus 2016, p. 37). These two institutions illustrate the limits of transplanting governance mechanisms and associated rule of law-based development. Despite the above efforts put forward by the Malagasy state in response to donor led programs and conditionalities to redress judicial corruption and engineer a rule of law environment, the perception of corruption within the judiciary has remained very high.

This section illustrates the consequences of implementing an uncontextualised rule of law. Arguably, the failure to account for relevant social, economic and political factors has compounded legal and judicial weaknesses in Madagascar. Notably, Malagasy judicial institutions still lack the presumed secondary supportive conditions that are necessary to support a strong judicial system, and ideal rule of law. This section denotes institutional and personal obstacles impeding effective judicial personnel functionality including, lack of independence, adequate compensation commensurate to skills and job and physical security, which are key for stemming corruption or coercion. Lastly, social influences based on class, ethnicities, caste, social relations and loyalties are most visible due to social norms such as *Fihavanana* underpinning institutional interaction, they even influence prosection trends for judicial corruption (Tamanaha 2011a, p. 222; Nathalie and Bart 2005). Clearly, whilst the orthodox view to rule of law-building prescribes more law and legal institutions, this section shows that in Madagascar, existing legal institutional mechanisms are ineffective, or are unused or worse, misinterpreted, misused and abused due to failure to comprehend social realities (Ouédraogo 2014, pp. 3–4).

[13] Created through a stronger law - Law No. 2016–020 of August 22 on the Fight against Corruption, and Law No. 2016-021 of August 22 on Anti-corruption Poles (PAC).

5 Rule of Law From Below?

International development policy and practice has marginalised the struggles that developing states encounter within an unjust international legal order. It has failed to acknowledge the uneven nature of its relationship with the sovereignty of developing states, their welfare or that of their people. This has implications for how international development initiatives, including rule of law programmes, are rolled out in developing countries. For instance, emphasis is placed on the depoliticization of governance issues, favouring standardised domestic rule of law building and modernisation for a liberal market economy (Rittich 2016, p. 3). In Madagascar, such depoliticization has disregarded the needs and roles of communities and their norms in defining new pathways in which their relations with the state can be redefined, negotiated and anchored. It has resulted in ineffective, misused and unused legal institutions. Since an ideal state-centred rule of law cannot be easily established within developing countries with weak state institutions and strong non-state normative systems like Madagascar, the option for complementing state approaches is conceptualising a rule of law from below, including through reliance on social movements or initiatives built through community organisations.

This section argues against uncontextualized development policy that underpins rule of law initiatives. It insists that the effectiveness of Malagasy legal institutions is dependent on acknowledging contextual moral values relevant to substantive outcomes, such as *Fihavanana*—which is local and non-state, and re-orienting it to discourage nepotism and corruption within state institutions. Malagasy legal institutions are encouraged to adapt to, acknowledge, co-exist with, and positively comprehend this local normative interpersonal system that is co-dependent on social networks and capital. It is argued that this framing should constitute a substantive rule of law that is specific to Madagascar. Such an approach might lead to socially just outcomes as opposed to the current disregard of *Fihavanana* by rule of law initiatives, which has left it to be deployed in entrenching elite capture of legal institutions to the detriment of justice accountability. However, the effectiveness of such proposal requires de-emphasising rule of law initiatives that presume a state led approach which only centers and strengthens the state and state agents with legal mandates.

Despite, its identified negative co-optation, *Fihavanana* is by nature an inclusive, moral concept which reflects values of solidarity, social harmony, tolerance, friendship, union, mutual responsibility, reciprocity, kinship, and hospitality, basically promoting pro-social behavior (McLain et al. 2021; Spath 2016, p. 101; Kneitz 2021, p. 328). In Madagascar, where trust tends to be localized and horizontal, *Fihavanana* could still be important for building and maintaining a substantive and contextualized rule of law environment, underpinned by peace and trust in local and eventually national institutions (Goetter 2016, p. 13). For instance, *Fihavanana* underpins local institutions and community organizations such as those for tillage, community rule-making (*Dina*) and funerals, which are active and important parts of daily life where trust is built and shared, social capital is negotiated and accumulated, and governance decisions are made (BTI 2020, p. 15). These institutions could be a starting point for identifying and conceptualizing a rule of law from below.

The advantage of relying on existing norms such as *Fihavanana* that originally embed positive social behavior through social participation, is that the issues raised within legal institutions above can be balanced out by a strong social norm that can discourage corruption and lend legitimacy and authority to state institutions that are currently untrustworthy, while ensuring that non-state institutions are not disregarded. This will help in positively re-orienting institutional values within state institutions. The point must not be to transplant and recreate an ideal rule of law environment, but a rule of law environment that is relevant and fit for Malagasy contexts (Hauge 2011). While it is important to structurally rebuild and re-enforce institutions such parliament and courts, and ensure inclusive reform and proper implementation of the constitution during the process of rebuilding the rule of law, such inclusivity makes it imperative to embrace the strong non-state norms that exist in Madagascar and rely on their social embeddedness and flexibility as a means to also positively transform institutional moral issues that exist in Madagascar. The purpose must be to promote socially just outcomes within state and non-state institutions as opposed to focusing almost exclusively on building state legal systems by assuming that the trajectory in Madagascar matches that of western countries—where law is consolidated within the state. This would require fostering direct engagement between the state and communities in order to deliberate on the indicators of, and most viable solutions to the national and local crises and rebuild trust and inclusion in formal legal institutions, while democratising and embracing the informal ones.[14] This return to a revived *Fihavanana* that contends with modernity and engages public issues such as impunity, insecurity and judicial independence, is being agitated for in Madagascar (Spath 2016, p. 109).

A good example of this has been the folkloric-inspired *Dahalo* amnesty, demobilisation, re-socialisation and reintegration program (*Dahalo miova fo*), that has seen former cattle bandits (*Dahalos*) intergrated into village (*fokonolonas*) security programs, assisting gendarmes and becoming justice collaborators.[15] Their former skills and insider knowledge of rural gang operations are being deployed to preempt attacks and structure defence strategies (Pellerin 2017, p. 20; DCAF-ISSAT 2017, pp. 3, 20). The Dina Melanky (*Dina n'y melaky tsy mipoly*) in the Melaky region, is an outstanding example of traditional rule making and traditional justice that has been headed by a former Dahalo and it has been extremely successful in maintaining security and resolving justice issues for the Fohara people.[16] However, the reintegration program is predomiantly state sponsored, forming part of rural Magadascar's contextualised rule of law initiatives around law, security and order,

[14] Interview conducted with Search for Common Ground Officer (SCG) Antananarivo, Madagascar in November 2015.

[15] *Dahalo* are Zebu cattle-raiding bandits prominent in Southern Madagascar.

[16] *Dina* are localised traditional justice agreements established by communities to maintain law and order.

in an attempt to secure the countryside. This has offered economic stability for the program, ensuring that Dahalos remain integrated, and offering them altenative survival and re-socialisation. Nevertheless, this threatens local ownership of the program, yet, the struggling Malagasy state cannot also assure long-term support (DCAF-ISSAT 2017, p. 3). Criticisms from an institutional rule of law angle have targeted the program's blanket amnesty without legal accountability, the eventual misuse of the program to reward even non-Dahalo detainees, and finally, the executive's politicised prerogative in pronoucing such program, circumscribing the criminal justice system (Ratsiazo 2014).

6 Conclusion

This chapter has engaged with rebuilding the rule of law in plural post-conflict societies. It has argued that western-styled intervention mechanisms are structured within a state-centric context and effectively fail in non-western plural contexts where rule of law intervention takes place. Madagascar illustrates the nature of normative pluralities and how they affect governance interaction. This goes to show that rule of law intervention programs centred only on state-based norms including law and its institutions, fail to contextualise rule of law building. The outcome is the constant depiction of corrupt institutions in developing countries, and a rule of law deficit. The chapter suggests approaching rule of law building from below by taking into account multiple co-existing and flexible normative systems with positive underlying moral values—that can influence pro-social institutional behaviours, which will be useful for building a rule of law culture that is also couched in local contexts.

Simultaneously, the chapter highlights the inherent failure to consolidate political, civil and traditional will in Madagascar. It illustrates how this is embedded in Madagascar's economic and political disparities, stemming centuries back into old Malagasy Kingdoms, coupled with a Malagasy political landscape that is represented by a few elites who have since independence failed to inspire credibility from the Malagasy community.[17] Consequently, vast class and other inequalities have left the majority of Malagasies in poverty, as their elites co-opt state institutions. While it is clear that constitutional design weaknesses and the co-optations thereof have led to institutional crisis, the chapter centres the role of *Fihavanana*.

It argues that the flexibility, authority and legitimacy of *Fihavanana* has been misused by elites, and its inbuilt trust mechanisms have been deployed to capture state institutions (Marcus 2008, p. 85). The chapter shows how such co-options have facilitated porosity within institutions of governance, for instance they have fanned perceptions of corruption within the judiciary-severely affecting trust (Tamanaha

[17] Interview conducted with Search for Common Ground Officer (SCG) Antananarivo, Madagascar in November 2015.

2011a, b; Mutua 2016; Zumbasen 2017). The chapter suggests that *Fihavanana* should be rejuvenated and its underlying social justice ideals deployed to keep formal institutions in check by emphasising pro-social behaviour. This would of course require understanding how *Fihavanana* works within informal institutions which are underpinned by negotiated authority, social consensus, social legitimacy and social justice, which easily offsets the consequences of its social embeddedness. However, this would not be a stretch, since *Fihavanana* is already nationally recognised, and is even being deployed in formal institutions, albeit, negatively. Nevertheless, this demands a less centralist approach to rule of law building, one which acknowledges other forms of normative rules and effectively respects pluralism.

References

Adelman S, Paliwala A (2020) Introduction. In: Adelman S, Paliwala A (eds) The limits of law and development: neoliberalism, governance and social justice. Routledge, Abingdon, pp 1–12

Bedford K (2020) Law, gender, and development: potent hauntings. Law Dev Rev 13(1):229–264

Bonar G (1997) Admiral Didier Ratsiraka and the Malagasy Socialist Revolution. J Mod Afr Stud 35:409

Brooks RE (2003) The new imperialism: violence, norms, and the "rule of law". Mich Law Rev 101:2275–2285

BTI BS (2020) Madagascar country report. Bertelsmann Stiftung, Gütersloh

Bulmer E (2017) Judicial appointments-International IDEA Constitution Building Primer 4. International Institute for Democracy and Electoral Assistance (International IDEA), Stockholm

Carothers T (2006) The problem of knowledge. In: Carothers T (ed) Promoting the rule of law abroad: in search of knowledge. Carnegie Endowment for International Peace, Washington, DC, pp 15–30

Chakrabarty D (2007) Provincializing Europe: postcolonial thought and historical difference, 2nd edn. Princeton University Press, New Jersey

Chan KT (2020) Personal responsibility and global justice. In: Brooks T (ed) The Oxford handbook of global justice. Oxford University Press, Oxford, p 476

Cohen A (2009) Thinking with culture in law and development. Buff Law Rev 57:511

CPEAC (n.d.) The National Coordination Directorate of Anti-Corruption Poles (DCN) and The Anti-Corruption Poles: From the Criminal Economic Anti-Corruption Chain (CPEAC) to the Anti-corruption Poles (PAC). [Online] Available at: www.dcn-pac.mg/historique.htm

Faundez J (2010) Rule of law or Washington Consensus: the evolution of the World Bank's approach to legal and judicial reform. In: Kessaris AP (ed) Law in the pursuit of development: principles into practice. Routledge, Abingdon, pp 180–181

Faundez J (2011) Legal pluralism and international development agencies: state building or legal reform? Hague J Rule Law 30(1):18–38

Fombad CM (2018) An overview of the crisis of the rule of law in Africa. Afr Hum Rights Law J 18(1):213–143

Fung C (2022) Legal Pluralism and the Rule of Law in Sub-Saharan Africa. Rule of Law Journal 3:18–24

Gannon F (2014) Le fihavanana comme capital social. In: Kneitz P (ed) Fihavanana – La vision d'une société paisible à Madagascar. Universitätsverlag Halle-Wittenberg, Halle an der Saale, p 326

Garth B (2002) Building strong and independent judiciaries through the new law and development: behind the paradox of consensus programs and perpetually disappointing results. DePaul Law Rev 52:383–400
Ginsburg T, Dixon R (2011) Introduction: comparative constitutional law. In: Dixon R, Ginsburg T (eds) Research handbook on comparative constitutional law. Edward Elgar, Cheltenham, p 1
Goetter JF (2016) The cattle raiders leave us no choice: new transhumance in the Mahafaly Plateau region in Madagascar. Madagascar Conservation & Development 11(1):12–22
Harding A (2019) The legal transplants debate: getting beyond the impasse? In: Breda V (ed) Legal transplants in East Asia and Oceania. Cambridge University Press, Cambridge, pp 13–33
Hauge W (2011) Madagascar between peace and conflict: domestic capabilities for peaceful conflict management. Conflict, Security & Development 11(5):509–531
HCC (2009) Decision No. 03-HCC-/D2, 2009 of April 23 2009
Humphreys S (2010) Theatre of the rule of law: transnational legal intervention in theory and practice. Cambridge University Press, Cambridge
ISSAT, (DCAF) GCfSSG (2017) Cattle rustling and insecurity in Africa: a comparative perspective. [Online] Available at: https://issat.dcaf.ch/download/117812/2146982
Jackson J, Hough M, Bradford B, Pooler T (2011) Trust in justice: topline results from round 5 of the European social survey. Eur Soc Surv 1:1–11
Jennings ET (2017) Perspectives on French Colonial Madagascar. Palgrave Macmillan, New York
Jowell J (2019) The rule of law. In: Jowell J, O'Cinneide C (eds) The changing constitution, 9th edn. Oxford University Press, Oxford, pp 3–28
Kneitz P (2021) A magic momentum: negotiating authority in the Bongolava region, Madagascar. In: Steinforth A, Klocke-Daffa S (eds) Challenging authorities: Ethnographies of legitimacy and power in Eastern and Southern Africa. Palgrave Macmillan, New York, pp 319–346
Kneitz P (2022) Negotiating modernity by concepts of relatedness: towards the construction of Malagasy Solidarity (Fihavanana Gasy). J South Afr Stud 48(4):727–745
Lwabukuna O (2022) Reconstructing the rule of law in plural Madagascar. In: Akinlabi O (ed) Policing and the rule of law in Sub-Saharan Africa. Routledge, London, pp 157–182
Madagascar-Govt (2015) Organic Act No. 2014-043 regarding the High Court of Justice. s.n., Antananarivo
Marcus RR (2008) Tokana: The collapse of the Rural Malagasy Community. Afr Stud Rev 51(1):85–104
Marcus RR (2016) The politics of institutional failure in Madagascar's Third Republic. Lexington Books, Maryland
McLain R et al (2021) An exploratory review of legal texts and literature on Living Tenure Systems in Madagascar. CIFOR, Antananarivo
Merry SE (1988) Legal pluralism. Law Soc Rev 22:869
Mutua M (2016) Africa and the rule of law. SUR Int J Hum Rights 13(23):159–173
Nathalie F, Bart M (2005) Security and perceptions on justice in Rural Madagascar. In: Dynamics in social service delivery and the rural economy of Madagascar: descriptive results of the 2004 commune survey. s.l.: (Ilo-Cornell Policy Brief), pp 5–6
Okoye A (2004) The rule of law and socio-political dynamics in Africa. In: Zeleza PT, McConnaughay PJ (eds) Human rights, the rule fo law and development in Africa. University of Pennysylvania Press, Philadelphia, pp 71–80
Ouédraogo É (2014) National security strategy development. Africa Center for Strategic Studies, Washington DC
Pellerin M (2017) Madagascar dealing with multifaced crime notes de l'ifri. s.l.: IFRI-SSAProgram
Randrianja S, Ellis S (2009) Madagascar a short history. Hurst, Chicago
Ratsiazo L (2014) Dahalo miova fo', Pandora's box. [Online] Available at: https://www.madagascar-tribune.com/Dahalo-miova-fo-la-boite-de,20508.html
Ratsimbaharison A (2016) The obstacles and challenges to democratic consolidation in Madagascar (1992–2009). Int J Political Sci 2(2):1–17

Ratsimbaharison AM (2017) The political crisis of March 2009 in Madagascar: a case study of conflict and conflict mediation. Rowman and Littlefield, Maryland

Ratsimbaharison A (2021) Didier Ratsiraka: The legacy of Madagascar's "Red Admiral". [Online] Available at: https://theconversation.com/didier-ratsiraka-the-legacy-of-madagascars-red-admiral-143017

Ravalomanda TH (2005) Corruption control in criminal justice: The Madagascar situation, problems and solutions and corruption cases. UNAFEI, Fyuchu

Razanadrakoto J (2020) The Fihavanana: myths and realities of a value that guarantees social peace. [Online] Available at: https://www.observatoirepharos.com/pays/madagascar/le-fihavanana-mythes-et-realites-dune-valeur-garante-de-la-paix-sociale/#_ftn1

Republic of Madagascar (2010) Madagascar's Constitution. Constitute Project. https://www.constituteproject.org/constitution/Madagascar_2010.pdf

Rittich K (2016) Theorizing international law and development. In: Orford A, Hoffman F (eds) The Oxford handbook of the theory of international law. Oxford University Press, Oxford, pp 820–843

Rodríguez-Garavito C (2016) Remapping law and society in Latin America: Visions and topics for a new legal cartography. In: Rodríguez-Garavito C (ed) Law and society in Latin America: A new map 1. Routledge, London, pp 1–20

Said E (1978) Orientalism. Pantheon Books, New York

Schatz F (2019) Madagascar's specialised anti-corruption court: the quest to end impunity. Retrieved February 2, 2022, from www.u4.no/publications/madagascars-speci. [Online] Available at: https://www.u4.no/publications/madagascars-specialised-anti-corruption-court-the-quest-to-end-impunity

Scheidecker G (2016) Cattle, conflicts and gendarmes in Southern Madagascar: a local perspective on fihavanana gasy. In: Kneitz P (ed) Fihavanana — La vision d'une société en paix à Madagascar: perspectives anthropologiques, historiques et socio-économique. Universitätsverlag Halle-Wittenberg, Halle an der Saale, pp 129–156

Sen A (2000, June 5) What is the role of legal and judicial reform in the development process? World Bank, Washington, DC

Siems M (2018) Malicious legal transplants. Leg Stud 38(1):103–119

Spath M (2016) Fihavanana 2010: National solidarity within the context ofMadagascar's 50th anniversary of Independence. In: Kneitz P (ed) Fihavanana — La vision d'une société en paix à Madagascar: perspectives anthropologiques, historiques et socio-économique. Universitätsverlag Halle-Wittenberg, Halle an der Saale, pp 101–128

Tamanaha B (2004) On the rule of law: history, politics, theory. Cambridge University Awards, Cambridge

Tamanaha B (2005) The tension between legal instrumentalism and the rule of law. Syracuse J Int Law Commerce 33(1):131–154

Tamanaha B (2008) Understanding legal pluralism: past to present, local to global. Sydney Law Rev 30:375

Tamanaha BZ (2011a) The primacy of society and the failures of law and development. Cornell Int Law J 44:209–247

Tamanaha B (2011b) The rule of law and legal pluralism in development. Hague J Rule Law 3:1–17

Trubek D (2006) Rule of law in development assistance: past, present and future. In: Trubek D, Santos A (eds) The new law and economic development: a critical appraisal. Cambridge University Press, Cambridge, pp 74–94

Twining W (2009) General jurisprudence: understanding law from a global perspective. Cambridge University Press, Cambridge

Twining W (2010) Normative and legal pluralism: a global perspective. Duke J Comp Int Law 20:473–517

United Nations (2019) Madagascar National Report submitted in accordance with paragraph 5 of the annex to Human Rights Council Resolution 16/21*. United Nations General Assembly, Geneva

VonDoepp P (2015) The rule of law and the courts. In: Cheeseman N, Anderson DM, Scheibler A (eds) Routledge handbook of African politics. Routledge, London, pp 37–48

Zumbasen P (2017) The rule of law, legal pluralism, and challenges to a western-centric view: some very preliminary observations, Osgoode legal studies research paper series, p 193

Rule of Law, Judicial Independence and International Development: Cambodia

Rhona Smith

Abstract Rule of law and judicial independence can be influenced and shaped by internal and external factors, not least international development activities. Arguably a focus of many 'western' states in their development work, securing written constitutional guarantees (de jure independence), overlooks the role of pre-existing local cultural approaches and practices which may preclude such de jure independence translating into practice, de facto independence. Other development partners a state may choose to work with may be less interested in constitutional development or democracy strengthening activities.

This chapter draws on a range of extant literature, including work on the role of courts and judicial independence in debates on rule of law v rule by law, judicialization of politics v politicisation of the judiciary and the difference between de jure judicial independence (a central goal of international organisation and bilateral 'western' development) and de facto independence. Cambodia is drawn on as a case study, with its recent evolution from a much-celebrated new democracy to a de facto one-party authoritarian, autocratic state considered, with reference to influential states supporting Cambodia's development.

Understanding the potential impact of external development influences on evolving judicial independence in fragile democracies offers insights into (unintended?) consequences of some international development approaches, suggesting a need for more focussed technical assistance partnerships.

R. Smith (✉)
School of Law, Newcastle University, Newcastle upon Tyne, UK
e-mail: rhona.smith@newcastle.ac.uk

N. Reayat, H. O. Yusuf (eds.), *Constitutionalism in Africa and Beyond*, Ius Gentium: Comparative Perspectives on Law and Justice 127,
https://doi.org/10.1007/978-3-032-01180-0_7

1 Introduction

Rule of law and judicial independence do not exist in a political and diplomatic vacuum in most states. Rather, they can be influenced and shaped not only by internal factors, but also by external factors, not least international development activities. Diverse international actors can undermine judicial independence in unstable or weakened democracies. Arguably a focus of many 'western' states in their development work, securing written constitutional guarantees (de jure independence), overlooks the role of pre-existing local cultural approaches and practices which may preclude such de jure independence translating into practice, de facto independence. Other development partners the state may choose to work with may be less interested in supporting such constitutional development or democracy strengthening activities. Understanding the potential impact of such external influences on evolving judicial independence in fragile democracies offers insights into (unintended?) consequences of some international development approaches, suggesting a need for more focussed technical assistance partnerships.

This chapter focusses on Cambodia, a country which experienced a tragic past, before re-establishing itself as a constitutional democracy following the 1993 elections (the first of its 'modern era'). Its progress towards the plural multiparty democracy foreseen by its modern constitution remains intensely monitored by the international community and of considerable interest to many protagonists, particularly 'western' and European states. The country's developing judiciary has long been tainted with allegations of corruption and a lack of actual, de facto, independence. Increasingly, the courts have been utilised by the ruling party through enforcing enacted laws in cases before them, to repress, even destroy, viable political opposition and to legitimise many constitutional changes and legislative initiatives which strengthen the position of the ruling party. Such a situation deepens popular perception of (political) bias within the judiciary, eroding public trust, and undermining judicial independence as foreseen in the constitution.

The interaction of rule of law/rule by law with de jure/de facto judicial independence, and the politicisation of judiciary by the executive provides a fast-moving context to analyse these challenges. Given the international scrutiny of the political situation by predominantly western development partners, and Cambodia's continuing and deepening development partnership with China, impacts on development partnerships and priorities are shifting. Whilst western countries regularly espouse the necessity of rule of law, democracy and judicial independence, others, in this context particularly China, evince a different approach to these concepts and, indeed, to development more generally.

Considering how judicial independence in weak or unstable democracies can be negatively impacted by international development assistance, this chapter will be structured as follows. The present international (UN) system does draw on a specific understanding of rule of law linked to a conception of democracy and separation of the powers of state. This is argued as being based on 'western approaches' and certainly such approaches dominate (are pseudo-imposed). 'Western' states, espousing that approach, are a major source of development funding, technical assistance and capacity-building. This chapter draws on a range of extant literature, including work on the role of courts and judicial independence in debates on rule of law v rule by law, judicialization of politics v politicisation of the judiciary and the difference between de jure judicial independence, a central goal of international organisation and bilateral 'western' development, and de facto independence. The latter is often compromised, to the detriment of the rule of law, as local conditions and traditions may not be compatible with that conception of the rule of law.

Next, Cambodia's constitutional, political and legal framework will be outlined, identifying key provisions which are discussed. The complexity of the Cambodian context offers a salutary and instructive case study on rule of law and judicial independence in an era of shifting global power and changing priorities.

The evolution of Cambodia in the modern era from a much-celebrated new democracy to a de facto one-party authoritarian, autocratic state will then be traced with reference to influential states supporting Cambodia's development as well as international organisations. As will be apparent, some elements of the Cambodian experience may resonate with experiences elsewhere.

Concluding this chapter, some reflections are offered as to ways in which technical assistance and capacity-building efforts of international organisations and development programming could be tailored to better support a convergence of de facto independence with the constitutional guarantees of de jure independence.

2 Judicial Independence, Rule of Law, Development: Current Understandings

Around the world, many political elites are strengthening and reinforcing their political power. Concepts of democracy and rule of law are evolving; constitutions are amended, and laws enacted to consolidate political power of the ruling elite and extend their periods of political dominance beyond that hitherto foreseen in the constitutional framework.[1] Courts are usually envisaged as offering a check on excessive political power, a neutral balance grounded in law. The doctrine of separation of powers has 'western' origins, usually attributed to French philosopher Charles-Louis de Secondat, Baron de La Brède et de Montesqieu in his seminal work, De L'Esprit des Loix.[2] Judicial independence free from political influence is posited as vital for democracies, ensuring that no-one is above the enacted law of the country and, in furtherance of the rule of law, giving effect to those laws in a just

[1] See, e.g., Amoah (2023); Fruhstorfer and Hudson (2022), pp. 93–112; McKie and Carlson (2022), pp. 133–153.

[2] See e.g. Montesqieu (1899), pp. 151–162, which discusses the English position.

manner.[3] Laws, however, can be deployed to support extensions of political power, and existing laws can even be changed in accordance with provisions of the constitutional framework, rendering courts almost impotent to challenge such political manoeuvres.[4] Law, especially in civil law orientated societies, arguably offers courts little scope for creative interpretation—the written law should be applied to the facts to offer a reasoned decision[5] (Common law, in contrast, is essentially 'judge made' so evolves with judicial interpretation). Courts find themselves engaged directly in political matters, for example when asked to offer opinions on constitutional affairs or to adjudicate cases challenging alleged excesses of political power.[6]

Whilst many countries claimed to embrace democracy (defined here as including a requirement for periodic free elections), in the wake of independence from colonial powers or emergence from periods of authoritarian and autocratic rule, there is considerable variation in understandings of 'democracy'.[7] Griffin writes of the term 'democracy' being used 'promiscuously' by some states, alluding to communist dictatorships,[8] whilst Ayers interrogates a USAID director's quote that 'we all know a democracy when we see one', concluding that indeed the democracy and good governance project is focussed on a neoliberal conceptualisation of democracy which should not be considered universal.[9] The role of the USA, advancing its particular 'brand' of democracy, is highly relevant in the development programming context. It often (or usually, depending on the President of the day) presents itself as a beacon of 'democracy', the model to be aspired to.[10] Certainly, its development programming is often focussed on rule of law, fair trial, electoral and civil society activities. Moreover, the USA government often publicly attempts to hold states to account for not following its model of democracy. For example, the Cambodia Democracy Act 2021 sought to impose sanctions 'on individuals responsible for acts to undermine democracy in Cambodia'.[11] As will be explained, that conceptualisation of democracy owes some understanding to the broadly US liberal model.

---

[3] On independence of the judiciary, see UN Basic Principles on the Independence of the Judiciary 1985, endorsed by General Assembly resolutions 40/32(29 November 1985) and 40/146 (13 December 1985) as complemented and developed by the Banglalore Principles of Judicial Conduct, ECOSOC resolution 2006/23.

[4] For example Russia's 2020 constitutional reforms, facilitating President Putin running for additional terms, were put to a 'national referendum' despite that not being required to offer the reforms additional 'legality'. President Putin was returned for a fifth term as President in March 2023.

[5] Judges can of course apply the law in light of evolving social circumstances: Hunter and Murison (1921), p. 11.

[6] Discussed elsewhere in this book and below re Cambodia.

[7] An early statement is by Thomas Jefferson, contemporary USA founder.

[8] Griffin (2008), at Chap. 14.3

[9] Ayers (2008), pp. 1–13 at 13.

[10] See, for example, The White House (2021).

[11] Cambodia Democracy Act of 2021, passed 28 September 2021, H.R.4686—117th Congress (2021–2022); see also United States Department of The Treasury, 'Treasury Targets Corrupt Military Officials in Cambodia' Press Release, 10 November 2021, available https://home.treasury.gov/news/press-releases/jy0475

On democratic governance, USAID is often overt on the aim of promoting democracy. Democracy is predicated on free elections, judicial independence and a strong (thick) rule of law.[12]

Evidence of growing populism in politics have often driven moves towards (or a return to) one party rule. In sum, the 'rule by people' derived from the etymology of the word democracy, is becoming continuous rule by the same people. Cambodia is no exception. Whilst Cambodia's contemporary governance system could be classed as coming towards the end of the third wave of democratisation,[13] it perhaps is now more properly categorised within the third wave of autocratisation, though Luhrmann and Lindberg did not include it in their 2018 classification of third wave states.[14] Their institute's most recent (2023) V-Dem report, following the 2018 election but before the 2023 one, considers Cambodia with its democratic decline an 'electoral autocracy'.[15] Several African countries have also moved in recent years towards more autocratic, and authoritarian regimes from embryonic (or indeed well established) democracies.[16] Such trends are covered in political science literature, with examinations usually geographically focussed, such as the situation in post-communist countries of Eastern Europe, in Asia, and in Latin America.[17]

Crucially, in many of the countries considered to be moving towards more authoritarian/autocratic rule, the post-colonial or post-transition (irrespective of the reason for the transition) constitution can be deployed by the ruling party (or regime) to justify strengthening political power. National courts often uphold the legitimacy of the measures taken, as rule of law become rules by law—a feature of many of these countries is legislative changes supporting the imminent or recent constitutional change/s and/or providing legal means to strengthen and secure political power. Legitimisation of political manoeuvring is often cited to justify legal changes. That the law is being used proactively is arguably positive, indicating respect for the power of law, even an element of adherence to the rule of law, standing in stark contrast to political elite adopting an overt dictatorial approach. Nevertheless, such rule by law politicises the decisions of the judiciary, even though they may only be applying the enacted laws, and undermines the conception of democracy so often enshrined in the country's constitutional provisions, a conception often embedded

---

[12] Tamanaha (2002).

[13] Huntington's work (1991), pp. 12–34 and (1993), would temporally include Cambodia at the end of the third 'wave'.

[14] Luhrmann and Lindberg (2019), pp. 1095–1113.

[15] Papada et al. (2023).

[16] See, for example, the datasets produced by V-Dem, Variations of Democracy, available https://v-dem.net/data_analysis/CountryGraph/; and the Open Society Initiative for West Africa, West Africa Autocratisation tracker, https://www.osiwa.org/publications/the-wes-africa-autocratization-tracker/

[17] See also, Laebens and Lührmann (2021), pp. 908–928; Lührmann (2021), pp. 1017–1039; Holesch and Kyriazi (2022), pp. 1–20; Castaldo and Memoli (2023); Benasaglio Berlucchi and Kellam (2023), pp. 815–835; Pernia (2023), pp. 63–85.

with the support of international development partners and the then prevailing views and practice advocated by the international community.

Of course, much of the English language literature is predicated on a distinct concept of democracy, one which can be traced to western theoretical and practical conceptualisations, albeit one also reflected in international human rights, rights which were debated and drafted in a world with considerably fewer independent states than today. Mutua highlights this, suggesting that the reluctance of the human rights movement to 'openly identify human rights with liberal democracy' is problematic, not least given that the 'human rights promise [….asks states to] follow a particular script […..advocating] liberal nationalism and democratic internal self-determination'.[18] This is reinforced by the bulk of development cooperation funding going from (neo)liberal democracies to states often with more fragile governance systems. With the UN firmly focussed on advocating the 'universal' human rights at its core, and human rights increasingly linked into the development framework,[19] the scope for conflicting narratives is clear. Indeed, the UN sustainable development goals' targets and indicators, which should be driving the world's development agenda, almost entirely map on to pre-existing human rights standards.[20] Especially relevant is SDG16—promote peaceful and inclusive societies for sustainable development, provide access to justice for all and build effective, accountable and inclusive institutions at all levels.[21] That goal includes a target on promoting the rule of law (16.3) albeit with indicators more centred on access to justice. This reinforces the centrality of human rights in development. As indeed does the Human Rights Based Approach to Development Cooperation: Towards a Common Understanding Among UN Agencies which was adopted in 2003 to guide and support a human rights based approach in the work of UN agencies.[22] It requires that 'programmes of development co-operation, policies and technical assistance should further the realisation of human rights as laid down in the Universal Declaration of Human Rights and other international human rights instruments….[and that] Development cooperation contributes to the development of the capacities of 'duty-bearers' to meet their obligations and/or of 'rights-holders' to claim their rights.'.[23] Promoting elements of democracies, including judicial independence, should be implicit in, or at least underpin, development.

Governance and rule of law is a common category of field activities for UNDP as well as integral to the field work of the Office of the High Commissioner for

[18] Mutua (2004), pp. 54 and 57.

[19] United Nations General Assembly, Transforming our world: the 2030 Agenda for Sustainable Development, Resolution A/RES/70/1 (2015).

[20] See, the Danish Institute for Human Rights, The Human Rights Guide to Sustainable Development Goals and database, available https://sdg.humanrights.dk/

[21] SDG 16 detailed by UN DESA at https://sdgs.un.org/goals/goal16

[22] UN Statement of Common Understanding Among UN Agencies, 2003, available https://unsdg.un.org/sites/default/files/6959-The_Human_Rights_Based_Approach_to_Development_Cooperation_Towards_a_Common_Understanding_among_UN.pdf

[23] UN Statement of Common Understanding Among UN Agencies, paras 1 + 3.

Human Rights. For the UN system, Antonio Guterres, currently Secretary-General launched his vision for the rule of law in June 2023.[24] 'The rule of law is essential for sustainable development and is a whole of society endeavour'[25] with SDG16 the key enabler. Moreover, the rule of law is required to align with human rights and so '[j]Judiciaries must be independent and free from political interference'.[26] Accordingly, for development cooperation, rule of law, good governance and judicial independence are important and inter-linked.

In Cambodia, as will be illustrated, democracy-centred, rule of law strengthening development activities (supported by the USA and EU for example) have faltered as the country moves towards autocracy. In their stead, development partners more focussed on trade and investment than democracy (eg China) or those taking a less interventionist approach (eg Japan) have maintained prominence. Independence of the judiciary is enshrined in the Cambodian constitution and regularly reiterated by the country's most senior government ministers. There is clear provision for de jure judicial independence, though as will be explained, that does not result in de facto independence. This chapter briefly considers USA, Japan and China, longstanding partners of Cambodia, and the EU which grew into an institutional partner. To understand the impact of these development partnerships and monitoring, however, an overview of the contemporary Cambodian context is useful, highlighting key events in the modern era.

3 Cambodia: A Complex Case Study in Democracy and Development

This section offers an understanding of the modern era of Cambodia, its constitutional framework and the evolution of its modern judiciary. Cambodia's tragic past, which is outlined below, inevitably shapes its present. Today, Cambodia is a net exporter of labour,[27] a net importer of energy[28] and an exporter of products (textile, footwear, agribusiness),[29] bolstering a fast-expanding economy. Cambodia can be categorised as a transitional democracy, with its current constitutionally democratic

[24] Guterres (2023).

[25] Ibid at page 5.

[26] Ibid at page 4.

[27] IOM (UN Migration), World Migration Report 2022, Geneva, 2022 report Cambodia had 79,000 migrants with it 'exporting' 1,012,674, more than half that number are in Thailand. These are official numbers, the actual number of migrant workers from Cambodia, including the informal figures, is considerably higher.

[28] ERIA Study Team (2022), pp. 1–12. Cambodia imports all petrochemicals, and remains import dependent across energy sectors, though domestic production has increased in some areas, e.g. hydropower.

[29] For an overview, World Bank, WITS, Cambodia database, though note exports have increased post covid, data available, https://wits.worldbank.org/countrysnapshot/en/KHM

framework influenced by the UN which administered the country in the early stage of its transition, the first and most substantial 'nation-building' programme of the UN to date. How Cambodia reached this point is relevant to understanding claimed challenges with the rule of law and judicial independence today, as well as its shifting development partnerships.

3.1 Historical Context

Whilst the Kingdom of Cambodia has a long history,[30] dating long before its famous Angkorian period, it also has a more tragic, recent past. In the last century it was still subject to French colonial rule.[31] For almost a century, the French derived civil law system was adhered to and, broadly, became the basis of the legal system. During the Second World War, Cambodia was occupied by Japanese forces who overthrew the French colonial powers in an effort to bolster support for Japan during what became the closing months of the conflict.[32] Although France re-established its protectorate after the Japanese surrender, there were increasing revolts against colonial rule.[33] This resulted in internal (civil) conflicts, often along ideological lines, which continued after Cambodia became the independent Kingdom of Cambodia in 1953.[34] Moreover, in the late 1960s, early 1970s Cambodia's civil unrest was exacerbated, and the country further destabilised, by the US military carpet-bombing parts of the country during its offensive against Vietnam.[35] A 1970 military 'coup' led by Lon Nol, himself a former Prime Minister, overthrew the monarchy. He self-appointed head of the new Khmer Republic,[36] and initiated a number of political and legal changes which were not supported by all sections of the then politically fragmented country.

Democratic Kampuchea was the next and deadliest incarnation of what is now modern Cambodia. Extensive devastation was wrought by Pol Pot,[37] the Marxist-Leninist nationalist who seized power with his Khmer Rouge and sought to institute a socialist agrarian society.[38] Virtually all pre-existing laws ceased to apply, most lawyers (and those with legal or law enforcement experience) fled the country or

---

[30] E.g. see Chandler (2008).

[31] E.g. see Tully (2003).

[32] E.g. see Nakano (2018).

[33] E.g. see Kiernan (1982).

[34] E.g. see Chandler (1991).

[35] Arne-Westad and Quinn-Judge (2006); US Government (2000).

[36] E.g. see Chap. 3 in Ayres (2000).

[37] Chandler (1999); Kiernan (2004).

[38] Tyner (2017).

were killed;[39] none continued in their previous occupations. Mass killings quelled dissent and sought to impose order,[40] during a tumultuous and desperate period of the country's history.[41] There followed a widespread famine.[42] (There have been successful (if limited) prosecutions for genocide,[43] as well as other international crimes. This was in a hybrid international/national criminal court established under the auspices of the UN.[44]) Subsequently Vietnam invaded (some claim liberated) Cambodia to bring to an end Pol Pot's regime,[45] though that establishment of the State of Cambodia heralded a further period of civil war, as well as famine and continued mass displacement of people (including returning population).[46]

The United Nations was heavily involved in the peace deal brokered by a number of countries which sought to bring the tumultuous civil war to a close; the Agreements on a Comprehensive Political Settlement of the Cambodia Conflict (the Paris Peace Agreement) signed in 1991 by eighteen countries and agreed by representatives of the different factions in Cambodia.[47] That heralded the UN Transitional Authority in Cambodia (UNTAC),[48] when 'the world invaded Cambodia'.[49] UNTAC oversaw the first 'democratic' elections of the modern era (in 1993)[50] and the drafting of the new Constitution (by those who were duly elected).

Arguably, the drafting of the Constitution was influenced by external (foreign) advisers, including through the United Nations Organisation. The result was described as a mix of the previous 1947 (colonial era) and 1989 State of Cambodia (SOC) constitutions combining 'the royalist electoral victors' conception of stable government with CPP[Cambodian People's Party]/SOC habits as [the then] de facto government', an arrangement which made sense in the then Cambodian political

---

[39] See, generally, Short (2004). Only a handful of legally qualified and experienced people remained in Cambodia.

[40] Locard (2005), pp. 121–143

[41] Becker (1998); Etcheson (1984); Vickery (1984).

[42] E.g. Defalco (2014).

[43] Nuon Chea and Khieu Samphan were convicted of genocide in the Extraordinary Chambers in the Courts of Cambodia, Case 002/02, with Khieu Samphan's conviction upheld on appeal on 23 December 2022 (Dossier No. 002/19-09-2007-ECCC/SC). Kiernan (2003), pp. 585–597.

[44] See, inter alia, General Assembly resolution 57/228B (2003) on the promulgation of the Law on the Establishment of the Extraordinary Chambers in the Courts of Cambodia for the Prosecution of Crimes Committed During the Period of Democratic Kampuchea; Agreement between the United Nations and the Royal Government of Cambodia, available http://www.unakrt-online.org/sites/default/files/documents/volume-2329-I-41723.pdf; concerning the prosecution under Cambodian law of crimes committed during the period of Democratic Kampuchea. Phnom Penh, 6 June 2003.

[45] Morris (1999).

[46] Chandler (2008); Strangio (2020).

[47] Endorsed by the UN Security Council in resolution 718 (1991).

[48] UN Security Council Resolution 745 (1992).

[49] Widyono (2008), p. 3.

[50] Election results were confirmed by the UNTAC and endorsed by the UN Security Council (Resolution 840 (1993)).

context.[51] There was a blend of the colonial French-influenced constitutional monarchy supported by the royalist FUNCINPEC party,[52] which won most of the seats in the 1993 election, and the post Khmer Rouge, socialist Vietnamese influenced framework of the Cambodian People's Party.[53] The constitution was, inevitably, a compromise agreed in a highly pressured situation as the UN oversaw the political transition and with all parties (internal and external) keen for the foundations of a peaceful modern Cambodia to be delineated.

Some key terms are not defined in the constitution, including 'liberal democracy',[54] a term required to be included by the Paris Agreement.[55] Marks suggests it was only included as King Sihanouk suggested it during the negotiations as 'he assumed it was what the Americans and other key participants in the Paris Conference wanted to hear'.[56] It is fair to assume that other terms and concepts may similarly have been included without extensive reflection and thought on the part of the newly elected Cambodian legislature. The lack of definition of key terms and concepts indirectly impacts the powers of the judiciary to protect constitutionally guaranteed rights and freedoms in a manner considered essential to advancing the rule of law, a principle which was also not defined.

Inevitably after 'the world had invaded Cambodia', it didn't all leave. In particular, international and national civil society flourished.[57] This was essentially 'new' in Cambodia which hitherto had (and still has) a strong network of pagoda-based associations focussed on supporting communities often through what would be termed now as volunteering. In Cambodia international development support nurtured the evolution of many national civil society organisations in the modern era. Civil society in Cambodia therefore was comparatively 'weak', with its 'grassroots' heavily supported by international entities (private parties, foreign governments, foreign civil society and non-governmental organisations etc). It was arguably a transplanted system, nurtured in a transitional environment and developed to address, monitor and support the transition of the country to its newly proclaimed democracy. Training was delivered by foreigners (for example on evidence gathering, logistics, resources, advocacy and record-keeping) and practical logistical and resource support was common. Some foreign organisations established bases in

---

[51] Marks (2010), pp. 207–244.

[52] Led by the King's son, Prince Norodom Rannariddh.

[53] Notably Hun Sen, who subsequently served as Prime Minister of Cambodia.

[54] See Article 51, Constitution.

[55] Framework for a Comprehensive Political Settlement of the Cambodia Conflict, 23 October 1991, A/46/608 S/23177, available https://peacemaker.un.org/cambodiaparisagreement91, Annexe 5, at para 4.

[56] Marks (2010), pp. 207–244, in 'The Influence of the Paris Agreements'.

[57] Michael Kirby, UN Special Representative of the Secretary-General in Cambodia in his final assessment commented on civil society: 'They are impressive. They are courageous. They spread the practical lessons of human rights to the homes and villages of Cambodia. There they provide an alternative model for society to the autocratic way of the past.', comments 'Cambodia - A Parting Assessment' 1 April 1996, available from https://www.michaelkirby.com.au/

Cambodia, including many focussed on democracy. Human rights training, constitutional, legislative, judicial and parliamentarian training, education training—Cambodia became almost a 'test centre' for development just as the internet was coming to prominence and as the world had recommitted in Vienna 1993 to the universality of international human rights and freedoms. There are over six thousand civil society organisations in the country. Now, as in so many countries, many members of that vibrant civil society are under threat with diminishing freedoms and increasing checks and surveillance.[58]

3.2 *Judicial Context*

As for judicial independence from the executive, it was a 'requirement', an onus on the drafters of the post 1991 modern era Constitution. As accepted by the Cambodian (and international) parties[59] to the Paris Peace Agreement, '[a]n independent judiciary will be established, empowered to enforce the rights provided under the constitution'.[60] Of course, it arguably reflects some of the prevailing (western) discourse during the negotiation of the peace agreement and seeks to embed a check on executive power such had as occurred during the Khmer Rouge period with devastating consequences. That would necessitate a sufficiently robust and resilient degree of independence to stand firm against political and internal/external pressures.[61]

Article 51 of the Cambodia Constitution provides that legislative, judicial and executive functions are to be separate. More specifically, Article 128 of the Constitution is explicit both that '[t]he Judiciary is an independent power' and that '[t]he Judiciary shall be impartial and protect the rights and freedom of citizens'. The principle is referenced repeatedly by senior members of government including the former Prime Minister, Samdech Techo Hun Sen, especially when challenged on apparent judicialization of politics.[62] Whilst critical legal scholars may argue that there are different conceptions of judicial independence, and certainly precise

[58] For a 2023 appraisal, see Vitit Muntarbhorn, Situation of human rights in Cambodia - Report of the Special Rapporteur on the situation of human rights in Cambodia, A/HRC/54/75 (September 2023).

[59] The negotiations included representatives of the principal political factions and so those elected in 1993.

[60] Point 5, Annex 5: Principles for a New Constitution for Cambodia, Agreement On A Comprehensive Political Settlement Of The Cambodia Conflict, Paris, 23 October 1991

[61] Gibler and Randazzo (2011), pp. 696–709.

[62] On file.

understandings may vary between the states party to the Paris Peace Agreement,[63] and indeed arguably also by factions within Cambodia,[64] the tenor is clear.

Availability of personnel with legal training and experience was extremely limited in the early era of the modern Cambodia. Indeed, Fernando commented (following interviews with those in country) that 'the whole concept of independence of the judiciary was alien to them' and that to secure independence as foreseen in the new Constitution, 'it would be necessary to abolish the judiciary as it exists now, completely'.[65] This can be an explanation for the early disconnect between de jure independence, as articulated in the Constitution, and de facto independence (or rather the lack thereof) as observed in reality in modern Cambodia. Of course, the Constitution and provisions on independence and separation of powers offer de jure independence. Transforming that into de facto judicial independence requires not only political commitment to an independent judiciary, but also the elimination of corruption and its causes.[66]

3.3 *Political Context*

Turning now to the political context, which is instrumental to appreciating the shift in development partnerships, as well as relevant to the evolution and demise of multiparty democracy. A constitutional monarchy through most of the modern era, Cambodia has had one constant Prime Minister, Samdech Techo Hun Sen—until August 2023.[67] Initially securing political power through the Vietnamese occupiers in 1979 (as foreign minister), he became leader in 1985 and, disputing the UN 1993 election results which credited the royalist FUNCINPEC party as the winner over his Cambodian People's Party (CPP), Hun Sen negotiated himself the role of second Prime Minister. He became outright Prime Minister in a 1997 coup, overthrowing the party of the first Prime Minister, Prince Norodom Ranariddh.[68] The CPP has since won outright every subsequent modern era election. Following the 2017/8 elections, Cambodia became a de facto one-party state, the main opposition party having been dissolved by the Supreme Court in November 2017, after the local level elections (which impacts the Senate membership) but before the National Assembly elections. That decision of the Court was made possible (and predictable) due to an

---

[63] Parties to the Agreement were drawn from common law, civil law and plural legal systems as well as postcolonial states and former colonising states.

[64] Royalist, Nationalist, and other political ideologies were represented.

[65] Fernando (1993), pp. 10 and 9. Cited in Marks (2010), pp. 207–244, fns 118–119

[66] See, generally, Diego García-Sayán, Report of the Special Rapporteur on the independence of judges and lawyers, UN Doc A/HRC/35/31, 9 June 2017, see also The Doha Declaration on Judicial Integrity 2020, available https://www.unodc.org/documents/ji/doha2020/Doha_Declaration_on_Judicial_Integrity_final_-_August_2020.pdf

[67] Mehta and Mehta (1999).

[68] See also, Strangio (2014), updated as Strangio (2020).

amendment to the electoral law a few months earlier. The then opposition party (CNRP—Cambodia National Rescue Party) had boycotted the National Assembly so the legislative change passed unopposed. This marked a new epoch of rule by law/man in the country, as the series of laws which had been enacted to facilitate the elimination of political dissent and the dissolution of the CNRP were applied by the courts, without consideration of whether the aims of the laws furthered or undermined the constitution.[69] They were the enacted laws of the country and so were applied by the courts, including the Supreme Court.

Such political impact may be better understood through an historic lens. Cambodian society was traditional characterised by patrimonial networks. James Scott offers an early analysis of the then more anthropologically analysed patron-client relationship considering its impact on politics.[70] His higher socio-economic status protector/provider patron and the lower status 'client' offering loyalty and service maps to the current political dynamic in Cambodia, strengthening under the rule of Hun Sen.[71] Progressively, the Prime Minister strengthened his authoritarian rule portraying himself as holder of power and bestower of favours/rewards echoing the status of historical absolute rulers. West suggests that '[a] civil law system in a neopatrimonial context is a legal-institutional structure highly susceptible to political interference'.[72] Dynastic rule was intimated in 2020 when the Prime Minister stated his intention to continue in post for another decade whilst preparing his son as a candidate for Prime Minister.[73] That son, Hun Manet, was selected by the CPP as their choice as next Prime Ministerial candidate (should his father demit office) in December 2021.[74] He was elected as an MP at the next general election in July 2023.[75] Having therefore satisfied the formal CPP internal and, following the election, the Cambodian constitutional requirements for Prime Minister,[76] his father intimated both his resignation and, following the King's appointment and Parliamentary approvals, his son's succession as Prime Minister.[77] Samdech Hun Manet formally became Cambodia's Prime Minister in August 2023.

---

[69] See, for examples, Report of the Special Rapporteur on the situation of human rights in Cambodia, Addendum 1, A/HRC/39/73/Add.1 (August 2018).

[70] Scott (1972), pp. 91–113; see also Neher (1981).

[71] As above, from 1993 as second/co-Prime Minister; from 1997 as sole Prime Minister.

[72] West (2019), pp. 537–553, at 538.

[73] See statement reported in RFA 'Cambodia's Hun Sen Confirms Eldest Son Hun Manet Being Groomed For Leadership' 22 June 2020, available https://www.rfa.org/english/news/cambodia/grooming-06222020172728.html

[74] 'CPP backs Manet as future PM candidate' Phnom Penh Post, 24 December 2021, available https://phnompenhpost.com/national-politics/cpp-backs-manet-future-pm-candidate

[75] 'Hun Manet officially becomes a candidate for Member of Parliament' Khmer Times, 1 April 2023, available https://www.khmertimeskh.com/501266284/hun-manet-officially-becomes-a-candidate-for-member-of-parliament/

[76] Article 119 of the Constitution.

[77] RFA Khmer 'Hun Sen's son chosen as Cambodia's new prime minister', Radio Free Asia, 22 August 2022, available https://www.rfa.org/english/news/cambodia/hun-manet-prime-minister-08222023161022.html

Noren-Nilsson had identified in the strengthening of power by Hun Sen a series of 'regal legitimisations'.[78] Hun Manet is set to have a similar impact, with the announcement of his new titles, Samdech Moha Bovorthipadi Hun Manet, redolent with regal tones.[79] Such titles deepen the alignment of the Prime Minister's power base to that of traditional kings and, of course, the patrimonial system, a system which compromises the democratic aspirations captured in the constitution, and advanced by key international protagonists. Those international protagonists were, in the main, 'western' developed states, who supported nation-rebuilding in Cambodia through extensive bilateral and multilateral development programmes from the 1990s.

Having outlined the evolution of Cambodia's constitutional democracy and some of the barriers to achieving a multiparty plural democracy, adhering to the rule of law, separation of powers and democratic governance, the role and impact of international development support will be considered. As will be explained, Cambodia has benefitted from a range of different development partnerships. These have included countries offering support/persuasion towards strengthening democracy and others focussing on finance and political alliances, rather more than democracy, rule of law and good governance. This has obvious implications on diplomatic and political imperatives to strengthen rule of law and independence of the judiciary in Cambodia.

4 International Development and Priorities

That the most early modern period development support in Cambodia followed a liberal democracy style model is without question. In part, that is attributable to the Constitution itself which provided for this. And so, development support furthers that expressed national aspiration. Of course, in the case of Cambodia, it can be argued that the then government was almost tied to a specific democratic model as outlined in the Paris Peace Agreement.[80] 'Western' attempts to strengthen (or build) a liberal democracy in Cambodia were initially welcomed, though arguably it is more accurate to suggest that that they were not publicly opposed. There was an influx of people, and a dramatic growth in civil society as the UN supported nation-building programme rolled out. Many countries supporting the democratic transition of Cambodia, supporting/providing law drafting and judicial training, implicitly or explicitly reinforcing the centrality of judicial independence to the modern

[78] Noren-Nilsson (2021), p. 3; this builds on her earlier analysis in Norén-Nilsson (2016).

[79] Royal Decree reported in 'Prime Minister Hun Manet granted the title "Samdech"', Khmer Times, 3 September 2023, available https://www.khmertimeskh.com/501353558/prime-minister-hun-manet-granted-the-title-samdech/

[80] See Letter dated 30 October 1991 from the Permanent Representatives of France and Indonesia to the United Nations addressed to the Secretary-general, A/46/698, S/23177, pp46–47, Part II, Annex 5 Principles for a new Constitution for Cambodia.

Cambodian state (as framed in the constitution). Support was desperately needed—the Special Representative of the Secretary-General noted in 1994 that when UNTAC was established, the country lacked, inter alia, an independent judiciary and even a functioning legal system.[81] There was no country-wide infrastructure of basic institutions of a state.

Human rights in Cambodia, including democratic rights and freedoms, remain subject to monitoring by a UN appointed Special Rapporteur,[82] as well as by UN treaty bodies reviewing compliance with the raft of core human rights treaties Cambodia has ratified and the peer review Human Rights Council universal periodic review process. Mostly dating from the UNTAC period, Cambodia also has a strong UN country team with many UN agencies active in the country.

The Cambodian government has over recent years increasingly refuted the 'westernised' model of democracy as per its constitution, and questioned its relevancy in the Kingdom. In a published report issued in the run up to the 2018 National Assembly elections, the government criticised authors of the Paris Peace Agreements and noted the attempt to 'transplant in one swoop a perfect model of liberal democracy in a country that never knew this kind of political system'

> For those who advocate that democracy is the panacea of all political, economic and social ills, they should be mindful that democracy can't trump the sacred sovereignty of a nation. The narrative of democracy and human rights is country specific and the forced transplantation of these principles are bound to fail, if the process is done in disregard to the national context… [and on rule of law]… politicians from the opposition are unable to express their opposing views through democratic means; the common understanding of the "rule of law" remains weak; the basic principles underlying law and order are largely ignored. All this is to make a case that the journey toward a conciliatory democracy remains still long, winding and arduous, and requires perhaps a generational transition.[83]

Whilst much of that document addresses the political situation, it also advocated strengths of the incumbent government, including peace and stability for 30 years. More so, the emphasis on Cambodian specific characteristics and approaches: 'the national context', the government refers to, is one respected by emerging preferred development partners.[84]

---

[81] Michael Kirby, A continued United Nations Presence in Cambodia, Report of the Special Representative of the Secretary-General, Mr. Michael Kirby (Australia) on the situation of human rights in Cambodia, submitted in accordance with Commission resolution 1993/6, E/CN.4/1994/73, at paras 25 and 21.

[82] Formerly Special Representative of the Secretary General, post created by the Peace Agreements. The author served as Special Rapporteur on the situation in human rights in Cambodia from 2015–2021.

[83] Ministry of Foreign Affairs and International Cooperation, 'Cambodia, Stability and Development First: To Tell The Truth Part II' Phnom Penh, MoFAIC, February 2018, page 3; Ministry of Foreign Affairs and International Cooperation, To Tell the Truth Version 1 (11 April 2017) and Version 2 (7 May 2018), available https://www.mfaic.gov.kh/Media/To%20Tell%20The%20Truth

[84] In February 2023, China reiterated its 'resolute support to Cambodian people's choice of development path that suits Cambodia's national conditions', Joint Statement between the People's Republic of China and the Kingdom of Cambodia on Building a China-Cambodia Community with a Shared Future in the New Era, China's State Council Information Office, 13 February 2023, at point 3, available http://english.scio.gov.cn/topnews/2023-02/13/content_85102645.htm

The necessity of adherence to the principles of democracy, the rule of law and good governance are not only enshrined in the Cambodian Constitution. They also find expression in the ASEAN Charter, with ASEAN and its members states (as well as its peoples) pledging 'adherence to the rule of law, good governance, the principles of democracy and constitutional government'.[85] There is considerable authority supporting a focus on strengthening democracy, rule of law and good governance in development programmes, albeit precision in definitions is missing. That opens the way for push-backs from (recipient) partner states, such as the views expressed by the Cambodian government, quoted above. As pre-existing international development assistance programmes morphed from a donation funding model to more outcome-driven programming, problems emerged. A shift of preferred partnerships from west to east became apparent and the erosion of democracy, rule of law and good governance, in effect, condoned.

This century, development funding has increasingly been tempered by conditions, highlighting the need for concretising outcomes, including measuring adherence to the rule of law, strengthening independence of civil society and political opposition, and, of course, judicial independence. Perhaps the defining epoch in Cambodia lies in politics, starting with the 'high point' of multiparty democracy following the 2013 elections and attempts at a culture of dialogue between the two main political parties achieving a split of power between them (CPP and CNRP).[86] Law, both the fast-track legislative process and the employment of laws in courts to shape political election outcomes played a substantial role in ensuring that political opposition was eliminated in advance of the 2018 elections. That posed a challenge to some of Cambodia's longstanding development partners—continue and be perceived as compromising on supporting democracy (and human rights) or withdraw support and simultaneously compromise the realisation of rights of many Cambodians and offer the opportunity of continuing financial support to states less concerned about establishing democracy than geopolitical influence and investment or trade gains.

4.1 Key Cambodian Development Partnerships

It is useful to delve further in to specificities of development programmes in Cambodia. Partnerships with the USA and the European Union typify the challenges and how rule of law and judicial independence strengthening programmes are threatened. The approach of 'western' programmes contrasts with the Asian approach typified by Japan and, particularly influential in the Cambodian context, China, which is outlined thereafter.

[85] Charter of the Association of South East Asian Nations 2007, eighth preambular paragraph and Article 2, Principle 2(h).

[86] Karbaum (2015).

Initial funding, donations and development support came from the most developed countries (though Japan and China also provided support). Those with the money initially framed their contributions as altruism, though inevitably the concept was tainted with politicisable aims such as countering communism/influence of other states or retaining power/oversight in former colonies. In the Cambodian context, the USA obviously had bombed the country heavily in the 1970s contributing to the instability which the Khmer Rouge sought to remedy. The USA and other western countries were part of the peace negotiation process in the 1990s and as signatories, were arguably supporting their commitments to the country with financial and technical assistance. Accurate inclusive figures are not available, but reports indicate tens of billions of USD have been received by Cambodia. For 2020–2021, the OECD records 3.8 billion USD in net receipts with the top ten donors of gross ODA Japan; the Asian Development Bank and EU; France; USA; Korea; Australia; Germany; and Switzerland.[87]

The Extraordinary Chambers in the Courts of Cambodia (the Khmer Rouge Tribunal) is worth singling out—it has been supported by almost 341 million USD of funding from a range of states.[88] Extensive legacy work focusses on not only international criminal law, but also on embedding good practice in terms of fair trial rights into the Cambodian national legal system (the court operated a hybrid format with international and national investigating judges, judges and lawyers).

Wealthier states were increasingly pressured within the UN to provide support to less developed and developing states and simultaneously, within their own borders, to evidence the difference made and justify their donations and support. This did give rise to conceptualisations of such programmes as predicated on 'white saviours'[89] and the famous 'post-colonial' articulation by Makau Mutua of the human rights framework in 'Savages, Victims and Saviors'.[90] Given the Cambodian experience of democracy building, and Western/Cambodian disconnects in understandings of the rule of law, the resonance is loud and clear. To illustrate the point, selected examples of development cooperation to support Cambodia follows.

Examples of 'Western' Development Partners: USA and the European Union

For the USA, a longstanding development partner, once a major investor in Cambodia and a substantial donor, there was a crisis of ethics, a 'decade of confusion' from 2013 to the present day.[91] Whilst the USA oscillated between dialogue and sanctions in response to the deteriorating democratic framework in Cambodia, the country has been targeted by the outgoing Prime Minister for criticism and ridicule. The USA was implicated in the treason charges (upheld) against the former

[87] OECD-DAC, Aid at a glance charts, Cambodia, available https://www.oecd.org/dac/financing-sustainable-development/development-finance-data/aid-at-a-glance.htm

[88] Figure as at 31 August 2023, taken from the ECCC funding report, available https://eccc.gov.kh/sites/default/files/08-Fund_Balance_31%20August%202023_final.pdf

[89] Khan et al. (2023).

[90] Mutua (2001), pp. 201–245.

[91] Poling et al. (2022).

leader of the former opposition party, CNRP, Kem Sokha. The government's case was predicated on a speech made in Melbourne, Australia in 2013 which referenced support/advice he had received from US democracy groups.[92] In 2017, this suddenly became a live political issue after the CNRP made gains in the local elections in June 2017, and with the National Assembly elections in July 2018 looming. Kem Sokha, arrested in September 2017 on treason related charges, was eventually convicted and sentenced in March 2023.[93]

USAID, the USA's International Development Agency is overt as to the aims of its work in Cambodia: 'The United States works with Cambodia to build a framework for lasting democracy and to improve the lives of all its citizens.'.[94] Of course, the US Government evinces a particular model of democracy, based on its own society. This is evident even through activities advertised by USAID: from 2018–2023, it claims to have 'laid the groundwork for building political will for change', including through 'Provid[ing] legal assistance that helped over 400,000 workers process their labor dispute cases. …Provid[ing] legal assistance to over 24,000 victims of human rights violations (pro-bono legal representation and legal advice). Help[ing] resolve high-profile land disputes for more than 1,000 families. Train[ing] and supply[ing] more than 9,600 grassroots human rights defenders, including more than 4,900 women, to carry out advocacy work. These human rights defenders helped 30,000 families involved in almost 400 land disputes across 19 provinces.'.[95] These are all current politically sensitive issues and, as is clear, link to a perception of democracy and to judicial independence and transparency of accountability of the executive. Moreover, the range of activities are, arguably, not addressing the root causes of de facto independence failures; they are simply addressing the results—land disputes, labour right issues and prosecution of/threats to human rights defenders.

Many civil society organisations and intergovernmental organisations which are highly critical of Cambodia's judicial independence (and wider civil and political rights) have a USA origin and evolved with primary or partial USA/USAID funding. Examples include the World Justice Project; Human Rights Watch,[96] National Democratic Institute,[97] and East West Management Institute.[98] These have all been

---

[92] In Khmer, see Cochrane (2017).

[93] See, e.g. comments in UN Press Release 'Cambodia: UN experts condemn verdict against opposition leader Kem Sokha', Geneva, 8 March 2023, available https://www.ohchr.org/en/press-releases/2023/03/cambodia-un-experts-condemn-verdict-against-opposition-leader-kem-sokha

[94] USAID, Country page, Cambodia, available https://www.usaid.gov/cambodia

[95] USAID, Cambodia, Democracy, Human Rights and Governance, Results, available https://www.usaid.gov/cambodia/democracy-human-rights-and-governance

[96] Human Rights Watch evolved from the Helsinki Watch (1978) established by American activists to monitor the Soviet Union and replicated in 'Watches' around the world.

[97] Independent of government, founded and based in USA, works around the world, see https://www.ndi.org/

[98] For an overview of the approach and Cambodia programme, see https://ewmi.org/ and https://ewmi.org/Countries/Cambodia

active in Cambodia from the early modern era. Each has a remit aligned with promoting democracy, including rule of law and judicial independence.

The Cambodian Government has terminated rights of several of these organisations in Cambodia. So, the National Democratic Institute, which worked in Cambodia since 1992, focussing on supporting and strengthening democratic institutions through inter alia accountability in government, was closed down (in Cambodia) in 2017.[99] Also in 2017, the Cambodia Daily, founded in 1993 by an American philanthropist as an independent English language paper, shut down. It had faced a large bill for allegedly unpaid taxes as well as increased scrutiny and pressure from the Government. It elected to close its operation, though its final edition went out proclaiming the end of democracy in Cambodia with a headline 'Descent into Outright Dictatorship,[100] as the leader of the (now former) CNRP (Kem Sokha) had just been arrested in a late night heavily policed operation. Radio Free Asia (RFA), a USA based media, funded by US Congress, states its focus is to 'provide independent, uncensored and accurate local news to a weekly audience of nearly 60 million who lack access to a free press or live in media environments vulnerable to authoritarian disinformation.'.[101] With such a mandate, it is unsurprising that RFA journalists have encountered challenges in Cambodia. Journalists have been arrested, particularly when seeking to report on contentious land issues ('land grabbing') and other politically sensitive matters. Two RFA journalists, Yeang Sothearin and Uon Chhin, were arrested on charges of espionage contemporaneously with the arrest of Kem Sokha and others in 2017.[102] Their arrests led to the closure of the Phnom Penh Bureau of RFA.

Human Rights Watch, working from their Bangkok and USA offices, remains active monitoring events Cambodia, publishing hard-hitting and extensively evidenced reports, and issuing fast commentary and critiques of the government.[103] Examples include substantive reports on the former Prime Minister's rise to power, subtitled 'Violence, Repression, and Corruption in Cambodia',[104] and reports on Chinese development initiatives,[105] while immediate response report subjects include political events[106] and labour rights.[107] Almost all include examples of

---

[99] NDI, 'Statement on Cambodian Government's Decision to Shut Down NDI's Office in Cambodia', 23 August 2017, available https://www.ndi.org/publications/statement-cambodian-government-s-decision-shut-down-ndis-office-cambodia

[100] Andrew Nachemson, 'The Cambodia Daily confirms it will close on Monday' Phnom Penh Post, 3 September 2017, available https://www.phnompenhpost.com/national/cambodia-daily-confirms-it-will-close-monday; Cambodia Daily, 4 September 2017, front page

[101] Radio Free Asia, About, available https://www.rfa.org/about

[102] Cambodian Center for Human Rights, 'The continued legal harassment of ex-RFA journalists Yeang Sothearin & Uon Chhin', April 2022, available https://cchrcambodia.org/storage/posts/4858/New_rjie_en.pdf

[103] Their country webportal links to their work, available https://www.hrw.org/asia/cambodia

[104] Adams (2015).

[105] Sifton (2021).

[106] Human Rights Watch (2023).

[107] Human Rights Watch (2022).

corruption and failures in judicial independence. Inevitably, they are dismissed by the government as inaccurate and biased, or simply ignored.[108]

The European Union has overtly tied its development support to democracy, rule of law and governance principles. Deterioration in protection of and respect for human rights, particularly civil, labour and political rights led, ultimately to the Union partially withdrawing trade preferences offered to Cambodia under its Everything But Arms (EBA) arrangement. EBA is available to least developed countries and aims at supporting the development of such countries by offering a suspension of Common Customs Tariff duties on goods entering the EU market.[109] However, that market access comes with conditions, including the strengthening of human rights.[110] Following the 'increasingly restricted' of civil society space, dissolution of the CNRP, and arrest of Kem Sokha, the European Union considered itself compelled to react.[111] The 2018 election process was a key factor, as the potential for democracy in Cambodia was quashed by the government, through legislation and policy decisions. Extensive diplomacy followed, as the EU sought to avoid any withdrawal of the country's access to the EU markets.[112] Regular discussions were held with the government and exhortations made on changing its practices to manifest stronger human rights protections, especially civil, labour and political rights.[113] On 12 February 2020, the European Commission determined it would partially suspend tariff preferences due to serious and systematic violations of human rights, including labour rights. Ultimately, despite some progress noted on labour rights and better cooperation with the EU re land rights relevant to sugar plantations, the European Commission withdrew trade preferences for key areas.[114] This exemplifies the linking of development cooperation to 'good' democracy, rule of law and human rights.

---

[108] On file.

[109] See Regulation (EU) No 978/2012 of the European Parliament and of the Council of 25 October 2012 applying a scheme of generalised tariff preferences and repealing Council Regulation (EC) No 732/2008, Official Journal of the European Union, L 303/1, 31 October 2012.

[110] Relevant conventions which must be complied with are listed in Annex VIII of the regulation.

[111] See, e.g., European Parliament Resolution of 13 September 2018 on Cambodia, notably the case of Kem Sokha (2018/2842(RSP)).

[112] For the process, see Article 19 Regulation (EU) No 978/2012.

[113] See EU Statement on Cambodia and EBA, 11 February 2019, available https://www.eeas.europa.eu/node/57920_en; see also the government response, Ministry of Foreign Affairs and International Cooperation, 'Statement of the Royal Government of Cambodia in response to the European Commission's decision to launch the formal procedure for the temporary withdrawal of the Everything But Arms (EBA) preferences for Cambodia', 12 February 2019, available https://www.mfaic.gov.kh/posts/post-26876

[114] Commission Delegated Regulation 2020/550 as regards the temporary withdrawal in respect of certain products originating in the Kingdom of Cambodia (12 February 2020) available https://eur-lex.europa.eu/legal-content/EN/TXT/PDF/?uri=CELEX:32020R0550&from=ENa—key 'serious and systematic violations' were found of the principles laid down in Articles 19, 21, 22 and 25 of the ICCPR, the latter being electoral rights.

Of course, as with sanctions, it is not necessarily the government that suffers. For EBA in Cambodia, the garment and textile industry was key and hundreds of thousands of predominantly rural women working in factories were at risk of losing their livelihood.[115] In human rights terms, extensive human rights, mostly social and economic, would be engaged by action taken to try to force the Cambodian government to comply with other human rights. At the time, the Cambodian government indicated that the trade loss from the EU would be mitigated by trade increase from China.[116] Of course, COVID-19 irrevocably changed the impact of the EBA changes as global trade shifted and faltered.

Interests of the USA and EU find resonance in the UN monitoring mechanisms on human rights and other international reviews. By way of examples, in 2022, the UN Human Rights Committee concluded that '[d]espite the measures taken by the State party to strengthen the independence of the judiciary, the Committee remains concerned about the persistent lack of an independent and impartial judiciary and about the high number of allegations of corruption within the judiciary. The Committee also notes with concern that some judges are openly members of the ruling party, often holding leadership positions, which seriously undermines their independence (art. 14).'.[117] Concern was also expressed during the countries universal periodic review.[118] Earlier, in 2015, the International Bar Association was highly critical of the lack of judicial independence.[119] Their high-level fact-finding team for that report included the current UN Special Rapporteur on the country, Professor Vitit Muntarbhorn.

Of course, the USA and the EU have engaged in a wide range of development projects in Cambodia over the decades, many warmly supported by the Cambodian Royal Government. The position of the USA and European Union epitomises Cambodian 'western' development partners, with their growing pre-conditions of strengthening democracy and human rights protection, contrasts with Asian approaches to development.

---

[115] On file.

[116] For example, the then Prime Minister heralded new trade agreements with China as offsetting the looming loss from the EU, RFA 'Cambodia's PM Hun Sen Touts China Deals as Loss of EU Trade Scheme Looms' 24 April 2019, available https://www.rfa.org/english/news/cambodia/deals-04292019163622.html

[117] Human Rights Committee, Concluding observations on the third periodic report of Cambodia, 18 May 2022, CCPR/C/KHM/CO/3, at para 32.

[118] For examples, see Report of the Working Group on the Universal Periodic Review, Cambodia A/HRC/41/17 (2019) recommendations of Austria at para 110.125, Belgium at 110.127, Italy at 110.118, Japan at 110.124, Lithuania at 110.122, and Norway at 110.121.

[119] International Bar Association' Human Rights Institute (IBAHRI), Justice versus corruption: Challenges to the independence of the judiciary in Cambodia, London: International Bar Association, 2015; an immediate Government response is found in the words of the Ministry of Justice spokesperson, Malin Chin, reported by Peter Zsombor, 'Legal Group Urges Review of Cambodia's Bar' Cambodia Daily, 18 September 2015, available https://english.cambodiadaily.com/news/legal-group-urges-review-of-cambodias-bar-94684/

4.2 *Examples of Asian Development Partners: Japan and China*

Asian development partners have long espoused a different model of support. This is often less 'democracy' focussed, more collaborative and components frequently include loans and shared financing, rather than the earlier donor orientated approach of western governments.[120] This reflects the Asian approach of non-interference in internal affairs of states.[121] It is useful to preface the following paragraphs by noting that that within East Asia, Japan and Korea are members of the OECD Development Assistance Committee, but China is not. Brautigam analysed the Chinese approach a decade ago, concluding that, with modest exceptions, it did not fall within the OECD framework's definition/scope.[122] It is submitted that position has not dramatically changed.

So, in Cambodia, Japan, a long-standing development partner, is working on a range of substantive infrastructure projects across the country, including building hospitals, teacher training colleges and many road projects.[123] Many of these are funded through loans from Japan International Cooperation Agency (JICA) or grants. Sitting alongside its technical cooperation programme, this illustrates the capacity building approach of Japan (and contrasts with the hitherto traditional donor approach of, e.g. USAID). Moreover, the Japanese government approach is much more collaborative and supportive, with quiet diplomacy, as contrasted with the more confrontational approach which is often the 'way' of 'western' states.[124] Democracy and rule of law are not overt centrepieces in their development and cooperation programmes. Peacebuilding and governance are nevertheless components. Japan has contributed to the development of laws in Cambodia, with a focus on the civil code and civil procedure code. It has supported elections too, though through technical assistance and (some years) election monitoring. Socio-economic progress and industrial development are, however, the main aims,[125] which contrasts with, for example, the USA approach discussed above.

Japan has habitually taken on the vexed role as pen holder for drafting the (now) biannual Human Rights Council resolution on Cambodia.[126] This requires dextrous

---

[120] Western governments also offered loans and preferential trade agreements.

[121] Article 2 Principles 2(a), (e) + (k), Charter of the Association of South East Asian Nations 2007; similar text appears in the earlier constituent documents of ASEAN. See also, Suzuki (2019), pp. 157–176.

[122] Brautigam (2011), pp. 752–764.

[123] Japan International Cooperation Agency (JICA), Map of JICA Major Projects: Cambodia, 1 May 2022, available https://libportal.jica.go.jp/library/Data/PlanInOperation-e/SoutheastAsia/021_Cambodia-e.pdf

[124] Hafner-Burton (2008), pp. 698–716; Lebovic and Voeten (2009), pp. 79–97.

[125] Government of Japan, Cambodia Development Cooperation Policy, 2017, available https://www.mofa.go.jp/files/000477240.pdf

[126] A/HRC/RES/48/23, 14 October 2021.

and deft fielding of competing approaches and usually involves a close connection with the Cambodian government as it builds support for each resolution.[127] The fact Japan secured support for resolutions during the 2013–2020 period encompassing fractious elections and a marked deterioration in the markers of 'democracy' evidences their diplomatic skill. These resolutions often reference rule of law and the need for Cambodia to strengthen laws to secure judicial independence.[128] Japan's interventions in the UN on Cambodia also reflect a nuanced approach though it has raised the need for an independent justice system, progress on democratisation and combatting corruption.[129]

China's approach to this development assistance is different than that taken by many other development partners Cambodia chooses to work with. It not only reinforces non-interference in national affairs, but comes with no human rights or good governance preconditions, in contrast to, for example, the EU's EBA scheme which was dependent on giving effect to fifteen core UN and ILO conventions.[130] China, as the then Cambodian Prime Minister commented, not only has an 'ironclad friendship' with Cambodia, but a relationship 'built on the foundation of a profound political trust and driven by a deep sense of mutual respect of each other's independence, sovereignty, territorial integrity, and non-interference in internal affairs.'.[131]

Cambodia has strengthened its longstanding good relationship with China over the years.[132] In August 2023, before handing over power, the former Prime Minister authored an Op-Ed in China Daily, noting

> China is currently Cambodia's top major trading partner, the main driver of foreign investment and a key contributor of development assistance. ….[and] China's BRI is the largest aid source for Cambodia's physical infrastructure development, which is the backbone for our economic growth and national development, both of which act as a vital catalyst for improving our people's livelihoods.[133]

---

[127] Technical Assistance. A/HRC/24/L.19, 20 September 2013; A/HRC/RES/30/23, 12 October 2015; A/HRC/RES/36/32, 5 October 2017; and A/HRC/RES/42/37, 9 October 2019.

[128] For example, A/HRC/RES/42/37, 9 October 2019 reaffirmed 'the need for the Government of Cambodia to strengthen efforts to consolidate and abide by the rule of law, including through the adoption, amendment and further implementation of essential laws and codes for establishing a democratic society and an independent judiciary', at para 10.

[129] Examples from recommendations made during universal periodic review, respectively, para 110.124 cycle 3, cycle 2 and cycle 1.

[130] For a summary, see European Commission, At a Glance "Everything but Arms': The case of Cambodia', available https://www.europarl.europa.eu/RegData/etudes/ATAG/2019/637931/EPRS_ATA(2019)637931_EN.pdf

[131] Samdech Akka Moha Sena Padei Techo Hun Sen, 'Cambodia-China ties cemented in BRI' China Daily 25 August 2023, available https://www.chinadaily.com.cn/a/202308/15/WS64daab71a31035260b81c12b.html?s=09

[132] China-Cambodia relations are claimed to be the oldest in southeast Asia—Hoang (2023).

[133] Samdech Akka Moha Sena Padei Techo Hun Sen, 'Cambodia-China ties cemented in BRI' China Daily 25 August 2023, available https://www.chinadaily.com.cn/a/202308/15/WS64daab71a31035260b81c12b.html?s=09

China also offers considerable military aid and cooperation to Cambodia, indeed, Cambodia tops the list of military support from China.[134] As implied above, the European Union support is explicitly 'everything but arms', so very limited as regards military cooperation.

Chinese support allowed Cambodia to pursue its own development path suitable to 'national characteristics', a refrain common in Chinese human rights and development dialogues.[135] Interestingly, Po and Sims negate China's oft-quoted claims on 'non-interference', fielding evidence China has repeatedly taken steps to reinforce (then Prime Minister) Hun Sen's leadership.[136] Lim and Kim considered a wider geographical approach, finding 'the leadership position at ASEAN [which rotates amongst members] appears to be significantly associated with an increase of official development aid flows from China'.[137] Nevertheless, for Cambodia, working with countries with an approach to the rule of law, democracy and judicial independence which is less onerous than that espoused by the USA or EU has attractions. Validation of progress is forthcoming and public, criticism less so.[138]

Extant academic analyses on Chinese development assistance often focus on Africa,[139] though there are some reviews of its longstanding and strengthening partnership with Cambodia.[140] What is notable is that China offers a different model for supporting development, not least a lot of direct investment. A free trade agreement was concluded, in October 2020,[141] following various packages of trade agreements. This was touted as a major investment into Cambodia and a major opportunity for exports, filling any gap from the reduction of preferential access to the EU from August 2020.

Whilst western countries may claim altruism for their support for Cambodia, this is tainted if viewed from a postcolonial lens. Their emphasis on judicial independence and rule of law is underpinned by legal transplantation, even though the UN arguably supports that stance. These evolving relationships can be viewed as

---

[134] Hundreds of millions of dollars in aid have been provided. See also Jack Lau, 'China, Cambodia look to upgrade military ties along with expanded naval base' South China Morning Post, 21 November 2022, available https://www.scmp.com/news/china/military/article/3200441/china-cambodia-look-upgrade-military-ties-along-expanded-naval-base

[135] Samdech Akka Moha Sena Padei Techo Hun Sen, 'Cambodia-China ties cemented in BRI' China Daily 25 August 2023, available https://www.chinadaily.com.cn/a/202308/15/WS64daab71a31035260b81c12b.html?s=09; see also comments of China in Human Rights Council re Cambodia, on file with author.

[136] Po and Sims (2022), pp. 36–54.

[137] Lim and Kim (2023), pp. 351–377.

[138] In UPR, China's recommendations are phrased as continuing to develop education, or strengthen health, maintain social stability and promote sustainable economic and social development. No mention of civic space, democracy or judiciary.

[139] Gu et al. (2016), pp. 24–34; Dong and Fan (2017), pp. 1–18; Broich (2017), pp. 180–207.

[140] Sato et al. (2011), pp. 2091–2104 (This was written by people working in JICA); Kilama (2016), pp. 76–91.

[141] China-Cambodia Free Trade Agreement October 2020, entering into force 1 January 2022, text available in English http://fta.mofcom.gov.cn/topic/encambodia.shtml

furthering SDG 17 on strengthening the means of implementation and revitalising the Global Partnership for Sustainable Development. With Cambodia's avowed aim of attaining upper middle-income status by 2030, having reached lower middle-income status in 2015, the country has more economic and political power to select development partners. Those imposing rule of law, democracy and judicial independence are unlikely to be top of their list. A more nuanced, cooperative collaborative with other Asian nations offers financial support to the country but without so many conditions. Of course, that support brings different pressure, not least that loans ultimately need repaid. Political and diplomatic support for their development partners may not be enough, though is welcome. Cambodia has certainly echoed and supported China when its human rights record is considered before the Human Rights Council,[142] and blocked the Association of South East Asian Nations from commenting at a high political level on maritime disputes in the South China Sea.[143]

5 Opportunities to Revisit Development Relationships and Strengthen Rule of Law, and Judicial Independence?

Cambodia is arguably in a unique position. No other country has been subject to such extensive nation-building on the part of the United Nations itself. The central positioning of a multiparty form of democracy possibly owes as much to timing as planning. The end of the 'cold war' which had restricted UN activities, not least as regards peacekeeping, was a key marker in international relations and politics. Contemporaneously, the UN's decolonisation project had dramatically changed the organisation's membership and secured transitions to independence for states around the world. Such states often embarked on independence with constitutions embedded with provisions on democracy, judicial independence and rule of law. The timing of the Paris Peace Accords also coincided with preparation for the UN World Conference on Human Rights in Vienna. Optimism and positivity dominated as the world approached the second millennium,[144] cumulating in the global agreement that 'priority be given to national and international action to promote democracy, development and human rights.'[145] and in furtherance thereof that.

Special emphasis should be given to measures to assist in the strengthening and building of institutions relating to human rights, strengthening of a pluralistic civil society and the protection of groups which have been rendered vulnerable. In this

---

[142] See for example, Statement of the Permanent Mission of the Kingdom of Cambodia to the United Nations Office and other International Organizations at Geneva during the General Debate on Human Rights attracted particular attention of the Council, Item 4, 42nd of the Human Rights Council, September 2019, Geneva http://www.cambodiaembassy.ch/statement/HR/20190917_Statement_HRC%2042_item%204.pdf

[143] Mogato et al. (2016).

[144] It is acknowledge that categorisation uses a western origin Christian calendar.

[145] Vienna Declaration and Programme of Action 1993, para 66.

context, assistance provided upon the request of Governments for the conduct of free and fair elections, including assistance in the human rights aspects of elections and public information about elections, is of particular importance. Equally important is the assistance to be given to the strengthening of the rule of law, the promotion of freedom of expression and the administration of justice, and to the real and effective participation of the people in the decision-making processes.[146]

It is understandable that with UNTAC concluding its goal of transferring authority after the first elections, elections supported by the UN with extensive engagement across states, and the Vienna Declaration fresh in all states' minds, strengthening the rule of law, promoting judicial independence and democracy were central to many development plans. Equally Cambodia was an obvious 'target' for these development opportunities. In the three decades since, Cambodia is not the only country whose version of 'democracy' does not fulfil the main requirements captured by the UN Declaration in 1993. Many countries in that so-called third wave of democratisation, not least from Eastern Europe and the former USSR block and across decolonised Africa, are moving away from (or at least not actively progressing towards) the liberal democracy model.

The non-interference approach to internal affairs of states, long advocated by China and adopted by ASEAN, as well as many African states, has held at bay attempts by 'western' governments and international organisations to push on democratic reforms and even human rights.[147]

Whilst the EU indicated a willingness to reinstate trade preference should the human rights situation in Cambodia improve,[148] there is little incentive for Cambodia to demonstrably enhance democracy, civil (freedom of expression and assembly and association) and political (electoral) rights when the country has concluded subsequent free trade agreements e.g. with China, which come with no rule of law, good governance or democracy conditions. Development need not include strengthening of democracy. After all, Cambodia has demonstrated strong economic growth year on year irrespective of its internal political position. Peace and stability, the 'win win', of former Prime Minister Hun Sen, have been maintained. Indeed, in 2022, 29 December was designated 'Win Win Policy Day', and a large Win Win memorial has been opened in Phnom Penh, the capital. On 1 January 2024, Win Win Policy Day was formally renamed Peace Day and added to the list of national holidays.

Democracy is not a term deployed regularly by Cambodian government ministers, peace, prosperity and stability, in contrast, are. Conachie mapped the democracy project in Cambodia up to the July 2023 elections, observing that 'Hun Sen's Legacy is the Defeat of Western Foreign Policy' with Hun Sen having demonstrated

---

[146] Id, para 67.

[147] On Africa, see for example, Arriola et al. (2023).

[148] Article 20 Regulation (EU) No 978/2012 of the European Parliament and of the Council of 25 October 2012 applying a scheme of generalised tariff preferences and repealing Council Regulation (EC) No 732/2008, Official Journal of the European Union, L 303/1, 31 October 2012.

that 'there is nothing natural or inevitable about the emergence of liberal democracy'.[149]

Development cooperation is predicated on a range of support options, including technical assistance and capacity building as well as direct investment. SDG17 identifies the centrality of partnerships to the successfully achieving the sustainable development goals. Those goals include SDG16 on peace, justice and strong institutions. However, countries are not obligated to build partnerships to advance specific goals or to accept assistance evincing specific political positions.

To return to the question posed at the outset, judicial independence can be strengthened or undermined by international influence and the ebb and flow of international development assistance from chosen development partners. It depends on those partners. Based on the Cambodian experience judicial independence and more generally the rule of law can be undermined by this ebb and flow of international development support. As countries choose to withdraw support when conditions of compliance with human rights are not met, other countries stand ready to fill the financial gap with no or few conditions. For authoritarian and autocratic regimes, especially those which may offer development partners additional benefits such as strategic alliances, trade, access to natural resources or support in international organisations, if western countries withdraw or reduce support, alternative sources of income and support are likely available. Whilst those other sources may come without human rights and democracy related conditions, they can bring other consequences, notably the risk of debt (for defaulting on loans) and diplomatic pressure on alignment in the UN or regional organisations.

In Cambodia, it can certainly be argued that some international partnerships are contributing to the undermining rather than strengthening of Cambodia's rule of law based democratic foundations. Written constitutional guarantees can be usurped and, increasingly, law has been deployed as a tool to erode the country's constitutionally proclaimed multiparty liberal democracy. Alongside this has been a shrinking civil society and civil society space in effect 'endorsed' by a judiciary increasingly involved in political and politicised trials.

Can judicial independence in weak or unstable democracies be influenced by international development assistance from chosen development partners? As global power shifts and international development priorities oscillate, judicial independence, rule of law and respect for international human rights can be strengthened or undermined depending in part on the approaches of each country's selected development partners.

[149] See Conochie (2023), and an updated oped after Hun Sen demitted office, 'Hun Sen's Legacy is the Defeat of Western Foreign Policy' The Diplomat 24 August 2024, available https://thediplomat.com/2023/08/hun-sens-legacy-is-the-defeat-of-western-foreign-policy/

References

Adams B (2015) 30 years of Hun Sen: Violence, repression, and corruption in Cambodia. Human Rights Watch

Amoah M (2023) Extending term limits, constitutional referendums and elections in francophone Africa. Soc Sci Humanit Open 7(1):100454. https://doi.org/10.1016/j.ssaho.2023.100454

Arne-Westad O, Quinn-Judge S (eds) (2006) The third Indo-China War; conflict between China, Vietnam and Cambodia 1972–79. Routledge, New York

Arriola L, Rakner L, van de Walle N (eds) (2023) Democratic backsliding in Africa? Autocratization, resilience, and contention. Oxford University Press, Oxford

Ayers A (2008) "We all know a democracy when we see one": (neo)liberal orthodoxy in the 'democratisation' and 'good governance' project. Policy Soc 27(1):1–13

Ayres D (2000) Anatomy of a crisis: education, development, and the state in Cambodia, 1953–1998. University of Hawai'i Press, Manoa

Becker E (1998) When the war was over: Cambodia and the Khmer Rouge revolution. Perseus Books

Benasaglio Berlucchi A, Kellam M (2023) Who's to blame for democratic backsliding: populists, presidents or dominant executives? Democratization 30(5):815–835

Brautigam D (2011) Aid 'with Chinese characteristics': Chinese foreign aid and development finance meet the OECD–DAC aid regime. J Int Dev 23(5):752–764

Broich T (2017) Do authoritarian regimes receive more Chinese development finance than democratic ones? Empirical evidence for Africa. China Econ Rev 46:180–207

Castaldo A, Memoli V (2023) Political support and democratic backsliding trends. The strange case of Central and Eastern European countries. J Contemp Eur Stud 32:138. https://doi.org/10.1080/14782804.2023.2206115

Chandler D (1991) The tragedy of Cambodian history: politics, war, and revolution since 1945. Yale University Press, New Haven

Chandler D (1999) Brother number one. A political biography of Pol Pot, revised edition. Westview

Chandler D (2008) A history of Cambodia, 4th edn. Westview

Cochrane L (2017) Australian speech the key 'treason' evidence against Cambodian opposition leader. Australian Broadcasting Cooperation news, 5 September 2017. Available https://www.abc.net.au/news/2017-09-06/australian-speech-evidence-of-treason-against-cambodia-kem-sokha/8876044

Conochie G (2023) A tiger rules the mountain: Cambodia's pursuit of democracy. Monash University Press, Melbourne

Defalco R (2014) Justice and starvation in Cambodia: the Khmer Rouge Famine. Cambodia Law Policy J 3. Available online https://cambodialpj.org/article/justice-and-starvation-in-cambodia-the-khmer-rouge-famine/

Dong Y, Fan C (2017) The effects of China's aid and trade on its ODI in African countries. Emerg Mark Rev 33:1–18

ERIA Study Team (2022) Review of current and future petroleum demand. In: ERIA and General Department of Petroleum, Ministry of Mines and Energy of Cambodia (eds) Cambodia Petroleum Master Plan 2022–2040. ERIA Research Project Report FY2021 No. 21. ERIA, Jakarta, pp 1–12

Etcheson C (1984) The rise and demise of Democratic Kampuchea. Westview

Fernando B (1993) The inability to prosecute: courts and human rights in Cambodia and Sri Lanka. Future Asia Link, Hong Kong

Fruhstorfer A, Hudson A (2022) Costs and benefits of accepting presidential term limits: "should I stay or should I go?". Democratization 29(1):93–112

Gibler D, Randazzo K (2011) Testing the effects of independent judiciaries on the likelihood of democratic backsliding. Am J Polit Sci 55(3):696–709

Griffin J (2008) On human rights. OUP, Oxford

Gu J, Zhang C, Vaz A, Mukwereza L (2016) Chinese state capitalism? Rethinking the role of the state and business in Chinese development cooperation in Africa. World Dev 81:24–34

Guterres A (2023) New vision of the secretary-general for the Rule of Law. UNP, New York. Available https://www.un.org/ruleoflaw/wp-content/uploads/2023/07/New-Vision-of-the-Secretary-General-for-the-Rule-of-Law.pdf

Hafner-Burton E (2008) Sticks and stones: naming and shaming the human rights enforcement problem. Int Org 6(4):698–716

Hoang N (2023) Cambodia–China economic relations in the context of BRI. In: Touch S, Wang L, Phea K, Zhao J, Jiayun G (eds) Cambodia-China comprehensive strategic partnership towards a community with a shared future. Springer, Singapore

Holesch A, Kyriazi A (2022) Democratic backsliding in the European Union: the role of the Hungarian-Polish coalition. East Eur Polit 38(1):1–20

Human Rights Watch (2022) Only "Instant Noodle" Unions Survive Union Busting in Cambodia's Garment and Tourism Sectors. 21 November 2022. Available https://www.hrw.org/report/2022/11/21/only-instant-noodle-unions-survive/union-busting-cambodias-garment-and-tourism

Human Rights Watch (2023) Cambodia: renewed attacks on political opposition-Hun Sen's campaign rhetoric prompts assaults, wrongful arrests. 24 April 2023. Available https://www.hrw.org/news/2023/04/24/cambodia-renewed-attacks-political-opposition

Hunter W, Murison A (1921) Introduction to Roman Law. Sweet and Maxwell, London

Huntington S (1991) Democracy's third wave. J Democr 2(2):12–34

Huntington S (1993) The third wave: democratization in the late twentieth century. University of Oklahoma Press

Karbaum M (2015) It's good to talk: Cambodia's culture of dialogue' Southeast Asia Globe. 1 September 2015. Available https://southeastasiaglobe.com/cambodia-culture-of-dialogue-southeast-asia-globe/

Khan T, Dickson K, Sondarjee M (eds) (2023) White saviorism in international development: theories, practices and lived experiences. Daraja Press, Wakefield

Kiernan B (1982) The Samlaut Rebellion 1967-68. In: Kiernan B, Boua C (eds) Peasants and politics in Kampuchea 1942–1981. Zed Press

Kiernan B (2003) The demography of genocide in Southeast Asia: the death tolls in Cambodia, 1975–79, and East Timor, 1975–80. Crit Asian Stud 35(4):585–597

Kiernan B (2004) How Pol Pot came to power: colonialism, nationalism and communism in Cambodia 1930–1975. Yale University Press

Kilama EG (2016) The influence of China and emerging donors aid allocation: a recipient perspective. China Econ Rev 38:76–91

Laebens MG, Lührmann A (2021) What halts democratic erosion? The changing role of accountability. Democratization 28(5):908–928

Lebovic J, Voeten E (2009) The cost of shame: international organizations and foreign aid in the punishing of human rights violators. J Peace Res 46(1):79–97

Lim T, Kim SE (2023) Buying influence? Rotating leadership in ASEAN and allocation of Chinese foreign aid. Int Relat Asia-Pac 23(2):351–377

Locard H (2005) State violence in Democratic Kampuchea (1975–1979) and retribution (1979–2004). Eur Rev Hist 12(1):121–143

Lührmann A (2021) Disrupting the autocratization sequence: towards democratic resilience. Democratization 28(5):1017–1039

Luhrmann A, Lindberg S (2019) A third wave of autocratization is here: what is new about it? Democratization 26(7):1095–1113

Marks S (2010) The process of creating a new constitution in Cambodia. In: Miller L, Aucoin L (eds) Framing the state in times of transition: case studies in constitution-making. US Institute of Peace, Washington, DC, pp 207–244

McKie K, Carlson E (2022) Do contravention attempts affect public support for presidential term limits?: evidence from sub-Saharan Africa. Democratization 29(1):133–153

Mehta H, Mehta J (1999) Hun Sen: strongman of Cambodia. Graham Brash, Singapore. (Republished as Mehta H, Mehta J (2013) Strongman: the extraordinary life of Hun Sen, from Pagoda Boy to Prime Minister of Cambodia. Cavendish, Singapore)
Ministry of Foreign Affairs and International Cooperation, To Tell the Truth Version 1 (11 April 2017) and Version 2 (7 May 2018). Available https://www.mfaic.gov.kh/Media/To%20Tell%20The%20Truth
Mogato M, Martina M, Blanchard B (2016) ASEAN deadlocked on South China Sea, Cambodia blocks statement. Reuters. 26 July 2016. Available https://www.reuters.com/article/idUSKCN1050F6/
Montesqieu B (1899) The spirit of laws (translated by Nugent T). The Colonial Press, New York
Morris S (1999) Why Vietnam invaded Cambodia – political culture and the causes of war. Stanford University Press
Mutua MW (2001) Savages, victims, and saviors: the metaphor of human rights. Harv Int Law J 42:201–245
Mutua MW (2004) The complexity of universalism in human rights. In: Sajo A (ed) Human rights with modesty: the problem of universalism. Martinus Nijhoff, Leiden
Nakano S (2018) Japan's colonial moment in Southeast Asia 1942–1945: The occupiers' experience. Routledge
Neher C (1981) Politics in Southeast Asia. Schenkman, Cambridge
Norén-Nilsson A (2016) Cambodia's second kingdom: nation, imagination, and democracy. Cornell University Press, Ithaca
Noren-Nilsson A (2021) A regal authoritarian turn in Cambodia. J Contemp Asia 52:715. https://doi.org/10.1080/00472336.2021.1974078
Papada E, Altman D, Angiolillo F, Gastaldi L, Köhler T, Lundstedt M, Natsika N, Nord M, Sato Y, Wiebrecht F, Lindberg SI (2023) Defiance in the face of autocratization: democracy report 2023. University of Gothenburg: Varieties of Democracy Institute (V-Dem Institute). Available https://www.v-dem.net/documents/29/V-dem_democracyreport2023_lowres.pdf
Pernia RA (2023) Populists in power: trust in public institutions and support for strong leadership in the post-authoritarian democracies of Indonesia and the Philippines. Asian J Polit Sci 31(1):63–85
Po S, Sims K (2022) The myth of non-interference: Chinese foreign policy in Cambodia. Asian Stud Rev 46(1):36–54
Poling G, Dunst C, Hudes ST (2022) Pariah or partner? Clarifying the U.S. approach to Cambodia. 14 June 2022. Center for Strategic and International Studies. Available https://www.csis.org/analysis/pariah-or-partner-clarifying-us-approach-cambodia
Sato J, Shiga H, Kobayashi T, Kondoh H (2011) "Emerging donors" from a recipient perspective: an institutional analysis of foreign aid in Cambodia. World Dev 39(12):2091–2104
Scott J (1972) Patron-client politics and political change in Southeast Asia. Am Polit Sci Rev 66(1):91–113
Short P (2004) Pol Pot – the history of a Nightmare. Hodder Headline
Sifton J (2021) Underwater - human rights impacts of a china belt and road project in Cambodia. Human Rights Watch
Strangio S (2014) Hun Sen's Cambodia. Silkworm Press, Singapore
Strangio S (2020) Cambodia: from Pol Pot to Hun Sen and beyond. Yale University Press, New Haven
Suzuki S (2019) Why is ASEAN not intrusive? Non-interference meets state strength. J Contem East Asia Stud 8(2):157–176
Tamanaha B (2002) On the rule of law history, politics, theory. Cambridge University Press, Cambridge
Tully J (2003) France on the Mekong: a history of the protectorate in Cambodia, 1863–1953. University Press of America
Tyner J (2017) From rice fields to killing fields: nature, life, and labor under the Khmer Rouge. Syracuse University Press, New York

US Government (2000) Air War over South Vietnam 1968–1975: comprehensive coverage from the Tet Offensive to the Collapse of South Vietnam, Waging War in South Vietnam, Cambodia, and Laos

Vickery M (1984) Cambodia 1975–1982. Allen and Unwin

West L (2019) The limits to judicial independence: Cambodia's political culture and the civil law. Democratization 26(3):537–553

White House (2021) Remarks by President Biden at the summit for democracy opening session. 9 December 2021. Available https://www.whitehouse.gov/briefing-room/speeches-remarks/2021/12/09/remarks-by-president-biden-at-the-summit-for-democracy-opening-session/

Widyono B (2008) Dancing in shadows. Sihanouk, the Khmer Rouge and the United Nations in Cambodia. Rowman and Littlefield

Courts as Sites of Political Contestation: A South African Perspective

Sfiso Benard Nxumalo and Dan Mafora

Abstract In South Africa, a nascent constitutional democracy, politics have migrated to the courtroom. South African courts, especially the Constitutional Court, have adjudicated political controversies under the guise of vindicating the Constitution and the rule of law, and fostering a culture of accountability, which has led to the steady judicialisation of politics. This chapter critically examines the effects of the judicialisation of politics and contends that this phenomenon poses a threat to the legitimacy of the judiciary. The chapter identifies constitutional supremacy, transformative constitutionalism and the extensive remedial powers of the courts as the factors that have influenced the judicialisation of politics in South Africa. It is argued that the courts' outcome-orientated approach to adjudication has led to a notable decline in the quality of the courts' jurisprudence, which itself has adverse implications for the rule of law, that lends credence to accusations of ad hoc reasoning in constitutional adjudication.

We are grateful to the generous and incisive comments of the attendees of the Socio-Legal Studies Association Conference held at the University of York on 6-8 April 2022 on an earlier draft of this paper, the University of Cape Town Public Law Discussion Group and attendees of the Postgraduate Seminar where a revised draft of this paper was presented. We also wish to thank Professor Sandy Fredman, Dr Meghan Campbell, Mandisa Shandu, Dr Gauri Pillai, Anjali Rawat, Jinghe Fan, Almas Shaikh, Dr Mónica Arango Olaya and Dr Sanya Samtani. We are also grateful to the editors for their invaluable comments. We remain responsible for any errors.

S. B. Nxumalo (✉)
Faculty of Law, University of Oxford, Oxford, UK

Linacre College, Oxford, UK
e-mail: sfiso.nxumalo@linacre.ox.ac.uk

D. Mafora
Faculty of Law, University of Cape Town, Cape Town, South Africa

Centre for Law and Society, University of Cape Town, Cape Town, South Africa
e-mail: dan.mafora@uct.ac.za

N. Reayat, H. O. Yusuf (eds.), *Constitutionalism in Africa and Beyond*, Ius Gentium: Comparative Perspectives on Law and Justice 127,
https://doi.org/10.1007/978-3-032-01180-0_8

1 Introduction

Despite its increasing prevalence, the phenomenon of the judicialisation of politics inheres a paradox. Addressing political and moral questions through the courts may create the perception of accountability through law but using the law to address these controversies may in fact undermine the legitimacy of the law as an institution. On one hand, the judicialisation of politics has created an additional accountability mechanism to review so-called "political questions," especially in countries with high levels of political corruption and where such states are on the brink of collapse. On the other hand, the judicialisation of politics tends to produce jurisprudence that is inconsistent and poorly reasoned, which undoubtedly has undeniable ramifications for the rule of law in the long term. Most times, judges opt for particular outcomes because they are exasperated with the state of affairs in the country.[1] Thus, while the judicialisation of politics has garnered praise because it has led to an additional measure of accountability, it has resulted in jurisprudence that has the potential to undermine the rule of law. This is the paradoxical nature of the judicialisation of politics. Our contribution seeks to delve into the adverse effects of this phenomenon, focusing specifically on South Africa.

In the last decade, South Africa has witnessed an exponential increase in the number of highly political matters that are being adjudicated in courtrooms, instead of being resolved on parliamentary floors.[2] This has led to courts generally, and the South African Constitutional Court in particular, expanding and shifting the boundaries and ambit of their authority, and potentially overreaching into areas beyond their constitutional competence. The judicialisation of politics has become commonplace.[3] Describing this phenomenon, John Comaroff and Jean Comaroff remark that the judicialisation of politics is marked by a migration of politics into courts, such that "conflicts once joined in parliaments, by means of street protests, mass demonstrations, and media campaigns, through labour strikes, boycotts, blockades, and other instruments of assertion, tend more and more … to find their way to the judiciary."[4]

For some scholars,[5] this phenomenon is a natural denouement of the adoption of the Constitution,[6] which expressly entrenches its own supremacy,[7] and confers, on the courts, the power to declare any law or conduct that is inconsistent with the Constitution invalid and to make any order that is just and equitable following

[1] O'Regan refers to this as the 'jurisprudence of exasperation'. See O'Regan (2011).

[2] Sibanda (2020), p. 287.

[3] Le Roux and Davis (2019), ch 1.

[4] Comaroff and Comaroff (2008), p. 17.

[5] Dube (2020), p. 293 and Gildenhuys (2020), p. 338.

[6] The Constitution of the Republic of South Africa, 1996 ('Constitution').

[7] Section 2 of the Constitution.

therefrom.[8] In this way, the courts are the ultimate guardian of the Constitution. Other scholars[9] have postulated that the acceptance of the doctrine of legality,[10] the rule of law,[11] the justiciability and enforcement of socio-economic rights,[12] the notion of transformative constitutionalism,[13] judicial independence,[14] and the courts' wide remedial powers are the factors that underpin the emergence of the judicialisation of politics in South Africa.[15] Putting aside the cause of this phenomenon for now, it is undeniably common cause that the South African judiciary has found itself dangerously, and perhaps impermissibly, wandering into the provinces of the other political branches of government. This, of course, is not to gainsay that in a constitutional democracy, one of the crucial functions of the courts is to ensure accountability for the exercise of public power.

Over the past decade, South Africa has experienced unimaginable corruption, which has led to the collapse of numerous state entities. Corruption is ubiquitous both in government and the private sector. Recently, a public inquiry was established to investigate allegations of corruption and fraud in government.[16] This public inquiry cost the state (read the taxpayers) approximately R1 billion (approximately £50 million).[17] After a sundry of delays, a lengthy report was released and implicated several government officials at every level. As a result of this corruption, some commentators have accused South Africa of being on the precipice of being a failed state, if it is not already a failed state.[18] The grand, rampant corruption that led to this public inquiry and the perceptions of South Africa being a failed state provide a backdrop to the political climate in which the judiciary operates. This environment has created the conditions necessary for the judiciary to step in and rein in the other two arms of government.

However, the question arises whether the South African courts have, over the years, crossed the bright line that separates law from politics proper and have steadily moved away from only fostering a culture of accountability to becoming active political players, engaging in political controversies ostensibly clothed in legal garb, in South African public life. We argue that the courts have crossed this

[8] Section 172 of Constitution. See also *Doctors for Life International v Speaker of the National Assembly* 2006 6 SA 416 (CC) at para 38.

[9] Le Roux and Davis, op. cit., n. 2.

[10] *Fedsure Life Insurance Ltd v Greater Johannesburg Transitional Metropolitan Council* 1999 1 SA 374 (CC). See also Hoexter (2004), p. 165.

[11] Kawadza (2018), p. 2.

[12] Davis (2006), p. 300.

[13] Kihbet and Fombad (2017), p. 341.

[14] Masengu (2017), p. 3.

[15] Section 172(1) of the Constitution.

[16] This was called the "Judicial Commission of Inquiry into Allegations of State Capture, Corruption and Fraud in the Public Sector including Organs of State". See its official website here: https://www.statecapture.org.za/.

[17] Gerber (2022) and Haffajee (2022).

[18] Malada (2022), Staff Writer (2022), and Moeng (2022).

bright line and have placed themselves in a position where there is no question that they may not resolve, widening the scope of justiciability to include those issues one might readily call political.[19] With this in mind, others have argued that this has led to the ascendence of the judiciary as a "super branch" of government.

It may also be argued that the trend towards the judicialisation of politics is a necessary response to rampant state corruption, a woefully incompetent executive, and a legislature that fails to hold the executive accountable. The judiciary, the argument proceeds, rescued the country from becoming a failed state during the so-called "Zuma years".[20] Thus, the judiciary should be celebrated as an institution that upholds South Africa's constitutional democracy. Proponents of such an argument may plausibly cite *Economic Freedom Fighters v Speaker of the National Assembly*[21] as an exemplary case of the Constitutional Court's outstanding defence of the Constitution and our democracy.[22] This case concerned lavish upgrades to then-President Zuma's private residence at state expense. These upgrades were justified as necessary security upgrades. However, the Public Protector,[23] a constitutionally established institution akin to an ombud, conducted an investigation which found that some of the upgrades were not security-related and that President Zuma had been unjustifiably and personally enriched by the upgrades, which were paid for using public funds.[24] The Public Protector ordered, as part of her remedial action, that President Zuma pay back some of the money used for the non-security upgrades, which he disregarded, arguing that the remedial action proposed by the Public Protector constituted mere non-binding recommendations.[25] The National Assembly, the lower house of Parliament, in response to opposition calls to implement the remedial action, established two ad hoc committees to review the Public Protector's report which, in turn, found that there was nothing amiss with the security upgrades and recommending that Parliament not take any action against President Zuma.[26]

Disgruntled, two opposition parties directly represented in the National Assembly approached the Constitutional Court and argued that the National Assembly had

[19] Wallis (2018).

[20] This phrase refers to the 9 years of Jacob Zuma's reign as the President of the South Africa from 9 May 2009–14 February 2018. These years are generally described as the wasted years, characterised by nepotism, corruption, failing state-owned entities; the systematic dismantling of law-enforcement agencies, such as National Prosecuting Authority and the South African Revenue Service; and poor service delivery. See Brett (2020), p. 131.

[21] *Economic Freedom Fighters v Speaker of the National Assembly; Democratic Alliance v Speaker of the National Assembly* 2016 (3) SA 580 (CC) ("*EFF I*").

[22] See Allison (2016).

[23] Sections 182 and 183 of the Constitution.

[24] Office of the Public Protector (2014) Secure in Comfort: Public Protector's Report on Nkandla: Report by the Public Protector on an Investigation into Allegations of Impropriety relating to the Installation and Implementation of Security Measures by the Department of Public Works at and in respect of the Private Residence of President Jacob Zuma at Nkandla in the Kwa-Zulu Province Report No: 25 of 2013/4.

[25] *EFF I*, op. cit., n 21, paras 8-14.

[26] *EFF I*, id., para 12.

breached its constitutional obligation to hold the President accountable.[27] The political parties framed the question as one of law, namely, whether the Public Protector had the power to issue binding orders in law, and whether, in turn, the President had breached his constitutional duty to uphold the Constitution by refusing to implement the remedial action. An affirmative answer to both questions would, in turn, mean that the National Assembly had failed to perform its own constitutional duty to hold the President accountable. The Court agreed with the political parties, holding that the Public Protector had the power to issue binding orders in law, and that President Zuma was obliged to implement the remedial action. The outcome of this decision was lauded and well-received. We argue, however, that this judgment epitomises the outcome-based approach to adjudication that the Court had increasingly adopted during the Zuma years, often leading to jurisprudentially unsound decisions.[28] In light of the political environment at the time, with widespread calls for President Zuma to "pay back the money" and/or resign from office, and faced with an ineffective legislature whose leadership was beholden to Zuma, the Court found itself with the opportunity to make a decision that would be popular and widely perceived as good. We argue that this consideration is the animating factor behind the Court's decision, which does not bear scrutiny when subjected to closer analysis based on settled constitutional principles.

We argue that the judicialisation of politics has had a deleterious impact on the legitimacy of the courts and is a cautious tale about the overzealous adjudication of political issues. But that is not all. We argue, too, that the Constitutional Court has forsaken sound judicial reasoning in favour of an overtly outcome-orientated approach, which has spawned inconsistent and incongruent decisions that can barely be defended on the application of settled legal principles or rules, such as *EFF I*. We will discuss these judgments below. We contend that, in the long term, this lack of analytical rigour is bound to have disastrous consequences, if it has not already. The Constitutional Court has essentially arrogated to itself immense power which permits it to depart from the text of the Constitution, statutes, and even its own past decisions, and to adjudicate any matter it wishes to adjudicate, in any manner it wishes to adjudicate it, unbounded by these usual constraints. Connected to this, we argue that the Court has unwittingly undermined the principle of the rule of law it purports to uphold. The Court's judgments often leave scholars, lawyers, government officials and the public confused about the content of the law as articulated by it. The application of the Constitution and the law has become uncertain. This amounts to a violation of the principle of certainty as a component of the rule of law.[29] It is essential to consider how the Court's expansive powers may be reconciled, if at all, with the rule of law to ensure that the rule of law is not replaced by the rule of, and by, courts.

[27] *EFF I*, id., para 13.

[28] For a discussion on the Constitutional Court's penchant for outcome-based reasoning, see Woolman (2007), p. 762.

[29] As will be demonstrated below, certainty is a vital strut to the rule of law. See Lifante-Vidal (2020), p. 456; Paunio (2009), p. 1469; and Kordela (2008), p. 587.

In the pages that follow, we seek to defend the propositions made in the preceding paragraphs. The structure will be as follows. Firstly, we set out the structure of the South African Constitution by employing a forward- and backward-looking approach where we look at the limited powers of the judiciary under apartheid and then at the wide powers courts now enjoy under the Constitution. Secondly, we define and problematise the phenomenon of the judicialisation of politics. Lastly, we will consider the detrimental effects of the judicialisation of politics, specifically on the rule of law, the separation of powers, and legal reasoning through an analysis of several cases from 2015 through to 2021 to provide a uniquely South African perspective on courts as sites of political contestation and the implications thereof for the future of constitutionalism and the rule of law.

2 Preliminary Issues

At this juncture, we set out some preliminarily issues. First, it is important to point out that while we predominantly focus on the cases of the Constitutional Court, this should by no means be construed as implying that the judicialisation of politics occurs solely at the level of that court. We largely restrict our discussion to Constitutional Court cases because of its authority as the highest court in the Republic, which axiomatically makes its decisions the most authoritative. Our arguments, we believe, are applicable to the judiciary generally.

Secondly, we set out some definitions. "Politics" is difficult to define and there is a sundry of definitions that have been given.[30] The question of what is political differs from polity to polity. For instance, what may be a religious and political question in a secular state may be relatively straightforward in non-secular states. There is thus no single definition of "politics" or for demarcating what is political and what is not. However, for purposes of this chapter, politics refers to matters that have been constitutionally reserved for the executive and the legislature, as well as questions of morality, public policy, and value, over which reasonable people in a political community may disagree, that would be properly addressed in participatory and deliberative democratic forums, and not courts.[31] This brings us to the notion of the separation of powers, which implies that certain issues are beyond the purview of the judiciary. There is no universal archetype of separation of powers, but at its most basic, it means that the powers and functions of the principal institutions of state, namely, the executive, legislature and judiciary, should be carefully delineated and functionally independent of each other in order to guard against tyranny and abuse of power.[32]

[30] Modebadze (2010), p. 39.

[31] Gildenhuys, op. cit., n. 5, p. 341.

[32] Montesquieu (1788). See also Madison (1788).

The South African conception of the separation of powers doctrine does not entail an absolute separation in that it anticipates a necessary intrusion by one arm of government onto the terrain of another. This is because the Constitution axiomatically provides for checks and balances between the different arms of government. However, it also requires that one arm of government should not usurp the power of another arm.[33] In *Ferreira v Levin NO*, Chaskalson P noted: "it is important that we bear in mind that there are functions that are properly the concern of the courts and others that are properly the concern of the legislature. At times these functions may overlap. But the terrains are in the main separate and should be kept separate."[34] In the cases we examine below, we aim to illustrate that the judiciary has concerned itself with matters that are beyond its concern, which is the inevitable outcome of the judicialisation of politics.

3 Understanding the South African Constitutional Design

Prior to the advent of constitutional democracy, South Africa rigidly adhered to the principles of the executive prerogative[35] and parliamentary sovereignty,[36] which traditionally inhered in the English monarch.[37] These principles severely constrained the powers of courts. Courts could not review the substance of the statutes, although the courts could adjudicate whether Parliament followed prescribed procedures in the legislative process. In short, the courts merely applied the law as enacted by the legislature, with no authority to inquire into its constitutionality. For instance, in *Johannesburg Consolidated Investment Co v Johannesburg Town Council*,[38] the court remarked that the doctrine of ultra vires was the overarching justification for judicial review. This means that courts could only interfere where power was being

[33] *In re: Certification of the Constitution of the Republic of South Africa* 1996 (4) SA 744 (CC); *Executive Council, Western Cape Legislature v President of the Republic of South Africa* 1995 (4) SA 877 (CC); *De Lange v Smuts* 1998 (3) SA 785 (CC); *South African Association of Personal Injury Lawyers v Heath* 2001 (1) SA 883 (CC); and Langa (2006), p. 2.

[34] *Ferreira v Levin NO* 1996 (1) SA 984 (CC).

[35] See for instance *President of the Republic of South Africa v Hugo* 1997 (4) SA 1 (CC).

[36] The doctrine of parliamentary sovereignty permitted the legislature to enact any statute or measure it desired, regardless of how arbitrary or unreasonable it was. The legislature was the ultimate law-making body and there was no law it could not make or repeal. See De Vos and Freedman (2014), pp. 42–44 and Marcus (1986), p. 17. Dicey (1959), p. 70 famously stated that the doctrine means:

> [N]either more nor less than this, namely that Parliament has under the English constitution the right to make or unmake any law whatever, further that no person or body is recognised by the law of England as has a right to override or set aside the Legislation of parliament.

[37] Du Plessis (2000), p. 228.

[38] *Johannesburg Consolidated Investment Company v Johannesburg Town Council* 1903 TS 111.

exercised beyond the contours of the law as set out by the Parliament. Similarly, this was confirmed in *Ndlwana v Hofmeyr*, where the Centilivres J (as he then was) held that "the Supreme Court has no power to pronounce upon the validity of an Act of Parliament duly promulgated and printed and published by proper authority."[39] In another case, Centilivres CJ asserted that if the provisions of a statute are clear and discernible, a court cannot interfere with the propriety of the legislation.[40] Courts could not second-guess the wisdom of the legislature; they merely had to implement the law. The implication of these restrictions meant that the judiciary was subordinated to the legislature and the executive. It could not review or strike down any laws, regardless of how absurd or morally objectionable they were. Ultimately, the judiciary was complacent in supporting and reinforcing a racist and evil apartheid state, as the jurisprudence of the former Appellate Division of the Supreme Court would later prove.[41] While, naturally, there are limited exceptions,[42] courts were largely inclined not to interfere with governmental power.[43] Accordingly, the maxim *iudicis est ius dicere sed non dare* (the duty of the judge is to apply the law, not to make it) prevailed.[44]

The adoption of the Constitution in 1996 caused radical departure from the position under apartheid. It entrenched its own supremacy and displaced the sovereignty of Parliament. South Africa became a constitutional democracy, founded on majority-rule with a justiciable bill of rights and a judiciary that enjoys extensive powers to interfere with governmental power and to strike down any law or conduct found to be constitutionally wanting.[45] Judicial review, once excluded under apartheid, is a key feature of our fledging constitutional democracy. As van der Schyff recognises, the judicial review of legislation is one of the cornerstones of the new constitutional dispensation that reinforced the view of the Constitution as a bridge to a new future.[46] The Constitution provides for an independent judiciary with wide remedial powers to make any order that it deems to be just and equitable. The constitutional text itself is open-ended and expansive. The appellate courts have wide

---

[39] *Ndlwana v Hofmeyr* 1937 AD 229, at 231. See also Griswold (1952), p. 1361.

[40] *Collins v Minister of the Interior* 1957 (1) SA 552 (A) at 567–568.

[41] See generally Chaskalson (2004), p. 590.

[42] Consider the landmark cases that formed part of the constitutional crisis of the 1950s: *Harris v Minister of the Interior* 1952 (2) SA 428 (A), *Minister of the Interior v Harris* 1952 (4) SA 769 (A) and *Collins* op. cit., n. 34.

[43] Corder and Hoexter (2017), p. 108.

[44] Singh and Bhero (2016), p. 1.

[45] It is worth noting that section 165 of the Constitution establishes one judiciary in South Africa. In terms of section 166 of the Constitution, the judiciary comprises the Constitutional Court, the Supreme Court of Appeal, the High Court of South Africa, the Magistrates' Courts and any other court established or recognised in terms of an Act of Parliament, including any court of a status similar to either the Hight Court of South Africa or the Magistrates' Courts. The Constitutional Court is the highest (apex) court in South Africa. In relation to judicial review, the High Court has jurisdiction to hear such matters and the Supreme Court of Appeal has jurisdiction over appeals arising from the High Court. We reiterate that this paper is concerned mostly with judgments from the Constitutional Court, which is the most authoritative court in the country.

[46] Van der Schyff (2010), p. 45.

jurisdiction to hear cases and an undefined and unfixed notion of the separation of powers which is itself given content and meaning exclusively by the courts. This has enabled courts to interfere with the substantive decisions of the other arms of government, which they previously could not do. The extension of the courts' terrain into the province of legislative and executive decisions is certainly one of the reasons behind the judicialisation of politics but is rightly considered a positive step from the position under apartheid.

Moreover, South Africa's Constitution has been described as "transformative," even though the word is not mentioned in the text itself.[47] Transformative constitutionalism has multiple meanings.[48] Certain elements and features of the concept have been identified to provide content and flesh to it. Klare proffers the following definition:

> [A] long-term project of constitutional enactment, interpretation and enforcement committed (not in isolation, of course, but in a historical context of conducive political developments) to transforming a country's political and social institutions and power relationships in a democratic, participatory, and egalitarian direction.[49]

For Klare, transformative constitutionalism is an enterprise of "inducing large scale social change through non-violent processes grounded in law."[50] In other words, it is a political and social project, which is pursued and achieved through law.[51] It is a concept that demands a change to the legal culture and socio-economic conditions. Under transformative constitutionalism, the constitution and the law—and therefore courts—are central to South Africa achieving social and political change. Former Chief Justice Ngcobo writes extra-curially that transformative constitutionalism envisages the three arms of government encroaching on each other's spheres, and that lines of division may occasionally be blurred.[52] The Constitution, he argues, contemplates a "constitutional dialogue" between the three arms of government and that this dialogue is what should inform the South African conception of the separation of powers doctrine.[53]

Another significant feature of transformative constitutionalism, as identified by Mureinik, is the shift from a legal culture of authority to a culture of justification.[54] Under apartheid a culture of authority prevailed: the government could enact racist and otherwise oppressive legislation with impunity and without fear of being required to substantively defend its exercise of public power.[55] In contrast, a culture

[47] Brickhill and van Leeve (2015), p. 146.

[48] Brickhill and van Leeve, id., p. 147.

[49] Klare (1998), p. 150.

[50] Klare, id.

[51] Sibanda (2011), p. 486.

[52] Ngcobo (2011), p. 38.

[53] Ngcobo, id., p. 39.

[54] Mureinik (1994), p. 33.

[55] Mureinik, id., p. 32, where he stated that: "[w]ithout a culture of authority it is difficult to imagine how its gardeners could have cultivated the forest of apartheid statutes whose most distinctive feature was their want of justification."

of justification provides that it is the role of the courts to ensure that every act or exercise of public power by the government is substantively justifiable.[56] A justiciable bill of rights is pivotal to this culture because citizens can rely on the bill of rights to challenge any exercise of public power that affects them and the courts have the responsibility of determining whether the impugned act or conduct is substantively justifiable. For Mureinik, the culture of justification is fundamental; as without it, the Constitution is meaningless.[57]

While accepting its importance in South Africa's constitutional law, Cachalia eschews an understanding of transformative constitutionalism that is court-centred.[58] In his view, the risk of turning transformative constitutionalism into a court-centred project might undermine the overall democratic project. He argues that a court-centred Platonic project would violate the doctrine of separation of powers. This court-centred approach to transformative constitutionalism, he argues, is a threat to a model of democracy where the legislature represents and responds to the demands of the public.[59] Thus, an overreliance on courts may not be in harmony with democratic accountability. Implicit in his argument is that the current transformative constitutionalism framework fosters a distrust for, and subverts, democratic processes.[60] In response to this argument, Davis argues that Cachalia's contention "ignores vast swathes of the Constitution".[61] He argues that the rights contained in the Constitution must be enforced by an independent institution, such as the judiciary. Thus, the Constitution is, by design, court centric.[62] He argues that the Constitution leaves it to the courts to determine the nature of the rules of substantive democratic participation, engagement, and governance. Moreover, where the other two arms of government attempt to alter these foundations, courts have a duty to vindicate these rules. Courts, essentially, are "vital to a democratic process which is under severe pressure."[63]

In a recent article, Dube argues that South Africa's constitutional design is predicated on a system of judicial supremacy.[64] He asserts that the Constitutional Court, due its *sui generis* institutional placement and wide powers, must be understood as being superior to the other arms of government.[65] Unlike the European Enlightenment conception of three arms of government of equal standing, Dube says, the Constitution elevates the role and importance of the Constitutional Court, bestowed with the requisite support to navigate and adjudicate legal as well as political questions.[66] He notes that the remedial powers of the Court are far-reaching and textually

[56] Mureinik, id., pp. 32–33; Möller (2020), p. 1078.

[57] Mureinik, id., p. 33.

[58] Cachalia (2015), p. 310.

[59] Cachalia, id., pp. 309–310.

[60] Cachalia, id.

[61] Davis (2016), p. 266.

[62] Davis, id., p. 267.

[63] Davis, id., pp. 270–271.

[64] Dube, op. cit., n. 5.

[65] Dube, id., p. 294.

[66] Dube, id., p. 299.

unconstrained.[67] Accordingly, the Constitutional Court can legitimately trespass into the terrain of the legislature and the executive without falling afoul of the separation of powers. For Dube, the Constitutional Court's judicial supervision over the executive cannot be reconciled with the European Enlightenment conception of the doctrine of separation of powers.[68] According to Dube, the counter-majoritarian dilemma does not arise in South Africa because our constitutional democracy has endowed the Constitutional Court with significant judicial review powers.[69] Considering all of this, we should embrace the Constitutional Court as a special institution and not merely a court of law.[70] The Constitutional Court's special status, Dube continues, is not due to some drafting oversight but was deliberately granted. Thus, South Africa's constitutional democracy is predominantly contingent on the vigilance of the Constitutional Court and its commitment to enforcing the values of accountability, responsiveness and openness, which underpin the Constitution.[71]

We do not align ourselves with the central position advanced by Dube, but it is beyond the scope of this paper to comprehensively respond to his claims. What is important for purposes of this chapter is the recognition that the judiciary, with the Constitutional Court at the apex, has wide remedial powers and is almost unencumbered with respect to what types of relief it may grant. These powers, coupled with the notion of transformative constitutionalism and a justiciable bill of rights, provide fertile ground for the judicialisation of politics in South Africa, to which we now turn.

---

[67] Dube, id., p. 304.

[68] Dube, id., p. 302.

[69] Dube, id., pp. 313–315.

[70] Dube, id., p. 317.

[71] Dube, id. Section 1 of the Constitution provides:

> 1. The Republic of South Africa is one, sovereign, democratic state founded on the following values:

a. Human dignity, the achievement of equality and the advancement of human rights and freedoms.
b. Non-racialism and non-sexism.
c. Supremacy of the Constitution and the rule of law.
d. Universal adult suffrage, a national common voters roll, regular elections and a multi-party system of democratic government, to ensure accountability, responsiveness and openness.

4 The Judicialisation of Politics: The South African Experience

The phrase "judicialisation of politics" has gained significant global popularity over the past few decades.[72] This notion has other names such as "lawfare", "judicial supremacy", "juristocracy" and "government by judges".[73] Despite this, there is no one single definition for the judicialisation of politics. Hirschl defines it as the increasing reliance on courts and judicial methods for resolving political controversies, fundamental moral predicaments and public policy questions.[74] Vallinder identifies two possible meanings of the judicialisation of politics: (i) the spread of judicial-decision means / methods to spheres outside of the judiciary; and (ii) the shift or expansion of the province of the courts into politics or decisions traditionally preserved for the legislature.[75] Sunkin contends that judicialisation may also refer to the importance placed on law and legal procedures as being central to efficient and effective government administration, which has resulted in the increased use of judicial review.[76]

For purposes of this chapter, we rely on the broader definition advanced by Hirschl and the second possible meaning advanced by Vallinder (that is, the expansion of the province of courts into political matters). Identifying this trend, Lord Roskill commented that "[t]oday it is perhaps commonplace to observe that … there has been a dramatic and indeed a radical change in the scope of judicial review."[77] Ultimately, judicialisation denotes a greater judicial involvement in matters or questions that were not conventionally classified as legal or of judicial concern.

The scope of judicial review has expanded, with the consequence that courts are now being called to address questions that would ordinarily have been beyond judicial competence. Endowing courts with the power of judicial review of legislation is crucial to the phenomenon of the judicialisation of politics. In South Africa for instance, where an opposition party or a member of the public is unhappy with a particular piece of legislation and believes that it is constitutionally wanting, they can approach a court and challenge the constitutionality of that legislation. Faced with this challenge, a court can strike down that legislation as unconstitutional or, alternatively, provide guidance on how to interpret statutory provisions in a

[72] Hamlin and Sala (2018) and Hirschl (2011), p. 1.

[73] We acknowledge that judicialisation of politics is a broader concept and is not accurately interchangeable with the other terms because they may be narrower and refer to specific instances. See Corder H and Hoexter C, op. cit., n. 37, p. 106; Schauer (2004), p. 1045; Knight and Epstein (1998), p. 87; Lemieux (2017), p. 1067; Davis D, op. cit., n. 53; Sweet (2000); and Hirschl (2004).

[74] Hirschl (2008), p. 94.

[75] Vallinder (1994), p. 91.

[76] Sunkin (1994), p. 126.

[77] *Council for Civil Service Unions v. Government Central Communication Headquarters* [1984] 3 AI E.R. 935 at 953.

manner that is constitutionally compliant,[78] which would invariably bind the other two arms of government. Similarly, courts may direct the other two arms of government on how to act in a constitutionally compliant manner to remedy the unconstitutionality.[79] In South Africa, courts have exercised supervisory jurisdiction through structural remedies in socio-economic rights cases.[80] Structural interdicts by their very nature require the continued participation and oversight of the court in the implementation of its orders by other state organs.[81] Various models of structural interdicts have been employed, from the report-back-to-court model[82] to the expert remedial formulation[83] model.[84] Examples of the South African courts exercising their supervisory role can be seen in the Court's judgment in *Black Sash Trust v Minister of Social Development*.[85]

The litigation history and facts of the *Black Sash Trust* case are complicated and morass. In a nutshell, a government agency, the South African Social Security Agency, that was constitutionally obligated to implement a monthly payment of social grants in terms of section 27(1) of the Constitution[86] had entered an unlawful procurement contract with a private company to pay out these social grants on its behalf. The Constitutional Court in an earlier decision held that the procurement process was invalid and at odds with the tenets of section 217 of the Constitution.[87] The Court however preserved the unlawful contract because it was of the view that if it had set the contract aside, it would have resulted in a public disaster where mil-

---

[78] See generally *Investigating Directorate: Serious Economic Offences v Hyundai Motor Distributors (Pty) Ltd In re: Hyundai Motor Distributors (Pty) Ltd v Smit NO* 2001 (1) SA 545 (CC).

[79] Petrov (2021), p. 1.

[80] Mbazira (2008), p. 1.

[81] Roach and Budlender (2005), p. 328.

[82] The report-back-to-court model essentially entails a court ordering government to perform certain obligations and report back to the court with a plan as to how they will implement the order and remedy the harm suffered. See *Brown v Board of Education of Topeka* 347 US 483; *Section 27 v Minister of Education* 20113 2 SA 40 (GNP); and Liebenberg (2016), p. 1.

[83] The expert remedial formulation model refers to a situation where a court appoints an expert or a panel of experts to create and develop a remedial plan to implement a court order. See Swanepoel (2017).

[84] For a broader discussion on the models of structural interdicts, see Maphosa (2020), p. 362.

[85] *Black Sash Trust v Minister of Social Development and Others (Freedom Under Law NPC Intervening)* 2017 (3) SA 335 (CC) ("*Black Sash Trust*").

[86] Section 27(1) of the Constitution provides:

1. Everyone has the right to have access to:

…

c. social security, including, if they are unable to support themselves and their dependants, appropriate social assistance.

[87] *Black Sash Trust*, op. cit., n. 75, para 3. The earlier decision is *AllPay Consolidated Investment Holdings (Pty) Ltd v Chief Executive Officer, South African Social Security Agency* 2014 (1) SA 604 (CC).

lions of people would be left without social grants. The Court then ordered that the contract remain in place until it was due to expire on 31 March 2017, at which point the government would take over the paying of grants or conduct a procurement process afresh and appoint a private company in line with section 217 of the Constitution to disburse the grants. Importantly, the Court held that the government agency had to submit a report to it on any procurement process undertaken and the outcome of such a process. The Court therefore assumed a supervisory role over an executive government agency through the report-back-to-court model.[88]

On the eve of 31 March 2017, it became apparent that the government agency would neither be able to directly make the payments itself, nor had it procured the services of any other entity to do so. It was evident that the government agency would not comply with the order, and would not be able to carry out its constitutional function. To avert a looming constitutional crisis, the Court gave a more extensive order. First, the Court ordered the extension of the unlawful contract for a further 12 months beyond its expiry date. Secondly, the Court directed the Auditor-General to review the operationalisation of the extended contract, to evaluate the steps to be taken by the government agency to administer and pay the social grants in the future.[89] The appointment of the Auditor-General also included the appointment of suitably qualified independent legal practitioners and experts to monitor and evaluate the implementation of the payment of social grants as well as the procurement process to secure a new contractor.[90] Third, the Court ordered that the government agency had to file detailed reports to the Court providing a chronology of deliverables.[91] The Court reasoned that this interference into the realm of matters that were preserved for the executive was necessary due to the government agency's systemic failure to guarantee social assistance for grant recipients.

The power of judicial review is particularly useful to opposition parties, who traditionally find themselves in a weaker political position than the governing party. When they lose a battle in relation to particular conduct of the state, or new legislation in Parliament, they can legally challenge the conduct or legislation, and secure a legal victory which aligns with their political goals. *EFF I*, discussed above is one such case. But we will also explore *EFF II* below, which will demonstrate how minority political parties used litigation in the Constitutional Court to win a political dispute. Barak remarked that there is no question that is beyond the reach of judicial review, and in a world premised on law, "anything and everything is justiciable".[92] The transformation of political questions into legal questions is a prevalent feature in many constitutional democracies. Naturally, due to the ease with which political questions can be reconfigured into legal questions, many political parties and organs of state in South Africa swiftly turned to the courts, causing a

---

[88] *Black Sash Trust*, id., paras 3–5.

[89] *Black Sash Trust*, id., para 69 and para 12 of the order.

[90] *Black Sash Trust*, id., para 12 of the order.

[91] *Black Sash Trust*, id., para 65.

[92] Hirschl, op. cit., n. 74, p. 95.

remarkable migration of political questions from more appropriate political forums to the courts.

However, if everything is capable of being transformed into a legal question and therefore justiciable, what does this mean for the doctrine of separation of powers? Surely the doctrine of the separation of powers presupposes that there are certain matters that cannot, or should not, be resolved by courts and should be left to other arms of government that are democratic and participatory in nature? The Constitutional Court's acceptance of separation of powers doctrine indicates that there are certain matters that it perceives as being beyond the scope of judicial review and adjudication. The law reports are replete with statements where the Constitutional Court has recognised the doctrine of the separation of powers and cautions against its violation.[93] For instance, the Constitutional Court in *National Coalition for Gay and Lesbian Equality v Minister of Home Affairs* (per Ackermann J) eloquently stated:

> The other consideration a court must keep in mind, is the principle of the separation of powers and, flowing therefrom, the deference it owes to the legislature in devising a remedy for a breach of the Constitution in any particular case. It is not possible to formulate in general terms what such deference must embrace, for this depends on the facts and circumstances of each case. In essence, however, it involves restraint by the courts in not trespassing onto that part of the legislative field which has been reserved by the Constitution, and for good reason, to the legislature.[94]

It can hardly be disputed that the respect for the separation of powers doctrine is vital in constitutional democracies. Woolman notes that South African courts have tested and pushed the boundaries of this doctrine, but that this was necessary to protect the broader politics of accountability.[95] Accordingly, it is implied that the judicialisation of politics may be prioritised to the detriment of the doctrine of the separation of powers in desperate times. Where fundamental rights are at risk, this doctrine may be rendered a casualty. For instance, certain applicants used the courts to challenge the appointment of the National Director of Public Prosecutions,[96] and cabinet reshuffles[97] on the basis that they were irrational and constitutionally improper exercises of public power.

Fowkes argues that the separation of powers doctrine and fundamental comity between the judiciary and the other arms of government were eroded during Jacob

---

[93] See for example: *In re: Certification of the Constitution of the Republic of South Africa* 1996 (4) SA 744 (CC) para 27; *Bato Star Fishing (Pty) Ltd v Minister of Environmental Affairs and Tourism* 2004 (4) SA 490 (CC) para 46; and *National Treasury v Opposition to Urban Tolling Alliance* 2012 (6) SA 223 (CC) para 65.

[94] *National Coalition for Gay and Lesbian Equality v Minister of Home Affairs* 2000 (2) SA 1 (CC) para 66.

[95] Woolman (2018), pp. 172–174.

[96] *Corruption Watch NPC v President of the Republic of South Africa; Nxasana v Corruption Watch NPC* [2018] (10) BCLR 1179 (CC).

[97] *President of the Republic of South Africa v Democratic Alliance* 2020 (1) SA 428 (CC).

Zuma's presidency. Zuma's presidency was, to say the least, disastrous.[98] The *Black Sash* case illustrates how the courts were called to interfere in the executive's exercise of its constitutional powers in discharging its obligations by invoking the courts' supervisory jurisdiction. Okpaluba and Mhango recognise the intrusive nature of the Constitutional Court's supervisory role over the executive, especially since the Court ordered that an unlawful contract must persist (and even subsequently extended it) under its supervision.[99] The Court effectively breathed life into a contract that would bind the executive, despite a manifest unlawfulness.

Nonetheless, it has been argued that courts are the last constitutional defence considering the dysfunction of the other two arms of government.[100] This view seeks to legitimise the courts' increasingly political decision-making. Similarly, Le Roux and Davis consider the judicialisation of politics through the lens of "lawfare" in South Africa, looking especially at the country's recent troubled past under Zuma's presidency. Theirs is a concern with the use and abuse of legal processes to resolve political problems. While acknowledging it as a form of displacing politics, lawfare, they argue, can be both positive and negative. It is good, they say, that adjudication is political "in the sense that it advances the constitutional project and is undertaken by litigants and judges as an instrument to ensure that the constitutional vision is realised." On the other hand, "when courts become the site of pure political contestation because politicians seek to usurp judicial powers to achieve their [political] objectives … it draws the judiciary far further into the political arena than has traditionally been the case."[101]

Furthermore, judicialisation was also accelerated by "state capture". State capture, at its simplest, refers to the capture or control of state institutions to direct and leverage state decision-making for the benefit of private interests.[102] Individuals who were part of the executive, under Zuma, and the legislature were implicated in the capture of the state by the infamous Gupta family. The general perception was that those two arms of government could not do anything to curb and root out corruption and state capture.[103] Differently put, they were supine. There was an accountability lacuna, and the courts filed that gap.

It is in the quest to fill this perceived lack of accountability (as well as the encouragement of lofty judicial rhetoric) that the courts have significantly trespassed into the political domain. Unfortunately, as we endeavour to show below, this has resulted in thinly reasoned judgments that lack analytical rigour and clarity. We will

---

[98] Johnson (2017), p. 39 and Southall (2016), p. 80.

[99] Okpaluba and Mhango (2017), p. 13.

[100] Tsele (2018), p. 197.

[101] Le Roux and Davis, op. cit., n. 2, 5. Another interesting perspective is offered by Sweet (1999), p. 164 where it is argued that one of the potential upsides of judicialisation is that the process of law-making becomes triadic, instead of dyadic, which progressively informs the behaviours and relationships of political actors.

[102] Daily Maverick (2017) 'State capture named SA word of the year'. https://www.dailymaverick.co.za/article/2017-10-16-state-capture-named-sa-word-of-the-year/.

[103] Brett, op. cit., n. 20, pp. 129–130.

call this the *Reasoning Problem*. One of the factors that contribute to a court's legitimacy is the content of its reasoning. It has been argued that courts' perceived legitimacy is at its highest when judges cite and rely on technical legal arguments, and at its lowest when they rely on extraconstitutional arguments and justifications.[104] Justice Elena Kagan of the Supreme Court of the United States recently stated that judges create legitimacy problems for themselves when they do not act like courts of law and stray into the terrain of politics.[105]

We argue that not only has the judiciary strayed into politics, but it has, in the process, sacrificed the quality of reasoning in favour of outcome-based decision-making. In highly political cases, the Constitutional Court has disregarded its previous decisions and neglected robust legal reasoning to reach outcomes that would be extolled by the public. As noted by Chaskalson P in *S v Makwanyane*, a court "should not allow itself to be diverted from its duty to act as an independent arbiter of the Constitution by making choices on the basis that they will find favour with the public."[106] We contend that in political cases as we have identified them, this is precisely what the Court has done, to the detriment of its jurisprudence. To demonstrate this, we consider the *EFF I* case.

Related to the Reasoning Problem is that the requisite features of the rule of law have been compromised and ignored in the creation of this new jurisprudence. We call this the *Rule of Law Problem*. While the rule of law is notoriously difficult to define and does not have a single definition, at the very least it requires of laws the following: clarity, relative stability, generality and equality. We contend that the courts' poor reasoning in pollical cases has meant that some of these key components of the rule of law have been subverted as a result. Courts create law through their decisions, as discussed below, and their decisions matter for the broader public, which is ultimately governed by such laws. If the reasoning of a court is inconsistent, unprincipled, and not constrained by the existing law, then naturally, the rule of law will be adversely impacted. In this regard, we discuss *Zuma I*[107] and *Zuma II*.[108]

We further contend that political controversies have caused a real divide between members of the Court, with the tenor of dissenting judgments increasingly calling into question the legitimacy of the Court. We refer to this as the *Political Dissent Problem*. We must not be understood to be taking issue with dissent in general. Judicial dissents represent a healthy judiciary in which judges think and decide cases independently. Dissents may also be of jurisprudential value, influence future decisions, and generally shape the development of the law.[109] The dissents we are referring to here are dissents that are not predicated on a disagreement over the legal

[104] For a broader discussion, see Farganis (2012), p. 206.

[105] Robinson (2022).

[106] *S v Makwanyane* 1995 (3) SA 391 at para 89.

[107] *Secretary of the Judicial Commission of Inquiry into Allegations of State Capture, Corruption and Fraud in the Public Sector including Organs of State v Zuma* 2021 (5) SA 1 (CC) ("*Zuma I*").

[108] *Secretary of the Judicial Commission of Inquiry into Allegations of State Capture, Corruption and Fraud in the Public Sector including Organs of State v Zuma* 2021 (5) SA 327 (CC) ("*Zuma II*").

[109] See Bilchitz (2015); Langa (2007), p. 362; Brennan (1985), p. 427; and Rogers (2022), p. 300.

principles or even the facts in a given case; these dissents are based on judges' political or other commitments not pertinent to the issues raised by the cases, reliance upon which undermines the legitimacy of the court. Here, we consider the following cases: *Afriforum*,[110] *EFF II*,[111] *Zuma II*, and *Zuma III*.[112]

5 Reasoning Problem

A great portion of the Constitutional Court's decisions have largely been lauded for the outcomes they secured. The *EFF I* case has been heralded as a vital decision that led to the ousting of an unpopular President.[113] As alluded to above, the Court was alive to the political climate and the outcry in relation to the excessive costs of the purported security upgrades, which were publicly funded. There was a desperate need for political accountability. There was public distrust in the National Assembly and its mechanisms. The fact that the two ad hoc committees it established contradicted the Public Protector's report and absolved the President did not bolster public confidence in the National Assembly. So, when the Court was asked to adjudicate the matter, it delivered a judgment that was tailored to protect the office of the Public Protector, and more specifically its incumbent at the time, considering the prevailing political environment. The Court unanimously held that no state actor can simply ignore the Public Protector's findings, recommendations, and remedies "willy-nilly" without obtaining a court order.[114] In reaching this conclusion, the Court emphasised that there was an obligation on organs of state to assist and protect the Public Protector's dignity through the enforcement of her remedial action. It also reiterated the importance of accountability in a constitutional democracy.[115]

From a reading of the judgment, it is apparent that the Court was responding to the political zeitgeist. As Woolman has argued, *EFF I* formed part of an ongoing attempt to ensure that state actors and well-connected private actors are held accountable to the Constitution and that they abide by the rule of law. Implicit in this

[110] *City of Tshwane Metropolitan Municipality v Afriforum* 2016 (6) SA 279 (CC) ("*Afriforum*").

[111] *Economic Freedom Fighters v Speaker of the National Assembly* 2018 (2) SA 571 (CC) ("*EFF II*").

[112] *Zuma v Secretary of the Judicial Commission of Inquiry into Allegations of State Capture, Corruption and Fraud in the Public Sector Including Organs of State* 2021 (11) BCLR 1263 (CC) ("*Zuma III*").

[113] Woolman, op. cit., n. 95.

[114] *EFF I*, op. cit., n. 21, para 67.

[115] *EFF I*, id., para 1. Mogoeng CJ remarked:

> For this reason, public office-bearers ignore their constitutional obligations at their peril. This is so because constitutionalism, accountability and the rule of law constitute the sharp and mighty sword that stands ready to chop the ugly head of impunity off its stiffened neck.

argument is the acknowledgement that the Court was outcome-driven in view of the prevailing phenomenon of state capture in South Africa. The Court adopted a functionalist approach in interpreting the constitutional provisions governing the office of the Public Protector to achieve a desirable outcome. The trouble with outcome-based reasoning is that once the facts that gave rise to the decision change, the legal consequences of the decision remain and may create unintended long-term consequences. Once Zuma was removed as President and a new Public Protector was appointed, the true effects of this decision became evident. For instance, the new Public Protector ordered that the National Assembly amend the provisions of the Constitution that regulate the central bank to alter the purpose of the South African Reserve Bank. This clearly offended the separation of powers doctrine as the National Assembly could not be directed to amend the Constitution by anyone, including the Public Protector.[116] However, this recommendation was only possible because of the Constitutional Court's judgment in *EFF I* which imbued the Public Protector with far-reaching powers, in order to hold Zuma accountable. The effects of this decision have been eloquently captured by Le Roux and Davis as follows:

> [This] ... shows how adjudication is inherently political in nature, responsive to its contemporaneous context. The [Constitutional] [C]ourt's uncompromising endorsement of the binding nature of the Public Protector's powers ... was applauded and welcomed – when Madonsela [the former Public Protector] was its occupant. However, once Mkhwebane [the current Public Protector] took over ... she, perhaps understandably, relied on the [*EFF I*] judgment for justification for her far-reaching remedial action. The latitude and authority defined by the [*EFF I*] decision were then abused by the current Public Protector ... This reflects the danger inherent in far-reaching court decisions on political questions in a system of precedent: what is desirable in one set of circumstances involving certain individuals can be wholly disastrous when circumstances change or other people are appointed.[117]

The problem identified by Le Roux and Davis is that judicial decisions are binding and persist in perpetuity, even after the composition of the executive and the legislature has changed. Therefore, sound judicial reasoning especially from an apex court, is paramount. *EFF I*, despite its importance, is unfortunately not a model of sound judicial reasoning. There are at least four issues with its reasoning. *First*, the Court's reasoning is circular. The Court held that allowing state actors accused of malfeasance to ignore the recommendations of the Public Protector would be at odds with "the rule of law".[118] This is circular because it rests on the assumption that the rule of law requires that the Public Protector's recommendations be binding in law. The Court was called to address and consider what the legal force of the

[116] Office of the Public Protector, Alleged Failure to Recover Misappropriated Funds: Report on an Investigation into Allegations of Maladministration, Corruption, Misappropriation of Public Funds and the Failure by the South African Government to Implement the CIEX Report and to Recover Public Funds from ABSA Bank Report 8 of 2017/2018. This report was successfully challenged in *South African Reserve Bank v Public Protector* 2017 (6) SA 198 (GP).

[117] Le Roux and Davis, op. cit., n. 3, p. 286.

[118] *EFF I*, op. cit., n. 21, para 72. The Court asserts that the rule of law demands that no power be exercised unless it is provided for by the law and no decision or conduct sanctioned by the law may be ignored based purely on a contrary view one holds. See *EFF I*, op. cit., n. 21, para 75.

recommendations was, and by stating that ignoring the recommendations would violate the rule of law the Court assumes the legal force of the recommendations, without deciding the matter or justifying that conclusion.[119] Regardless of its conception of the rule of law, the Court had to address an anterior question: are the powers of the Public Protector binding? Once this question was addressed, only then could the court grapple with considerations of the rule of law.

Second, the Court employs a functionalist approach in that it answers the question of the binding nature of the recommendations by looking at the overall function of the Public Protector in a constitutional democracy. As a result of this, the Court does not undertake a close reading of the text of the Constitution or the Public Protector Act, the regulatory legislation.[120] It must be noted that the Constitution is silent on the effect and force of the Public Protector's powers. Little to no attention is given, by the Court, to locating where the binding nature of the remedial action is to be found—either in the Constitution or the Public Protector Act. This is particularly troubling considering the express wording of the Constitution, which provides that powers of the Public Protector are regulated by national legislation[121] and that the Public Protector has any additional powers and functions prescribed by national legislation.[122] Since the Court did not engage in any meaningful textual analysis of the Constitution or the Public Protector Act, it is not evident whether Parliament can restrict the binding powers through national legislation. If the binding nature of the powers is sourced from the Constitution, Parliament is constrained and cannot, through legislation, make any amendments changing the effect of the Public Protector's powers. However, if the binding nature flows from the Public Protector Act, or any other legislation, then Parliament is at large to amend the legislation, and remove the binding nature of those powers. Huq notes that the wide legislative authority to regulate the Public Protector may plausibly indicate that the powers of the Public Protector are not constitutionally binding, and that if the Court dealt with these provisions, the outcome would have been markedly different.[123] We are inclined to agree. The functionalist approach misconstrued and subverted the true question. The Court focused on whether the binding nature of the Public Protector's powers would enhance the ability of the Public Protector to hold state actors accountable. However, the true question was whether her powers are binding in law, through an interpretation of the Constitution or the Public Protector Act.

Third, the Court endeavours to ensure that the Public Protector's powers are effective but appears to conflate effectiveness with the binding nature of the powers of the office. The Court states that it is incomprehensible that the Public Protector could be considered effective without having binding powers.[124] Yet, the Court does

---

[119] Huq (2019), p. 35.

[120] Act 23 of 1994.

[121] Section 182(1) of the Constitution.

[122] Section 182(2) of the Constitution.

[123] Huq, op. cit., n. 119, p. 36.

[124] *EFF I*, op. cit., n. 21, para 49.

not do the hard work of justifying this logic. There are many institutions, which are constitutionally mandated to strengthen constitutional democracy and uphold the Constitution, such as the Auditor-General, the South African Human Rights Commission, the Electoral Commission and the Commission of Gender Equality,[125] which do not have binding powers, but which are effective in executing their constitutional obligations.[126] The Court's argument also ignores the fact that the Public Protector had until that point existed since 1994 without having any binding powers, and was never accused of being ineffective. Bishop and Woolman make exactly this point and write that, at the time, even though the Public Protector did not make binding decisions, the application of reason had resulted in infinitely more powerful results than using coercion.[127] The averment that only binding decisions are effective lacks grounding in any empirical evidence as well as being logically and legally flawed. The questionable logic of the judgment evinces that the Court was preoccupied with reaching a desirable outcome and reasoned the case back to front.

Fourth, by holding that the decisions are binding and can only be set aside by a court of law, the Court shifted the burden from the Public Protector to the state actor accused of acting in a manner contrary to the Constitution. Before *EFF I*, the Public Protector would have to approach a court to compel a state actor to implement its remedial action where the state actor had refused to comply (this is the case with the South African Human Rights Commission which is established under the same chapter in the Constitution as the Public Protector). However, because of *EFF I*, the state actor must approach a court to set aside the decision. Again, the Court fails to justify the burden shift. In fact, the Court does not address this point at all in its judgment. If the Court is concerned with accountability, does requiring the Public Protector to approach a court to enforce her remedial action denude her of the function to hold state actors accountable? Was the burden shift necessary for achieving accountability? If the Public Protector implicates a relatively powerless state bureaucrat for their involvement in corruption, it is on that bureaucrat to challenge the findings of the Public Protector. It is plausible that such a person would not have recourse to the law, for financial or other reasons. This seems to buttress the argument that the Court decided with a particular person in mind (that is, President Zuma) after being exhausted by his evasive tactics.[128]

[125] Section 188 of the Constitution.

[126] It is interesting to note that the Auditor-General is established in terms of Chapter 9 of the Constitution alongside the Public Protector and the Court does not seem to suggest that the binding nature of the Public Protector's powers extends to other institutions such as the Auditor-General. Others have made this argument, see for instance Govender and Swanepoel (2020), p. 1.

[127] Bishop and Woolman (2005), ch 24A, 3. See a recent contribution: Woolman, op. cit., n. 85, p. 180.

[128] For a discussion on this, see Woolman, op. cit., n. 95, p. 176–177.

Fifth, the Court fails to sufficiently engage with two other competing decisions delivered by the High Court[129] and Supreme Court of Appeal.[130] While both cases concerned different facts from the *EFF I*, the courts had addressed the same question—does the Public Protector have binding powers? The High Court found that her powers are not binding in nature as the Constitution did not confer such powers on her.[131] Schippers J reasoned that while the powers were not binding, they could not be ignored or disregarded without a rational basis. However, the Supreme Court of Appeal disagreed and held that the powers of the Public Protector are binding considering the constitutional and legislative structure of her office. The Constitutional Court briefly (in two paragraphs) engaged with these decisions, preferring the decision of the Supreme Court of Appeal without any reasoning. However, Mogoeng CJ appears to have mischaracterised the High Court judgment as permitting self-help by offending state actors,[132] whereas the High Court was at pains to hold that the decisions can only be ignored when there is a rational basis for ignoring them. Rationality is part and parcel of our legal system, and it is unclear how requiring state actors to comply with a recommendation by the Public Protector unless they have a rational reason for not doing so amounts to self-help.[133] What is even more curious about the Court's preference for the Supreme Court of Appeal decision is that the Court held that:

> The judgment of the Supreme Court of Appeal is correct in recognising that the Public Protector's remedial action *might at times have a binding effect*.[134]

In that statement, the Court seems to endorse the reasoning of the Supreme Court of Appeal that the remedial action might occasionally be binding, but then goes on to hold that the remedial action is always inherently binding (unless set aside). There is no reason furnished for this manifest difference. Connected to this, the Court pegs most of its argument on accountability but fails to furnish a definition of accountability, nor does it explain why legal accountability, as opposed to political accountability, should be preferred in cases involving the Public Protector's remedial action.[135] This decision, as Huq contends, is based on the political risks that South Africa faced at the time. It is discernibly a decision based on a purported functional analysis of the Public Protector's powers and not on close reading of the Constitution's specific text.[136] The Court was concerned with sending a message at a time when the state was generally corrupt and incompetent and there was public distrust of state institutions.

---

[129] *Democratic Alliance v South African Broadcasting Corporation* 2015 (1) SA 551 (WCC) ("*Democratic Alliance*").

[130] *South African Broadcasting Corporation Soc Ltd v Democratic Alliance* 2016 (2) SA 522 (SCA).

[131] *Democratic Alliance*, op. cit., n. 129, para 74.

[132] *EFF I*, op. cit., n. 21, paras 72–75.

[133] Tsele, op. cit., n. 100, pp. 214–215.

[134] *EFF I*, op. cit., n. 21, para 73.

[135] Huq (2018), p. 4.

[136] Huq, op. cit., n. 100, p. 36.

Ideally, when courts decide a matter, they set out principles or rules that will apply to future cases arising from similar facts. These principles are discernible from a court's reasoning. The danger with outcome-based decisions is that they lack the very essence of what makes a judgment important—sound judicial reasoning that sets out or applies proper legal principles. In a legal system that adheres to the principle of *stare decisis* (the idea that courts are bound their own previous decisions or those of higher courts than themselves), the significance of coherent reasoning is self-evident and cannot be gainsaid. Courts do not command an army, nor do they control the fiscus.[137] Their legitimacy is dependent on principled adjudication, underpinned by sound, coherent and consistent reasoning. The judicialisation of politics tends, at least in South Africa, to threaten the very essence of courts. While we do not argue that the Constitutional Court has descended from the realm of legal reasoning down "to the aphorisms of the fortune cookie",[138] we contend that the reasoning of the Constitutional Court, in politically charged matters like *EFF I*, tends to deliver incoherent jurisprudence that causes more confusion than provides clarity. By appealing to public sentiment, the Court strayed away from settled legal principles and the text of the Constitution. While this was a political victory, which led to the fall of a President, the shaky logic on which the decision rests reminds us that courts are not and should not be sites for political struggle.[139]

6 Rule of Law Problem

Judicial decision-making generates rules. These rules are binding on all of us within the jurisdiction of that court and provide us with directions on how to lawfully regulate and live our lives.[140] Former Constitutional Court judge, Justice Kate O'Regan writes that "as a member of the bench, I am required to issue a judgment; and in that judgment, I am required to lay down a rule of law that binds both the parties before the court and South African society as a whole."[141] The judiciary is not alone in its rule-generating enterprise. It is trite that the legislature and the executive also make rules.[142] The judicialisation of politics in South Africa, we argue, has led to the courts' failure to lay down clear, cognisable, and principled legal rules. In turn, we argue that the courts' decisions increasingly and worryingly run counter to the rule of law.

137 Hamilton (1961).

138 Scalia J dissenting in *Obergefell v. Hodges* 135 S Ct 2584, 2628 (2015).

139 *Merafong Demarcation Forum v President of the Republic of South Africa* 2008 (5) SA 171 (CC), at paras 303–310

140 Scalia (1989), p. 1177.

141 O'Regan (2007).

142 Woolman, op. cit., n. 28, p. 788.

The rule of law has multiple meanings.[143] Dicey described the rule of law as referring to, *inter alia*, the notion of the absolute supremacy of the law and the equality of individuals before the law.[144] Everyone is bound by the law and should be treated equally before the law, regardless of their rank, office or status.[145] Raz notes that the rule of law demands that people exercising public power or who have political authority must be subjected to mandatory, predetermined rules that will constrain arbitrary governance.[146] Fuller identifies the formal aspects of the rule of law or what he referred to as the "inner morality of law".[147] The rule of law, according to Fuller, requires the state to act in a manner that is orderly, predictable and with sufficient notice given and that it should consistently apply these standards and not arbitrarily depart from them.[148] The multiple meanings of the rule of law have inspired numerous scholars to conclude that the rule of law has both substantive and procedural components.[149] For purposes of this chapter, we do not intend to enter that debate but we merely advance the view that the rule of law encompasses at least four principles to which law must conform: clarity, relative stability, generality and equality.[150]

To the extent that courts generate rules and make law, this law must be clear, public, general, prospective, and stable. This will ensure that people know in advance how to plan and govern their lives.[151] The Constitutional Court, in its pursuit to uphold the rule of law against the other arms of government mired in political controversies, has unwittingly undermined the rule of law by rendering judgments that create uncertainty, that are imprecise, and focused or geared towards certain political ends. The Court has also on numerous occasions,[152] abandoned judicial precedent, departing radically from its previous decisions, and not treating like cases alike, without properly justifying why it does so.

The principle of generality requires that rules and laws apply to all legal subjects in a principled manner. The same laws should apply to similar sets of facts. The principle of equality simply denotes that people should be subjected to the same laws in the same way. In a recent triad of decisions concerning former President Jacob Zuma that resulted in his imprisonment, the Constitutional Court has once

143 Waldron (2008), p. 6.

144 Dicey, op. cit., n. 36, p. 193.

145 Allan (1985), p. 113.

146 Raz (2009), p. 224.

147 Fuller (1968).

148 Fuller, id.

149 Craig (1997), p. 467.

150 Endicott (1999), pp. 1–2.

151 Raz (2019), pp. 3–5; Rawls (1996), pp. 235–243; Fuller, op. cit., n. 147, ch 2.

152 See the Court's conflicting decisions in *Fredericks v MEC for Education and Training, Eastern Cape* 2002 2 SA 693 (CC), *Chirwa v Transnet Limited* 2008 4 SA 367 (CC) and *Gcaba v Minister for Safety and Security* 2010 1 SA 238 (CC). See also *State Information Technology Agency Soc Limited v Gijima Holdings (Pty) Ltd* 2018 (2) SA 23 (CC) and the critical discussion of this judgment in Boonzaier (2018), p. 642.

again sacrificed these principles at the altar of outcome-based adjudication. Until recently, South Africa was subjected to a prolonged commission of inquiry since 2018, which was tasked with investigating allegations of state capture, corruption and fraud in the public sector, including organs of state ("the Commission").[153] The Commission was a site of political struggle, with numerous opposition parties using it as a tool to score political points against the ruling party, the African National Congress. The Commission was specifically tasked with uncovering the extent of the rot under the Zuma presidency. Former President Zuma was implicated as an active participant in, and enabler of, corruption.

After briefly participating in the proceedings, Zuma refused to continue giving testimony for a myriad of reasons. The Commission then elected to approach the Constitutional Court to seek an order compelling Zuma to appear before it and to give testimony (bypassing the High Court, which was competent to hear the matter and to issue a warrant of arrest in terms of the Commissions Act[154]).[155] It is worth noting that the Commission was chaired by the then-Deputy Chief Justice Raymond Zondo, a member of the Constitutional Court. The choice to bypass the High Court as alluded to above, suggests that it was a deliberate strategic decision given the profiles of the parties involved. The Commission approached the Court with a constitutional question, namely, whether there was a constitutional duty on Zuma, in his capacity as former President and head of the national executive, to give testimony before the Commission and to account for the exercise of public power during his term of office.[156] The Constitutional Court, aware of the political storm surrounding the Commission, entertained the matter and held in favour of the Commission, compelling Zuma to appear before the Commission. However, the Court, in doing so, did not decide the constitutional question and disposed of the matter on purely statutory grounds, deciding the question whether the Commissions Act compelled Zuma's presence at the Commission.

One of the key issues in the judgment was jurisdiction. The Constitutional Court, as a super-appellate court, has limited jurisdiction and does not have carte blanche to adjudicate any matter it desires. It is constrained to hear constitutional matters or matters that raise an arguable point of law of general public importance that ought to be decided by it.[157] Once the jurisdictional threshold has been met, the Court must also decide whether it is in the interests of justice for it to grant leave to appeal. However, the Constitution also provides an alternative procedure through which a litigant may seek direct access to the Court, bypassing the other superior courts below it, on interests of justice grounds and with the leave of the Court.[158]

---

[153] Commission of Inquiry into State Capture, Our Mandate. https://www.statecapture.org.za/site/about/mandate.

[154] Act 8 of 1947.

[155] *Zuma I*, op. cit., n. 108.

[156] The Commission's founding papers in the Constitutional Court can be accessed here: https://www.statecapture.org.za/site/files/judgments/5/CC_JGZ_Papers.pdf.

[157] *Paulsen v Slip Knot Investments 777 (Pty) Limited* 2015 (3) SA 479 (CC) ("*Paulsen*").

[158] Section 167(6)(a) of the Constitution.

On a reading of the judgment, it is evident that the Court crafts a specific test for jurisdiction to accommodate the Commission's case. Compelling Zuma to appear before the Commission was neither a constitutional issue nor did it raise an arguable point of law of public importance (none of the parties contested the meaning or legal effect of the provisions of the Commissions Act). The Commission had powers in terms of the Commissions Act to compel Zuma's testimony, but for whatever reason, it elected not to. The Court relied on the argument that the public has an interest in having the allegations against Zuma settled to assume jurisdiction.[159] At most, this argument might go to indicating that it was in the interests of justice to grant the Commission leave to bring a direct access application. That, however, is not enough to establish jurisdiction (which, again, is a separate question). It must be noted that the High Court was competent to hear the case, and as a rule, the Commission ought to have approached the High Court first. It is only in exceptional circumstances where a party can bypass the High Court and directly approach the Constitutional Court. The Court has on numerous occasions held that direct access is not simply for the taking.[160]

As previously alluded to, the Court's relationship with the chairperson of the Commission (who was their colleague) and the profiles of the parties involved may have played a key role in the Court deciding both to take up the case and to render the judgment that it did. Certainly, the Court eschewing the constitutional question squarely raised by the Commission in its application—which would have engaged its specialist jurisdiction—for a statutory question on which the parties were agreed should raise some concern. On the Court's own test for jurisdiction,[161] neither its specialist (constitutional) nor general jurisdiction was engaged, and it was thus enjoined to dismiss the application. Its failure to do so is a stark and unjustified departure from previous cases where it declined to assume jurisdiction even where the parties were not agreed on the interpretation of the legal rule in question.[162] This offends against the rule of law requirement that laws be stable and clear.

The Commission's application gave birth to two more judgments of the Court, which laid bare the politics at the heart of the dispute and further revealed that the fault lines of dissent at the Court are at the level of politics and not law. We discuss this in more detail below. For now, it must be noted that Zuma publicly disregarded the court order compelling him to appear before the Commission. This led to the Commission approaching the Court seeking a declaration that Zuma was guilty of the crime of contempt of court for failure to comply with the order. A majority of the Court held that Zuma was indeed guilty of contempt and sentenced him to 15-months' imprisonment.

---

[159] *Zuma I*, op. cit., n. 108, para 70.

[160] *United Democratic Movement v Speaker of the National Assembly* 2017 (5) SA 300 (CC) at para 23.

[161] *Gcaba v Minister for Safety and Security* 2010 (1) SA 238 (CC) and *Paulsen*, op. cit., n. 128.

[162] For example: *Jacobs v S* 2019 (1) SACR 623 (CC) and *General Council of the Bar of South Africa v Jiba* 2019 (8) BCLR 919 (CC).

The issue here is that the Court, despite Zuma's public statement indicating that he had no intention in participating in the Court proceedings and was prepared to the "first prisoner" of the Court,[163] issued directives to Zuma, effectively asking him to make written submissions on what an appropriate sanction would be should he be found guilty.[164] This was an unusual step. Generally, when parties have indicated that they have no interest in participating in proceedings, the courts proceed with the matter on that basis. While the Court attempts to argue that it issued these directions because of the severity of the sanction (imprisonment) and that it had to afford Zuma an opportunity to make representations, this ignores that Zuma decidedly rejected participating in the proceedings from the beginning. It would be reasonable to question whether the Court would have extended the same courtesy to another party. It would be dishonest to suggest that the fact that Zuma was a former president played no role in him being treated differently. This demonstrates how the judicialisation of politics and being drawn into political issues may create inequality in the sense that certain individuals (who wield political power) will be treated differently to those who do not wield any political power.

The Court defended its decision by stating that offering Zuma this opportunity to make representations was an "unexceptional, commonplace entitlement to a fair process dictated by section 12 of the Constitution in a manner comparable to the section 35 residual fair trial right".[165] Despite claiming that this is commonplace, the Court fails to cite a case to support this proposition. It must be recalled that Zuma explicitly denounced the Court and stated that he would not be participating in the proceedings at all. One could say he broke himself into prison. There is no record of a court extending this courtesy to a contemnor who has completely waived their right to participate in the case, which highlights the exceptionality of the Court's conduct in the matter.

7 Political Dissent Problem

Up until recently, dissent in South African courts had always been cordial and informed largely by judges' approach to legal method. However, the tone and frequency of dissent in the Constitutional Court have begun to change, generously peppered with political rhetoric which reveals the judges' political sympathies and their impact on how cases are adjudicated. We stress tone here not to police the way in which judges choose to dissent from their colleagues but simply to highlight that because the issues that lie at the heart of the dissents are often political, as opposed to legal, the tone of these dissents takes on a more emotive tenor.

[163] Ferreira (2021).

[164] *Zuma II*, op. cit., n. 198, at paras 63–70.

[165] Ibid, para 70.

For instance, in a case concerning a metropolitan council's decision to change street names that paid homage to the country's apartheid and colonial leaders, Cameron and Froneman JJ, both white judges, dissented from the Court's judgment and laid bare the fraught nature of dissent at the Court. The relevant facts are that Afriforum NPC, a self-styled Afrikaner civil rights organisation, sought to interdict the City of Tshwane's decision to change the names of some 25 streets, asserting a claim that the culture and heritage of its members were being assaulted. The High Court granted the interim interdict pending finalisation of judicial review proceedings and the municipal council, after two failed attempts to appeal to two other appellate courts, found favour at the Constitutional Court. There, the case was ostensibly about the appealability of interim orders and the requirements for granting interdicts. However, given the polarising facts that underlay the dispute, descent into the realm of the political proved unavoidable.

In arguing that its members would suffer irreparable harm if the interdict were not granted, Afriforum contended that even the removal of the old street names on a temporary basis would cause untold emotional hurt and suffering to those who drew from them a "sense of place and a sense of belonging".[166] Mogoeng CJ, writing for a majority, characterised the submission variously as "insensitive," "divisive," and "somewhat selfish" and held that it disregarded "the centuries old deprivation of 'a sense of place and a sense of belonging' that black people have had to endure."[167] In their dissent, Cameron and Froneman JJ took exception to this, stating that Mogoeng CJ had implied that "any reliance by white South Africans, particularly white Afrikaner people, on a cultural tradition founded in history, finds no recognition in the Constitution, because that history is inevitably rooted in oppression."[168] While disavowing Afriforum's view of history which minimised colonialism and apartheid, Cameron and Froneman JJ held that Afriforum's members had a real and constitutionally cognisable interest because "the Constitution creates scope for recognising an interest or right based on a sense of belonging to the place where one lives, rooted in its particular history, and to be involved in decisions affecting that sense of place and belonging."[169]

Responding to this latter claim, Jafta J penned a judgment concurring in the majority which, in very strong terms, accused the two dissentient judges of advancing an interpretation of the Constitution which is "rooted in oppression"[170] and declaring that "there can be no justification for recognition of cultural traditions or interests 'based on a sense of belonging to the place where one lives' if those interests are rooted in the shameful racist past."[171] One would do well at this point to remember that the case was ostensibly about the requirements for a grant of an

---

[166] *Afriforum*, op. cit., n. 110, at para 57.

[167] *Afriforum*, id., para 58.

[168] *Afriforum*, id., para 81.

[169] *Afriforum*, id., para 124.

[170] *Afriforum*, id., para 176.

[171] *Afriforum*, id., para 169.

interdict and whether or not Afriforum had met the test. However, all three judgments engaged in ideological and political posturing about the underlying facts of the case, which were to a very large degree irrelevant to the ultimate resolution of the dispute, in very strong and unusually emotive language. The *Afriforum* judgment marked a noticeable change in the tone and content of dissents (and 'counter-concurrences') in the Constitutional Court.

In *EFF II*,[172] the sequel to *EFF I*, opposition parties sought a declaration that the National Assembly had failed to fulfil some of its constitutional obligations by not having in place parliamentary rules to facilitate the removal or impeachment of the President. In terms of section 89 of the Constitution, the National Assembly may remove the President by resolution of a two-thirds majority of its members only on the grounds of a serious violation of the Constitution or the law; serious misconduct; or inability to perform the functions of office. The Court was confronted with two questions. The first was whether the National Assembly was under a constitutional obligation to have a mechanism in place to facilitate a section 89 removal and whether such obligation had been breached by the failure to have a mechanism in place. The second was whether the National Assembly had failed to hold the President accountable in terms of section 89 insofar as it did not seek to establish whether the President had violated the Constitution by not complying with the Public Protector's report that was the subject of the litigation in *EFF I*.

On both questions the Court was split. In a majority judgment by Jafta J the Court held that the Constitution did require that the National Assembly have rules in place to facilitate a section 89 removal. For the majority, section 89 required the National Assembly to satisfy itself that the jurisdictional grounds listed in section 89(1) exist before putting a removal motion to a vote. This, the majority argued, requires a preliminary enquiry by the National Assembly to establish the existence of a removal ground prior to tabling a resolution in terms of section 89. Anything outside of that, including the ad hoc committee procedure that was previously employed by the National Assembly, was unconstitutional. Following from this, the majority concluded that "the [National] Assembly has failed to hold the President to account following delivery of this Court's judgment [in *EFF I*], as was required by section 89(1)."[173]

In its order, the Court declared the failure of the National Assembly to have rules regulating the removal of the President in terms of section 89 unconstitutional and directed that it make the rules without delay.[174] In dissent, Mogoeng CJ accused the majority of being guilty of judicial overreach, an "impermissible intrusion by the judiciary into the exclusive domain of Parliament."[175] In his view, the Court had impermissibly prescribed a procedure in terms of which an inquiry *always* had to be held prior to a section 89 motion being voted upon which, in turn, deprived the

[172] *EFF II*, op. cit., n. 111.
[173] *EFF II*, id., para 208.
[174] *EFF II*, id., para 222.
[175] *EFF II*, id., para 223.

National Assembly of relying "only on readily available documented or recorded evidential material" in order to establish a ground of removal.[176]

For Mogoeng CJ, a requirement that there be an "institutional predetermination" of the existence of a removal ground regulated by rules of the National Assembly was "inflexible" and an imposition, by the majority, of its preferred procedure on Parliament,[177] and "an unprecedented and unconstitutional encroachment into the operational space of Parliament by judges."[178] This accusation of unconstitutional conduct on the part of the majority by a dissentient judge would later prove to be a useful rhetorical tool deployed where desired outcomes were not reached.

The two cases that followed the initial *Zuma I* judgment illustrate this. Having been compelled by the Court to appear before the Commission Zuma still refused to appear, arguing that the Commission's summons was not lawfully issued. To this, the Commission responded by approaching the Court again. This time it sought an order that Zuma was in contempt of the Court's earlier order. This would be the first time that the Court would hear a contempt application as a court of first instance. In addition, the Commission sought Zuma's direct committal (i.e., imprisonment) as a sanction for the contempt, also a first. Zuma responded with a media statement accusing the Commission of political expediency and stating that he would not participate in the contempt proceedings.

In its judgment, the Court was again split. The Court unanimously found Zuma guilty of contempt of court for his failure to appear and give testimony before the Commission, however only seven of the nine judges agreed that he should be sentenced to a 15-month term of imprisonment. It must be noted at this point that civil contempt law in South Africa had until this point been settled and the jurisprudence was univocal.[179] In dissent, Theron J (with Jafta J concurring) accused the majority judgment of being unconstitutional and of "trammel[ing] over the constitutional rights of [Zuma]."[180] It accused the majority judgment of not just being bad law, but unconstitutional.[181] The divergence was on the question of sanction. Having found Zuma guilty of civil contempt, the majority imposed direct imprisonment. For the dissentients, this was impermissible. According to Theron J, Zuma's rights not to be detained without trial[182] and to have a fair trial[183] were violated by the order. Despite accepting a civil court's competence to determine guilt for contempt in application or motion proceedings, the minority argued that no imprisonment could follow from

[176] *EFF II*, id., para 224.

[177] *EFF II*, id., para 250.

[178] *EFF II*, id., para 254.

[179] See *Burchell v Burchell* [2005] ZAECHC 35; *Fakie N.O v CCII Systems (Pty) Ltd* 2006 (4) SA 326 (SCA); *Victoria Park Ratepayers' Association v Greyvenouw CC* 2004 JDR 0498 (SE); *Mashiya v Matshikawe* [2002] ZAECHC 10, [2005] JOL 14725 (E); *S v Mamabolo* 2001 (3) SA 409 (CC); and *Pheko v Ekurhuleni City* 2015 (5) SA 600 (CC).

[180] *Zuma II*, op. cit., n. 108, para 143.

[181] *Zuma II*, id., para 262.

[182] Section 12 of the Constitution.

[183] Section 35 of the Constitution.

a finding of guilt absent a criminal trial. This finding was contrary to existing jurisprudence to the effect that a court deciding a civil contempt case was competent to issue any order it saw fit.[184] The dissent continued to strenuously argue this point, at various points accusing the majority of acting unconstitutionally.

After the judgment was handed down, chaos ensued. Many of Zuma's supporters embraced the minority judgment's rhetoric that the majority had acted unconstitutionally and rallied around this point to mobilise for action. In the days that followed, South Africa experienced violent unrest unlike any the country had seen since 1994, and it is believed that Zuma's followers played a key role in instigating the violence and looting.[185] In that time, Zuma filed an application for the rescission of the Court's contempt judgment, *Zuma II*, on the basis that the judgment contained "rescindable errors and/or omissions" which rendered it vulnerable to attack. Meanwhile, he sought to appeal the Court's judgment and to introduce new evidence to defend himself against the contempt charge.[186]

Again, the Court was split along the same lines as in *Zuma II* with Jafta J now writing the dissent. This time, the dissentients took the opportunity to relitigate their earlier arguments and essentially refusing to accept the holding in *Zuma II* as binding on them. They looked beyond the law on rescission (whose principles had also been settled)[187] to international law to found a basis on which to both overturn the Court's earlier decision and to provide Zuma with advice on how to proceed further in international tribunals. They persisted in their claim that the Court acted unconstitutionally and would have set the order in *Zuma II* aside.

Each of these cases demonstrates where the fault lines of dissent at the Court currently lie, and it is not to do with legal doctrine. On a close reading of each judgment, the judges are almost always agreed on what the law is but seem more preoccupied with finding alternative pathways to achieving their desired outcomes. In each case, dissent is animated not by fidelity to the law per se, but by a sense of apprehension that the law as it stood yielded outcomes that were politically unpalatable. This is especially true of *Zuma II* and *Zuma III*, where much was made of the fact that violent riots had erupted in response to the judgments, almost as if to cow the Court into submission. To its credit, the Court did not retreat. However, the tone of the dissents is cause for concern. Where previously judges saw dissenting opinions as evincing a diversity of interpretational approaches or judicial philosophies, it has now become fashionable to accuse fellow judges of unconstitutional conduct, and to refuse to accept majority judgments as binding authority. This situation does

---

[184] See *Victoria Park Ratepayers' Association*, op. cit., n. 179 and *Cape Times Ltd v Union Trades Directories (Pty) Ltd* 1956 (1) SA 105 (N) at 121D-125H.

[185] Report of the Expert Panel into the July 2021 Civil Unrest. https://www.thepresidency.gov.za/download/file/fid/2442.

[186] *Zuma III*, op. cit., n. 112.

[187] Consider the following cases: *Erstwhile Tenants of Williston Court and Another v Lewray Investments (Pty) Ltd and Another* 2016 (6) SA 466 (GJ); *Colyn v Tiger Food Industries Ltd t/a Meadow Feed Mills Cape* [2003] 2 All SA 113 (SCA); and *Van Heerden v Bronkhorst* [2020] ZASCA 147.

not bode well for the legitimacy of the Court in the eyes of the public, who see these tendencies as nothing more than politics by other means and who are increasingly questioning the moral and constitutional authority of the Court.

The prevailing approach by the Court to adjudicate matters by focusing on outcomes poses a greater danger of political displacement as more and more parties approach the Court in the hopes that, the provisions of the law notwithstanding, the Court will always make the "right" decision (i.e., one which the affected party desires). An instance of this was the attempt by South Africa's electoral commission to have the Court order the postponement of the local government or municipal elections which had to be held before 1 November 2021.[188] Constitutionally, newly elected councils had to be elected by that date.[189] The electoral commission, citing challenges presented by the COVID-19 pandemic, asked the Court to suspend its constitutional obligations and to allow it to hold elections outside of the window provided for in the Constitution. It invoked the Court's broad remedial jurisdiction to justify such an order. The Court dismissed the application and found that it had no power to postpone the elections, or to order that they be held outside of the constitutionally mandated timelines. What is concerning is that the Court enrolled the matter for a hearing in the first place (as opposed to dismissing the matter outright based on the papers) that the electoral commission seemed to have some sympathy from members of the bench, and that a retired judge of the Court[190] had advised the electoral commission to take that route as opposed to seeking an amendment of the Constitution to allow for a postponement.

We review these cases to show a steady arrogation of power by the Court which increasingly treads into areas previously reserved only for Parliament or the executive. This is a logical consequence of the judicialisation of politics which includes the rampant invocation of the courts' wide remedial jurisdiction to craft new and unusual remedies for disputes that are quintessentially political, the retreat of the political from public life, and the increasingly visible and prominent role that judges now play in public life.

8 Conclusion

In this chapter, we have attempted to demonstrate that while the phenomenon of the judicialisation of politics in South Africa is generally celebrated as a triumph for accountability and the vindication of the Constitution and the rule of law, this comes at a grave cost. The ascendence of the judicialisation of politics has been accompanied by a decline in the quality of jurisprudence of the superior courts generally, and

[188] See *Electoral Commission v Minister of Cooperative Governance and Traditional Affairs* 2022 (5) BCLR 571 (CC).

[189] Section 159(2) of the Constitution.

[190] See Moseneke (2021).

the Constitutional Court in particular. This can largely be attributed to outcome-based adjudication, where judges employ grand legal and political rhetoric to justify their decisions without setting out clear and cogent legal rules. This in turn has an adverse effect on the rule of law because courts, which invariably make law through their decisions, do not make rules that are general, certain, clear and which apply equally to everyone. Further, the migration of politics into the courtroom has resulted in an increase in judicial dissents that are peppered with political rhetoric that reveals that the fault lines of dissent are drawn according to the political sympathies of the judges and have nothing to do with genuine and principled disagreements about the law. These effects of the judicialisation of politics cannot merely be disregarded as casualties of constitutional democracies founded on the value of accountability. On the contrary, they call for a reversal of the displacement of politics by lawfare and for a return to democratic modes of conflict resolution in political institutions and not the imposition of will by force of law.

Case Law

Bato Star Fishing (Pty) Ltd v Minister of Environmental Affairs and Tourism 2004 (4) SA 490 (CC)

Black Sash Trust v Minister of Social Development and Others (Freedom Under Law NPC Intervening) 2017 (3) SA 335 (CC)

Brown v Board of Education of Topeka 347 US 483

Burchell v Burchell [2005] ZAECHC 35

Cape Times Ltd v Union Trades Directories (Pty) Ltd 1956 (1) SA 105 (N)

Chirwa v Transnet Limited 2008 4 SA 367 (CC)

City of Tshwane Metropolitan Municipality v Afriforum 2016 (6) SA 279 (CC)

Collins v Minister of the Interior 1957 (1) SA 552 (A)

Colyn v Tiger Food Industries Ltd t/a Meadow Feed Mills Cape [2003] 2 All SA 113 (SCA)

Corruption Watch NPC v President of the Republic of South Africa; Nxasana v Corruption Watch NPC [2018] (10) BCLR 1179 (CC)

Council for Civil Service Unions v. Government Central Communication Headquarters [1984] 3 AI E.R. 935

De Lange v Smuts 1998 (3) SA 785 (CC)

Democratic Alliance v South African Broadcasting Corporation 2015 (1) SA 551 (WCC)

Doctors for Life International v Speaker of the National Assembly 2006 6 SA 416 (CC)

Economic Freedom Fighters v Speaker of the National Assembly; Democratic Alliance v Speaker of the National Assembly 2016 (3) SA 580 (CC)

Economic Freedom Fighters v Speaker of the National Assembly 2018 (2) SA 571 (CC)

Electoral Commission v Minister of Cooperative Governance and Traditional Affairs 2022 (5) BCLR 571 (CC)
Erstwhile Tenants of Williston Court and Another v Lewray Investments (Pty) Ltd and Another 2016 (6) SA 466 (GJ)
Executive Council, Western Cape Legislature v President of the Republic of South Africa 1995 (4) SA 877 (CC)
Fakie N.O v CCII Systems (Pty) Ltd 2006 (4) SA 326 (SCA);
Ferreira v Levin NO 1996 (1) SA 984 (CC)
Fedsure Life Insurance Ltd v Greater Johannesburg Transitional Metropolitan Council 1999 1 SA 374 (CC)
Fredericks v MEC for Education and Training, Eastern Cape 2002 2 SA 693 (CC)
Harris v Minister of the Interior 1952 (2) SA 428 (A),
Gcaba v Minister for Safety and Security 2010 (1) SA 238 (CC)
General Council of the Bar of South Africa v Jiba 2019 (8) BCLR 919 (CC)
In re: Certification of the Constitution of the Republic of South Africa 1996 (4) SA 744 (CC)
Jacobs v S 2019 (1) SACR 623 (CC)
Johannesburg Consolidated Investment Company v Johannesburg Town Council 1903 TS 111
Investigating Directorate: Serious Economic Offences and Others v Hyundai Motor Distributors (Pty) Ltd In re: Hyundai Motor Distributors (Pty) Ltd v Smit NO 2001 (1) SA 545 (CC)
Mashiya v Matshikawe [2002] ZAECHC 10, [2005] JOL 14725 (E)
Merafong Demarcation Forum v President of the Republic of South Africa 2008 (5) SA 171 (CC)
Minister of the Interior v Harris 1952 (4) SA 769 (A)
National Coalition for Gay and Lesbian Equality v Minister of Home Affairs 2000 (2) SA 1 (CC)
National Treasury v Opposition to Urban Tolling Alliance 2012 (6) SA 223 (CC)
Ndlwana v Hofmeyr 1937 AD 229
Paulsen v Slip Knot Investments 777 (Pty) Limited 2015 (3) SA 479 (CC)
Pheko v Ekurhuleni City 2015 (5) SA 600 (CC)
President of the Republic of South Africa v Democratic Alliance 2020 (1) SA 428 (CC)
President of the Republic of South Africa v Hugo 1997 (4) SA 1 (CC)
S v Makwanyane 1995 (3) SA 391
Section 27 v Minister of Education 20113 2 SA 40 (GNP)
Secretary of the Judicial Commission of Inquiry into Allegations of State Capture, Corruption and Fraud in the Public Sector including Organs of State v Zuma 2021 (5) SA 327 (CC)
Secretary of the Judicial Commission of Inquiry into Allegations of State Capture, Corruption and Fraud in the Public Sector including Organs of State v Zuma 2021 (5) SA 1 (CC)
South African Association of Personal Injury Lawyers v Heath 2001 (1) SA 883 (CC)
South African Broadcasting Corporation Soc Ltd v Democratic Alliance 2016 (2) SA 522 (SCA)

South African Reserve Bank v Public Protector & Others 2017 (6) SA 198 (GP)
State Information Technology Agency Soc Limited v Gijima Holdings (Pty) Ltd 2018 (2) SA 23 (CC)
United Democratic Movement v Speaker of the National Assembly 2017 (5) SA 300 (CC)
Van Heerden v Bronkhorst [2020] ZASCA 147
Victoria Park Ratepayers' Association v Greyvenouw CC 2004 JDR 0498 (SE)
Zuma v Secretary of the Judicial Commission of Inquiry into Allegations of State Capture, Corruption and Fraud in the Public Sector Including Organs of State 2021 (11) BCLR 1263 (CC)

Legislation

Commissions Act 8 of 1947
Public Protector Act 23 of 1994

References

Books

Bishop M, Woolman S (2005) Public protector. In: Woolman S, Bishop M (eds) Constitutional law of South Africa, 2nd edn. Juta, Cape Town, ch 24A
De Vos P, Freedman W (eds) (2014) South African constitutional law in context. Oxford University Press, Cape Town
Dicey AV (1959) Introduction to the study of the law of the constitution, 10th edn. Liberty Fund, London
Fuller L (1968) Morality of the law. Oxford University Press, Oxford
Hirschl R (2004) Towards Juristocracy. Harvard University Press, Cambridge
Hirschl R (2011) The Judicialization of politics. In: Goodin RE (ed) The Oxford handbook of political science. Oxford University Press, Oxford
Montesquieu C (1788) The spirit of laws. Cambridge University Press, Cambridge
Rawls J (1996) A theory of justice. Harvard University Press, Cambridge
Raz J (2009) The authority of law. Oxford University Press, Oxford
Sweet AS (2000) Governing with judges: constitutional politics in Europe. Oxford University Press, Oxford

Conference Papers

O'Regan K (2007) Dignity, application and the rule of law. Conference on dignity and the jurisprudence of Laurie Ackermann. University of Cape Town
Wallis M (2018) Can Judges (and Ombuds) overreach? http://supremecourtofappeal.org.za/index.php/speeches-and-conxferences/category/14-conference-papers (2018, World Bar Conference)

Constitution

Constitution of the Republic of South Africa, 1996

Journal Articles

Allan TRS (1985) Legislative supremacy and the rule of law: democracy and constitutionalism. Camb Law J 44:111–143

Bilchitz D (2015) Humility, dissent and community: exploring chief Justice Langa's political and judicial philosophy. Acta Juridica: 88–119

Boonzaier L (2018) A decision to undo. South Afr Law J 4:642–677

Brennan Jr WJ (1985) In defense of dissents. Hast Law J 37:427–438

Brett P (2020) Politics by other means in South Africa today. J Law Soc 47:126–144

Brickhill J, van Leeve Y (2015) Transformative constitutionalism—guiding light or empty slogan? Acta Juridica:141–171

Cachalia F (2015) Separation of powers, active liberty and the allocation of public resources: the Etolling case. South Afr Law J 132:285–312

Chaskalson A (2004) From wickedness to equality: the moral transformation of South African law. Int J Const Law 1:590–610

Comaroff J, Comaroff J (2008) Law and disorder in the postcolony. Chicago University Press, Chicago

Corder H, Hoexter C (2017) "Lawfare" in South Africa and its effects on the judiciary. Afr J Legal Stud 10:105–126

Craig P (1997) Formal and substantive conceptions of the rule of law: an analytical framework. Public Law 467–487

Davis D (2006) Adjudicating the socio-economic rights in the South African constitution: towards "deference lite". S Afr J Hum Rights 22:301–327

Davis D (2016) Separation of powers: Juristocracy or democracy. South Afr Law J 133:258–270

Du Plessis M (2000) The legitimacy of judicial review in South Africa's new constitutional dispensation: insights from the Canadian experience. Comp Int Law J South Afr 33:227–247

Dube F (2020) Separation of powers and the institutional supremacy of the constitutional court over parliament and the executive. S Afr J Hum Rights 36:293–318

Endicott TAO (1999) The impossibility of the rule of law. OJLS 19(1):1–18

Farganis D (2012) Do reasons matter? The impact of opinion content on supreme court legitimacy. Polit Res Q 65:206–216

Gildenhuys L (2020) Esoteric decision-making: judicial responses to the judicialisation of politics, the constitutional court and EFF II. S Afr J Hum Rights 36:338–361

Govender K, Swanepoel P (2020) The powers of the Office of the Public Protector and the South African human rights commission: a critical analysis of *SABC v DA* and *EFF v Speaker of the National Assembly* 2016 3 SA 580 (CC). Potchefstroom Electr Law J 23:1–32

Griswold E (1952) The "Coloured Vote Case" in South Africa. Harv Law Rev 65:1361–1374

Hamilton A (1961) The judiciary department. In The Federalist No. 78. https://avalon.law.yale.edu/18th_century/fed78.asp

Hamlin R, Sala G (2018) The judicialization of politics disentangled. Politics. https://doi.org/10.1093/acrefore/9780190228637.013.746

Hirschl R (2008) The judicialization of mega-politics and the rise of political courts. Ann Rev Pol Sci 11:93–118

Hoexter C (2004) The principle of legality in South African administrative law. Macquarie Law J 4:165–186

Huq A (2018) Legal or political checks on apex criminality: an essay on constitutional design. Univ Calif Los Angeles Law Rev 65:1506–1530

Huq A (2019) A tactical separation of powers doctrine. Const Court Rev 9:19–44
Johnson RW (2017) The Fall of Jacob Zuma and the crisis of South Africa. Quadrant 61:39–41
Kawadza H (2018) Attacks on the judiciary: undercurrents of a political versus legal constitutionalism dilemma? Potchefstroom Electr Law J 21:1–23
Kihbet E, Fombad C (2017) Transformative constitutionalism and the adjudication of constitutional rights in Africa. Afr Human Rights Law J 17:340–366
Klare K (1998) Legal culture and transformative constitutionalism. S Afr J Hum Rights 14:146–188
Knight J, Epstein L (1998) On the struggle for judicial supremacy. Law Soc Rev 30:87–120
Kordela M (2008) The principle of legal certainty as a fundamental element of the formal concept of the rule of law. La Revue Du Notariat 110:587–605
Langa P (2006) "A delicate balance": the place of the judiciary in a constitutional democracy—the separation of powers in the South African Constitution. S Afr J Hum Rights 22:2–9
Langa P (2007) The emperor's new clothes: Bram Fischer and the need for dissent. SAJHR 23:362–372
Lemieux SE (2017) Judicial supremacy, Judicial power, and the finality of constitutional rulings. Persp Polit 15:1067
Le Roux M, Davis D (2019) Lawfare: judging politics in South Africa. Jonathan Ball Publishers, Johannesburg
Liebenberg S (2016) Remedial principles and meaningful engagement in education rights disputes. PERL 19:1–43
Lifante-Vidal I (2020) Is legal certainty a formal value? Int J Legal Polit Thought 11:456–467
Madison J (1788) The particular structure of the new government and the distribution of power among its different parts. In: The Federalist Papers: No. 47. https://avalon.law.yale.edu/18th_century/fed47.asp
Maphosa R (2020) Are judicial monitoring institutions a legitimate remedy for addressing systemic socioeconomic rights violations. S Afr J Hum Rights 36:362–385
Marcus G (1986) Challenging injustice: the role of the judiciary. Indicator SA 4:17–19
Masengu T (2017) The vulnerability of judges in contemporary Africa: alarming trends. Africa Today 63:3–19
Mbazira C (2008) From ambivalence to certainty: norms and principles for the structural interdict in socio-economic rights litigation in South Africa. S Afr J Hum Rights 24:1–28
Modebadze V (2010) The term politics reconsidered in the light of recent theoretical developments. IBSU Sci J 1:39–44
Moller K (2020) Justifying the culture of justification. Int Const Law 17:1078–1097
Mureinik E (1994) A bridge to where?—introducing the interim bill of rights. S Afr J Hum Rights 10:31–48
Ngcobo S (2011) South Africa's transformative constitution: towards an appropriate doctrine of the separation of powers. Stellenbosch Law Rev 22:38–49
O'Regan K (2011) A forum for reason: reflections on the role and work of the constitutional court. Helen Suzman Memorial Lecture. Available at: https://hsf.org.za/publications/lectures/HSF%20Memorial%20Lecture%202011_data/helen-suzman-memorial-lecture-november-2011.pdf
Okpaluba C, Mhango M (2017) Between separation of powers and justiciability. Law Democr Dev 21:1–24
Paunio E (2009) Beyond predictability—reflections on legal certainty and the discourse theory of law in the EU legal order. Germ Law J 10:1469–1493
Petrov J (2021) (De-)judicialization of politics in the era of populism: lessons from Central and Eastern Europe. Int J Human Rights 1–26
Raz J (2019) The law's own virtue. OJLS 39: 1–15
Roach K, Budlender G (2005) Mandatory relief and supervisory jurisdiction: when is it appropriate, just and equitable. South Afr Law J 122:325–351
Rogers O (2022) "I beg to differ": are our courts too agreeable? SALJ 139:300–339
Scalia A (1989) The rule of law as a law of rules. Univ Chicago Law Rev 56:1175–1188
Schauer F (2004) Judicial supremacy and the modest constitution. Calif Law Rev 92:1045–1067
Sibanda S (2011) Not purpose-made! Transformative constitutionalism, post-independence constitutionalism and the struggle to eradicate poverty. Stellenbosch Law Rev 22:482–500

Sibanda S (2020) Introduction to special issue: separation of powers, the judiciary and the politics of constitutional adjudication. S Afr J Hum Rights 36:287–292

Singh A, Bhero MZ (2016) Judicial law-making: unlocking the creative powers of judges in terms of section 39(2) of the constitution. PERJ 19:1–22

Southall R (2016) The coming crisis of Zuma's ANC: the party state confronts fiscal crisis. Rev Afr Polit Econ 43:73–88

Sunkin M (1994) Judicialization of politics in the United Kingdom. Int Polit Sci Rev 15:126–133

Sweet AS (1999) Judicialization and the construction of government. Comp Pol Stud 32:147–184

Tsele M (2018) "Coercing virtue" in the constitutional court: neutral principles, rationality and the *Nkandla* problem. Const Court Rev 8:193–220

Vallinder T (1994) The judicialization of politics. A world-wide phenomenon: introduction. Int Polit Sci Rev 15:91–99

Van der Schyff G (2010) Judicial review of legislation: a comparative study of the United Kingdom, The Netherlands and South Africa. Springer, London

Waldron J (2008) The concept and the rule of law. Georgia Law Rev 43:1–61

Woolman S (2007) The amazing, vanishing bill of rights. South Afr Law J 124:762–794

Woolman S (2018) A politics of accountability: how South Africa's judicial recognition of the binding legal effect of the public protector's recommendations had a catalysing effect that brought down a president. Const Court Rev 18:155–192

Newspaper Articles

Allison S (2016) Nkandla verdict shows South Africa's democracy is alive and kicking. Guardian. Available at: https://www.theguardian.com/world/2016/mar/31/south-africa-nkandla-verdict-jacob-zuma

Daily Maverick (2017) State capture named SA word of the year. https://www.dailymaverick.co.za/article/2017-10-16-state-capture-named-sa-word-of-the-year/

Ferreira E (2021) Zuma threatens uprising against courts in latest attack on judiciary. https://mg.co.za/news/2021-03-26-zuma-threatens-uprising-against-courts-in-latest-attack-on-judiciary/

Gerber J (2022) Five years and R1bn later: civil society unpicks Ramaphosa's plans after the Zondo Commission. News24. Available at: https://www.news24.com/news24/politics/government/five-years-and-r1bn-later-civil-society-unpicks-ramaphosas-plans-after-the-zondo-commission-20221025

Haffajee F (2022) State Capture Inquiry cost almost R1bn, but it saved billions more – Judge Zondo. Daily Maverick. Available at: https://www.dailymaverick.co.za/article/2021-06-30-state-capture-inquiry-cost-almost-r1bn-but-it-saved-billions-more-judge-zondo/

Malada B (2022) Let's not beat about the bush – Africa is a failed state, now let's all stand up and fix it. Daily Maverick. Available at: https://www.dailymaverick.co.za/opinionista/2022-09-05-lets-not-beat-about-the-bush-south-africa-is-a-failed-state-now-lets-all-stand-up-and-fix-it/

Moeng S (2022) SA is a failed state, and we're paying for it in the cost of living. News24. Available at: https://www.news24.com/fin24/opinion/solly-moeng-sa-is-a-failed-state-and-were-paying-for-it-in-the-cost-of-living-20220710

Robinson KS (2022) Disregarding precedent can harm judicial legitimacy, Kagan says. Bloomberg Law. Available at: https://news.bloomberglaw.com/us-law-week/disregarding-precedent-can-harm-judicial-legitimacy-kagan-says

Staff Writer (2022) South Africa is practically a failed state: CEO. BusinessTech. Available at: https://businesstech.co.za/news/business-opinion/565926/south-africa-is-practically-a-failed-state-ceo/

Reports

Moseneke D (2021) A Report to the Electoral Commission of South Africa in terms of section 14(4) read with section 5(2)(a) of the Electoral Commission Act. https://www.elections.org.za/freeandfair/

Office of the Public Protector (2014) Secure in Comfort: Public Protector's Report on Nkandla: Report by the Public Protector on an Investigation into Allegations of Impropriety relating to the Installation and Implementation of Security Measures by the Department of Public Works at and in respect of the Private Residence of President Jacob Zuma at Nkandla in the Kwa-Zulu Provinc*e* Report No: 25 of 2013/4

Office of the Public Protector (2018) Alleged Failure to Recover Misappropriated Funds: Report on an Investigation into Allegations of Maladministration, Corruption, Misappropriation of Public Funds and the Failure by the South African Government to Implement the CIEX Report and to Recover Public Funds from ABSA Bank Report 8 of 2017/2018

Report of the Expert Panel into the July 2021 Civil Unrest. https://www.thepresidency.gov.za/download/file/fid/2442

Zondo R (2022) Judicial Commission of Inquiry into Allegations of State Capture, Corruption and Fraud in the Public Sector including Organs of State. https://www.statecapture.org.za/

Miscellaneous Sources

Commission of Inquiry into State Capture, Our Mandate. https://www.statecapture.org.za/site/about/mandate

The Commission's founding papers in the Constitutional Court. https://www.statecapture.org.za/site/files/judgments/5/CC_JGZ_Papers.pdf

Thesis

Swanepoel P (2017) The potential of structural interdicts to constitute effective relief in socio-economic rights cases. LLM Dissertation, Stellenbosch University

Conclusion

Nauman Reayat

Abstract This chapter synthesises the core challenges to constitutionalism identified across the book and evaluates how they manifest in different social, political, and legal contexts. It highlights persistent obstacles—such as weak or strong judicial leadership, popular decision-making, executive dominance over judicial processes, the influence of international actors in constitution-making, the role of non-state institutions in constitutional governance, the judicialisation of politics, and the politicisation of the judiciary—that hinder the effective functioning of constitutional systems. Drawing on comparative insights from the volume, the chapter outlines how these challenges interact and evolve, shaping the nature and durability of constitutional practices in Africa and beyond. It offers practical recommendations for strengthening constitutionalism, emphasising the importance of integrated social, political, and legal approaches to sustaining constitutional governance.

Developments discussed in this book illustrate how constitutions operate under both national and international pressures and highlight the complexities of accountability in different legal and political contexts. Issues such as the relationship between constitutionalism and federalism, the judicialization of politics, and judicial independence discussed in this book are not confined to any single geographic region. These are global challenges that manifest in various forms and ways across almost every country. They underscore the fact that constitutionalism is a dynamic and ongoing global phenomenon.

Nonetheless, it is crucial to focus on countries with unstable political and legal systems, as developments in these contexts provide important and up-to-date insights into the challenges facing constitutionalism. These developments also spark debates on how to address such challenges effectively. In this regard, analyzing distinct aspects of constitutionalism in Africa is particularly significant, as the

N. Reayat (✉)
Leicester Law School, University of Leicester, Leicester, UK
e-mail: nr210@leicester.ac.uk

N. Reayat, H. O. Yusuf (eds.), *Constitutionalism in Africa and Beyond*, Ius Gentium: Comparative Perspectives on Law and Justice 127,
https://doi.org/10.1007/978-3-032-01180-0_9

continent is home to many countries with unstable constitutional frameworks. Consequently, much of this book focuses on African jurisdictions, with one chapter comparing an African jurisdiction (Egypt) and an Asian jurisdiction (Pakistan), and another chapter examining an Asian jurisdiction (Cambodia).

This book explained constitutionalism in a number of countries, including Pakistan, Egypt, Ethiopia, Nigeria, Madagascar, Cameroon, Cambodia, and South Africa. This chapter examines the challenges to constitutionalism as discussed in this book and provides recommendations for addressing them.

1 Judicial Leadership

One of the most distinctive topics explored in this book is the relationship between judicial populism and judicial independence (as examined by Reayat in Chapter 2). It also examines the role of judicial leadership in either strengthening or weakening this relationship and analyzes how this dynamic shapes the nature and scope of constitutionalism in Africa and beyond. The chapter comparing Egypt and Pakistan is one of very few studies that presents a comparative analysis of judicial populism and judicial independence across an African and an Asian jurisdiction, offering new insights into these phenomena.

The study reveals that judicial populism—characterized by a combination of judicial leadership, political divisions, mass demonstrations against the regime in power and in support of judges, and anti-regime litigation—strengthened judicial independence in Pakistan. In contrast, the absence of some of these key elements in Egypt hindered the strengthening of judicial independence. This comparative analysis highlights the varying impacts of judicial populism on constitutional governance across different contexts.

The challenge to constitutionalism posed by the emergence of strong and strategic judicial leadership lies in judges prioritizing public support over their primary duty of interpreting laws and rules. A strategic judge leading the judiciary in African jurisdictions and beyond may engage with the public to garner support, but this risks centralizing judicial power in the hands of individual judges, potentially undermining institutional integrity. This issue can be addressed through two approaches: (a) either by removing constitutional provisions that grant the public direct access to supreme courts in matters of public interest or by establishing strict criteria for *locus standi* in such cases; or (b) developing mechanisms to prevent judges from engaging directly with the general public. While codes of conduct for judges exist in almost every country, most fail to comprehensively define the permissible nature and scope of judges' interactions with the public. Therefore, it is essential to refine the contents of these codes and ensure their strict implementation.

Another significant challenge to constitutionalism in Africa and beyond is the risk that judicial populism may lead to decisions influenced by popular desires rather than being grounded solely in laws, rules, and evidence. This trend could erode judicial independence, weaken the rule of law, and destabilize constitutional governance. This challenge is discussed in greater detail in the next section.

2 Judicial Decision-Making and the Influence of Popular Expectations

There is a pressure of popular decision-making, which compels judges to make rulings in a context shaped by divided society. Judges, lacking the power of the purse or the sword, may feel discouraged from making decisions solely based on the law if they perceive risks to their safety or face mass protests against their rulings. Under this pressure judges make decisions that avoid public reprisals and gain public support (as examined by Reayat in Chapter 2). This questions judges neutrality in decision making. A recent example is the Federal Supreme Court of Iraq's handling of the General Amnesty Law and Personal Laws.[1] The General Amnesty Law aimed to reconcile extremists with the Iraqi government, while the Personal Law lowered the minimum age of marriage for girls from 15 to puberty. Initially, the court suspended these laws pending a final decision, but widespread protests erupted soon after. The court subsequently approved the laws,[2] creating the impression that the judges' decision was influenced by public opinion rather than legal principles. This sequence of events underscores the challenges judges face in maintaining judicial independence amid societal pressures.

3 Inter- and Intra-Governmental Disputes in Federal States: The Absence of Impartial Institutions

Another important challenge discussed across multiple chapters of this book, in various contexts is the political influence exerted over institutions responsible for decision-making and interpreting the law. While this issue has been widely discussed in nearly every text on constitutionalism, this book emphasizes its effects within unstable political and legal contexts. When institutions designed to mediate decisions among diverse societal factions are influenced by politicians, they risk losing public trust (as examined by Yusuf in Chapter 4). If politicians manipulate decision-making in disputes among different factions in a federal state to serve their political objectives (as discussed by Fiseha in Chapter 3), the outcomes will inevitably be challenged by opposing groups. This resistance can lead to disorder and destabilize constitutional frameworks. Therefore, it is crucial to allocate the authority to resolve disputes in a federal state to an institution that commands the trust of all stakeholders.

[1] Ochab (2025).

[2] Shafaq News (2025).

4 Government Influence Over Judicial Appointments

One of the most crucial ways to influence the judiciary is to introduce a judicial appointment process that gives politicians greater scope to place judges whom they believe will serve their political interests. This constitutes an ongoing challenge to constitutionalism. Although this issue has been discussed in various other works, several chapters of this book examined it specifically within the context of unstable legal and political systems of Africa and beyond, where external control over bodies responsible for judicial appointments is particularly pronounced. When judges are appointed without undue influence, they are more likely to make decisions independently. Therefore, an independent and transparent process for judicial appointments can significantly contribute to judicial independence, the rule of law, and stable constitutionalism.

The Higher Judicial Council (HJC) of Cameroon has not been granted sufficient powers to appoint judges independently (as discussed by Enonchong in Chapter 5). This limitation undermines the independence of the judiciary and weakens the rule of law. However, the inclusion of representatives from other branches of the state and civil society within the HJC could create an opportunity for the council to operate more independently. Input from diverse state and societal actors would enhance the quality of the judicial appointment process, build trust among various stakeholders, and contribute to the stabilization of the system.

Therefore, it is recommended that the organization responsible for appointing judges undergo diversification by involving actors from various sectors of society. However, an equally important issue for constitutionalism is the removal of judges. The process of removing judges must be conducted in accordance with the law and for reasons that safeguard the integrity of the judiciary and the state. Strengthening this process will help strike a balance between judicial independence and judicial accountability. The issue of how to strike an appropriate balance between judicial independence and judicial accountability has not been addressed in this book. This could be a potential area of inquiry for the next volume in this collection.

5 The Influence of International Actors in Constitution-Making Processes

One of the most significant challenges explored in detail in this book, yet often overlooked in other works, is the role of international actors in constitution-making (as discussed by Smith in Chapter 7). International actors bring their own understanding of concepts such as constitutions, the rule of law, and judicial independence, which are often rooted in Western values and culture. While their collaboration with national actors aims to strengthen governance, the steps they take can have unintended consequences for national institutions deeply embedded in local culture, norms, values, and social structures. These unintended consequences may include a decline in public trust in constitutions and reduced engagement of political and social actors with constitutions framed with international assistance. Ultimately, this can lead to the failure of constitutions in fragile states.

6 Non-State Institutions and Their Role in Constitutional Governance

Similar to the challenge of constitutions failing due to excessive input from international actors is the lack of recognition of the importance of non-state institutions (as examined by Lwabukuna in Chapter 6). Depending on various social, political, and economic circumstances, non-state institutions can either facilitate or undermine the Western concept of the formal rule of law. These institutions have the potential to both limit and increase state powers.

Non-state institutions can limit state powers when they effectively carry out governance and resolve disputes in a manner acceptable to the majority of the community, thereby reducing the need for state intervention. Conversely, they can increase state control over society when their activities undermine the functioning of formal state institutions. In such cases, the state may justify expanding its powers to ensure law and order, further consolidating its authority.

The phenomena described above are not exclusive to Madagascar. Similar dynamics exist in Asian countries as well. For instance, institutions such as *jirgas* or *panchayats*—non-state, informal bodies rooted in cultural norms—are designed to resolve disputes and facilitate local governance. However, when the activities of these institutions undermine those of formal state institutions, state intervention often follows.

This presents an opportunity to raise awareness about the utility and potential of the rule of law as promoted by non-state institutions. It also highlights the need to explore ways to reconcile the activities of state and non-state institutions, ensuring that they complement rather than undermine each other.

7 The Judicialisation of Politics and the Politicisation of the Judiciary

Another challenge to constitutionalism, which appears to be a global issue and has been extensively discussed in comparative constitutional law literature, is the tendency of courts to adjudicate political issues. This phenomenon not only judicializes politics but also politicizes the courts (as discussed in Chapter 8 by Nxumalo and Mafora and in Chapter 4 by Yusuf). While the judicialization of politics may, in some contexts, empower courts to limit government powers, it can, in other contexts, erode public trust in the judiciary. A decline in public confidence may exacerbate judges' apprehensions about potential retaliation from powerful societal groups if court rulings go against their interests. This fear can discourage courts from imposing necessary limits on government powers, undermining their role as guardians of constitutional principles.

This challenge can be addressed if politicians cultivate a culture of resolving political issues through appropriate forums and political mechanisms, such as meetings of relevant parliamentary committees and debates during parliamentary sessions. Often, politicians shift the burden of responsibility by deferring contentious and unpopular political issues to the courts. However, they could achieve the same objective by invoking the advisory jurisdiction of the courts, where the judiciary is asked to provide guidance on the legality of specific matters. This approach would allow the government to retain control over political issues while preventing courts from becoming arenas for political disputes.

The list of challenges discussed here is not exhaustive. These challenges evolve under varying social, economic, political, legal and historical circumstances, continually taking on new shapes and forms. This evolution necessitates regularly providing fresh insights into the nature, scope, and varieties of constitutionalism. Given the complexity and diversity of constitutionalism across different jurisdictions, a single edited volume cannot comprehensively analyze all its aspects and manifestations. Other aspects of, and new developments in, constitutionalism in Africa and beyond will be discussed in next volume of this collection.

References

Ochab EU (2025) Iraq Parliament Passes Controversial Personal Status And General Amnesty Laws. Forbes 26 January https://www.forbes.com/sites/ewelinaochab/2025/01/26/iraqi-parliament-passes-controversial-personal-status-and-general-amnesty-laws/ accessed 19 October 2025

Shafaq News (2025) Iraq' Supreme Judicial Council Orders to enforce Amnesty Law. 20 February https://shafaq.com/en/Iraq/Iraq-s-Supreme-Judicial-Council-orders-to-enforce-Amnesty-Law accessed 2 October 2025

MIX
Papier aus verantwortungsvollen Quellen
Paper from responsible sources
FSC® C105338

If you have any concerns about our products, you can contact us on
ProductSafety@springernature.com

In case Publisher is established outside the EU, the EU authorized representative is:
Springer Nature Customer Service Center GmbH
Europaplatz 3, 69115 Heidelberg, Germany

Printed by Libri Plureos GmbH
in Hamburg, Germany